T0338526

Advanced Research on Biologically Inspired Cognitive Architectures

Jordi Vallverdú
Universitat Autònoma de Barcelona, Spain

Manuel Mazzara
Innopolis University, Russia

Max Talanov
Kazan Federal University, Russia

Salvatore Distefano
University of Messina, Italy & Kazan Federal University, Russia

Robert Lowe
University of Gothenburg, Sweden & University of Skövde, Sweden

A volume in the Advances in Computational Intelligence and Robotics (ACIR) Book Series

www.igi-global.com

Published in the United States of America by
    IGI Global
    Information Science Reference (an imprint of IGI Global)
    701 E. Chocolate Avenue
    Hershey PA 17033
    Tel: 717-533-8845
    Fax: 717-533-8661
    E-mail: cust@igi-global.com
    Web site: http://www.igi-global.com

            Library of Congress Cataloging-in-Publication Data

Names: Vallverdú, Jordi, editor. | Mazzara, Manuel, editor. | Talanov, Max, 1974- editor. | Distefano,
Salvatore, editor.
Title: Advanced research on biologically inspired cognitive architectures / Jordi Vallverdú, Manuel
Mazzara, Max Talanov, and Salvatore Distefano, editors.
Description: Hershey, PA : Information Science Reference, [2017] | Includes bibliographical
references.
Identifiers: LCCN 2016049249| ISBN 9781522519478 (hardcover) | ISBN
  9781522519485 (ebook)
Subjects: LCSH: Natural computation. | Software architecture. | Artificiall intelligence. | Conscious
automata. | Computational intelligence. | Cognitive science.
Classification: LCC QA76.9.N37 A385 2017 | DDC 005.1/2--dc23
LC record available at https://lccn.loc.gov/2016049249

This book is published in the IGI Global book series Advances in Computational Intelligence and
Robotics (ACIR) (ISSN: 2327-0411; eISSN: 2327-042X)

British Cataloguing in Publication Data
A Cataloguing in Publication record for this book is available from the British Library.

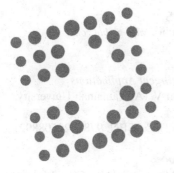

Advances in Computational Intelligence and Robotics (ACIR) Book Series

ISSN:2327-0411
EISSN:2327-042X

MISSION

While intelligence is traditionally a term applied to humans and human cognition, technology has progressed in such a way to allow for the development of intelligent systems able to simulate many human traits. With this new era of simulated and artificial intelligence, much research is needed in order to continue to advance the field and also to evaluate the ethical and societal concerns of the existence of artificial life and machine learning.

The **Advances in Computational Intelligence and Robotics (ACIR) Book Series** encourages scholarly discourse on all topics pertaining to evolutionary computing, artificial life, computational intelligence, machine learning, and robotics. ACIR presents the latest research being conducted on diverse topics in intelligence technologies with the goal of advancing knowledge and applications in this rapidly evolving field.

COVERAGE

- Adaptive and Complex Systems
- Synthetic Emotions
- Artificial Life
- Computational Logic
- Fuzzy systems
- Robotics
- Evolutionary Computing
- Machine Learning
- Computer Vision
- Cyborgs

IGI Global is currently accepting manuscripts for publication within this series. To submit a proposal for a volume in this series, please contact our Acquisition Editors at Acquisitions@igi-global.com or visit: http://www.igi-global.com/publish/.

Titles in this Series

For a list of additional titles in this series, please visit: www.igi-global.com

Multi-Core Computer Vision and Image Processing for Intelligent Applications
Mohan S. (Al Yamamah University, Saudi Arabia) and Vani V. (Al Yamamah University, Saudi Arabia)
Information Science Reference • copyright 2017 • 292pp • H/C (ISBN: 9781522508892) • US $210.00 (our price)

Developing and Applying Optoelectronics in Machine Vision
Oleg Sergiyenko (Autonomous University of Baja California, Mexico) and Julio C. Rodriguez-Quiñonez (Autonomous University of Baja California, Mexico)
Information Science Reference • copyright 2017 • 341pp • H/C (ISBN: 9781522506324) • US $205.00 (our price)

Pattern Recognition and Classification in Time Series Data
Eva Volna (University of Ostrava, Czech Republic) Martin Kotyrba (University of Ostrava, Czech Republic) and Michal Janosek (University of Ostrava, Czech Republic)
Information Science Reference • copyright 2017 • 282pp • H/C (ISBN: 9781522505655) • US $185.00 (our price)

Integrating Cognitive Architectures into Virtual Character Design
Jeremy Owen Turner (Simon Fraser University, Canada) Michael Nixon (Simon Fraser University, Canada) Ulysses Bernardet (Simon Fraser University, Canada) and Steve DiPaola (Simon Fraser University, Canada)
Information Science Reference • copyright 2016 • 346pp • H/C (ISBN: 9781522504542) • US $185.00 (our price)

Handbook of Research on Natural Computing for Optimization Problems
Jyotsna Kumar Mandal (University of Kalyani, India) Somnath Mukhopadhyay (Calcutta Business School, India) and Tandra Pal (National Institute of Technology Durgapur, India)
Information Science Reference • copyright 2016 • 1015pp • H/C (ISBN: 9781522500582) • US $465.00 (our price)

Applied Artificial Higher Order Neural Networks for Control and Recognition
Ming Zhang (Christopher Newport University, USA)
Information Science Reference • copyright 2016 • 511pp • H/C (ISBN: 9781522500636) • US $215.00 (our price)

www.igi-global.com

701 E. Chocolate Ave., Hershey, PA 17033
Order online at www.igi-global.com or call 717-533-8845 x100
To place a standing order for titles released in this series,
contact: cust@igi-global.com
Mon-Fri 8:00 am - 5:00 pm (est) or fax 24 hours a day 717-533-8661

Table of Contents

Detailed Table of Contents

Chapter 1
Francis Fallon, St. John's University, USA

This chapter aims to evaluate Integrated Information Theory's claims concerning Artificial Consciousness. Integrated Information Theory (IIT) works from premises that claim that certain properties, such as unity, are essential to consciousness, to conclusions regarding the constraints upon physical systems that could realize consciousness. Among these conclusions is the claim that feed-forward systems, and systems that are not largely reentrant, necessarily will fail to generate consciousness (but may simulate it). This chapter will discuss the premises of IIT, which themselves are highly controversial, and will also address IIT's related rejection of functionalism. This analysis will argue that IIT has failed to established good grounds for these positions, and that convincing alternatives remain available. This, in turn, implies that the constraints upon Artificial Consciousness are more generous than IIT would have them be.

Chapter 2
Jordi Vallverdú, Universitat Autònoma de Barcelona, Spain
Max Talanov, Kazan federal University, Russia

The purpose of this chapter is to delineate a naturalistic approach to consciousness. This bioinspired method does not try to emulate into a 1:1 scale real mechanisms but instead of it, we capture some basic brain mechanisms prone to be implemented into computational frameworks. Consequently, we adopt a functional view on consciousness, considering consciousness as one among other cognitive mechanisms useful for survival purposes in natural environments. Specifically, we wish to capture those mechanisms related to decision-making processes employed by brains in order to produce adaptive answer to the environment, because this is the main reason for the emergence and purpose of consciousness.

Vincent T. Cialdella, Illinois State University, USA
Emilio J. C. Lobato, Illinois State University, USA
J. Scott Jordan, Illinois State University, USA

In this chapter, the authors focus on cognitive architectures that are developed with the intent to explain human cognition. The authors first describe the mission of cybernetics and early cognitive architectures and recount the popular criticism that these perspectives fail to provide genuine explanations of cognition. Moving forward, the authors propose that there are three pervasive problems that modern cognitive architectures must address: the problem of consciousness, the problem of embodiment, and the problem of representation. Wild Systems Theory (Jordan, 2013) conceptualizes biological cognition as a feature of self-sustaining embodied context that manifests itself at multiple, nested, time-scales. In this manner, Wild Systems Theory is presented as a particularly useful framework for coherently addressing the problems of consciousness, embodiment, and representation.

Leonard Johard, Innopolis University, Russia
Vittorio Lippi, University Medical Center Freiburg, Germany
Larisa Safina, Innopolis University, Russia
Manuel Mazzara, Innopolis University, Russia

A purely reductionist approach to neuroscience has difficulty in providing intuitive explanations and cost effective methods. Following a different approach, much of the mechanics of the brain can be explained purely by closer study of the relation of the brain to its environment. Starting from the laws of physics, genetics and easily observable properties of the biophysical environment we can deduce the need for dreams and a dopaminergic system. We provide a rough sketch of the various a priori assumptions encoded in the mechanics of the nervous system. This indicates much more can be learnt by studying the statistical priors exploited by the brain rather than its specific mechanics of calculation.

Robotic developments are seen as a next level in technology with intelligent machines, which automate tedious tasks and serve our needs without complaints. But nevertheless, they have to be fair and smart enough to be intuitively of use and safe to handle. But how to implement this kind of intelligence, does it need feelings and emotions, should robots perceive the world as we do as a human role model, how far should the implementation of synthetic consciousness lead and actually, what is needed for consciousness in that context? Additionally in Human-Robot-Interaction research, science mainly makes use of the tool phenomenography, which is exclusively subjective, so how to make it qualify for Artificial Intelligence? These are the heading aspects of this chapter for conducting research in the field of social robotics and suggesting a conscious and cognitive model for smart and intuitive interacting robots, guided by biomimetics.

Computer simulations have become a very powerful tool for scientific research. Given the vast complexity that comes with many open scientific questions, a purely analytical or experimental approach is often not viable. For example, biological systems comprise an extremely complex organization and heterogeneous interactions across different spatial and temporal scales. In order to facilitate research on such problems, the BioDynaMo project aims at a general platform for computer simulations for biological research. Since scientific investigations require extensive computer resources, this platform should be executable on hybrid cloud computing systems, allowing for the efficient use of state-of-the-art computing technology. This chapter describes challenges during the early stages of the software development process.

In particular, we describe issues regarding the implementation and the highly interdisciplinary as well as international nature of the collaboration. Moreover, we explain the methodologies, the approach, and the lessons learned by the team during these first stages.

Chapter 7

Software development is critically dependent on a number of factors. These factors include techno-logical and anthropic-oriented ones. Software production is a multiple party process; it includes customer and developer parties. Due to different expectations and goals of each side, the human factors become mission-critical. Misconceptions in the expectations of each side may lead to misbalanced production; the product that the developers produce may significantly differ from what the customers expect. This misbalanced vision of the software product may result in a software de-livery crisis. To manage this crisis, the authors recommend using software engineering methods. Software engineering is a discipline which emerged from the so-called "software crisis" in the 1960s: it combines technical and anthropic-oriented "soft" skills. To conquer the crisis, this chapter discusses general architecture patterns for software and hardware systems; it provides instances of particular industries, such as oil and gas and nuclear power production.

Chapter 8

In this chapter, different notions of allostasis (the process of achieving stability through change) as they apply to adaptive behavior are presented. The authors discuss how notions of allostasis can be usefully applied to Cybernetics-based homeostatic systems. Particular emphasis is placed upon affective states – motivational and emotional – and, above all, the notion of 'predictive' regulation, as distinct from forms of 'reactive' regulation, in homeostatic systems. The authors focus here on Ashby's ultrastability concept that entails behavior change for correcting homeostatic errors (deviations from the healthy range of essential, physiological, variables). The authors consider how the ultrastability concept can be broadened to incorporate allostatic mechanisms and how they may enhance adaptive physiological and behavioral activity. Finally, this chapter references different Cybernetics frameworks that incorporate the notion of allostasis. The article then attempts to untangle how the given perspectives fit into the 'allostatic ultrastable systems' framework postulated.

Chapter 9

According to Spinoza, "Love is nothing else but pleasure accompanied by the idea of an external cause". Author proposes that desire is nothing else but a change of pleasure accompanied by the idea of its cause, that terms 'desire', 'want' and their cognates describe change of the pleasantness of the state of a subject (PSS in short) associated with X, that if change of PSS is positive/negative, then X is called desirable/undesirable correspondingly. Both positive and negative desires can be strong, so strength of desire characterizes its magnitude. Need of X is defined here as a cyclical desire of X that gets stronger/weaker with dissatisfaction/satisfaction of its need. Author also explores an idea that the stronger is desire of X by a subject, the more attention this subject pays to X. Distribution of attention and influence on it by the will effort are analyzed in this paper.

Preface

It has been observed how the technological progress of our civilization mimics the extraordinarily smart design choices of the nature surrounding us. As scientists have been inspired by the cosmos to observe and understand its mechanics from the deepest to the smallest particle, so engineers have found inspiration in biological systems to design the artificial systems that support our daily life.

With the massive technological advancement of the last few decades we are close to a potential shift in our perception of the world, and our role in it. It is certainly not the first time in history that our position with respect to the universe has had to be adapted, reconsidered and, to some extent, regrettably marginalized. The possibility of eventually creating a real-life computational equivalent of the human brain is no longer a remote possibility. Numerous scientists around the globe are relentlessly working day and night in order to realize this possibility which should no longer be seen as an unreachable mirage.

As active part of the scientific community we, as representatives of cognitive science, philosophers, and software engineers had some time ago the idea to join forces and collect contributions of colleagues working towards the dream of reproducing what is the most complex existing object in the know Universe: the human brain and the mind. These two entities are considered separable by some (dualists) while others consider the former a manifestation of the latter (monists). The different chapters in this book offer alternative perspectives on brain and mind that we hope will offer new insights into cognition and architectures thereof.

There are four major disciplines covered in this book offering exciting and potentially synergistic perspectives: cognitive science, cybernetics, computer science and software engineering, and neuroscience. These are the four pillars of Biologically Inspired Cognitive Architectures. In fact, it is not possible to pursue such an ambitious objective without interdisciplinary teams and research at the cutting edge of all these areas. We have invited some of the best representatives of these communities to guide you during your investigation.

OBJECTIVES

Current systems are melting pots of interacting parts mixing economical, philosophical and socio-technical issues and interests, thus calling for adequate management approaches of the ecosystem as a whole. Trans-/inter-disciplinary methodologies are therefore required for dealing with such issues. The objective of this book is to establish a new domain: *Anthropic-oriented computing,* and attract the attention of a broader audience in inter/cross/trans-disciplinary areas such as philosophy, sociology, psychology, anthropology, neurophysiology and computer science. This way we aim at initiating the discussion on the Anthropic-oriented computing is by exploiting the expertise of several specialists from different domains of the cognitive and social sciences.

Chapter 1
Integrated Information Theory (IIT) and Artificial Consciousness

Francis Fallon
St. John's University, USA

ABSTRACT

This chapter aims to evaluate Integrated Information Theory's claims concerning Artificial Consciousness. Integrated Information Theory (IIT) works from premises that claim that certain properties, such as unity, are essential to consciousness, to conclusions regarding the constraints upon physical systems that could realize consciousness. Among these conclusions is the claim that feed-forward systems, and systems that are not largely reentrant, necessarily will fail to generate consciousness (but may simulate it). This chapter will discuss the premises of IIT, which themselves are highly controversial, and will also address IIT's related rejection of functionalism. This analysis will argue that IIT has failed to established good grounds for these positions, and that convincing alternatives remain available. This, in turn, implies that the constraints upon Artificial Consciousness are more generous than IIT would have them be.

DOI: 10.4018/978-1-5225-1947-8.ch001

INTRODUCTION

The functionalist account of mind holds that mental events are functions, rather than fundamental properties attaching to or arising from particular physical arrangements. According to functionalism, it may be the case that only a limited set of physical systems will be practically capable of realizing mental events, such as consciousness. It stresses, at the same time, that these physical systems will realize, e.g., consciousness, in virtue of their functional characteristics. Function may constrain physical form, but function, rather than physical properties themselves, adequately explains consciousness.

IIT departs from functionalism, claiming that consciousness is a fundamental property of certain kinds of physical systems. Systems that integrate information – combine different kinds of information into a unified whole – produce consciousness. The brain does this by reentrant processing. IIT claims that the production of consciousness by integrated information systems is a feature of the physical communication among the parts of the whole, reentrant system. IIT, then, understands consciousness not as a set of functions which can be achieved by any system with the right functional capacity and organization. Rather, IIT identifies consciousness as a fundamental feature only of systems (that integrate information) whose anatomy is physically reentrant. Subjective experience is a property of these systems in the same fundamental way as mass or charge is a property of particles. IIT, then, rules out feed-forward or otherwise insufficiently reentrant systems as having the potential to generate consciousness, which limits the options available to the field of Artificial Consciousness.

This chapter will forego a general evaluation of IIT and focus on its claims concerning the neurophysiological constraints on modelling Artificial Consciousness. This will involve, after laying out the background,

1. Clarifying its anti-functionalist commitments,
2. Tracing the link between those commitments and the conclusion that consciousness emerges as a basic property of reentry systems only,
3. Challenging the anti-functionalist position, and
4. Revisiting the possibilities for Artificial Consciousness architecture, arguing for a more generous interpretation of the parameters for future work (in Solutions and Recommendations).

BACKGROUND

This chapter gives a critical analysis of those dimensions of Integrated Information Theory (IIT) that bear most directly on the possibilities and constraints of Artificial Consciousness. Although its proponents cautiously qualify their claims, the scope of IIT is tremendously ambitious. In short, IIT proposes a framework for defining, explaining, and measuring consciousness.

It is worth noting at the outset that, despite its relative youth (see Tononi 2004 and 2008, for IIT's first explicit publications), IIT has support from major scientific figures, strong links to very well-funded organizations, and a growing body of literature. Its creator, Giulio Tononi, serves as principle investigator of the Center for Sleep and Consciousness at the University of Madison, Wisconsin, overseeing more than forty researchers. The Center includes an IIT Theory Group, which addresses the neural substrates of consciousness. The Center continues to fill postdoctoral positions specific to IIT. Arguably the most visible champion of IIT, Christof Koch runs the Allen Institute for Brain Science, which has ties to the White House Brain Research through Advancing Innovative Neurotechnologies (BRAIN) Initiative, and the European Human Brain Project (HBP). (Before this, Koch held positions at MIT in Artificial Intelligence and at Caltech in Cognitive and Behavioral Biology, and published extensively with Francis Crick, co-discoverer of the double-helix, on the neural correlates of consciousness.) Tononi, Koch, and others both within and outside their Centers have generated a wealth of publications, and IIT informs programs for cognitive modelling. (It has also attracted considerable media attention: see Marcus (2013) and Zimmer (2010) for just two examples.)

The theory occupies a unique place in the broader, interdisciplinary debate concerning consciousness. IIT engages explicitly with the philosophical issues surrounding attempts to explain consciousness, but only to a limited extent. For example, its proponents routinely align themselves with Cartesian claims concerning the essential unity of subjective experience (see, e.g., Tononi & Koch, 2015). The IIT literature also associates itself in a qualified way with the modern philosophical movement of panpsychism (ibid. This association is, again, in a qualified way, reciprocated; see Chalmers (in press).) IIT does not so much argue for these connections as take them as self-evident (in the case of the Cartesian claims) or as basic consequences of IIT's methodology (in the case of the association with panpsychism). So, while the doctrine is situated in the broader debate, its situation remains largely unjustified. IIT's rejection of functionalism involves more explicit defense (Edelman & Tononi, 1998, 2000), but, as this chapter will argue, this defense takes the form of an attack on a 'straw man', a version of functionalism no longer entertained by most functionalists. In any case, it is striking that IIT, a theory created by scientists and advertising itself as scientific in nature, should reject the naturalism of functionalism (which posits no new fundamental natural entities in its explanation of consciousness) in favor of a form of panpsychism that augments the naturalistic ontology by positing consciousness as a fundamental physical property.

The basics of the theory are as follows:

Methodologically, IIT chooses not to move from the analysis of brain mechanisms toward an explanation of consciousness, but from an identification of consciousness's essential properties to an account of how physical systems could realize these. So, IIT proceeds from axioms asserting and characterizing the fundamentally subjective, or first-person, nature of consciousness. This consciousness is identical to integrated information.

Integrated information can be illustrated by example: Our visual experience of an apple, for example, integrates its redness and its shape inseparably. The brain's neurons' communication with one another performs the integration. By contrast, a digital camera's many photodiodes do not communicate with one another, so the information is not integrated, and the camera is not conscious: it has no experience of the apple it photographs.

Two different kinds of information are at play here. In the case of the camera, the information is observer-relative: it exists exactly insofar as an outside observer could experience it. (This is Shannonian information.) The brain's information, on the other hand, is not observer-relative; the brain experiences the information that it integrates. So, "IIT introduces a novel, non-Shannonian notion of information… which can be measured as "differences that make a difference" to a system from its intrinsic perspective" (Koch & Tononi, 2013).

The degree of consciousness depends upon the quantity of the integrated information, which IIT identifies with differentiation. A human's visual experience, even of a blank wall, has great richness, because it is differentiated from countless other prior and possible experiences (Tononi 2014). By contrast, a photodiode has minimal information because it is sensitive to only two states, differentiating only between light and dark. The amount of integrated information is mathematically quantifiable, according to IIT's *phi* metric (see Oizumi, Albantakis, & Tononi, 2014 for a recent version).

IIT's proponents believe that their approach is vindicated by its ability to account for why neurons in the cerebellum do not contribute to consciousness, while cortical neurons do (for example), or by experimental confirmation of its prediction that instances of loss of consciousness correlate to breakdown in integrated information (Oizumi, Albantakis, & Tononi, 2014).

More relevantly for the purposes of this chapter, IIT assigns definite parameters to work in Artificial Consciousness. According to the proponents of IIT, functionalism fails to appreciate the physical features necessary for a system to instantiate consciousness. The specification by a physical system of an integrated informational structure constitutes consciousness. A dynamic core (in brains, the neurons physically communicating with each other) realizes qualia space (the domain of subjective experience). Consciousness is a basic feature of this physical process: fundamental in a way analogous to mass or charge. As a consequence, IIT predicts that feed-forward networks, and conventional circuit-based networks generally, no matter how high their functional capacity, will never realize consciousness (but only simulate it). Such networks, on IIT, simply do not have the right 'anatomy' for it: the physical connections are not rich enough to realize the integration necessary for consciousness. Only reentry networks are even in principle able to do this. (This is much stronger than the claim that reentry networks *do* realize it or even that they are likely to be the *best* at this.)

ANALYSIS

Characterizing IIT

IIT's methodology involves, from the outset, claiming certain properties as essential to consciousness. "[A]s long as one starts from the brain and asks how it could possibly give rise to experience…the problem [of consciousness] may not only be hard, but almost impossible to solve." (Tononi & Koch, 2015) Instead, we should start with what is most basically known (even "transcendental" (Tononi, 2015). Here, IIT aligns itself with the Cartesian tradition: "That I am conscious, here and now, is the one fact I am absolutely certain of—all the rest is conjecture. This is, of course, the gist of the most famous deduction in Western thought, Descartes' *je pense, donc je suis.*" (Tononi & Koch, 2015) IIT claims various axioms concerning this consciousness (see Tononi & Koch, 2015 and Oizumi, Albantakis, & Tononi, 2014 for recent discussions of these). For the purposes of this chapter, these axioms, "which are taken to be immediately evident," can be distilled in the claims that consciousness exists (following Descartes), that each experience "consists of multiple aspects in various combinations", with "each experience differ[ing] in its particular way from other[s]", where each experience is "irreducible to non-interdependent components," and has unique borders (Oizumi, Albantakis, & Tononi, 2014). So, a person's experience of a red apple exists, involves different elements and differs from other experiences, and cannot be reduced to independent experiences of redness and shape, etc., as mentioned above.

Now, these remarks on their own may read like nothing more than an idiosyncratic expression of a traditional Cartesian position. But note that, as described in the 'Background' section above, IIT further identifies consciousness as integrated information, a novel characterization. The person's experience of the red apple is intrinsic to the integration of the *information* of redness and shape. Much of the purported contribution of IIT lies in its arguments concerning what physical systems could realize the axiomatic properties of consciousness, understood as integrated information.

Because anything with existence must have causal power, and because conscious systems must possess their consciousness intrinsically (in a non-observer-relative way), a conscious system (or 'complex') "must have cause-effect power upon itself" (Tononi & Koch, 2015. The authors do not supply an account of causal powers or an explicit justification of their necessity to existence.). The system has a range of possible states in its cause-effect repertoire, constituting its cause-effect structure. Recall that the axiomatic description of consciousness included that each experience cannot be reduced to independent parts. Accordingly, the integration of information requires that the system "specify a cause-effect repertoire (information) that is *irreducible* to independent components" (Oizumi, Albantakis, & Tononi, 2014). This "implies that every part of the system must be able to both affect and be affected by the rest of the system". (Tononi & Koch, 2015)

"[T]his convergence between neurobiology and phenomenology is no mere coincidence" (Edelman & Tononi, 2000). Indeed, a central paper within the IIT literature is entitled "From the Phenomenology to the Mechanisms of Consciousness" (Oizumi, Albantakis, & Tononi, 2014). The argument is claiming that phenomenology, as described axiomatically, very directly determines the physical mechanisms of conscious systems. Brains – neurobiological conscious systems – have their consciousness in virtue of their physical causal powers operating upon themselves in ways irreducible to component mechanisms. "Note that the notion of information in IIT…is faithful to its etymology: information refers to how a system of mechanisms in a state, through its cause-effect power, specifies a form ('informs' a conceptual structure)"; "the quantity and quality of an experience are an intrinsic, fundamental property [of such information] just as it is considered to be intrinsic to a mass to bend space-time around it" (Tononi & Koch, 2015. The reader should bear in mind that the very notion of fundamental physical properties is itself controversial; the IIT literature does not engage that controversy explicitly, and this chapter's critical discussion of IIT will focus on other possible problems.).

IIT is arguing – not that only neurobiological systems can be conscious – but that only systems that, like neurobiological brains, have the ability to cause physical changes to themselves, where each part can affect each other part physically, can be conscious. Why? Because consciousness is a property intrinsic to such systems, fundamental to them (as the bending of space-time is fundamental to mass). This constitutes a unique and strong claim.

IIT's observation concerning the convergence of neurobiology and phenomenology could have led to a less radical claim. For example, it might have claimed that the convergence of the brain's reentrant systems with the axiomatic properties of consciousness is an efficient physical way to realize those properties functionally. This would obviate the need to venture the radical claim that consciousness is a fundamental property of (certain causal systems in) the world. It would also leave open the possibility that non-reentrant systems could realize consciousness.

So, why does IIT commit itself to the unusual (although, as will become apparent below, not unheard-of) idea that we must account for consciousness by positing it as a fundamental property in the physical world? The answer lies in its rejection of the alternative interpretation, functionalism, which holds that consciousness is not a fundamental property, but rather explicable by primary reference to functions (where the physical properties of the system matter only insofar as they sustain those functions). The remainder of this section identifies the motivations behind this rejection.

Before developing IIT, Tononi published with the influential neuroscientist Gerard Edelman. (Edelman & Tononi, 2000) Edelman himself had already written of the "insufficiency of functionalism" (1989, p. 28). Edelman takes Putnam's machine state functionalism as representative of functionalism as a whole. He also notes that Putnam himself eventually rejected this position on the grounds that internal states alone do not suffice for fixing meaning, but require reference to the environment. For this reason, Edelman dismisses functionalism. He then contrasts this with the "sufficiency of selectionism" (pp. 31-2).

Edelman and Tononi's *A Universe of Consciousness* (2000) offers very little discrete attention to functionalism, although its anti-functionalism is clear from its other explicit commitments. Edelman and Tononi do claim "any information-processing, strictly functionalist approach to consciousness has little to say about the fact that consciousness requires the activity of specific neural substrates. These substrates are actually the central concern of neuroscientists" (2000, p. 7). The brain is not a computer: among other differences, it is less exact, more diverse, and uses ambiguous, non-Turing signals (p. 48). Again taking it as contrasting with other approaches, including functionalism, Edelman and Tononi endorse a selectionist outlook, searching for the properties of conscious systems by reference to principles of Darwinism at the neural level (p. 78).

Edelman and Tononi adopt a methodology that strongly anticipates IIT. Their strategy involves starting with the general properties of consciousness, and then proceeding to explain its neural basis (p. 20). They have ruled out reference to function as a possible explanation of consciousness, and seek the explanation in the physical structures of evolved neural systems. In *A Universe of Consciousness*, the familiar IIT themes of consciousness as integrated information with varying levels of differentiation emerge here explicitly for the first time (complete with the example of a camera) (pp. 23-32).

So, to summarize: IIT observes that evolved neural reentrant systems possess a physical causal structure that converges with the phenomenological (experiential) properties of consciousness. It also makes the further, bold, and novel claim that consciousness is a fundamental property of systems with such causal properties. The motivation for interpreting the convergence in this radical way rests upon a rejection of functionalism. Although IIT literature does not explicitly engage the issue of functionalism, this section has traced its rejection of that alternative to earlier arguments in Edelman (1989) and Edelamn & Tononi (2000).

IIT and Artificial Consciousness

This section reveals the relevance of IIT's claims to Anthropic Oriented Computing (AOC), and Artificial Consciousness in particular.

One finding of IIT that bears relevance for Artificial Consciousness lies in a claim concerning the causal properties of 'silent' neurons. In order to appreciate the nature of this claim, recall that IIT claims that a complex specifying a cause-effect repertoire gives rise to consciousness. IIT characterizes this physically, not functionally, so this is a process of a physical system realizing in physical space a set of elements that have the potential for physical causation over one another. This is the integration of information, and consciousness is a fundamental property of it. This generates a counterintuitive prediction: non-firing neurons will still have the ability to shape consciousness, because "Inactive elements of a complex specify a cause–effect repertoire…just as much as active ones" (Tononi & Koch, 2015). (Here, the authors remind us of the Sherlock Holmes story, where the fact that a dog did not bark (although it could have) holds meaning: the dog's silence signifies its prior knowledge of an intruder, an important clue.) On the other hand, if neurons were *rendered incapable* of specifying a cause-effect repertoire – e.g. optogenetically – the result would be different. In this case, the silence of the neurons would not contribute to consciousness, because the silence is not a result of neuronal inactivity within the complex, but rather the result of certain neurons' exclusion from the complex. To belong to the complex, neurons must be physically able to make a difference to the rest of the system: this causal capacity, IIT claims, is a physical requirement of realizing the phenomenology of consciousness. By extension, any genuine Artificial Consciousness would have to respect that elements of the system which enjoy potential causality with respect to the system may still, even when inactive, contribute to consciousness.

Even more relevant to Artificial Consciousness is IIT's claim that no feed-forward system could realize consciousness at all (and that largely non-reentrant systems will not achieve anything close to human consciousness). This position stems from IIT's bold, novel claim that consciousness is a fundamental property of causal systems with certain physical characteristics, which, as described above, rests on a rejection of functionalism.

Again, a consideration of earlier material reveals the origin of this claim. Edelman argues that reentry is a ubiquitous and vital mechanism in relating neural mappings to one another (1989, p. 90). Criticizing connectionist models of perception for not committing to particular biological cortical anatomy (pp. 71-2), Edelman further claims that primary consciousness requires reentrant mapping (p. 245). Tononi and Edelman (1998) claim that reentrant mechanisms are necessary for consciousness. Later, (Edelman & Tononi, 2000), they support this position in various ways: Reentry is a "*unique* feature of higher brains" (p. 49), and allows for integration without a "central coordination area" (p. 44). (This allows Edelman and Tononi to avoid positing a homunculus that experiences integrated information. The claim for such homunculi is vulnerable to the objection from infinite regress.) Only a subset of the brain's mechanisms contributes to consciousness; this 'dynamic core' is reentrant (p. 144). Reentry is "necessary for conscious experience to emerge", which is why subliminal priming is not conscious (pp. 67-8). Referencing Edelman (1989) directly, they claim that reentry "assures the integration that is essential to the creation of a scene in primary consciousness" (2000, p. 106, Chapter Ten). Here, Edelman and Tononi's claim that reentry is necessary to consciousness anticipates IIT's more specific claims regarding consciousness as integrated information.

The IIT literature explicitly lays out the claim that non-reentrant systems will never realize consciousness: IIT "predicts that feed-forward networks, even complex ones, are not conscious…. Also, in sharp contrast to widespread functionalist beliefs, IIT implies that digital computers, even if their behaviour were to be functionally equivalent to ours…would experience next to nothing" (Tononi & Koch, 2015). Even systems that are not totally feed-forward -- CPUs where each transistor only communicates with a few others – would have negligible levels of consciousness (or low *phi,* in IIT's terms). Koch (2015) holds that computers' arithmetic-logic units (ALUs), e.g., have too low a connectivity to generate high *phi*.

Here it becomes useful to revisit IIT's claim that consciousness has unique borders. This 'exclusion axiom' is not trivial as interpreted by the theory. Recall that consciousness is integrated information. This characterization is accurate but incomplete. As mentioned in the axiomatic description, consciousness has unique borders. These borders describe which groupings of elements integrate information such that it is conscious. An informational system may have subsets of elements whose cause-effect power integrates information. Of all the groupings of elements within a system of mechanisms that have cause-effect power, only one will do so maximally, specifying a conceptual structure that is conscious. (This is called the maximally irreducible conceptual structure, or MICS, and is mathematically distinguishable as having the largest *phi* value of any partitioning of the system.)

So, in the brain, for example, only a subset of the mechanisms contribute to consciousness – the 'dynamic core' mentioned earlier in this section. Neurons in the cerebellum, for example, contribute to the functioning of the brain, but do not belong to the MICS, and so do not contribute to consciousness. Feed-forward systems by definition do not have reentry and therefore do not have groupings of elements that make differences to themselves. Of course, most computers have large amounts of feedback and reentry, but they are still not designed in a way that sustains a significant MICS. There will be comparatively localized groupings with some amount of *phi*; where these do not overlap, they will constitute their own local maxima, and so will be MICS with some amount of consciousness, but the absence of a large MICS means that conventional computational efforts that mimic human operations will not have actually achieved human-level consciousness. Deep convolutional neural networks like GoogLeNet are therefore unable to contribute to Artificial Consciousness, and ambitious projects such as Blue Brain may achieve *intelligence* but not consciousness.

So, IIT's constraints upon Artificial Consciousness are an implication of its anti-functionalism. It is not the operation (function) of a system that constitutes consciousness; rather, a system embodies consciousness by making a difference to itself. The complex reentry of the brain, each of whose 'dynamic core' neurons may make thousands of connections with others, does just this, sustaining a rich, unitary consciousness. Mere local feedback integrates relatively little information and so sustains far less consciousness. Feed-forward systems do not have the architecture to do this at all: "In a feed-forward network, the input layer is always determined entirely by external inputs and the output layer does not affect the rest of the system, hence neither layer can be part of a complex…. According to IIT, then, a feed-forward network does not exist intrinsically—for itself—but is a zombie—carrying out tasks unconsciously." Such systems may compute very well, and could in principle "replicate the input-output behavior of the human brain," but will never experience as the human brain does.

The allusion to zombies is no mere rhetorical flourish, and is significant enough to merit attention in its own right. Oizumi, Albantakis, & Tononi (2014) describe non-reentrant systems that replicate human function along similar lines, as "true "zombies" – unconscious feed-forward systems that are functionally equivalent to conscious complexes". These references to zombies draw on an anti-functionalist tradition well-known in philosophy of mind (see Chalmers, 1996, e.g.). The argument runs as follows: If zombies – understood as entities that are mechanically identical to humans but that have no subjective experience – are possible, then consciousness cannot be identical to the function of those mechanisms. Therefore, (given the possibility of zombies) functionalism leaves something crucial out in its attempts to address the problem of consciousness. (The precise extent to which IIT and other anti-functionalist doctrines converge is a live issue. Aside from a few references to Chalmers in IIT, including the line about 'true zombies' just cited (Oizumi, Albantakis, & Tononi, 2014), and some allusions to IIT (e.g. from Chalmers, in press), there is little sustained formal discussion in print, although a recent workshop at New York University, organized by Chalmers, Tononi, and Hedda Hassel-Morch, brought together IIT theorists and panpsychists, and one can expect the published literature on this to grow.) The relevant lesson for this chapter lies in the strong link of IIT's exclusion of non-reentrant systems as candidates for Artificial Consciousness with IIT's anti-functionalist commitments.

IIT's anti-functionalism therefore implies not only that reentry systems are good or even optimal for generating consciousness artificially, but that they are *necessary*. This narrows the parameters in which the field of Artificial Consciousness must work. Tononi and Koch (2015) note that Artificial Consciousness is still possible: "there is no reason why hardware-level, neuromorphic models of the human brain that do not rely on software running on a digital computer, could not approximate, one day, our level of consciousness". Still, if IIT is correct, this places very serious constraints on the Artificial Consciousness.

Defending Functionalism

Despite the heading of this section, what follows will not attempt a complete defense of functionalism, a task suited for a much longer work; this section aims to undermine the particular arguments against functionalism offered by the literature associated with IIT, and to clarify functionalism's commitments. The expectation is that the functionalist position will emerge as at least a plausible (and very possibly a superior) alternative to IIT's interpretation of consciousness. In any case, those interested in Anthropic Oriented Computing (AOC) should have the opportunity of knowing their options, and the functionalist option does not receive a proper hearing in the IIT literature. (For a different philosophical critique of IIT, see Searle (2013).

The section entitled "Characterizing IIT" (above) addressed comparatively early rejections of functionalism that had influence on IIT's development. Edelman (1989) bases his opposition to functionalism on a negative evaluation of machine state functionalism. Machine state functionalism, broadly, argued that cognition, which is realized by a physical system, can be understood as the functional state of that system. In other words: The brain is operating in a way analogous to a computer. We can understand the workings of a computer not only at the physical level of circuitry, etc., but at the higher level of the operations that circuitry is performing. In fact, the particulars of the hardware are to an extent incidental, because different hardware can operate – function – identically. As Edelman rightly notes, Putnam, who initially conceived this doctrine (1960) rejected it later (1988). Putnam himself advanced the position that meaning is not fixed completely by the state of a system (brain): imagine a world otherwise identical to our own where, e.g., what was called 'water' actually had different a molecular structure. When our 'twin earth' counterparts use the word 'water', although their functional state is the same as ours when we use the word, they are referring to something different. Their 'water' means something different from our 'water', so meaning is not just a matter of internal states (1975a). Edelman belongs to a broad consensus that includes Putnam in opposing machine state functionalism. The problem is that machine state functionalism is a 'straw man'. More robust, contemporary versions of functionalism do not include the commitment to a completely internal determination of meaning. Moreover, while Edelman contrasts what he takes to be functionalism with selectionism, non-machine-state versions of functionalism easily accommodate commitments to natural selection: on these, selective pressures account for both function and the particular ways in which our brains neurophysiologically realize function.

Edelman and Tononi's subsequent remarks (2000) betray a similarly narrow conception of functionalism. As in Edelman (1989), they draw a false contrast between functionalism and selectionism. New instances of misunderstanding functionalism arise too. The fact that neuroscience is concerned with the neural substrates of consciousness (2000, p. 7), while functionalist accounts normally do not reference neuroanatomy in much depth, implies no tension between the two. Identifying neural substrates, any functionalist will agree, advances understanding of the particular physical nature of the brain. The functionalist is claiming that these particular substrates achieve consciousness in virtue of realizing certain functions. Edelman and Tononi's claim that the brain is not a computer (p.48) really amounts to claim that the brain is not a particular kind of computer. As Dennett expresses it, "Minds will turn out not to be *simple* computers, and their computational resources will be seen to reach down into … subcellular resources…but the theories that emerge will still be functionalist in the broad sense" (2005, p. 21). The conflation of machine state functionalism with functionalism in general has prevented Edelman and Tononi from appreciating that functionalism has broad appeal. In general, functionalism understands the relevance of physical matter to thought in terms not of matter's intrinsic properties but rather in terms of what that matter is doing. This claim "is so ubiquitous in science that it is tantamount to a reigning presumption of all of science" (2005, p. 17).

IIT continues to conceive too narrowly of functionalism. Referencing Hofstadter (2007), Oizumi, M., Albantakis, L., & Tononi, G. (2014) write "The idea that "feed-back", "reentry", or "recursion" of some kind may be an essential ingredient of consciousness has many proponents". But Hofstadter, actually a functionalist, explicitly distances himself from the idea that consciousness is a fundamental physical property: "[the functional recursion of conscious operations] is no more a pinpointable, extractable physical object than an audio feedback loop" (2007, p. 180).

As noted, IIT's claim that a non-reentrant system that replicates the function of a brain would be a zombie participates in a well-known anti-functionalist tradition. Dennett claims that positive allusions from the scientific community to the literature on zombies evidence not a commitment to deep anti-functionalism, but rather are motivated by opposition to understanding the mind as a simple computer, and constitute "an artefact of interdisciplinary miscommunication and nothing more" (2005, p. 22). Now, Edelman and Tononi clearly do oppose the mind-as-simple-computer idea, but their alignment with the zombie arguments is part of an opposition to functionalism in general. Their position may rest on a misunderstanding of functionalism, but they certainly do share some metaphysical convictions with those who argue from the possibility of zombies against functionalism.

Chalmers (1996) argues that we can conceive of a creature that is human-like in every physical way, but that has no experience. It would still operate in the same way – reporting beliefs, expressing emotion, etc. – but it would not be conscious. Because such a being is conceivable (and so, according to the argument, possible), consciousness is something other than physical parts operating in a certain way. This illustrates what has become widely known as the 'hard problem' of consciousness: coming to understand its physical substrate is difficult, but the truly hard problem is to understand the 'further fact' of consciousness (Chalmers, 1995). IIT does not parallel Chalmers' argument. On IIT, a creature physically human-like in every way would possess neuroanatomy that integrated information physically and would be conscious. But both IIT and Chalmers reject that systems that perform the same functions as humans would thereby be conscious. In both cases, this rejection leads to novel claims. Chalmers has developed a metaphysical system – panpsychism - that attributes mental properties to the basic elements of the structure of existence. IIT has claimed that consciousness is fundamentally inextricable to systems that embody integrated information. Of course, the latter is this chapter's concern, but it is worth noting that the rejection of functionalism – of, as Dennett calls it, "the reigning presumption of all science" – leads in both cases to claims that depart radically from the standard scientific ontology.

Both IIT and those who follow Chalmers routinely cite Descartes as having captured an essential and unavoidable truth, that "I am conscious, here and now" (Tononi & Koch, 2015). As discussed at various points above, IIT regards this as so basic that it takes whatever properties this basic consciousness has – its existence in itself, its integration, etc. – as axiomatic; the subjective phenomenology serves as a starting point. Because it overlooks the viable forms of functionalism, it does not so much explain this phenomenology as observe the convergence of it with our neurobiology (and claim the former as fundamental to the latter).

Functionalism affords the Cartesian gloss on experience a different kind of respect. Yes, it seems as though consciousness is immediate, essentially subjective, integrated such that it cannot be explained by reference to its functional elements operating in concert. But where IIT posits its existence as a special fundamental property, functionalism has other resources. That consciousness seems to have these properties is itself explicable. *Belief*, although historically a topic of great interest and controversy, does not have the reputation of being impervious to functional explanation that consciousness clearly still enjoys. (People do not much discuss the 'hard problem' of belief.) Beliefs are among a system's "dynamically interacting data-structures, with links of association…suggesting new calls to memory, composing on the fly new structures with new meanings and powers". This "system of internal operations" allows for complex behaviors, and is essentially computational in nature (Denett, 2005, pp. 12-13). Functionalism can address consciousness adequately because it can *explain* the Cartesian intuition about consciousness by reference to beliefs (Dennett, 2005, p. 44). Our experience of immediacy, subjectivity, integration, etc. is not sufficient to motivate the position that these are simple, brute facts (to be accounted for by the positing of a fundamental property), but are themselves beliefs. We believe that our experience is immediate, but that is a belief that in principle can be accounted for functionally, including by reference to evolutionary and developmental pressures. We believe that consciousness is essentially subjective, but that need not lead us to the conviction that objective explanation (that does not make recourse to positing fundamental entities new to science) will be unavailable. Functional elements working in concert suffice to produce in us the (false) conviction that experience could never be composed of these. "This 'I' you speak of is not some pearly something outside the physical world [NB – 'physical world' is understood here as not including the fundamental property posited by IIT] or something in addition to the team of busy, unconscious robots whose activities compose you" (2005, p. 75). Those who reject functionalism having at least encountered it in this form do so on the grounds that this account seems too deflationary, but, since functionalism claims all such beliefs as falling under its explanatory domain, this objection itself may deflate, and more accurately be regarded as the expression of jarred intuition. As Dennett puts it, "I don't maintain, of course, that human consciousness does not exist; I maintain that it is not what people often think it is" (2005, p. 71).

(Although there has been little explicit critical discussion of IIT to date, there are relevant connections to the debate surrounding the relationship between consciousness and 'access'. Some anti-functionalists, such as Ned Block, separate phenomenal consciousness (how it feels) from access consciousness ("a representation is access-conscious if it is made available to cognitive processing") (Block, 2011, p. 567). Koch and Tsuchiya (2007) defend this position, as one might expect: access-consciousness is totally explicable by reference to function, and Koch, as an IIT proponent, takes functionalism as inadequate. Indeed, Tononi (2015) explicitly links IIT with Block's arguments because both similarly account for the existence of many (phenomenal) concepts. Cohen and Dennett (2011) argue (as the title of their paper suggests) that "consciousness cannot be separated from function". Block (2011) and Fahrenfort & Lamme (2012) press further the anti-functionalist case, which is amenable to IIT, but, for a functionalist rejoinder in keeping with overall analysis of this section, see Cohen and Dennett (2012).

SOLUTIONS AND RECOMMENDATIONS

As has been addressed, IIT implies two related claims of great relevance to Artificial Consciousness. First, parts of a system that can make a difference to itself but remain 'silent' still contribute to consciousness, by differentiating the actual state from many possible alternatives. This accords with accounts (Koch & Tsuchiya, 2007; Block, 2011; Fahrenfort & Lamme, 2012) that take the richness of human phenomenology to be under-described by functionalist accounts that have recourse only to 'access'; large components of a system remaining silent do not affect function (by definition), but they still endow enrich phenomenology. The functionalist approach argues that reports of and convictions about one's rich phenomenology, which seems on the face of it to include more than what the subject has access to, themselves bear explanation functionally (Cohen & Dennett, 2011, 2012). There is no need to appeal to new fundamental physical/causal properties of silent system components (in the case of the brain, silent neurons). If we have a rich experience staring at blank wall, it is not (as Tononi would have it) because of the inactivity of many system elements that could make a difference but remain silent, but because even in the simple act of staring at a wall, various functional dispositions (associations, data structures amounting to calm or impatient attitudes etc.) are at work, which suffice to characterize the phenomenology. If IIT is correct, then Artificial Consciousness would have to take this into account, and would also be able to exploit the construction of potentially- but not currently-active system elements (so long as they have the proper physical architecture, of course) to enrich conscious experience (perhaps even indefinitely). If, as the last section suggests, functionalism is correct, then Artificial Consciousness would have to engineer rich experience in simple sensory cases by layering those with various functional associations. On the face of it, this is more demanding, but seems more principled than the IIT move, because one could link the presence of functional dispositions to phenomenology, rather than making appeal to 'realizing qualia space'.

Second, and more significantly, IIT claims that feed-forward architecture will not be conscious at all, and artificial systems that include reentrant architecture will probably have some complexes with small MICS, but will be unlikely to have a major MICS with a high level of *phi*. Attempts at artificial consciousness should be massively reentrant, generating a large MICS with high *phi*.

Given the depth of disagreement between IIT and functionalism, one would expect dramatically different expectations for the practical realization of Artificial Consciousness, but this is not necessarily so. Recall that Tononi and Koch (2015) claim that "neuromorphic models of the human brain that do not rely on software running on a digital computer could…approximate…our level of consciousness". Compare Dennett (p. 21, 2005), cited in brief above but fully here: "Minds will not turn out to be *simple* computers, and their computational resources will be seen to reach down into subcellular molecular resources available only to organic brains, but the theories will still be functionalist in the broad sense." Here, Tononi and Koch make similar claims to Dennett's (if anything, theirs are slightly *less* conservative than the functionalist's) about what kind of system will be conscious. The reason for this convergence lies in the willingness of the functionalist position to accept that practical engineering concerns will likely favor architecture similar to the brain. Modern functionalism can self-consistently hold that Artificial Consciousness should emulate nature's solution to engineering mental thought, including consciousness.

Given this convergence, IIT's *phi* metric may have value independent of IIT's ontological claims. That is, even if IIT is incorrect in understanding consciousness as a fundamental property of certain causal systems, given that the functional realization of consciousness does employ these causal systems, *phi*, which is intended to measure the quantity of integrated information within these systems, may pick out a genuine property about consciousness. Readers optimistic about this may consult Oizumi, M., Albantakis, L., & Tononi, G. (2014) for a recent version of *phi* calculation. *Phi*, even considered apart from the rest of IIT, does attract controversy. Aaronson (2014 May 21 and 30, 2015 November) claims that uninteresting expander graphs, or at least the grids based on them, could have *phi* values higher than human levels, a point that Tononi has accepted (2014, 2015 November), but that for many constitutes a reductio ad absurdum of the current *phi* metric. Even more pessimistically, Maguire, P., Moser, P., Maguire, R., & Griffith, V. (2014) argue that the integration required for unitary consciousness is not computable at all.

Whatever the utility of *phi* as a quantifier of consciousness-level, and however much the practical expectations of IIT and functionalism may converge, they remain committed to deeply different explanations of consciousness, and imply different scopes for its possible realization in Artificial Consciousness. Since (as Sections 1 and 2 of this chapter show), IIT's anti-functionalism implies accepting rigid constraints on Artificial Consciousness, a defense of functionalism over IIT's objections (Section 3) opens the possibility of conceiving of the constraints on Artificial Consciousness differently. Even if, as Dennett has it, the functional realization of Artificial Consciousness would do well to emulate the reentry architecture of the brain, as selected for by natural processes, Artificial Consciousness engineers may depart from this emulation in the service of more conveniently achieving the relevant functional operations. (Aaronson (2014, June 2), also briefly criticizes IIT's requirement of reentry for consciousness (Koch, 2014, June 1, inter alia).)

FUTURE RESEARCH DIRECTIONS

IIT is a fertile research area. As mentioned, IIT proponents and philosophers such as David Chalmers, aligned with the 'panpsychist' tradition, have begun to explore whether they share metaphysical commitments. Physicists have also taken note of IIT, asking whether IIT might best be understood with reference to fundamental fields (Barrett, 2014), or whether consciousness, on IIT, counts as a state of matter, describable in terms of quantum systems (Tegmark, in press). Within IIT, the measurement of *phi* for complex systems remains elusive; several refinements to *phi* measurement have already been made and the issue will likely attract further speculation (e.g., Hoel & Marshall, 2015, are working on this). It would be surprising if IIT proponents declined to attempt to refute the claim (Maguire, Moser, Maguire & Griffith, 2014) that unitary consciousness is not computable, given IIT's general stance on the computability of consciousness given the right physical systems.

Of course, such research may be premature, especially if one takes the functionalist alternative to IIT. Further neuroscience might clarify whether Koch and Tsuchiya (20017) and Block (2011) are right to claim that phenomenology 'overflows' access, or vindicate the functionalist claim (Cohen & Dennett, 2011, 2012) that phenomenology can on all counts be understood as (functional) access to information. Those already satisfied with the functionalist approach will take comfort that Artificial Consciousness is not necessarily tethered to analog reentry at every turn. Without IIT's strict requirements, low connectivity CPU features such as arithmetic-logic units and feed-forward convolutional systems such as GoogLeNet become engineering options available for designing Artificial Consciousness. As Steve Furber (chief designer of the SpiNNAker computer architecture, inspired by the brain) puts it, "as speedy and efficient as analog circuits are, they're not very flexible; their basic behavior is pretty much baked right into them. And that's unfortunate, because neuroscientists still don't know for sure which biological details are crucial to the brain's ability to process information and which can be safely abstracted away" (Furber, in Courtland, 2014). If the functionalist paradigm proves viable, then Artificial Consciousness research will overlap with and benefit from more of the work going on in the Blue Brain Project, the Human Brain Project, and the White House BRAIN initiative. Given the latitude afforded by functionalism in the realization of mental events, the direction that research will take would become difficult to predict with precision.

CONCLUSION

Those interested in designing Artificial Consciousness have an interest in understanding IIT. IIT is an influential and well-argued theory, and if correct, implies strict constraints for any computational program aimed at generating consciousness. Those in the field of Artificial Consciousness should also have the resources to assess IIT. Although it is not fully and directly apparent from IIT's literature, IIT bases its claims on controversial philosophical positions, and an informed evaluation of IIT includes an awareness of the alternatives to those positions. This chapter has sought to provide a fair hearing of IIT as well as a good indication of its possible weaknesses.

IIT observes a convergence between phenomenology – subjective, unitary experience of integrated information – and neurobiology, which, it argues, physically integrates information in an irreducible way. This on its own may constitute an insight into the natural engineering of consciousness.

IIT's particular philosophical commitments lead it to further and arguably less defensible claims. Those commitments--to certain dimensions of experience as essential, and to a separate domain of phenomenal consciousness--preclude a genuine explanation of consciousness, and IIT must therefore assert that consciousness attaches fundamentally to physical structures of a particular kind. But because the 'phenomenal' aspect of consciousness – its subjective, immediate feeling – can be characterized in terms of access (i.e. access to certain information within the system), a system that functionally realizes the right kind of access will be conscious. On the functionalist account, consciousness is a system operating in a certain way, not a fundamental property analogous to mass or charge that attaches only to the physical structure of reentry systems.

A more defensible position may involve characterizing the convergence of phenomenology and neurobiology as evidence of how natural selection has realized conscious functioning, while leaving open whether artificial approaches must emulate natural selection in its physical particulars. On this account, attempts at Artificial Consciousness will have functional principles as their guide in generating experience, which will rule out the ability to enrich phenomenology via 'silent' subsystem elements, but will provide much more practical guidance than IIT's reference to 'qualia space'. More importantly, this account preserves the possibility that Artificial Consciousness will benefit from largely following nature's example, implementing functions via reentrant architecture. At the same time, according to the functionalist position, those in the field of Artificial Consciousness should have the option of using feed-forward or less reentrant systems/subsystems, when doing so would better realize conscious functioning.

REFERENCES

Aaronson, S. (2014a, May 21). *Why I am not an integrated information theorist (or, the unconscious expander)* [Web log post]. Retrieved from Shtetl-Optimized, http://scottaaronson.com/blog

Aaronson, S. (2014b, May 30). *Giulio Tononi and me: a phi-nal exchange* [Web log post]. Retrieved from Shtetl-Optimized, http://scottaaronson.com/blog

Aaronson, S. (2015, November). *The Unconscious Expander*. Paper presented at The Integrated Information Theory of Consciousness: Foundational Issues, Workshop, New York, NY.

Barrett, A. (2014). An integration of integrated information theory with fundamental physics. *Frontiers in Psychology*, *5*(63). PMID:24550877

Block, N. (2011). Perceptual consciousness overflows cognitive access. *Trends in Cognitive Sciences*, *15*(12), 567–575. doi:10.1016/j.tics.2011.11.001 PMID:22078929

Chalmers, D. (1995). Facing up to the problem of consciousness. *Journal of Consciousness Studies*, 2.

Chalmers, D. (1996). *The Conscious Mind*. New York: Oxford University Press.

Chalmers, D. (in press). The combination problem for panpsychism. In L. Jaskolla & G. Bruntup (Eds.), *Panpsychism. Oxford University Press*.

Cohen, M., & Dennett, D. (2011). Consciousness cannot be separated from function. *Trends in Cognitive Sciences*, *15*(8), 358–364. doi:10.1016/j.tics.2011.06.008 PMID:21807333

Cohen, M., & Dennett, D. (2012). Response to Fahrenfort and Lamme: Defining reportability, accessibility and sufficiency in conscious awareness. *Trends in Cognitive Sciences*, *16*(3), 139–140. doi:10.1016/j.tics.2012.01.002

Courtland, R. (2014). Can the human brain project succeed? *IEEE Spectrum*, *9*(July). Retrieved from http://spectrum.ieee.org/tech-talk/computing/hardware/can-the-human-brain-project-succeed

Dennett, D. (2005). *Sweet dreams: Philosophical obstacles to a science of consciousness*. Cambridge, MA: The MIT Press.

Edelman, G. (1989). *The remembered present: A biological theory of consciousness*. New York: Basic Books.

Edelman, G., & Tononi, G. (2000). *A universe of consciousness: How matter becomes imagination*. New York: Basic Books.

Fahrenfort, J., & Lamme, V. (2012). A true science of consciousness explains phenomenology: Comment of Cohen and Dennett. *Trends in Cognitive Sciences*, *16*(3), 138–139. doi:10.1016/j.tics.2012.01.004 PMID:22300549

Hoel, E., & Marshall, W. (2015, November). *How the macro beats the Micro*. Paper presented at The Integrated Information Theory of Consciousness: Foundational Issues, Workshop, New York, NY.

Hofstadter, D. (2007). *I am a strange loop*. New York: Basic Books.

Koch, C. (2014, June 1). *Giulio Tononi and me: a phi-nal exchange* [Web log post]. Retrieved from Shtetl-Optimized, http://scottaaronson.com/blog

Koch, C. (2015, November). *Some Counterintuitive Predictions Arising from IIT*. Paper presented at The Integrated Information Theory of Consciousness: Foundational Issues, Workshop, New York, NY.

Koch, C., & Tononi, G. (2013). Can a photodiode be conscious? *The New York Review of Books*, *3/7*(13).

Koch, C., & Tsuchiya, N. (2007). Phenomenology without conscious access is a form of consciousness without top-down attention. *Behavioral and Brain Sciences*, *30*(5-6), 509–510. doi:10.1017/S0140525X07002907

Maguire, P., Moser, P., Maguire, R., & Griffith, V. (2014) Is consciousness computable? Quantifying integrated information using algorithmic information.*Proceedings of the 36th Annual Conference of the Cognitive Science Society*. Austin, TX: Cognitive Science Society.

Marcus, G. (2013, June 6). How much consciousness does an iphone have? *The New Yorker*. Retrieved October 28, 2015, from www.newyorker.com/tech/elements/how-much-consciousness-does-an-iphone-have

Oizumi, M., Albantakis, L., & Tononi, G. (2014). From the phenomenology to the mechanisms of consciousness: Integrated information theory 3.0. *PLoS Computational Biology*, *10*(5), e1003588. doi:10.1371/journal.pcbi.1003588 PMID:24811198

Putnam, H. (1960). Minds and machines. *Republished in Putnam, 1975b*, 362–385.

Putnam, H. (1975a) The meaning of 'meaning'. In Mind, language, and reality (pp. 215-71). Cambridge, UK: Cambridge University Press. doi:10.1017/CBO9780511625251.014

Putnam, H. (1975b). *Mind, Language, and Reality*. Cambridge, UK: Cambridge University Press. doi:10.1017/CBO9780511625251

Putnam, H. (1988). *Representation and Reality*. Cambridge, UK: Cambridge University Press.

Searle, J. (2013, January 10). Review of the book *Consciousness: confessions of a romantic reductionist*, by C. Koch. *New York Review of Books*.

Tegmark, M. (in press). Consciousness as a state of matter. *Chaos, Solitons, and Fractals*.

Tononi, G. (2004). An information integration theory of consciousness. *BMC Neuroscience*, *5*(1), 42. doi:10.1186/1471-2202-5-42 PMID:15522121

Tononi, G. (2008). Consciousness as integrated information: A provisional manifesto. *The Biological Bulletin*, *215*(3), 216–242. doi:10.2307/25470707 PMID:19098144

Tononi, G. (2014, May 30). *Why Scott should stare at a blank wall and reconsider (or, the conscious grid)* [Web log post]. Retrieved from Shtetl-Optimized, http://scottaaronson.com/blog

Tononi, G. (2015, November). *Integrated Information Theory: An outline and some ontological considerations*. Paper presented at The Integrated Information Theory of Consciousness: Foundational Issues, Workshop, New York, NY. doi:10.4249/scholarpedia.4164

Tononi, G., & Edelman, G. (1998). Consciousness and complexity. *Science, 282*(5395), 1846–1851. doi:10.1126/science.282.5395.1846 PMID:9836628

Tononi, G., & Koch, C. (2015). Consciousness: here, there and everywhere? *Philosophical Transactions of the Royal Society, Philosophical Transactions B.* doi:10.1098/rstb.2014.0167

Zimmer, C. (2010, September 20). Sizing up consciousness by its bits. *The New York Times*. Retrieved October 28, 2015, from www.nytimes.com/2010/09/21/consciousnesss.html

KEY TERMS AND DEFINITIONS

Access Consciousness: Characterizes mental states that are available for cognitive processing. Purportedly contrasted with 'phenomenal consciousness' (below).

Cartesian: Descriptive of ideas associated with philosopher Renee Descartes (1596-1650), especially, in this context, the conviction that experience is immediately known in certain ways. Descartes took the position that the mental was a separate substance from the physical.

Feed-Forward: A system (computational or neural) that processes information in one direction only, taking input and giving output.

Functionalism: The position that mental states, including consciousness, may in principle be explained by reference to how a system functions, rather than to its particular material constitution. 'Machine State Functionalism' is an early form of functionalism that identified a mental state with an internal functional or 'machine' (e.g. Turing) state.

Maximally Irreducible Conceptual Structure (MICS): The grouping of elements within a system with the greatest cause-effect power to integrate information. The MICS is conscious.

Panpsychism: Refers to a metaphysical system that attributes mental properties to the basic elements of the structure of existence.

Phenomenology: A word with many associations, here used to denote experience as encountered subjectively.

Phi: IIT's metric for quantifying consciousness. Mathematically, *phi* is very difficult to calculate for anything but simple systems given current techniques, but enters into heuristic descriptions: e.g. 'low vs. high *phi*'.

Qualia: Plural of 'quale'; the raw feelings of conscious experience.

Reentry/Reentrant: A system (computational or neural), composed of feedback loops, where information processing involves signals travelling in both directions, i.e. where output can serve as input also.

Chapter 2
Naturalizing Consciousness Emergence for AI Implementation Purposes:
A Guide to Multilayered Management Systems

Jordi Vallverdú
Universitat Autònoma de Barcelona, Spain

Max Talanov
Kazan federal University, Russia

ABSTRACT

The purpose of this chapter is to delineate a naturalistic approach to consciousness. This bioinspired method does not try to emulate into a 1:1 scale real mechanisms but instead of it, we capture some basic brain mechanisms prone to be implemented into computational frameworks. Consequently, we adopt a functional view on consciousness, considering consciousness as one among other cognitive mechanisms useful for survival purposes in natural environments. Specifically, we wish to capture those mechanisms related to decision-making processes employed by brains in order to produce adaptive answer to the environment, because this is the main reason for the emergence and purpose of consciousness.

DOI: 10.4018/978-1-5225-1947-8.ch002

INTRODUCTION

The purpose of this chapter is to delineate a naturalistic approach to consciousness. This bioinspired method does not try to emulate into a 1:1 scale real mechanisms but instead of it, we capture some basic brain mechanisms prone to be implemented into computational frameworks. Consequently, we adopt a functional view on consciousness, considering consciousness as one among other cognitive mechanisms useful for survival purposes in natural environments. Specifically, we wish to capture those mechanisms related to decision-making processes employed by brains in order to produce adaptive answer to the environment, because this is the main reason for the emergence and purpose of consciousness (Ross, 2010; vanGaal et al 2012). From an evolutionary perspective, consciousness is cognitive mechanism useful for self-evaluation processes as well as for taking somehow elaborated decisions and managing attention processes (Damasio, 1999; Taylor, 2010). Thanks to the neuromodulators involved into attention processes, we can establish a clear connection between neuromodulatory activities and consciousness emergence (Montemayor & Haladjian, 2015). Despite of the previous ideas, in no case we suggest that consciousness is the highest and privileged way to manage multi-haptic data received by an organism. It is one of the several ways that employs the brain to process valuable information, although it is clear that consciousness owns several self-monitoring mechanisms and usually it makes possible to guide the whole system towards a required action.

We propose the crucial mechanism for emotional information processing, the neuromodulation, which must be placed into the multi-dimensional architecture of the cognition. The neuromodulators influence several emotional, intentional and processing mechanisms in the brain. For example: the presence of the DRD4 (the gene of dopamine receptor D4) is involved in subtle, and complex behavior. We use the naturalistic approach to consciousness and its emergence that is related to the active and determinant role of neuromodulators and we propose modeling consciousness emergence pathways. Our research is oriented towards the design of multi-dimensional cognitive systems into AI research. Some of our previous results (from NEUCOGAR project Vallverdu et al, 2016) are presented here as validation of our foundational ideas in the field.

THE DEBATES ON THE MEANING OF WORD 'CONSCIOUSNESS'

David Chalmers' Online database on consciousness is exhaustive and "monumental" (http://consc.net/online), indicating the great interest for this topic, expressed by philosophers, psychologists, neurologists, anthropologists or computer scientists.

The complexity of this study has been identified as "the hard problem" (Chalmers, 1995). De Gardelle & Kouider (2009) have described the historical and conceptual evolution of the cognitive debates around the notion of consciousness. Well known homunculus paradox (Gregory, 1988) that is used as the central control system of mind justifying the existence of consciousness indicates a lack of understanding of cognitive process of a consciousness. Several models have been proposed to identify the consciousness: the Global Workspace Theory (Baars 1988), the Intermediate Level Theory (Prinz, 2005 following Jackendoff, 1987), the Information Integration Theory of Consciousness (Tononi, 2008, Edelman, 1989),the Multiple Drafts Model (Dennet, 1991), the Theory of Apparent Mental Causation (Wegner, 2002) and more recently,the Sensory-Motor Theory of Consciousness (O'Regan & Noë, 2001),Radical Plasticity thesis (Cleereman, 2008) or Bayesian Decision Theory (Lau, 2008). For the reason of the complexity of the understanding (Crick, 1995) and description of consciousness, some authors propose an indirect approach, being focused on the neural correlates of (human) consciousness (Crick & Koch 2003). The neurologist Antonio Damasio described the self-conscious feeling in his book "The feeling of what happens" (Damasio, 1999), it is directly intertwined with the emotional semantics that any embodied living system has. This is reflected in the recent rise of the interest of AI experts into emotional AI (Minsky, 2007).

Considering all the previous ideas about the nature of consciousness, we assume that consciousness is the result of natural evolutionary processes. As a physically instantiated process, a naturalized approach is a sound method for its analysis. The study of the natural emergence or presence of consciousness across living entities has been a research topic for animal experts, especially among cognitive ethologists. It has been proved that several animals like great apes, asian elephants, bottlenose dolphins, magpie and, among fishes, giant manta rays, show mirror self-recognition awareness (Ari & D'Agostino, 2016). Besides, as a consequence of this naturalistic framework, it must be understood from a functional perspective: it is a mechanism that improved the survival ratio of their hosts, not only affecting bodily-individual aspects but also to the social activities of these living systems (Skoggard & Waterson, 2015). The understanding of the reasons why consciousness emerged can help us to design more complex AI systems, implementing new ways of information processing. We consider a consciousness as complex mechanism to analyze and process inbound and internal information with different tools or heuristics (Turner & Fauconnier, 2002; Gigerenzer et al, 2011). This process can be conscious or even unconscious, as shows us the "Broken escalator" phenomenon: brains process very complex patterns in an inbound information flow without conscious control (Reynolds & Bronstein, 2003). Consequently, we present here two strongly connected ideas: a) consciousness relays on embodied mechanisms, b) consciousness is not the highest level of informational filtering and appraisal, action-decision of living systems.

THE EMERGENCE OF CONSCIOUSNESS IN LIVING ENTITIES

Following a naturalistic approach, we look at biological evolution and existing nature to analyze the nature of consciousness as well as to elucidate the possible mechanisms that made possible the emergence of consciousness into some animals. On the basis of these ideas we propose a naturalized perspective about the emergence of consciousness. We will provide an explanation of its basic mechanisms via a bottom up approach which could inspire robotics and AI programmers for the creation of conscious machines.In their work, Hills and Butterfill (2015: 368) have proposed the following idea: "The capacity to adapt to resource distributions by modulating the frequency of exploratory and exploitative behaviors is common across metazoans and is arguably a principal selective force in the evolution of cognition". Both behaviors are triggered and controlled by processes of self-evaluations. As the part of a self-awareness, we could identify a simpler mechanism to cope with ones body interactions: autonoetic consciousness. According to Tulving (1985:1), autonetic consciousness is the name given to the kind of consciousness that mediates an individual's awareness of his or her existence and identity in subjective time extending from the personal past through the present to the personal future. On the other hand, we can identify a neurochemical way to understand foraging actions: dopamine releasement. At the level of simple living entities goal-directed actions are the result of embodied requirements and create intentional actions within these systems (Hills, 2006). Thus, dopamine acts like a regulator of these actions, managing the goals achievement via 'reward', 'interest' or 'novelty' values (Costa et al., 2014; Bromberg-Martin and Hikosaka, 2009). These neurochemical reactions and as the result behavioral patters are observed across variety of species including humans (Barron et al., 2010). Therefore, we can establish a correlation between self-awareness, goal-directed actions and neuromodulation, all together triggering the emergence of consciousness.

NEUROTRANSMITTERS, CONSCIOUSNESS AND COMPUTATIONAL SIMULATIONS: NEUCOGAR

One of the main aims of Artificial Intelligence designers is the creation of a rational machine able to perform any cognitive activity with at least the same competence of a human (expert). Creativity and innovation are also fundamental pieces of this interest. such machines should be capable to: create new knowledge, deal with complex situations/dynamic environments and self-learn. We assume that this cognitive machine should have consciousness as well as emotions, both related mechanisms which help human agents to select strategies and perform appraisal of inbound information. We address roots of conscious processes into neurochemical circuitry of a human brain. We work in the project to implement ideas of a neuromodulation into a computational system, creating NEUCOGAR (NEUromodulating COGnitive ARchitecture) (Vallverdu et al 2015). The objective of NEUCOGAR project is to create the model of computational emotions using analogy of the influence of basic affective states via three neuromodulators: serotonin, dopamine and noradrenaline on thinking processes; to the influence of machine affective states over computational processes of Von Neumann machine. As a basis of the modeling we used and extended the "Cube of Emotion" by Hugo Lövheim (Lövheim, 2012) with mapping to parameters of a Von Neumann architecture. Validation was conducted via simulation on a computing system of dopamine neuromodulation and its effects on a motor cortex. During experiments of the project we indicated that the increase of consumed computing power and storage redistribution modulated by the dopamine system, confirmed the soundness of our model. Thus, we indicated that the mechanisms of a brain involved in several cognitive tasks could be reproduced successfully in modern computer system.

We consider the NeuCogAr initial success, as the first step to the implementation of a framework, based on similar neuro-bio-inspired bottom up approach to AI architectures, that potentially will be capable of emergence of a machine consciousness similar to mammalian consciousness. Our neuromodulatory approach provides an intentionality to a intelligent system and defines a syntax for the information evaluation, filtering and appraisal, that are crucial for a organism existence as an informational entity. Proposed cognitive architecture is compatible with the Multiple Drafts Model (Dennet, 1991), and with Sensory-Motor Theories (Barsalou, 2008) and justifies transverse Information Integration (Tononi, 2008). We suppose that the neuromodulatory mechanism could be at the core of several cognitive mechanisms like: behavior, emotions, attention, information filtering, memories and behavior strategy selection, among others. The role of artificial consciousness in the whole map of cognitive functions of a brain, natural or artificial, will be explained in the next section.

CONSCIOUSNESS AS ONE OF THE COGNITIVE DOMAINS, BUT WHICH ONE?

One of the most surprising facts of human cognition is that conscious processes are not placed on any top layers of general control over the body and mind, but they are placed among several mechanisms that uses the body to achieve its survival (Van Gaal & Lamme, 2012): subliminal negation (Armstrong & Dienes, 2013), word processing (Hollenstein et al 2012), vision (Ansorge, Kunde & Kiefer, 2014; Kouider

& Dehaene, 2007). In fact, can be stated that almost the vast amount of brain cognitive activity is not under conscious control (Donchin & Coles, 1998), and this huge unconscious activity run several fundamental cognitive activities (Weiss, 1997). These statements should not led us to the abandon of the interest on consciousness not the undervaluation of its role across cognitive processes. Clearly, consciousness allows an informational sphere of decision-making that makes possible scientific and formal reasoning. On the other side, it is also true that consciousness is not directly involved into several fundamental cognitive processes that happen into living systems that interact with the world. Perhaps we should look at which kind of functions consciousness is necessary. The basic necessity for a predictive mechanisms, used for example in purposes of locomotion, could be used to explain and justify the necessity in extended control system that is called usually 'consciousness' (Cleermans, 2011). The prediction is one of the key functions of some brains, including human one (Llinás, 2001) and it runs simultaneously at a conscious as well as at a unconscious levels (Kihlstrom, 1987, 1994). We propose that unconscious cognition is the processing of perception, memory, learning, thought, and language without being aware of it (Barg and Morsella, 2008). This process runs into individual as well as social levels (Winkielman & Schooler, 2011). Think for example in music performing: several conscious and unconscious mechanisms interoperate and provide the final output (Zatorre, Chen & Penhune, 2007). We can also consider living systems with cognitive systems without consciousness that nevertheless are well adapted to changing environments, as in the case of several minimal cognition studies can explain. Then...If consciousness is not the highest or more fundamental function of human brains, why do we want to implement it in the machines? Because it provides an option to operate with symbolic and cultural informational mechanisms, these mechanisms are rich, diverse, and provide human beings multiple heuristic ways to create meaning of events. We propose the integrated perspective to conscious and unconscious mechanisms based on the intentional design of the system. The conscious level is the dynamic analysis and regulation of multiple processes, that are monitored by the whole system simultaneously. We propose the understanding of a mind as a sum of cognitive processes, conscious processes just one group of them, useful for symbolic and precisely analysis processes.

THE SAME NEUROMODULATIVE MACHINERY FOR EMOTIONS AND COGNITION

For animals to be conscious means not only to 'know about myself' but actually have "feeling myself" as something existent. We have to admit that using the concept of self awareness, lead us to the shifting sands of *qualia* (Dennet, 1990). Underlying mechanisms of neuronal functioning that regulate all types of cognitive strategies, and emotional filtering and appraisal are at the core of any mammalian brain. Especially on unconscious level (Kihlstrom, 2000), emotions play important role in information filtering and appraisal.Emotions plays significant role in conscious and rational processes (Damasio, 1994). Nevertheless, there are a lot of cognitive architectures implementations adding 'emotional' modules that manage part of the information required by the program/robot (usually for Human-Robot Interaction), instead of building a whole cognitive architecture based on emotional mechanisms (Vallverdú, 2012). The new architecture implies a more efficient cognitive modeling as well as the creation of novel generation of machines with moods, affective predispositions and unique personalities. It could improve emotional interactions between humans and machines, once we validated and weighted artificial architectures with human-like responses.

QUANTITATIVE AND QUALITATIVE ELEMENTS OF CONSCIOUSNESS

As we've seen, consciousness studies are very complex and affect several academic domains: psychology, neuroscience, ethology, philosophy or anthropology, among others. Besides, the complexity of the phenomenal nature of this process, the experience of one-self, turns the analysis somehow complex. Nevertheless, we can defend a quantitative and formal approach. We are close to the Integrated Information Theory (IIT) held by neuroscientist Giulio Tononi (Oizumi, Albantakis & Tononi, 2014). IIT allows a mathematical approach to consciousness establishing some axioms and postulates about the nature of consciousness: existence, composition, information, integration, and exclusion. Thus, consciousness exists, and it is structured, as well as differentiated, unified and singular.At the same time, consciousness flows over time and must be understood as a dynamic system in constant change. All these process do not imply automatically self-conscious processes, because several cognitive processes run beyond direct control. Without abandoning materialism, we could affirm the each "person" (who experiences a "me") is an specialized ghost in a shell controlled by another general-purpose ghost. We make several cognitive estimations implied into sensorimotor processes as well as thinking processes that are processed most of time unconsciously: avoiding an obstacle while walking, evaluating best strategies to be happy in a future according to the decision about which bachelor we will choose, or identifying a sound as a provable menace. This late process includes a very important aspect: the predictive capacity of minds. It implies some kind of models about reality as well as probability functions. At a biological level, several animals run probability estimations instinctively, that is, using amodal techniques.

Natural statistics is then processed by cognitive systems, without any symbolic or formal mechanism. Regarding statistics evaluations there is a second important key aspect to consider for: these evaluations imply a comparison, and it is possible thanks to semantic values. The cognitive system not only process, but compare and estimate according to previous real or imagined data. Our previous researchers with NEUCOGAR provide a naturalistic approach to cognition that could allow to implement semantic mechanisms to guide the cognitive processes. Neuromodulators make possible to assign values to information data as well as to manage the data with several heuristics. From this perspective, neuromodulators emerged evolutionary as functional and useful short-cuts mediators for agent actions: from mind processes to real embodied practices or actions. Such computational approach allows to maintain basic axiomatic concepts that makes possible information processing entities with semantic and intentional relations with the information. The naturalistic approach to the involved statistical procedures must be clearly flavored with Bayesian methods, but using different and embodied approach (Vallverdu, 2016).

A MULTILAYERED MODEL OF COGNITIVE SYSTEMS FOR AGI PURPOSES

Perhaps the best model that captures the several intricacies of cognitive systems is the one of Minsky (Minsky, 2007) (Figure 1).

It can be seen as the best approximation to the multidimensional and layered range of informational actions performed by human beings. Previous models from

Figure 1. Minsky

31

computer or cognitive scientists, such as CogAff are still interesting, but under-value the role of emotional mechanisms into cognitive processes.

On the other side, the more recent LIDA model (Baars & Franklin, 2009) captures with a better modularity approach the differences between conscious and unconscious levels:

But these general modular approaches need to be defined at a bottom level, explaining the mechanisms by which a bottom up architecture is possible. To give an answer we find several approaches that tries to explore this approach:

1. **Mechanistic Emulation:** Projects like Markram's Blue Brain Project (BBP) is focused into building a large-scale brains models which emulates in detail biological (neurological) processes. This bottom up construct is based on the assumption that the more complex behavioral features will emerge, although it is a disembodied approach without an obvious intentional drive for the system. Several and serious critics towards BBP were launched in 2014 by a huge net of European neuroscientists (http://www.neurofuture.eu/). Frégnac & Laurent (2014) made a review of this project, considered by a lot of experts of cognitive sciences communities as a waste of money and scientific senseless activity.

2. **Mechanistic Simulation:** Still interested on neural processes, but without the emulation requirements, other approaches can be found which try to describe a theory for cognitive processes, including a theory of consciousness. Very briefly:

    a. **Neural Engineering Frameworks (NEF):** According to Komer & Eliasmith (2016) NEF identify three quantitatively specified principles and then implement nonlinear dynamical systems in a spiking neural substrate, allowing thus that this neural spiking neural network approximates the original dynamical system. These systems are focused into how neural systems compute, without an interest in the semantic content. This approach uses very often non-biological optimization methods.

    b. **Semantic Pointer Architecture (SPA):** Gossman & Eliasmith (2016) consider that the semantic content (perceptual, motor, and cognitive) is expressed through neural representations that compress information via lossy operators. This approach allows to allows then to take into account the meaning of the information. At the same time, SPA works with biologically plausible spiking models that allow better learning procedures.

    c. **Information Integration Theory (IIT):** Oizumi et al (2014), make a different approach, trying to integrate an informational architecture that deals mathematically with the mechanisms that happen into phenomeno-logical experiences (existence, composition, information, integration, and exclusion), that is: in consciousness. Very curiously, the very first attempts to describe mathematically consciousness have provided the first clues to the understanding of the basic cognitive mechanisms that operate all throughout cognitive levels. A comparison of SAP and IIT can be found at Thagard & Steward (2014). 1.NEUCOGAR: our approach (Talanov et al, 2016; Vallverdu et al, 2016) offers to previous models a way to give valences and to regulate main informational processes, following a bioinspired architecture based on neuromodulators. This approach makes possible the bottom up and scalable integration of emotional mechanisms into cognitive systems, at subconscious and conscious levels. Because most of mathematical approaches forget that living entities integrate and guide their actions according to structural necessities, and neuromodulators are the grammatical rules that build the grammatical values of cognition. This functional approach (a key aspect pointed by Cohen & Dennet, 2011) fulfill at the same embodiment influence, and a framework for the dynamical regulation of informational values. Perhaps the notion of 'qualia' can be mathematically explained as an unique informational state, but the feeling of it can only be expressed using an emotional architecture. This is a fundamental approach that most theoreticians of mathematical modeling are neglecting, maintaining their interests into the necessary but narrow domains of defining the formal syntax of neural processes. ON the other hand, general approaches, like those of Sloman or even Minsky lack from a mechanistic theory that connects all the cognitive layers.

Anyhow, from the previous models can be affirmed that:

- There are modular approaches to the informational processing run by cognitive machinery, but following formal rules at different layers. Neucogar could provide the same rules for all cognitive domains, the computational bricks from which any kind of derived architecture could emerge.
- Conscious processing is overvalued: the key point here, when we try to create conscious AGI, is to understand which real role that has the consciousness into human cognitive processes, in order to design better operational systems. From our perspective, consciousness is too expensive from the side of resources and information managing and for such reasons its role is limited to some kind of special activities. These activities can local be adapted to local and temporary situations (danger, illness, social pressure,...).
- Finally, we need to assume that artificial consciousness is still not functionally defined. Why should a machine to have consciousness or a similar mechanism? With more computational power, is still this mechanism necessary?

With NEUCOGAR, we suggest a model that uses the same syntax for all computational levels, as happens with neuromodulators in human brain. The key point here is to define the levels of self-awareness and the function of this process for a multidimensional AGI. Possibly, the coexistence of several cognitive processes (visual analysis, internal scanning, tactic analysis, language analysis,...) is the key to understand the mechanisms by which at certain point one discourse is merged and the upper level of information processing is devoted at that activity (meanwhile: sensorimotor activities, among other ones, are still under process).

ENDING REMARKS

This chapter has explained the connections between neurotransmitters, and self-awareness for information appraisal, as well as the intimate connection between cognitive and emotional informational processing. We explained the nature of cognitive processing, at low/high and conscious/unconscious levels. The cognitive mapping we've explained describes the existence of several layers of informational analysis and, consequently, the co-existence of parallel heuristics for the search of best solutions. Our proposal of a naturalistically inspired architecture, based on neurotransmitters, provides an option to design novel AI systems, more complex in their behavior and skills. It also captures the biologically non-linearity of cognitive and brain processes, making possible artificial cognitive systems able to generate values that help them to integrate, combine and recombine data according to their own internal states. This implies a more adaptive and rich heuristic approach to action-decision in complex environments. Our NEUCOGAR approach offers a biologically inspired way to integrate mathematical theories of informational evaluation with semantic ways to generate dynamic approaches to the cognitive processes (emotional), and a scalable way to connect basic operations with interconnected layers of decisions. This research line possibly will trigger a creation of creative machines (once stated that creativity is the ability to create new and unique ways to deal with information), able to generate their own semantic values and feelings about the world.

ACKNOWLEDGMENT

Part of this research has been possible thanks to the funding provided by the project "Creatividad, revoluciones e innovación en los procesos de cambio científico" (FFI2014-52214-P).

REFERENCES

Ansorge, U., Kunde, W., & Kiefer, M. (2014). Unconscious vision and executive control: How unconscious processing and conscious action control interact. *Consciousness and Cognition, 27,* 268–287. doi:10.1016/j.concog.2014.05.009 PMID:24960432

Ari, C., & DAgostino, D. P. (2016). Contingency checking and self-directed behaviors in giant manta rays: Do elasmobranchs have self-awareness? *Journal of Ethology, 34*(2), 1–8. doi:10.1007/s10164-016-0462-z

Armstrong, A. M., & Dienes, Z. (2013). Subliminal understanding of negation: Unconscious control by subliminal processing of word pairs. *Consciousness and Cognition, 22*(3), 1022–1040. doi:10.1016/j.concog.2013.06.010 PMID:23933139

Baars, B. (1988). *A Cognitive Theory of Consciousness.* Cambridge, UK: Cambridge University Press.

Baars, B. J., & Franklin, S. (2009). Consciousness is computational: The Lida model of global workspace theory. *International Journal of Machine Consciousness, 1*(1), 23–32. doi:10.1142/S1793843009000050

Bargh, J. A., & Morsella, E. (2008). The Unconscious Mind. *Perspectives on Psychological Science: A Journal of the Association for Psychological Science, 3*(1), 73–79.

Barron, A. B., Søvik, E., & Cornish, J. L. (2010). The roles of dopamine and related compounds in reward-seeking behavior across animal phyla. *Frontiers in Behavioral Neuroscience, 4,* 1–9. doi:10.3389/fnbeh.2010.00163 PMID:21048897

Barsalou, L. W. (2008). Grounded cognition. *Annual Review of Psychology, 59*(1), 617–645. doi:10.1146/annurev.psych.59.103006.093639 PMID:17705682

Bayne, Y., Cleeremans, A., & Wilken, P. (2009). *The Oxford Companion to Consciousness.* Oxford, UK: OUP. doi:10.1093/acref/9780198569510.001.0001

Bromberg-Martin, E. S., & Hikosaka, O. (2009). Midbrain dopamine neurons signal preference for advance information about upcoming rewards. *Neuron, 63*(1), 119–126. doi:10.1016/j.neuron.2009.06.009 PMID:19607797

Chalmers, D. J. (1995). Facing up to the Problem of Consciousness. *Journal of Consciousness Studies, 2,* 200–219.

Cleeremans, A. (2008). Consciousness: the radical plasticity thesis. *Prog Brain Res., 168,* 19-33.

Cleeremans, A. (2011). The Radical Plasticity Thesis: How the Brain Learns to be Conscious. *Frontiers in Psychology, 2*, 86.

Cohen, M. M., & Dennet, D. (2011). Consciousness cannot be separated from function. *Trends in Cognitive Sciences, 15*(8), 358–364. doi:10.1016/j.tics.2011.06.008 PMID:21807333

Costa, V. D., Tran, V. L., Turchi, J., & Averbeck, B. B. (2014). Dopamine modulates novelty seeking behavior during decision making. *Behavioral Neuroscience, 28*(5), 556–566. doi:10.1037/a0037128 PMID:24911320

Crick, F. (1995). *Astonishing Hypothesis: The Scientific Search for the Soul*. Scribner.

Crick, F., & Koch, C. (2003). A framework for consciousness. *Nature Neuroscience, 23*(2), 119–126. doi:10.1038/nn0203-119 PMID:12555104

Damasio, A. (1994). *Descartes*. New York: Gosset/Putnam Press.

Damasio, A. (1999). *The Feeling of What Happens. Body and Emotion in the Making of Consciousness*. London: Heinemann.

de Gardelle, V., & Kouider, S. (2009). Cognitive theories of consciousness. In W. Banks (Ed.), *Elsevier Encyclopedia of Consciousness*. Elsevier. doi:10.1016/B978-012373873-8.00077-3

Dennett, D. (1990). *Quining Qualia*. In W. Lycan (Ed.), *Mind and Cognition* (pp. 519–548). Oxford, UK: Blackwell.

Dennett, D. C. (1991). *Consciousness Explained*. Boston: Little, Brown and Company.

Donchin, E., & Coles, M. G. H. (1998). Context updating and the p300. *Behavioral and Brain Sciences, 21*(1), 152–154. doi:10.1017/S0140525X98230950

Edelman, G. (1989). *The Remembered Present: A Biological Theory of Consciousness*. New York: Basic Books.

Frégnac, Y., & Laurent, G. (2014). Where is the brain in the Human Brain Project? *Nature, 513*(7516), 27–29. doi:10.1038/513027a PMID:25186884

Gigerenzer, G., Hertwig, R., & Pachur, T. (Eds.). (2011). *Heuristics: The foundations of adaptive behavior*. New York: Oxford University Press. doi:10.1093/acprof:oso/9780199744282.001.0001

Gossman, J., & Eliasmith, E. (2016, February22). Optimizing Semantic Pointer Representations for Symbol-Like Processing in Spiking Neural Networks. *PLoS ONE*, 1–18.

Gregory, R. L. (1988). Consciousness in science and philosophy: conscience and con-science. In Consciousness in Contemporary Science. Oxford, UK: Oxford Science Publications.

Hills, T. (2006). Animal foraging and the evolution of goal-directed cognition. *Cognitive Science*, *30*(1), 3–41. doi:10.1207/s15516709cog0000_50 PMID:21702807

Hills, T., & Butterfill, S. (2015). From foraging to autonoetic consciousness: The primal self as a consequence of embodied prospective foraging. *Current Zoology*, *61*(2), 368–381. doi:10.1093/czoolo/61.2.368

Hollenstein, M., Koenig, T., Kubat, M., Blaser, D., & Perrig, W. J. (2012). Non-conscious word processing in a mirror-masking paradigm causing attentional distraction: An ERP-study. *Consciousness and Cognition*, *21*(1), 353–365. doi:10.1016/j.concog.2012.01.005 PMID:22289507

Jackendoff, R. (1987). *Consciousness and the computational mind*. Cambridge, MA: MIT Press.

Kihlstrom, J. F. (1987). The cognitive unconscious. *Science*, *237*(4821), 1445–1452. doi:10.1126/science.3629249 PMID:3629249

Kihlstrom, J. F. (1994). The rediscovery of the unconscious. In H. Morowitz & J. L. Singer (Eds.), *The mind, the brain, and complex adaptive systems* (pp. 123–143). Reading, MA: Addison-Wesley Publishing Co, Inc.

Kihlstrom, J. F., Mulvaney, S., Tobias, B. A., & Tobis, I. P. (2000). The emotional unconscious. In E. Eich, J. F. Kihlstrom, G. H. Bower, J. P. Forgas, & P. M. Niedenthal (Eds.), *Cognition and emotion* (pp. 30–86). New York: Oxford University Press.

Komer, B., & Eliasmith, C. (2016). A unified theoretical approach for biological cognition and learning. *Current Opinion in Behavioral Sciences*, *11*, 14–20. doi:10.1016/j.cobeha.2016.03.006

Kouider, S., & Dehaene, S. (2007). Levels of processing during non-conscious perception: A critical review of visual masking. *Philosophical Transactions of the Royal Society of London. Series B, Biological Sciences*, *362*(1481), 857–875. doi:10.1098/rstb.2007.2093 PMID:17403642

Lau, H. C. (2008). A Higher-Order Bayesian Decision Theory of Perceptual Consciousness. *Progress in Brain Research*, *168*, 35–48. doi:10.1016/S0079-6123(07)68004-2 PMID:18166384

Limb, C. J., & Braun, A. R. (2008). Neural Substrates of Spontaneous Musical Performance: An fMRI Study of Jazz Improvisation. *PLoS ONE*, *3*(2).

Llinás, R. R. (2001). *I of the Vortex. From neurons to Self.* Cambridge, MA: MIT Press.

Lövheim, H. (2012). A new three-dimensional model for emotions and monoamine neurotransmitters. *Medical Hypotheses, 78,* 341–348.

Minsky, M. (2007). *The emotion machine: Commonsense thinking, artificial intelligence, and the future of the human mind.* Simon & Schuster.

Montemayor, C., & Haladjian, H. H. (2015). *Consciousness, Attention, and Conscious Attention.* Cambridge, MA: MIT Press. doi:10.7551/mitpress/9780262028974.001.0001

Oizumi, M., Albantakis, L., & Tononi, G. (2014, May). From the Phenomenology to the Mechanisms of Consciousness: Integrated Information Theory 3.0. *PLoS Computational Biology, 10*(5), e1003588. doi:10.1371/journal.pcbi.1003588 PMID:24811198

Olsson, J. (2015). *An evaluation of the integrated information theory against some central problems of consciousness, Bachelor Degree Project.* University of Skövde.

ORegan, J. K., & Noë, A. (2001). A sensorimotor account of vision and visual consciousness. *Behavioral and Brain Sciences, 24*(5), 883–917. doi:10.1017/S0140525X01000115 PMID:12239892

Prinz, J. J. (2005). A neurofunctional theory of consciousness. In A. Brook & K. Akins (Eds.), *Cognition and the brain: Philosophy and neuroscience movement* (pp. 381–396). Cambridge, UK: Cambridge University Press. doi:10.1017/CBO9780511610608.012

Reynolds, R. F., & Bronstein, A. M. (2003). The broken escalator phenomenon: Aftereffect of walking onto a moving platform. *Experimental Brain Research, 151*(3), 301–308. doi:10.1007/s00221-003-1444-2 PMID:12802549

Rolls, E. T. (2010). *Consciousness, Decision-Making and Neural Computation.* In A. Hussain & J. G. Taylor (Eds.), *Cutsuridis, Vassilis* (pp. 287–333). Perception-Action Cycle, Germany: Springer.

Skoggard, I., & Waterson, A. (2015). Introduction: Toward an Anthropology of Affect and Evocative Ethnography. *Anthropology of Consciousness, 26*(2), 109–120. doi:10.1111/anoc.12041

Talanov, M. (2015). Neuromodulating Cognitive Architecture: Towards Biomimetic Emotional AI. *2015 IEEE 29th International Conference on Advanced Information Networking and Applications*. http://doi.ieeecomputersociety.org/10.1109/AINA.2015.240

Taylor, J. G. (2010). Article. In V. Cutsuridis, A. Hussain, & J. G. Taylor (Eds.), A Review of Models of Consciousness (pp. 335–357). Perception-Action Cycle, Germany: Springer.

Thagard, P., & Steward, T. C. (2014). Two theories of consciousness: Semantic pointer competition vs. information integration. *Consciousness and Cognition, 30*, 73–90. doi:10.1016/j.concog.2014.07.001 PMID:25160821

Tononi, G. (2008). Consciousness as integrated information: A provisional manifesto. *The Biological Bulletin, 215*(3), 216–242. doi:10.2307/25470707 PMID:19098144

Tononi, G., & Koch, C. (2015). Consciousness: here, there and everywhere? *Phil. Trans. R. Soc. B, 370*. DOI: .10.1098/rstb.2014.0167

Tulving, E. (1985). Memory and consciousness. *Canadian Psychology, 26*(1), 1–12. doi:10.1037/h0080017

Turner, M., & Fauconnier, G. (2002). *The Way We Think. Conceptual Blending and the Mind's Hidden Complexities*. Basic Books.

Vallverdú, J. (2012). Subsuming or Embodying Emotions?. In J. Vallverdú (Ed.), *Creating Synthetic Emotions through Technological and Robotic Advancements*. IGI Global Group. doi:10.4018/978-1-4666-1595-3

Vallverdu, J. (2015). *A cognitive architecture for the implementation of emotions in computing systems*. Biologically Inspired Cognitive Architectures. doi:10.1016/j.bica.2015.11.002

Vallverdú, J. (2016). *Bayesians Versus Frequentists. A Philosophical Debate on Statistical Reasoning*. Springer. doi:10.1007/978-3-662-48638-2

Vallverdu, J., Talanov, M., Distefano, S., Mazzara, M., Manca, M., & Tchitchigin, A. (2016). NEUCOGAR: A Neuromodulating Cognitive Architecture for Biomimetic Emotional AI. *International Journal of Artificial Intelligence, 14*(1), 27–40.

van Gaal, S., de Lange, F. P., & Cohen, M. X. (2012a). The role of consciousness in cognitive control and decision making. *Frontiers in Human Neuroscience, 6*, 121. doi:10.3389/fnhum.2012.00121 PMID:22586386 van Gaal, S., & Lamme, V. A. (2012). Unconscious high-level information processing: Implication for neurobiological theories of consciousness. *The Neuroscientist, 18*(3), 287–301. doi:10.1177/1073858411404079 PMID:21628675

Wegner, D. (2002). *The Illusion of Conscious Will*. Cambridge, MA: MIT Press.

Weiss, J. (1997). The role of pathogenic beliefs in psychic reality. *Psychoanalytic Psychology, 14*(3), 427–434. doi:10.1037/h0079734

Winkielman, P., & Schooler, J. W. (2011). Splitting consciousness: Unconscious, conscious, and metaconscious processes in social cognition. *European Review of Social Psychology, 22*(1), 37–41. doi:10.1080/10463283.2011.576580

Zatorre, R. J., Chen, J. L., & Penhune, V. B. (2007). When the brain plays music: Auditory–motor interactions in music perception and production. *Nature Reviews. Neuroscience, 8*(7), 547–558. doi:10.1038/nrn2152 PMID:17585307

Chapter 3
Wild Architecture:
Explaining Cognition via Self-Sustaining Systems

Vincent T. Cialdella
Illinois State University, USA

Emilio J. C. Lobato
Illinois State University, USA

J. Scott Jordan
Illinois State University, USA

ABSTRACT

In this chapter, the authors focus on cognitive architectures that are developed with the intent to explain human cognition. The authors first describe the mission of cybernetics and early cognitive architectures and recount the popular criticism that these perspectives fail to provide genuine explanations of cognition. Moving forward, the authors propose that there are three pervasive problems that modern cognitive architectures must address: the problem of consciousness, the problem of embodiment, and the problem of representation. Wild Systems Theory (Jordan, 2013) conceptualizes biological cognition as a feature of self-sustaining embodied context that manifests itself at multiple, nested, time-scales. In this manner, Wild Systems Theory is presented as a particularly useful framework for coherently addressing the problems of consciousness, embodiment, and representation.

DOI: 10.4018/978-1-5225-1947-8.ch003

INTRODUCTION

For some time now, one of the leading assumptions in the development of cognitive architectures has been Marr's (1982) tri-level theory of explanation; the idea that the proper approach in developing a cognitive architecture (and thus explaining cognition) is to

1. Determine the computations necessary to completing a cognitive task (e.g., sorting a list of numbers from lowest to highest),
2. Generate a representation of the inputs, outputs, and algorithms an information-processing system would need to complete the task, and
3. Actually build (i.e., implement) a system capable of executing the algorithms.

The purpose of the present paper is to examine issues that have proven challenging to Marr's implementation approach to explaining cognition. Three particular challenges are the issues of consciousness, embodiment, and representation. After examining these challenges, we will present an approach to describing cognitive architectures (Wild Systems Theory—WST, Jordan, 20213) that addresses each challenge, while simultaneously shifting the focus of modeling from looking to biology for inspiration, to looking at a more fundamental property that biological systems share with many other types of systems, including chemical, psychological, and cultural—specifically, the ability of certain far from equilibrium systems to generate catalysts that feedback into and sustain the processes that produced them; what Kauffman (1995) refers to as 'autocatalytic' systems, and what Jordan (2013) refers to as self-sustaining, or *wild* systems.

PROBLEMS WITH "IMPLENTATION AS EXPLANATION"

While Marr's (1982) approach to developing cognitive architectures has inspired research that has given rise to a host of new technologies, there are those who have expressed doubts regarding his assertion that implementation constitutes explanation. In his seminal paper, *Quantitative analysis of purposive systems: Some spadework at the foundation of scientific psychology*, William T. Powers (1973) expressed his belief that psychologists were working under the confused assumption that control-theoretic concepts had been developed to explain the behavior of organisms. According to Powers, control-theoretic concepts were developed so that engineers could develop systems capable of doing what organisms do; namely, maintain ordered states with their environment by offsetting environmental disturbances to those ordered states. Powers referred to this ability to maintain ordered states as *input control*, and he further stated that in order for engineers to be able to build input control systems, they had to develop a conceptual scheme that captured the dynamics of organismic input control in a way that allowed the dynamics to be transformed into functioning, artificial, input-control systems, what have come to be known as servomechanisms. Thus, the conceptual scheme created by engineers includes phrases such as reference signal, which represents the state the system is to sustain. For example, when one dials in a room temperature on a thermostat, one is basically specifying the reference signal for the system. Or, said another way, one is setting the input level the system should keep constant. In order to keep its input at a pre-specified level, the system must be able to counteract environmental events that move the input (i.e., sensed temperature) away from the value of the reference signal. For example, when one opens a window and allows cold air into the room, the air temperature will change. If it varies from the pre-specified level, the system must be able to offset such disturbance. The system's ability to generate disturbance-offsetting events is referred to as output. In the case of the thermostat, the system's output is the turning on of the furnace. As the system continues to generate output (e.g., the furnace stays on) the difference between the input and the reference signal decreases. From the perspective of an engineer, who is actually trying to build such a system, this means the system has to be able to compare its current input state (i.e., sensed room temperature) to its reference signal. Engineers refer to the system component that accomplishes this function as a comparator. They also refer to the result of the comparison as an error signal. Collectively then, servomechanisms are constructed such that the error signal drives the system's disturbance-offsetting outputs (i.e., the difference between the sensed temperature and the reference signal determines when and for how long the furnace is active). As a result of this architecture, the error signal actually serves to negate itself (i.e., make itself become zero), and this explains why engineers also refer to servomechanisms as negative-feedback control systems.

The reason for analyzing the nature of servomechanistic concepts so thoroughly was to underline Powers' (1973) point that concepts such as *reference signal*, *disturbance*, *input*, *output*, *comparator*, *error-signal*, and *negative-feedback* were created by engineers so they could create systems capable of doing what organisms do (i.e., maintain ordered relationships). That is, the concepts were created for the purpose of *implementation*, not *explanation*. Implicit in Powers' argument is a take on the relationship between implementation and explanation that is counter to Marrs' (1982) position.

From Cybernetics to Cognitive Architecture

Following the cybernetic movement referred to by Powers (1973), cognitive psychologists began to work toward developing computational systems (i.e., architectures) meant to model human cognition. While some architectures were and are developed with the sole intention of enabling artificially intelligent behavior, others were and are developed in the hopes of explaining the architecture that underlies human cognition. Thus, as was the case in Powers' (1973) critique of the cybernetics movement, there are those whose approach to developing cognitive architectures entails two related, but distinct, goals: the technological goal and the explanatory goal. The former refers to the practicality of using artificial systems to complete tasks that require human level competence or, perhaps, a level of performance that goes beyond the limitations of humans (Duch, Oentaryo, & Pasquier, 2008). Cognitive scientists operating within the field of Artificial Intelligence (AI) are particularly interested in building systems that can realize the same cognitive functions that are achieved by humans. To some extent, the focus on modeling and building cognitive systems renders this approach an engineering perspective on cognition. On the other hand, the explanatory goal refers to the possibility of using what was learned while building an artificial cognitive system to explain the achievements of natural cognitive systems such as humans. That is, success in building an artificially cognitive system might be taken as an indication that human cognition is actualized by the same mechanisms that were used to produce artificial cognition (Anderson et al., 2004).

According to contemporary AI researchers, *cognitive architecture* can be described as the invariant properties that underlie cognition (Douglass & Mittal, 2013). While contexts inevitably vary, the principles by which a system engages the world exhibit consistency; that is, they are invariant. This consistency may be attributed to the system's stable architecture. Examples of cognitive architectures include Soar (Laird, 2008; Laird, Newell, & Rosenbloom, 1987), LIDA (Baars & Franklin, 2009; Franklin et al., 2013), and ACT-R (Anderson, 1996; Anderson et al., 2004). While these architectures may, to some extent, exhibit similarities, they diverge in their implementation, the authors' motivations and goals for their architectures, and the phenomena to which they are commonly applied. Laird (2012) described this divergence in reasons for development: Some developers design their architectures specifically with a more technical, engineering focus in order to support the development of agents, whereas others are designed with the goal of explaining cognition. In addition to their variable purpose, architectures also differ in their fundamental assumptions about cognition; they may differ in the mechanisms by which they learn, the way in which knowledge is represented, or even the types of knowledge that can be represented.

To be sure, it is often the case that the same architecture is used to pursue both the technical and the explanatory goal. In the past, Soar has been used to model human behavior (Lewis, 1993; Miller & Laird, 1996), but the developers are now predominantly concerned with demonstrating its real-time functionality in artificial systems (Laird, 2012; Langley, Laird, & Rogers, 2009). In this sense, the developers are largely interested in achieving the technological goal of AI. In contrast with Soar, a majority of work in ACT-R seems to reflect an interest in the explanatory goal of AI. Although it has seen applied use in intelligent tutors (Koedinger, Anderson, Hadley, & Mark, 1997) and robotics (Trafton et al., 2013), ACT-R has largely been used to model a wide variety of data obtained from work in experimental psychology (e.g., Halbrügge, Quade, Engelbrecht, 2015; Wirzberger & Russewinkel, 2015). Despite the use of some architectures to achieve both technical and explanatory goals, we now focus on one particular architecture (i.e., ACT-R) and the issues that have arisen as research have attempted to use it as an explanation of cognition.

ACT-R as Explanation

The ACT-R architecture (Anderson et al., 2004) is composed of a number of components called modules, which each handle different types of information. Examples of ACT-R modules include an intentional module that maintains goal states and intentions, a declarative module that handles the retrieval of information from memory, a visual module that supports information about entities in the visual field, and a manual module that affords control over hands. Each module contains a buffer that maintains information relevant to the task currently being addressed. Two kinds of knowledge are represented in ACT-R: declarative knowledge and procedural knowledge. Declarative knowledge is represented using *chunks*: knowledge units that accommodate key-value pairs. Procedural knowledge is represented using *productions*: condition-action rules.

During run-time, buffers of each module can be manipulated by way of a central production system that recognizes when the chunk in a buffer meets certain conditions. When a pattern is matched, the production system can make changes to that buffer or the buffers of other modules. Buffers are updated by the productions that 'fire' when their conditions are met. For example, if a chunk in the visual buffer matches conditions specified in a production, the model might alter the chunk in the manual buffer to make a request to move the hands toward an identified object. In ACT-R, only one production can fire at a time. To resolve this conflict, a utility calculation determines which production will be most likely to achieve the current goal and consequently fire. Apart from the inter-module communication that is afforded through the central production system, these modules operate independently of one another.

According to ACT-R's implementers, the ACT-R architecture affords the development of software agents as well as a unified theory of human cognition (Anderson et al., 2004). That is, the authors strive toward the explanatory goal of cognitive architectures. As any good theory of human cognition should, the theory is used to explain a large body of data obtained in experimental psychology. In a comprehensive presentation of the ACT-R theory and related empirical work, Anderson and colleagues (2004) presented data from a number of behavioral and neuroimaging studies to identify the neural correlates of various ACT-R modules by tracking how and when information is updated in buffers while engaging in tasks. Since then, ACT-R models have been used in concert with fMRI data to localize the updating of working memory and the retrieval of declarative memory by using the activity of ACT-R's modules as a predictor of neural activity in a regression analysis (Borst & Anderson, 2013). Another study has simulated the process of learning a new song, demonstrating robust primacy and recency effects that are similar to those observed in human subjects (Chikhaoui et al., 2009). Results from modeling efforts have also motivated the development of richer theoretical accounts of associative memory (Thomson, Pyke, Trafton, & Hiatt, 2015).

In other experiments, researchers have measured participants' ability to estimate the amount of time that has passed while multitasking. Comparing these results with ACT-R models has highlighted the importance of considering the influences of multiple contextual factors (Moon & Anderson, 2013). Researchers investigating action control while driving an automobile have evaluated the performance of novice and experienced drivers by using ACT-R to model the influence of driving experience on collision avoidance and lateral control skills (Cao, Qin, Jin, Zhao, & Shen, 2014; Cao, Qin, Zhao, & Shen, 2015). Additionally, comparison of models with human reaction-time data in a task-switching paradigm has generated possible, concrete accounts of psychological constructs such as flow (Altmann, & Trafton, 2007). In sum, by comparing the data exhibited by ACT-R models to the data collected from human participants, researchers are not only afforded the ability to generate possible explanations of observed phenomena but are also able to enhance their theoretical perspective.

Despite ACT-R's ability to computationally model experimental human data, there are those who express concerns regarding its ability to constitute an explanation of human cognition. For example, it is recognized (e.g., Bösser, 1987, 2013) that there exists more than one set of values for chunking parameters in Soar that can fit a single data set. This also applies to the parameterization in ACT-R. Others have criticized the practice of parameter estimation on the grounds that any pattern of data can be fit (Roberts & Pashler, 2000), and these criticisms have been appropriately responded to (see Anderson et al., 2004). Johnson-Laird expresses further suspicions regarding the explanatory capabilities of models:

The reason for the suspicion is complex. In part it derives from the fact that any large-scale program intended to model cognition inevitably incorporates components that lack psychological plausibility.... Certain aspects of any such program must be at best principled and deliberate simplifications or at worst ad hoc patches intended

merely to enable the program to work. The remedy... is not to abandon computer
programs, but to make a clear distinction between a program and the theory that it
is intended to model. (1980, p. 110, emphasis in original)

Choices about what should be modeled (e.g., the types of knowledge) and how
to model it will necessarily reflect the constraints and affordances of the technology
that are made available to the developers. In order to obtain a functioning model,
decisions might be made during implementation so as to accommodate for technological limitations. For this reason, as Johnson-Laird advises, one should be wary
of equating a description (i.e., the model) with the explanation (i.e., the theory).

To be sure, the authors of ACT-R do not present their architecture as *the* truth about
human cognition. Anderson and colleagues note, "just because such architectures
aspire to account for the integration of cognition, they should not be interpreted as
claiming to have the complete truth about the nature of the mind" (2004, p. 1057).
Instead, the hallmark of cognitive architectures is their ability to force researchers
to think about how all these various, independently studied functions can all be
brought together under one cohesive framework. Focusing on the architecture of
cognition draws attention to the problems that are neglected when theorists fail to
concern themselves with the implementation of cognition.

CONTEMPORARY ISSUES WITH IMPLEMENTATION

Contemporary attempts to explain human cognition via implemented architectures
have begun to place more emphasis on the biological substrate of human cognition
(Franklin, Strain, McCall, & Baars, 2013). The BICA (Biologically Inspired Cognitive Architectures) movement, as represented by the journal of the same name,
describes its mission as follows: "The focus of the journal is on the integration of
many research efforts in addressing the challenge of creating a real-life computational equivalent of the human mind." Along the way, BICA researchers have also
had to address the issue of whether the goal is to implement an architecture that can
produce the same output as a biological organism, or is the goal to implement an
architecture that serves to explain biological cognition? If the goal is the former, then
issues with implementation are predominantly pragmatic. Specifically, the challenge
of implementation largely, if not entirely, concerns finding the algorithms that will
provide the right kind of output. If the goal, however, is explanatory, then all of the
issues in the behavioral, cognitive, and social sciences necessarily become issues for
instantiating a particular model of cognition. In the following sections, we outline
three general topics that we feel need to be addressed by any explanatory cognitive
architecture. These topics are consciousness, embodiment, and representation.

The Problem of Consciousness

A more recent cognitive architecture has been developed in response to the pursuit of biologically inspired artificial intelligence systems: the Learning Intelligent Distribution Agent (LIDA; Franklin et al., 2007). LIDA was developed to implement the Global Workspace Theory (GWT) of consciousness to integrate both conscious and unconscious aspects of biological, in particular human, cognition (Baars & Franklin, 2009). GWT proposes that cognition results from the culmination of many specialized and distributed processes within the brain. Conscious cognition is enabled and constrained by unconscious cognitive processes, in particular perceptual processes, which are recursively influenced by the focal content of conscious cognition feeding back to these unconscious processes (for review, see Baars, 1988). What LIDA attempts to do is to computationally model and implement GWT. Specifically, the LIDA model focuses on the notion of cognition as resulting from cognitive cycles, which are rapid sensory samplings by the cognitive agent of the environment (both external and internal) to update the agent's representation of the environment. During this rapid sampling process, the agent's unconscious processing determines what aspects of the environment are sufficiently salient enough to draw conscious attention toward, which is then fed back to the lower-level processes so that subsequent appropriate action selection and execution can occur.

The developers of the LIDA model have also recently proposed LIDA as a referent architecture for the broader community of scholars interested in artificial intelligence by outlining the conceptual commitments of the model (Franklin et al., 2013). The major draw of doing so is that LIDA, which is an outgrowth of GWT, is committed to the importance of consciousness as a necessary component of cognition, in contrast to other architectures like ACT-R or Soar (Chella, 2013; Franklin et al., 2013).

The Problem of Embodiment

Curiously, the authors of the LIDA model, in explicating the conceptual commitments of the system, express a commitment to embodiment as significant for their model without necessarily insisting on physical, robotic implementation (Franklin et al., 2013). This is due to their broad interpretation of embodied cognition as just the structural coupling of the agent with its environment. Their view is that general intelligence is a sufficiently abstract enough entity to not necessitate robotic instantiation, and embodiment still occurs as long as the agent and environment are coupled in some way (Franklin, 1997; Franklin et al., 2013). Commenting on this curiosity of a disembodied form of embodiment, Wiltshire and colleagues (2013) noted that physical embodiment of an AGI model such as LIDA would enhance the capacities of the model. Morphology prescribes and constrains an agent's ability to perturb and interact with its environment (Anderson, 2003), particularly with regards to more complex and dynamic forms of agent-environment interactions such as social cognition. Architectures that aim to be used for the development of artificially intelligent agents might be more successful if they were to directly address the complexity of embodied cognition.

To be sure, this is easier said than done. The complexity of the embodied cognition perspective is partially due to the lack of a firm or precise description of what constitutes a body (Anderson, 2003). The most radical claim of the embodied cognition perspective is that "the brain is not the sole cognitive resource we have available to use to solve problems" (Wilson & Golonka, 2013, p. 1). As dramatic as that claim is, which itself cannot be understated currently, the claim does require further elaboration on what constitutes a body. This issue is addressed only indirectly, by describing what bodies do, such as "move and act in rich real-world surroundings" (Clark, 1998, p. 506) or describing the role of the body in constraining the form that behavior takes via an organism's perceptual-motor capabilities (Anderson, 2003; Varela, Thompson, & Rosch, 1991; Wilson & Golonka, 2013).

The Problem of Representation

In addition to consciousness and embodiment, another on-going critique of the cognitive architecture literature is its total reliance on the notion of "representation." Common to most such criticisms is a commitment to some form or another of dynamical systems theory and the assertion that the work of cognition is to be found in the self-organizing, synergetic, circular causality of continuous interactions between brain, body and world (Clark, 1997; Jordan, 2003; Kelso, 1995; O'Regan & Noe, 2001; Tschacher & Dauwalder, 2003; Thelen & Smith, 1994; van Rooij, Bongers & Haselager, 2002; Varella, Thompson & Rosch, 1991; van Gelder, 1998). A classic example of a self-organizing system is a convection roll. If one applies heat to a pan of cool oil, a rather complex system of convection rolls will emerge as the heated oil rises to the top and the cooler oil sinks to the bottom.

The resulting convection rolls are what physicists call a collective or cooperative effect, which arises without any external instructions... Such spontaneous pattern formation is exactly what we mean by self-organization: the system organized itself, but there is no 'self', no agent inside the system doing the organizing. (Kelso, 1995, pp. 7-8)

Van Gelder (1998) strongly rejects the computationalist notion that behavior is controlled (i.e., regulated) by internal structures such as codes and plans. Instead, he proposes it is possible for a system to give rise to regulatory behavior solely on the basis of self-organizing dynamics. He presents the Watt Governor as an example.

A Watt Governor is a mechanism that keeps the velocity of a fan constant. It does so because the velocity of the fan's flywheel influences itself recursively. That is, the faster the flywheel moves, the more it slows itself down. This is because the movements of the flywheel cause two weighted arms, attached to the flywheel via a spindle, to rise as the flywheel moves faster. These movements cause a valve, connected to a steam-engine driving the flywheel movement, to close, thereby reducing the amount of steam released which, in turn, slows the flywheel and allows the weighted arms to lower. Because of the constant, mutual influence all the components have on one another, fan velocity can be held fairly constant. Van Gelder proposes the Watt Governor as a prime example of regulated behavior emerging out of purely self-organizing processes. At no point in the Watt Governor systems is there a 'code', a 'representation', or information being processed. As a result, he argues it should be possible to model cognitive systems solely in terms of self-organizing dynamics. (Jordan & Ghin, 2007. P. 183-184)

Jaeger (1998) later criticized theorists who asserted that dynamical systems such as the Watt Governor constituted the proper way to explain cognition. Specifically, he believed that the current state of mathematics in dynamical systems theory was not sophisticated enough to effectively model organisms:

First, DST principles like attractors and bifurcations are not of much help in wild systems with fast stochastic input varying on the system's own characteristic time scale. Second...DST handles high-dimensional domains by reducing them to low-dimensional descriptions...this reduction to some collective parameters is helpful in some respects but still poses a limit to the study of high-dimensional systems. (1998, p. 643-644, emphasis added)

Collectively, critiques of the ability of currently available cognitive architectures to explain cognition imply that while modeling efforts such as those in the ACT-R and LIDA communities have demonstrated considerable progress toward the technological goal of AI, the extent to which the efforts display progress toward the explanatory goal remains unclear. That is, such efforts surely have the potential to yield artificial systems that can do what we do, but successful modeling does not necessarily demonstrate that these artificial systems do what we do *in the way that we do it*. At their core, cognitive architectures engage cognition as a purely computational process. This conception of biological cognition has existed for decades (e.g., Miller, Galanter, & Pribram, 1960), arising in part from a desire to broaden psychological science as more than strict behaviorism. However, this assumption of cognition as computation is not universally accepted (e.g., Gibson, 1979), and there exist useful and productive lines of research that incorporate non-computational explanatory mechanisms in their theorizing of human cognition, either as true alternatives to purely computational models of information processing (e.g., Marsh, Richardson, & Schmidt, 2009) or as additional components into pluralistic frameworks that propose both computational and non-computational mechanisms to explain aspects of human cognition (e.g., Wiltshire et al., 2014; see also Gallagher, 2015). It is our contention that progress in the development of cognitive architectures that are intended to explain human cognition, rather than "simply" mimic the output of human cognition, would benefit greatly from attempting to model such non-computational components. In particular, we propose that the Wild Systems Theory (WST) put forward by Jordan (2013) serves as an especially useful framework for such an endeavor. In the following section, we will present and describe WST as a way to conceptualize human cognition that may aid in the development of a biologically inspired cognitive architecture that supports intelligence by means similar to those which result in natural cognitive systems.

WILD ARCHITECTURE

Jordan and Day (2015) describe organisms as multi-scale self-sustaining systems. This means that the work that organisms do is self-sustaining, or autocatalytic. That is, the work produces products that further promote the work. Put simply, an autocatalytic reaction between chemicals A and B will produce a catalyst for the A-B reaction (Kauffman, 1995). Such reactions continue to occur by the nature of their self-sustaining work. As networks of autocatalytic reactions are sustained, the stability maintained by this level of autocatalysis enables the emergence of larger-scale autocatalytic processes. When one level of autocatalytic order is achieved, another can emerge. One might conceptualize living systems as large-scale organizations of autocatalytic processes or multi-scale systems of self-sustaining work. The tree-climbing behavior of a monkey (i.e., the work) to obtain a banana will yield energy in the form of food that will further promote the energy-obtaining work of the monkey. Importantly, within each organism, self-sustaining work is occurring at multiple time scales simultaneously (Jordan, 2013). The monkey exhibits self-sustaining work at the behavioral level while the organs, tissues, and cells exhibit self-sustaining work at various different biochemical levels and time scales.

As these living systems emerge, they alter their environment by the nature of their autocatalytic work, providing a new context in which other self-sustaining systems can emerge. For example, the emergence of plants afforded the emergence of a life form that harvests plants for energy, and the emergence of herbivores afforded the emergence of a life form that harvests herbivores for energy. Given that organisms emerge out of the context in which they are embedded, the work they do necessarily reflects the kind of energy transformation that is required for self-sustainment in that context; the fuel source dictates the consumer (Jordan & Ghin, 2006). An organism (i.e., a self-sustaining energy transformer) sustains itself using the energy that is made available in its environment. Conceptualizing organisms in this way, nature is illustrated as a self-organizing energy-transformation hierarchy in which each organism alters its context such that it can continue to sustain itself and consequently creates a context in which another organism can obtain, transform, and dissipate the newly available energy. At each level, energy transformation is not what a system *does*; it is what a living system *is*.

Following from the notion that the fuel source dictates the consumer, Jordan and Day (2015) argue that all organisms constitute embodiments of their context. That is, organisms embody the dynamics in which they emerged and in which they continue to sustain themselves. As an example of an embodied context, the herbivore embodies the contextual constraints that determine what kind of work must be done for an organism to sustain itself in an environment furnished with plants. A carnivore embodies the constraints of its context, namely that it must be able to catch a moving energy source in order to sustain itself. For the carnivore, this requires anticipation of where the prey *will be* rather than where the prey *is* in order to be successful.

Jordan and Day (2015) contend that this anticipatory form of aboutness (i.e., embodiment) is what one might refer to as mind. However, it is important to note that there is a fundamental similarity between the abstract, anticipatory aboutness that we experience as a mental life and the aboutness of a plant. Both emerge out of the constraints that determine the work that must be done for an organism to sustain itself in a context. It just so happens that, because of the constraints of the context that fostered the emergence of humans, humans embodied the dynamics of temporally distal events. This allows humans to live rather anticipatory lives in which we can organize ourselves about abstract events such as 'tomorrow' (Jordan & Vinson, 2012).

What Does WST Afford AI Research?

From the WST perspective, one is afforded a new way of describing what it is that intelligent behavior entails: multi-scale, self-sustaining energy transformation. In architectures like ACT-R, wherein the basic mechanisms work in concert to produce a rich combination of symbolic and sub-symbolic knowledge (through the acquisition and curation of knowledge units), Wild Systems Theory (WST) proposes that knowledge exists at every scale of work because every level is about the context in which that order is maintained. In this way, knowledge is not something that intelligent agents *have*; it is what they *are*. This leads to two related statements that could be taken as invariant principles for a biologically inspired, artificial cognitive system: (1) behavior embodies contextual constraints and affordances; a system's work reflects the kind of energy transformation that is necessary for sustainment in that context, and (2) the system consists of multiple levels (e.g., sub-personal; personal; supra-individual; see Bohl & van den Bos, 2012; Wiltshire et al., 2014) of self-sustaining work; each level of order is achieved and maintained by work that adheres to principle (1). We argue that these two statements coherently capture what it is that intelligent systems are: multi-scale, self-sustaining embodiments of context. Thus, adherence to these principles effectively integrates all of human behavior (and cognition).

In order to better clarify how we believe the notion of multi-scale, self-sustaining embodiment of context provides a biologically inspired approach to cognition and cognitive architecture, we need to more thoroughly describe how the architecture of self-sustaining systems qualifies as "cognitive." Take, for example, a rock. A rock can be considered an embodiment of its context. That is, animals, plants, and rocks could all be considered instantiations of the demands or forces that their environments exert on them. In this sense, the rock is much like animals and plants; the rock also constitutes embodied context. So what makes the embodied context of living organisms different from the embodied context of a rock? Jordan and Vinson (2012) assert that the internal dynamics of an organism are coupled to the dynamics of the organism as a whole such that changes occurring at the micro scale bring about events at the macro scale that recursively affect the micro scale and serve to sustain both the micro and macro scales of organization. For example, energy depletion at the cellular level will influence behaviors at the organismic level to increase the amount of available energy at the cellular level. This recursion enables the sustainment of the internal and whole-organism dynamics. Like organisms, the rock is an embodiment of its context (i.e., the constant tension between the strong and weak atomic forces, electromagnetism, and gravity), but the micro-macro coupling does not serve to sustain the order achieved at either the micro or macro scale. In WST, it is the self-sustaining recursion of the micro-macro coupling that distinguishes the embodied context of organisms from that of rocks and affords a particularly interesting means of being 'about' the world. It is through this self-sustaining work that organisms maintain relationships with their environment. Rocks, desks, and computers do not share this feature with organisms. From this, we argue that the WST framework provides a unique avenue for addressing the problems of consciousness, embodiment, and representation that still challenge the development of cognitive architectures.

WST and Consciousness

Some researchers are not only interested in the processes that give rise to intelligent behavior, but are also interested in identifying those properties that afford a phenomenal consciousness (Reggia, 2013). Such an investigation first requires an adequate description of what consciousness is. Following from the conceptualization of organisms as self-sustaining embodiments of context, Jordan and Ghin (2006) propose that consciousness is the 'aboutness' inherent in self-sustaining embodied context. That is, if a self-sustaining system constitutes an embodiment of its context, it follows that system is naturally and necessarily *about* its context. The authors consider the aboutness of a single-celled organism a "proto-consciousness" because it is the evolutionary precursor to human, embodied aboutness. This suggests that phenomenal consciousness is achieved by humans through their work's natural property of being *about* sustaining a relationship with the world. Accordingly, any system—natural or artificial—that has self-sustaining embodied aboutness would have what we call consciousness.

The problem of implementing consciousness is important to a few AI researchers (e.g., Baars, 1998; Baars & Franklin, 2009). Alternatively, others might operate under the assumption that one can ignore the "Hard Problem" of consciousness (Chalmers, 1995) and solely address the comparatively "easy" work of building an artificial system that can perceive, deliberate, and act. Such an approach could go on doing its work and create artificial systems that behave intelligently without a phenomenal consciousness. By contrast, from the perspective of WST, the problem of artificial cognition and the problem of artificial consciousness are, essentially, one and the same. In other words, if one produces an artificial system that is intelligent by the same means as organisms, one necessarily has implemented a phenomenal consciousness because the system would constitute the self-sustaining kind of embodied aboutness. To be sure, the distinction between the first perspective and WST is not intended as a criticism of the former but, rather, as an opportunity to clarify the difference between creating an artificial system that can do what we do and creating an artificial system that can do what we do *in the way that we do it*. In WST, consciousness is necessary for cognition because it is what we are (i.e., self-sustaining embodied aboutness).

WST and Embodiment

Hypothetically, one can attach arms and legs to a modern computer and program various behaviors into this robot. On the condition that its battery is nearly depleted, the robot might act so as to recharge its battery by navigating to a charging station. To be sure, one can refer to such behavior as self-sustaining. However, we would not grant this system the same self-sustaining, embodied aboutness that we ascribe to organisms. While the behavior of such a robot is self-sustaining at the organismic level, the stability at every other level of scale is taken for granted and is relatively independent of the self-sustaining work of the system as a whole. The chassis, for example, does not generate dynamics that sustain its work or serve to sustain the work of the robot. On the other hand, human neuromuscular architecture works to sustain its own integrity while simultaneously sustaining the integrity of the human. Changes that occur at the level of our neuromuscular architecture give rise to changes at the level of the organism, which, in turn, influences the neuromuscular architecture. This recursion simultaneously sustains the work of the neuromuscular architecture and the human organism, preserving their stability. Such self-sustaining micro-macro coupling would not be observed in the self-charging robot as described. One might say that the robot we described merely *has the ability* to recharge its own battery (i.e., obtain energy) while obtaining energy (i.e., self-sustainment) is what organisms *are*.

In sum, the human body is not merely a "container" for cognition. A body is yet another scale of self-sustaining work that emerges from and is sustained by all the levels of work of which it is constituted. In addition, the various levels of self-sustaining work that constitute a body are simultaneously embodiments of the contextual constraints that need to be addressed in order to afford sustainment. As a result, the human body can be coherently conceptualized as an amalgamation of internal and external dynamical constraints, such as the multi-scale constraints that have to be addressed in order to propel oneself toward an energy source. Accordingly, unlike other embodiment perspectives which emphasize the importance of the body but fall short of defining exactly what a body is (Anderson, 2003), WST addresses the issue of embodiment by unifying bodies and cognition under the conceptual framework of self-sustaining systems.

Furthermore, this perspective clarifies exactly why bodies matter for cognition. Put simply, the body is an ever-present context for the brain and serves as a definable border between the entity and the external environment, albeit a border that is amenable to change (the development from a tadpole into a frog or the growth of a human newborn into an adult human as examples of typical changes to bodies' borders; loss of a limb due to an accident, surgery, or predation as an example of atypical changes to a body's border). The nature of the body as a defined border allows for cognition and behavior to reflect the simultaneous incorporation of or approach towards parts of the environment that facilitate self-sustainment as well as the rejection or avoidance of parts of the environment that destabilize self-sustainment. The self-sustaining work of a body is among the vast constellation of contextual constraints that a brain has to embody in order to sustain itself and the body to which it is recursively coupled. In short, bodies matter to brains because brains, as embodiments of context, are inherently *about* bodies.

WST and Representation

We have noted that there are those who abstain from the use of representation in describing the work of cognitive systems (e.g., Van Gelder, 1998). Specifically, researchers committed to a dynamical account of cognition tend not to refer to internal states with causal powers and, instead, view cognition as a self-organizing process spanning brain, body, and world. While WST does not refer to representations, it does not deny that cognition is constituted of content-bearing internal states. In fact, given the conception of cognitive systems as embodiments of contexts, cognition necessarily entails content (Jordan & Ghin, 2006). The internal dynamics of an organism must be about the contexts in which they are sustained, and for this reason, the internal dynamics of the organism are inherently meaningful. In other words, the internal work of an organism naturally refers to its context (i.e., it is an internalization of the contingent constraints). By replacing the notion of representation with the notion of *self-sustaining embodied context*, WST provides a means of addressing how the internal can be related to the external: "In short, the *inside* is an embodiment of the *outside*. Thus, there is no need to ask how internal states map onto external states....synchronies between internal and external events constitute resonances" (Jordan & Ghin, 2006, p. 58). The use of the word resonance—instead of representation—highlights the dynamic, interdependent relationship of the internal and external. The benefit of approaching the problem of representation from the perspective of WST is that one does not need to ask how cognitive systems represent their environments. Ultimately, self-sustaining systems entail embodied content. To clarify, from this perspective, representation is ubiquitous. Representation (i.e., embodiment) is not unique to brain dynamics or the putatively cognitive processes. It is a feature of all embodiments of contexts as they all effectively "represent" their contexts. The multi-scale self-sustaining processes that constitute a human body represent the phylogenetic, cultural, and ontogenetic contexts in which the body emerged and in which it sustains itself (Jordan & Vinson, 2012). As an embodiment of its context, it naturally and necessarily is *about* its contexts. In other words, one might say that the human body maintains "internal" states that reflect the contingent constraints. What distinguishes brains from other embodiments of context is the time scale at which they can reorganize themselves or change what they are "representing." The importance of treating representation as a natural characteristic of embodied contexts is that it leads to the realization that bodies, like cognitions, are information-laden because they are saturated with *aboutness*. Strictly speaking, information is not unique to brains or cognitive systems; all embodiments of context entail information. Another way to say this is that self-sustaining embodiments are inherently semiotic systems (Emmeche, 2002; Jordan, 2008)

CONCLUSION

The description of Wild Systems Theory (Jordan, 2013; Jordan & Day, 2015) introduced an alternative way to conceptualize what it is that intelligent behavior entails. While other approaches (e.g., Soar, LIDA, and ACT-R) have made considerable progress toward developing architectures that enable intelligent behavior, Wild Systems Theory provides a glimpse at the fundamental principles that might support artificial intelligence if one is interested in creating systems that exhibit intelligent behavior *in the same way* as natural cognitive systems. In this chapter, we have set the foundation for the development of a biologically inspired cognitive architecture—a Wild architecture—one that is grounded in the notion of self-sustaining embodiment of context. Further, the proposal of consciousness as a property of self-sustaining systems sheds light on the nature of artificial systems that might potentially constitute phenomenal consciousness.

REFERENCES

Altmann, E. M., & Trafton, J. G. (2007). Timecourse of recovery from task interruption: Data and a model. *Psychonomic Bulletin & Review*, *14*(6), 1079–1084. doi:10.3758/BF03193094 PMID:18229478

Anderson, J. R. (1996). A simple theory of complex cognition. *The American Psychologist*, *51*(4), 355–365. doi:10.1037/0003-066X.51.4.355

Anderson, J. R., Byrne, M. D., Douglass, S., Lebiere, C., & Qin, Y. (2004). An integrated theory of the mind. *Psychological Review*, *111*(4), 1036–1060. doi:10.1037/0033-295X.111.4.1036 PMID:15482072

Anderson, M. L. (2003). Embodied Cognition: A Field Guide. *Artificial Intelligence*, *149*(1), 91–130. doi:10.1016/S0004-3702(03)00054-7

Baars, B. J. (1988). *A Cognitive Theory of Consciousness*. Cambridge, UK: Cambridge University Press.

Baars, B. J., & Franklin, S. (2009). Consciousness is computational: The LIDA model of global workspace theory. *International Journal of Machine Consciousness*, *1*(01), 23–32. doi:10.1142/S1793843009000050

Bohl, V., & van den Bos, W. (2012). Toward an integrative account of social cognition: Marrying theory of mind and interactionism to study the interplay of Type 1 and Type 2 processes. *Frontiers in Human Neuroscience*, 6. PMID:23087631

Borst, J. P., & Anderson, J. R. (2013). Using model-based functional MRI to locate working memory updates and declarative memory retrievals in the fronto-parietal network. *Proceedings of the National Academy of Sciences of the United States of America*, *110*(5), 1628–1633. doi:10.1073/pnas.1221572110 PMID:23319628

Bösser, T. (1987). Learning in man-computer interaction: A review of the literature. In *Esprit Research Reports* (Vol. 1). Heidelberg, Germany: Springer-Verlag. doi:10.1007/978-3-642-83233-8

Bösser, T. (2013). A discussion of 'The Chunking of Skill and Knowledge' by Paul S. Rosenbloom, John E. Laird & Allen Newell. In B. A. Elsendoorn & H. Bouma (Eds.), *Working Models of Human Perception* (pp. 411–418). San Diego, CA: Academic Press.

Cao, S., Qin, Y., Jin, X., Zhao, L., & Shen, M. (2014). Effect of driving experience on collision avoidance braking: An experimental investigation and computational modelling. *Behaviour & Information Technology*, *33*(9), 929–940. doi:10.1080/0144929X.2014.902100

Cao, S., Qin, Y., Zhao, L., & Shen, M. (2015). Modeling the development of vehicle lateral control skills in a cognitive architecture. *Transportation Research Part F: Traffic Psychology and Behaviour*, *32*, 1–10. doi:10.1016/j.trf.2015.04.010

Chalmers, D. J. (1995). Facing up to the problem of consciousness. *Journal of Consciousness Studies*, *2*, 200–219.

Chella, A. (2013). LIDA, Committed to Consciousness. *Journal of Artificial General Intelligence*, *4*(2), 28–30.

Chikhaoui, B., Pigot, H., Beaudoin, M., Pratte, G., Bellefeuille, P., & Laudares, F. (2009). Learning a song: An ACT-R model. *International Journal of Computer, Electrical, Automation, Control and Information Engineering*, *3*, 1784–1789.

Clark, A. (1997). *Being there: putting brain, body, and world together again*. London, UK: MIT Press.

Clark, A. (1998). Embodied, situated, and distributed cognition. In W. Bechtel & G. Graham (Eds.), *A companion to cognitive science* (pp. 506–517). Malden, MA: Blackwell.

Douglass, S. A., & Mittal, S. (2013). A framework for modeling and simulation of the artificial. In A. Tolk (Ed.), *Ontology, Epistemology, and Teleology for Modeling and Simulation* (pp. 271–317). Heidelberg, Germany: Springer-Verlag; doi:10.1007/978-3-642-31140-6_15

Duch, W., Oentaryo, R. J., & Pasquier, M. (2008). Cognitive architectures: Where do we go from here? In P. Wang, B. Goertzel, & S. Franklin (Ed.), *Proceedings of the First AGI Conference* (pp. 122-136). Memphis, TN: IOS Press.

Emmeche, C. (2002). The chicken and the Orphean egg: On the function of meaning and the meaning of function. *Sign Systems Studies*, *30*, 15–32.

Franklin, S. (1997). Autonomous Agents as Embodied AI. *Cybernetics and Systems*, *28*(6), 499–520. doi:10.1080/019697297126029

Franklin, S., Ramamurthy, U., D'Mello, S. K., McCauley, L., Negatu, A., Silva, R., & Datla, V. (2007). LIDA: A computational model of global workspace theory and developmental learning. In *AAAI Fall Symposium on AI and Consciousness: Theoretical Foundations and Current Approaches* (pp. 61-66). Arlington, VA: AAAI Press.

Franklin, S., Strain, S., McCall, R., & Baars, B. (2013). Conceptual commitments of the LIDA model of cognition. *Journal of Artificial General Intelligence*, *4*(2), 1–22. doi:10.2478/jagi-2013-0002

Gallagher, S. (2015). The new hybrids: Continuing debates on social perception. *Consciousness and Cognition*, *36*, 452–465. doi:10.1016/j.concog.2015.04.002 PMID:25952957

Gibson, J. J. (1979). *The Ecological Approach to Visual Perception*. Hillsdale, NJ: Lawrence Erlbaum Associates.

Halbrügge, M., Quade, M., & Engelbrecht, K.-P. (2015). A predictive model of human error based on user interface development models and a cognitive architecture. In N. A. Taatgen, M. K. van Vugt, J. P. Borst, & K. Mehlhorn (Ed.), *Proceedings of the 13th International Conference on Cognitive Modeling* (pp. 238-243). Groningen, The Netherlands: University of Groningen.

Jaeger, H. (1998). Todays dynamical systems are too simple (Commentary on Tim van Gelders The dynamical hypothesis in cognitive science). *Behavioral and Brain Sciences*, *21*, 643–644. doi:10.1017/S0140525X98401730

Johnson-Laird, P. N. (1980). Mental models in cognitive science. *Cognitive Science*, *4*(1), 71–115. doi:10.1207/s15516709cog0401_4

Jordan, J. S. (2003). Emergence of self and other in perception and action. *Consciousness and Cognition*, *12*(4), 633–646. doi:10.1016/S1053-8100(03)00075-8 PMID:14656506

Jordan, J. S., & Ghin, M. (2007). The role of control in a science of consciousness: Causality, regulation, and self-sustainment. *Journal of Consciousness Studies*, *14*(1-2), 177–197.

Jordan, J. S. (2008). Toward a theory of embodied communication: Self-sustaining wild systems as embodied meaning. In I. Wachsmuth, M. Lenzen, & G. Knoblich (Eds.), *Embodied Communication in Human and Machines* (pp. 53–75). Oxford, UK: Oxford University Press. doi:10.1093/acprof:oso/9780199231751.003.0003

Jordan, J. S. (2013). The wild ways of conscious will: What we do, how we do it, and why it has meaning. *Frontiers in Psychology*, *4*. doi:10.3389/fpsyg.2013.00574 PMID:24027543

Jordan, J. S., & Day, B. (2015). Wild systems theory as a 21st century coherence framework for cognitive science. In T. Metzinger & J. M. Windt (Eds.), *Open MIND: 21*. Frankfurt am Main, Germany: MIND Group; doi:10.15502/9783958570191

Jordan, J. S., & Ghin, M. (2006). (Proto-) consciousness as a contextually-emergent property of self-sustaining systems. *Mind & Matter*, *4*, 45–68.

Jordan, J. S., & Vinson, D. (2012). After nature: On bodies, consciousness, and causality. *Journal of Consciousness Studies*, *19*(5-6).

Kauffman, S. (1995). *At Home in the Universe*. New York, NY: Oxford University Press.

Kelso, J. A. S. (1995). *Dynamic patterns*. Cambridge, MA: MIT Press.

Koedinger, K. R., Anderson, J. R., Hadley, W. H., & Mark, M. A. (1997). Intelligent tutoring goes to school in the big city. *International Journal of Artificial Intelligence*, *8*, 30–43.

Laird, J. E. (2008). Extending the Soar cognitive architecture. In P. Wang, B. Goertzel, & S. Franklin (Ed.), *Proceedings of the First AGI Conference* (pp. 224-235). Memphis, TN: IOS Press.

Laird, J. E. (2012). *The Soar cognitive architecture*. Cambridge, MA: MIT Press.

Laird, J. E., Newell, A., & Rosenbloom, P. S. (1987). Soar: An architecture for general intelligence. *Artificial Intelligence*, *33*(1), 1–64. doi:10.1016/0004-3702(87)90050-6

Langley, P., Laird, J. E., & Rogers, S. (2009). Cognitive architectures: Research issues and challenges. *Cognitive Systems Research*, *10*(2), 141–160. doi:10.1016/j.cogsys.2006.07.004

Lewis, R. L. (1993). An architecturally-based theory of sentence comprehension. *Proceedings of the Fifteenth Annual Conference of the Cognitive Science Society* (pp. 108-113). Boulder, CO: Lawrence Erlbaum.

Marr, D. (1982). *Vision: A computational investigation into the human representation and processing of visual information*. San Francisco, CA: W. H. Freeman.

Marsh, K. L., Richardson, M. J., & Schmidt, R. C. (2009). Social connection through joint action and interpersonal coordination. *Topics in Cognitive Science*, *1*(2), 320–339. doi:10.1111/j.1756-8765.2009.01022.x PMID:25164936

Miller, C. S., & Laird, J. E. (1996). Accounting for graded performance within a discrete search framework. *Cognitive Science*, *20*(4), 499–537. doi:10.1207/s15516709cog2004_2

Miller, G. A., Galanter, E., & Pribram, K. H. (1960). *Plans and the structure of behavior*. New York: Holt, Rinehart and Winston. Inc. doi:10.1037/10039-000

Moon, J., & Anderson, J. R. (2013). Timing in multitasking: Memory contamination and time pressure bias. *Cognitive Psychology*, *67*(1-2), 26–54. doi:10.1016/j.cogpsych.2013.06.001 PMID:23892230

ORegan, J. K., & Noë, A. (2001). A sensorimotor account of vision and visual consciousness. *Behavioral and Brain Sciences*, *24*(5), 939–1031. doi:10.1017/S0140525X01000115 PMID:12239892

Powers, W. T. (1973). Quantitative analysis of purposive systems: Some spadework at the foundation of scientific psychology. *Psychological Review*, *85*(5), 417–435. doi:10.1037/0033-295X.85.5.417

Reggia, J. A. (2013). The rise of machine consciousness: Studying consciousness with computational models. *Neural Networks*, *44*, 112–131. doi:10.1016/j.neunet.2013.03.011 PMID:23597599

Roberts, S., & Pashler, H. (2000). How persuasive is a good fit? A comment on theory testing. *Psychological Review*, *107*(2), 358–367. doi:10.1037/0033-295X.107.2.358 PMID:10789200

Thelen, E., & Smith, L. B. (1994). *A dynamic systems approach to the development of cognition and action*. Cambridge, MA: MIT Press.

Thomson, R., Pyke, A., Trafton, J. G., & Hiatt, L. M. (2015). An account of associative learning in memory recall.*Proceedings of the 37th Annual Conference of the Cognitive Science Society*. Austin, TX: Cognitive Science Society.

Trafton, J. G., Hiatt, L. M., Harrison, A. M., Tamborello, F., Khemlani, S. S., & Schultz, A. C. (2013). ACT-R/E: An embodied cognitive architecture for human robot interaction. *Journal of Human-Robot Interaction*, 2(1), 30–55. doi:10.5898/JHRI.2.1.Trafton

Tschacher, W., & Dauwalder, J.-P. (Eds.). (2003). *The dynamical systems approach to cognition: concepts and empirical paradigms based on self-organization, embodiment, and coordination dynamics*. Singapore: World Scientific. doi:10.1142/5395

van Gelder, T. J. (1998). The dynamical hypothesis in cognitive science. *Behavioral and Brain Sciences*, 21(05), 1–14. doi:10.1017/S0140525X98001733 PMID:10097022

van Rooij, I., Bongers, R. M., & Haselager, F. G. (2002). A non-representational approach to imagined action. *Cognitive Science*, 26(3), 345–375. doi:10.1207/s15516709cog2603_7

Varella, F., Thompson, E., & Rosch, E. (1991). *The embodied mind: cognitive science and human experience*. Cambridge, MA: MIT Press.

Wilson, A. D., & Golonka, S. (2013). Embodied cognition is not what you think it is. *Frontiers in Psychology*, 4. PMID:23408669

Wiltshire, T. J., Lobato, E. J., McConnell, D. S., & Fiore, S. M. (2014). Prospects for direct social perception: A multi-theoretical integration to further the science of social cognition. *Frontiers in Human Neuroscience*, 8. PMID:25709572

Wiltshire, T. J., Lobato, E. J. C., Jentsch, F. G., & Fiore, S. M. (2013). Will (dis)embodied LIDA agents be socially interactive? *Journal of Artificial General Intelligence*, 4(2), 42–47.

Wirzberger, M., & Russwinkel, N. (2015). Modeling interruption and resumption in a smartphone task: An ACT-R approach. *i-com, 14*, 147-154. doi:10.1515/icom-2015-0033

Chapter 4
Mind and Matter:
Why It All Makes Sense

Leonard Johard
Innopolis University, Russia

Vittorio Lippi
University Medical Center Freiburg, Germany

Larisa Safina
Innopolis University, Russia

Manuel Mazzara
Innopolis University, Russia

ABSTRACT

A purely reductionist approach to neuroscience has difficulty in providing intuitive explanations and cost effective methods. Following a different approach, much of the mechanics of the brain can be explained purely by closer study of the relation of the brain to its environment. Starting from the laws of physics, genetics and easily observable properties of the biophysical environment we can deduce the need for dreams and a dopaminergic system. We provide a rough sketch of the various a priori assumptions encoded in the mechanics of the nervous system. This indicates much more can be learnt by studying the statistical priors exploited by the brain rather than its specific mechanics of calculation.

DOI: 10.4018/978-1-5225-1947-8.ch004

INTRODUCTION

The best minds of man's short history on Earth have been thrown into the bottomless pit of a single question: What is the relation between the inner and outer worlds of our experience? Is the universe purely a product of the mind, nothing but an illusion in the mind of an ancient dreamer? Or, on the contrary, is the mind but a small piece of machinery in God's cosmic clockwork?

The rise of materialism in the last centuries has certainly favoured the latter view but, as the technological progress continues to blur the lines separating imagination and reality, the fragility of our current understanding of the relation between mind and matter is again becoming unsettlingly apparent.

The spearhead in this transformation has been information technology. Rather than, as in older scientific visions, molding the world around our fantasies the scientific development has moved in a diametric direction. We have liberated the flow of information and, to some extent, our subjective experience from the physical world.

Be it literature, cinema or computer games, increasing amount of time is being spent in purely imaginative and virtual worlds. To many of us, direct experience of the material world remains just a necessity and distraction. Likewise, the centers of the economy and power is equally being transferred into the virtual realm. While accepting a materialist world view, we have been moving into an idealist reality. The material world, although commonly accepted as the higher reality, has been greatly reduced in its importance in our daily lives.

However important this digital transformation has been, what awaits us next will dwarf it. In handling the growing amount of information we have recruited the help from self-learning systems and thus triggered the probably irreversible development of artificial intelligence.

Compared to information technology, artificial intelligence is a very different beast. Instead of liberating the mind from its material obligations, we liberate the material obligations from the human mind.

Further, as mathematical formula and the human minds inevitably grow ever more similar to each other, the question of what a mind is becomes ever more urgent. So being developed in the materialist reductionist tradition, artificial intelligence seeks to explain the mind as a movement of molecules, a transmission of substances, a network of synapses that all give rise to images in the mind. Instead of imagining the world roughly as the realization of a set of ideal physical laws, as in traditional physics, we imagine thoughts themselves as a set of physical structures.

This new field of science is no longer about explaining the world in theoretical terms but in explaining the mind in material terms. What then is a mind? Let us not resist the zeitgeist and instead follow the materialist path to its natural conclusion. The mind is just an illusion of the material brain. The brain is there to help us humans survive and reproduce, if you can excuse the teleology. The brain is there to adapt to the universe, to predict it and to tame it.

In machine learning it has long been known and accepted that no single prediction is universally supreme in all possible worlds. An intelligent mind is inevitably tied together with the world in which it is considered intelligent. We, as children of our cosmos, are intelligent but intelligent in this world alone. The very structure of the cosmos and our lives here on earth are mirrored in our very definition of what intelligence is.

LIMITS OF REDUCTIONISM

Reductionism is the dominant doctrine in neuroscience. It seeks to divide the mind's function into ever smaller parts and figure out how they work with the intention to sometime in the future put them all back together. Consequently, every time we are unable to grasp how the brain functions at a certain scale level we go into a smaller scale. Current efforts are down to the scales of individual ion channels and models of the genetic expression. This approach is bound to eventually hit some problems. A complete mapping of the phenotype of even a single cell still lies far into the future. As the objects of our attention grow smaller and smaller the cost and difficulty of obtaining new information inevitably goes up. It is with current technology it is also unfeasible to simulate the brain at anything resembling a molecular level.

There is a growing need to apply different scientific methods and to create high-level abstract models in order to fill in the blanks where direct measurements have not been made. By comparison, the predominant method in biology is, for good reasons, entirely different: teleology, i.e. the study of purpose. As an example, we might be unaware of the exact mechanisms of intracellular molecular signaling in the heart. Still, the heart is considered much less of a mystery than the brain and this is because we can imagine what it does. We see it through its purpose: to pump blood. We reach this conclusion not by studying the microscopic mechanisms of the heart itself, but through seeing it in the context of its environment.

The scientific understanding of the mind is gradually moving away from the old interpretation of the brain as a complex machinery consisting of many distinct subfunctions. We are instead moving toward a blank slate interpretation with its new brand name: plasticity. Yet the heritage from reductionism is a tendency to again divide plasticity models into specific subsystems, each with their own teleology, be it V1 neurons or be it sparse spatial maps of the environment. Such reductionism in plasticity seems excessive in light of the ease at which tasks are redistributed in the brain after physiological changes and the complexity of precisely encoding the tasks assigned to each subsystem. The teleological division of the brain has a direct impact on the learning mechanism and hence demands due attention to be paid.

To critics of teleology we must note the obvious, that the metaphysical notion of the purpose of objects is of course nothing but a simplified model of the underlying evolutionary process. As we will see, however, there is a good biological reason why talking about the purpose of evolution makes sense to us. We will claim that our minds are by their nature in constant search for states with high approximate genetic fitness. Although genes are not psychological beings, teleology will inevitably be a good approximation due to the similarity between reinforcement learning and genetic algorithms, as well as the approximate equality of the reward functions and the genetic fitness. Teleology remains an imperfect model, but it is a model that, like Newtonian physics, is of great utility.

OUR PURPOSE

What, then, is the purpose of the animal brain? From an evolutionary perspective, plasticity arises from the need to learn at a pace that our slowly adapting genes are able to keep up with. As human we have passed through the stone ages, iron ages, information ages while keeping our genome substantially intact. Since the arrival of the first animals, nervous systems have been dealing with constantly changing environments far too complex to adapt to across generations. Neural plasticity is thus a way to accelerate the adaptation of our behavior beyond what is possible with genetic means.

This adaptation, however, cannot be made without a priori assumptions. How do we combine the need to make accurate predictions in an unpredictable world with the need to predict how the world will behave?

This seeming paradox can be resolved in only one way: The way our mind adapts encodes knowledge about the a priori distribution of all learnable systems. Somehow, all patterns that we are able to understand share some common properties that are originally defined in part by the cosmic laws that unfold our space-time and in part by the emergent laws of nature that determine the relation of animals to themselves and each other.

Hence, the study of the mind is the study of its environment. However, while our mind is completely free in the realm covered by its a priori assumptions, it remains hopelessly unable to grasp anything outside of it. Our scientific process is unfortunately bound by endless recursion; we are born blind to whatever reality lies beyond the borders of the mind's narrow eye. There may be many significant patterns in the cosmic distribution that we are unable to exploit and we will be unaware of this. In other cases, the patterns are picked up by our scientific methods and we should be able to mathematically outline the relation between our minds and the aspects of the cosmos that are visible to us. Thus, one part of the coin is that the nature of the visible cosmos is inherently dependent on the nature of the mind.

The more interesting side of the coin is the opposite relation. The study of our environment might give us better insight into the functioning of the mind. The purpose of this work is such: to summarize our knowledge of the purpose of the mind. We will search for the underlying a priori assumptions that are necessary for the mind to function and deduce how these influence the development of the human brain. You can follow the reasoning with our approximate map of our deduction presented in Figure 1 and Figure 2.

First, a warning. This overview necessarily covers a great number of complex scientific topics and thus is prone to error, oversimplifications and omission.

THE COSMOS

Let us start with the following question: Are there any physical laws that govern a priori probabilities of events around us?

First, we would wisely start by defining more formally what we mean by a learning system. In this case we can start with the supervised learning formulation from the machine learning field, where we adapt a slightly non-customary notation in order to homogenize the notation across the different topics covered.

Figure 1. Map

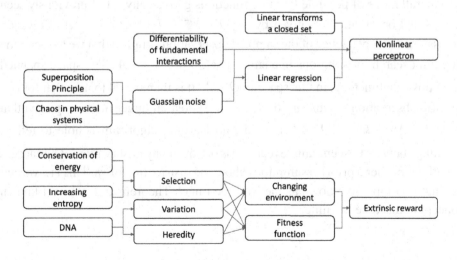

Figure 2. Map

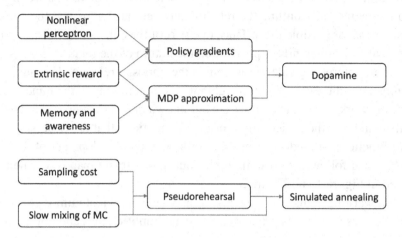

Let us start with the naive approach. Given a set of targets $t_{all} = t_1, t_2...t_n$, a set of observations $o_{all} = o_1, o_2...o_n$ and a set of example actions $a_{all} = a_1, a_2...a_n$. We denote the corresponding spaces of the variables T, O and A.. We further assume that they are all sampled from some static distribution so that all sets a_n, o_n, t_n are independent from each other for all n. For simplicity of notation we also assume that there exist some deterministic target function g. such that $t_n = g(o_n)$ for all n and that $o_k \neq o_m$ for all $k \neq m$.

We assume the observations and actions are independent. Assume a prediction a of the next data point produced by a prediction algorithm f:
$a_{n+1} = f(o_n, a_{n-1}, t_{n-1}, o_{n-1}...a_1, t_1, o_1)$.

The full range of possible learning functions g given any set of previously seen actions and observations is given by $f : O \times A^{n-1} \times T^{n-1} \times O^{n-1} \mapsto A$. However, the assumed independence of the sampled observations implies that we at each time step limit search for solutions in a smaller set: $f(t) : O \mapsto A$. The space spanned of all possible functions in this space is $O \times A$. It is then trivial to note that for any specific observation o_n and a_n there exists a potential target function g such that $o_k = f(a_k) \forall k : k \leq n$. In other words, no learning algorithm is able to tell us anything about an unseen sample regardless of how many observations it has access to without further a priori assumptions about the distribution of g. This is a variant of what is commonly known as the No Free Lunch Theorem and is a well-known concept in machine learning.

Any learning system must thus implicitly or explicitly exploit a priori knowledge about the data in order to make successful predictions. In particular the human mind, with its extreme range of applications, must within its learning mechanisms encode some a priori knowledge about the a priori distribution of the cosmos. We will list some of that knowledge below.

$$E\left[(y-t)^2\right] = \infty$$

Bounds

One of the simplest and most powerful observations which lies in the very foundation of our understanding of the universe is the assumption that everything is bounded. Although we can somehow understand infinity in the terms of limits, bounded entities come much more natural to us. Improving our foresight based on this simple fact is elementary.

Let us now assume that the universe is bounded. Although debatable in the light of singularities, this is still an assumption that is valid almost everywhere. We do not directly observe infinite energies or temperatures in the universe.

Even such a simple a priori knowledge allows us to create a prediction that is infinitely better than a random guess in R. We simply pick a number in the existing range and can rest assured that it is in the admissible range of values and that our distance from this point to any future point is less than the range of admissible values. This concept allows us to create the immensely powerful concepts of averages or other central tendency. By picking any value within the domain the expected error is reduced from infinite to finite:

$$y := t_i$$

for any i

$$E\left[y - t_j\right] \leq t_{max} - t_{min}$$

Order and Chaos

A deeper search for the meaning of our thoughts will take us back to the primordial struggle between two conflicting forces of nature. The brave claim is that the mind's predictive ability is solely derived from the interaction between order and chaos. Intelligence is by definition our ability to tell one apart from the other.

Further, the cause for existence of order and chaos on every level of the universe can, at least in part, be traced back to the fundamental forces themselves. These well-known physical laws necessarily create a universe that is in part predictable and in part stochastic no matter what scale we are looking at.

A key to unlocking these secrets lies in the simple observation that the most basic laws of physics, the fundamental interactions, are differentiable in time and space. This means that on some small scale in space and time these forces can be accurately predicted by a linearization.

Next, we proceed with another observation to explain the creation of chaos: Practically every physical system is chaotic, which essentially means it will be in-distinguishable from a stochastic system when viewed over large time scales. The time scale at which this transition takes place is called Lyapunov time. Further, the decay of the fundamental interactions over distance means that the time scale of systems is a monotonically increasing function of the spatial scales, without going into a deeper discussion of scale symmetry. Consequently, as we increase the spatial scale of our observed physical system more and more of the orderly and determin-istic interactions from smaller systems will be practically transformed into chaos. Quantum mechanics would guarantee a pure stochastic initial seed of randomness in this seeming fractal of order and chaos.

Chaos can, however omnipresent, be tamed. This consists of additivity, or taken the complex nature of quantum mechanics into account, the superposition principle:

$$f(x + y) = f(x) + f(y)$$

$$f(ax) = af(x)$$

The success for reductionism in physics arises from the fact that physical systems can be divided into spatially separated subsystems. Due to the locality of interac-tions these subsystems have a tendency to mix independently and their long-distance interactions add together as per the superposition principle. Regardless of the dis-tribution of their interaction they will add up to a Gaussian distribution as a result of the central limit theorem.

We can summarize these principles that remain for any scale we are looking at as follows:

1. Interactions arising from collections of small physical systems will be approximately stochastic and have a Gaussian distribution.
2. Interactions arising from large patterns will be approximately linear.

The universe is for these reasons trapped in a conflict between linear and stochastic forces. No matter at what scale we are looking we will have influences from large systems that can be effectively linearized. To do so we must sort out the Gaussian noise inevitably arising from small processes. This is for these reasons a well-studied problem and the solution can be found in a linear regression:

$$\arg\max_{a,b} P\left(a,b\right) \quad \mathrm{x} = \left\{x_1, x_2 \ldots x_n\right\}, y = \left\{y_1, y_2 \ldots y_n\right\}$$

where $y_i = a + bx_i + \epsilon$ and ϵ is the normal distribution $N\left(0, sigma^2\right)$. Linear regression is one of the most essential scientific methods and a natural first step in any modelling attempt. As not all systems are mathematically large in relation to our own lives it is often possible to create significantly better models using more detailed information, but the strength of linear regression is that it is applicable to such a wide range of problems. In studying the mind we can find the principles of linear regression embedded into most biologically inspired statistical methods. The first model of neural learning, the linear perceptron (Rosenblatt 1958), uses this method to perform a range of learning tasks.

Beyond the Obvious

Linear models are a closed set under composition, which means that a network is limited of linear perceptrons perform an equivalent mapping as a single perceptron. Likewise, biological neurons likely hit a limit in their evolution when linear models could not progress further. Although large systems are predictable, we also have the power to predict systems working on a similar scale as the learning agent itself. To do this we have to break free of the linear constraints.

While gaining the ability to make nonlinear predictions we would like our expanded priori to preserve the ability to predict linear systems. The most obvious way of doing this is to have a prior over differentiable functions, i.e. functions that a priori are likely to be approximately linear. Common examples are tangent sigmoid, logarithmic sigmoid and radial basis functions. For this the model pays the necessary price for generality in performing less well on the many tasks which remain linear. In return the advantage is substantial. A superposition of models can approximate any continuous function to any degree of accuracy (Hornik, Stinch-combe, and White 1989).

These non-linear functions, known in neural models as activation or transfer functions, are piecewise differentiable and thus contain the linear models as a subset. As the a priori likelihood for approximately linear models is still high, these non-linear perceptrons still have an advantage on linear problems. At the same time, they are able to approximate any continuous function. Minimization with a square error function will provide the maximum likelihood estimate given Gaussian noise, but the a priori distribution over physical systems is now a continuous set of candidate functions, which is often very complicated to derive analytically. Any specific choice of activation function lacks the solid support that the assumption of differentiability does and consequently there has been little progress in finding an optimal activation function and parameter settings generally superior to other choices.

THE MIND

Life and Death

The cycle of life and death is the counterpoint to the linear and progressive nature of learning. Seen from a single lifetime death is but the ultimate nemesis and destroyer of our minds; a crowning, anticlimactic moment of our lives where every memory and all the knowledge painfully accumulated in a life time is forever lost.

Seen from a multigenerational perspective the cycle instead spirals into the very essence of intelligence: the fitness function. This Darwinian derivative is a numerical estimate of how well each organism is able to reproduce in the environment per unit of time.

Given an environment with limited resources the average fitness function regresses to zero. Add some random mutations and the result is a continuous search in the gene pool for candidates with a higher fitness function. Evolution is a direct analogue to function optimization in mathematics, where many contemporary methods borrow heavily from its Darwinian ancestry. Formally, the existence of universal Darwinism is dependent three components:

1.   Variation,
2.   Selection, and
3.   Heredity.

Let us examine the underlying assumptions in biological Darwinism further. The natural variation and selection process is guaranteed by the DNA replication process. The requirements for its spontaneous formation in nature is still a topic of intense and complex debate that is best left out of the scope of this discussion.

The selection process, on the other hand, can be traced back directly to physical laws. The first and the second law of thermodynamics work together to make exergy a limited resource in any closed system. With the larger pattern of the sun supplying the Earth with a steady stream of exergy we have the basics of a selection process in place.

However, without further assumptions this evolution will simply sample random points in the fitness landscape taking the maximum. For evolution to be more effective than a naive strategy in a single step we need to assume a certain sense of continuity, in particular that genes close to each other, as determined by the distribution of mutations around a population, have similar fitness values.

For the genetic algorithm to be successful across several steps we would need slightly stronger assumptions that brings our problem closer to those used in the optimization of differentiable functions. A simple example can be seen by attempting optimization of the Weierstrass function using genetic algorithms, where genetic distributions will be stuck in a local optimum.

The genetic optimization gives us the basis for our existence. Life will adapt and survive.

Mortals and Immortals

Still the answers to several questions surrounding our inevitable deaths are hidden from us. One of the most important questions is perhaps the naivest one: Why do we die?

Up until recently it has been assumed that death is a failure of the organism to stay alive. The idea is simple: This world is a harsh one and life is unlikely to last until old age. The cellular mechanisms necessary to achieve immortality have simply never been exposed to evolutionary pressure since the life span's impact on the fitness function has been negligible. Until now. With the development of modern civilization humans have been able to support life to its natural end. As a consequence of new evolutionary pressure on the aging process people will get older and older.

The renewing aspects of the life and death cycles are excluded from the above narrative and the interpretation can be diametrical when included. Several recent studies best summarized by Goldsmith (Goldsmith 2014) support the old notion that the limitation of our life span is not the result of an absence of evolutionary pressure, but rather the direct result of it.

Given certain conditions, such as a changing environment and group selection, death accelerates the intelligent adaptation of life, the evolvability. Moreover, the changing environment of a specific organism can be derived from the cyclical, competitive or chaotic nature of evolution itself (Van Valen 1973) (Doebeli and Ispolatov 2014; Van Valen 1973). Preprogrammed mortality allows us to evolutionary outrun species with longer life spans and stay adapted to our environments. In a rapidly developing society it is actually possible that our life spans will be reduced.

The existence of group selection in practice is an intensely debated topic. The question we are facing is the nature of the extrinsic rewards function. The suggested range of such self-destructive mortal pleasures range from sex (Fisher 1930) and music (Wallin and Merker 2001) to morality (Sober and Wilson 1999).

A blank slate interpretation of the brain as a statistical machinery does not in any way rule out inheritability. Rather, the No Free Lunch Theorem states precisely that the choice of statistical model affords us infinte flexibility given a fixed data. In particular, the reward function might differ significantly between individuals or groups. The conflict between nature and nurture is not a mathematical concept.

The Brain

The brain itself originates at a very specific moment in evolutionary history: the development of voltage-gated sodium channels (Sakarya et al. 2007). At this moment started the development of proper neural nets that later evolved into complete nervous systems. Although earlier animals displayed some motility and probably some of the adaptive properties of neuron, the development of signaling mechanisms in neural nets provided a sophisticated information infrastructure for the organisms that allowed the rapid evolution in adaptive behavior that followed.

Today, all animals, except for the Philae sponges and placozoa, have neurons and all animals are motile at one stage or another of the life cycle. The original role of neurons was exactly this: to provide information for the motor control of the animal. Precise and complex motor control has since remained a defining property in their survival.

The need for more complex definition of the behavior applied evolutionary pressure. We see a rather continuous scale of behavioral complexity ranging from simple nematodes and insects to more complex vertebrates and humans. It seems reasonable to assume that this is likewise springs from a continuous development of motor learning rather than conceptually different roles being added within the same processing units.

It can be noted that the most common formulations of the learning tasks used within the context for motor learning, observable or partially observable Markov decision processes, are indeed general enough to motivate similar formulations for essentially any human behavior. Neural development since the first neurons might thus simply be bigger and faster versions of the same fundamental mechanism.

The teleological concept of motor learning is essential in guessing the function of the nervous system. In a motor learning task the animal optimizes its behavior according to a rough approximation of its genetic fitness. The total genetic fitness of animal behavior then becomes a function of both inherited behavior and adaptation to previous experiences within its lifetime.

Pleasure

The evolutionary principles actually mimic certain learning principles hypothesized in the brain almost exactly(Heidrich-Meisner and Igel 2008). Both consist of a local exploration of their behavior in order to maximize a function known as either fitness or reward.

Formally, the brain is known as an agent in the reinforcement learning. The state of the environment that the agent lives in generates some limited information accessible to the agent. This information is called an observation, o. At every moment the agent generates an output called its action, a. The agent then seeks to maximize its fitness or reward r by changing the distribution that generates actions from observations. It is able to change this function by adjusting a number of parameters, θ.

Such a system can be described as:

$$\arg \max_{\theta} r = \int_{0}^{\infty} r\left(a,s\right) dt$$

where $a = a\left(\theta,o\right), o = o\left(s\right)$ and $\frac{\partial}{\partial \tau} s = f\left(a,s\right)$, where f is some distribution. All distributions here are also implicitly dependent on time, τ.

The genetic fitness function is directly mirrored in the extrinsic reward that approximates it. An action that intuitively seems to have a purpose to us is one that approximately increases the fitness. This is the reason why teleology is a successful method in biology; we constantly think about approximate genetic fitness in our pursuit of happiness.

Memories

We could imagine memory as a way to selective study moments in the past. What exactly is it that makes memory useful to us? Memories need to capture certain aspect of our past lives that is neither otherwise incorporated in the current state of the animal, nor taken fully into consideration into the learning mechanisms.

Substantial differences between short and long term memories are known (Cowan 2008). While the mechanics of short-term memory can be fully implemented by recursive connections in a neural network, the long term memory continues to elude us. Promising hypotheses are either the neuron based model, such as LSTM neurons (Hochreiter and Schmidhuber 1997) or the energy based models derived from Hebbian frameworks and later stochastic counterparts being popularized through (Hinton, Osindero, & Teh 2006).

Short-term memory needs no further explanation than the non-observability of the universe. We are limited in what we are able to sense in an instant and thus memories become a way to compensate by increasing the range of the observation at any instant.

The separate mechanisms of long-term memories could be caused by the computation infeasibility of otherwise saving information over long time spans with conventional methods (Hochreiter et al., n.d.). Further, it is hard to say for certain whether this memory is a separate dedicated mechanism or somehow emergent from other learning principles.

Memories themselves can be evolutionarily motivated solely through the partial observability of the environment at each instant. An additional benefit is the change in learning type possible when the accessible memory is large, which we will cover next.

Desire

In order to accelerate the learning process, we could add some additional a priori assumptions. One such example is that the animal has access to all the information it needs to take the right decision, which is equivalent to changing our problem formulation from a POMDP to a MDP approximation. This is a subtle transition that motivates further explanation. In the terms of a single neuron the MDP assumption is unreasonable. It needs to take action dependent on its immediate inputs and results regarding success of the signal will not be available until later when it receives feedback from other parts of the nervous systems. At any specific moment the neuron will not be able to observe the success of its past actions and is unable to exactly reconstruct the input-output pairs for learning purposes.

If we move up in scale to an animal as the atomic unit, the picture changes. Although an animal might have taken an action, such as pushing a button in an experiment, whose result might not be observable until much later, the animal has access to memories that are able to tell it whether it has pushed the button or not.

This subtle difference allows to exploit the assumption that the surroundings are observable. Although the MDP assumptions are not true for the surrounding world for a memoryless agent (Singh, Jaakkola, and Jordan 1994), they will however be applicable if we allow for a complete memory of previous events.

This is easy to see if we note that best possible estimate of the current state given all previously observed information is a function of all past observation and actions. This theoretical function can be approximated to any desired accuracy given a universal function approximator. The presence of a memory seems to allow for a variant of the universal function approximation theorem where we can learn anything as long as we scale up the memory together with the neural network.

The main advantage from moving from MDP to POMDP assumptions is that the learning mechanisms can move from slow reinforcement learning to the much faster supervised learning algorithms. These rely on analytical derivation from past experiences rather than the explicit trial-and-error approach of policy gradients that requires a substantial amount of behavioral noise for local policy exploration.

Realizing the validity of the MDP assumptions on the scale of an animal but certainly not on the scale of individual motor neuron is of great importance to our understanding of how the central nervous system treats information. The presence of memory is an observation about the immediate environment of the learning agent that in terms of scale seems the opposite to physical principles such as continuity. In the perspective of a specific brain structure through evolutionary history they are equally universal.

These experiments seem to validate the concept in motor learning tasks. In this case our observation about the nature of the external world would be validated through the imitation of a mechanism exploiting the MDP approximation in a rat brain.

There are different ways to work under a MDP approximation. A weaker assumption is to sample the reward from observables and make a monte carlo estimate of the reward r_{int}. In this case a choice between states that are indistinguishable from each other through observation might lead the actor to take the wrong action. Regardless, it does give the best estimate of its reward possible given the information in the observation.

A stronger assumption is to assume that $E\left[\dfrac{\partial r}{\partial \tau}\right] = 0$, which is indeed true for the optimal solution in a fully observable MDP. This relation is exploited by the popular TD-learning algorithms (Sutton 1988) where the stronger assumption allows more efficient bootstrapping and an optimal prediction given limited training data.

However, the above relation breaks in cases where we are not able to perfectly estimate the MDP. The stronger assumption in TD-learning leads to rewards estimates that are suboptimal given the information available. This inability to perfectly estimate the MDP is caused not only by non-observable state differences, but also by limits in the function approximation. A POMDP problem resulting in a suboptimal solution given the available observations under TD-learning is shown in Figure 3 and Figure 4, where blocks represent states and numbers the observable visible to the agent. Figure 4 is clearly not solvable by TD-algorithms, as the two actions leading to an observable 1 will be considered equivalent.

In practical algorithms, the theoretical issues with TD-learning become even more severe. As noted in (Geist & Pietquin 2013) most algorithms, such as residual, bootstrapping and projected-fixed point approaches rely on further approximations or introduces biases which weakens the theoretical foundation of the algorithms.

Not surprisingly, measurements done in live animals have indeed revealed an extrinsic reward signal in the animal brain that perfectly matches what could be expected by an MDP approximation (Pan et al. 2005). With all the problems arising from TD-learning, it is also encouraging that biological measurements tend to rule out at least pure temporal difference learning without traces.

Figure 3. TD-Learning

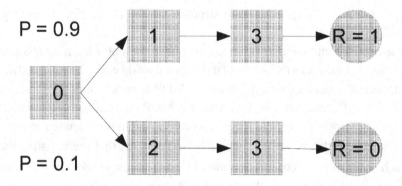

Figure 4. TD-Learning

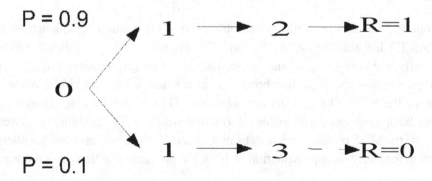

Dreams

Even in the light of all the scientific progress a third of our lives remains unexplored. One obvious reason is that we have very few memories of it and another is that it is a part of our lives that we largely face alone. Dreams are an entire existence independent from our daily lives and we reach it just through the glimpses that are still in our memory when we awaken. How little we understand of the phenomena is best illustrated by the variety of hypotheses it has generated, which is far too long to exhaustively list. Of these none offer anything even resembling a complete mathematical model. Unknown to many, one such model has nonetheless been proposed (Robins 1995). In this model, dreams are a way to safely interact with an environment that resembles our own. Even though our understanding is noisy and far from perfect, this training resembles reality just enough to enable us to receive valuable lessons from it. Its defects in terms of accuracy are compensated by our control over it.

More generally, pseudorehearsal shows that even very crude statistical models of the world work as an efficient substitute for real training data. Feeding noise and exploiting the distribution crude world model already inherent in the function approximator showed remarkable (Baddeley 2008)

The study of pseudorehearsal is still in its infancy and its true potential remains to be explored. Although it passed under the radar of most scientists, similar ideas have indeed been explored by Hinton (Hinton et al. 1995) and it later developed into the popular algorithms for pretraining in deep learning (Hinton & Salakhutdinov 2006), which was the algorithm which triggered the recent interest in Deep Learning. The weakness of the model is the shared weights which seemingly differs from what we observe in real neurons. It is in any case very possible that we can develop analogue algorithms even for symmetric weights.

Deep Boltzmann Machine models are generative models that approximate the input distributions, which is ideal for imitating the environment in a dream. One significant theoretical issue of the contrastive divergence is that it approximates the Markov chain and that the approximating truncation causes a bias in the estimate. The stated reason for using this approximation is that the true Markov chain mixes too slowly. A suggestive solution for the slow mixing that avoids bias is borrowed from numerical optimization: simulated annealing (Kirkpatrick et al. 1983). This method alternates between high temperature and low temperature mixings of the Markov chain. In the context of dreams, this means that it would change between less noisy and noisier dream modes. The role of the noisier dream modes is to allow the dreams to jump between completely different types of dream experiences (mixing the Markov chain) without altering the underlying distribution. The role of the less noisy dreams is to accurately describe a certain subset of experiences. This mixing possibly has an analogue to dream cycles observed in humans.

Thus, although we still lack the precise mechanisms for understanding dreams we do possess an approximate computational hypothesis. The benefit is derived partly from our limited memory capacity. In contrast to the MDP assumptions, where we assume that we have access to enough knowledge to learn the right decisions, we here assume that we do not have enough memories to accurately calculate the gradient. The assumption is that the gradient estimate that we get from our generative model is sufficient to learn meaningfully.

Another benefit is that the generative model can learn from unlabeled data. Although the Markov chain we construct through observations is different from the real world it is similar enough to be learnt effectively. The cost of sampling from it is significantly less than sampling from the real world. Actions which are especially difficult or expensive to sample would provide the greatest benefit. If the brain has access to methods to affect the mixing process by affecting the temperature, it would be expected to generate a higher number of such experiences. An increased prevalence of nightmares be a natural way for the mind to establish a behaviour for experiences too dangerous to experience.

CONCLUSION

We set out to improve the teleological explanations of the brain by reevaluating its role from a statistical perspective and identifying the priors it exploits. The rough outline of the priori assumptions on which our intellect is based has been presented and the main ideas are summarized in Figure 1 and Fe2igur 1 for the reader's convenience.

The conclusions and assumptions illustrated in our map is obviously incomplete, but at the same time inevitable together with reasonable assumptions at each step. This illustrates that the development of the high-level structure and mechanism of the brain could be a direct and inevitable result of the laws of physics.

The idea that human intelligence is best understood holistically by studying the priors of its environment then stands in contrast to the common reductionist perspective, i.e. that the brain should be understood as a collection of independent processes each with their own teleological explanation and history of evolutionary adaptation. One perspective obviously does not rule out the other and, even if our explanation of human intelligence was to be entirely correct, the modulation of the rewards system is left to reductionist explanations.

Our hope is that the approach presented here will facilitate exchange between the artificial intelligence fields and neuroscience. It also provides additional motivation for the further study of basic principles and symmetries in physics, as well as more precisely defining evolutionary principles; what we can state about the distribution of energies and matter in the universe can directly impact the way we build intelligent systems.

REFERENCES

Baddeley, B. (2008). Reinforcement learning in continuous time and space: Interference and not ill conditioning is the main problem when using distributed function approximators. *Systems, Man, and Cybernetics, Part B: Cybernetics. IEEE Transactions on*, *38*(4), 950–956.

Cowan, N. (2008). What are the differences between long-term, short-term, and working memory? *Progress in Brain Research*, *169*, 323–338. doi:10.1016/S0079-6123(07)00020-9 PMID:18394484

Fisher, R. A. (1930). *The genetical theory of natural selection: a complete variorum edition*. Oxford University Press. doi:10.5962/bhl.title.27468

Geist, M., & Pietquin, O. (2013). Algorithmic survey of parametric value function approximation. *Neural Networks and Learning Systems. IEEE Transactions on*, *24*(6), 845–867.

Goldsmith, T.C. (2014). *The evolution of aging*. Academic Press.

Heidrich-Meisner, V., & Igel, C. (2008). Similarities and differences between policy gradient methods and evolution strategies. *ESANN*, 149–154.

Hinton, G. E., Dayan, P., Frey, B. J., & Neal, R. M. (1995). The wake-sleep algorithm for unsupervised neural networks. *Science*, *268*(5214), 1158–1161. doi:10.1126/science.7761831 PMID:7761831

Hinton, G. E., Osindero, S., & Teh, Y. (2006). A fast learning algorithm for deep belief nets. *Neural Computation*, *18*(7), 1527–1554. doi:10.1162/neco.2006.18.7.1527 PMID:16764513

Hinton, G. E., & Salakhutdinov, R. R. (2006). Reducing the dimensionality of data with neural networks. *Science*, *313*(5786), 504–507. doi:10.1126/science.1127647 PMID:16873662

Hochreiter, S., Bengio, Y., Frasconi, P., & Schmidhuber, J. (2001). Gradient flow in recurrent nets: the difficulty of learning long-term dependencies. *A field guide to dynamical recurrent neural networks*.

Hochreiter, S., & Schmidhuber, S (1997). Long short term memory. *Neural Computation, 9*(8), 1735–1780.

Hornik, K., Stinchcombe, M., & White, H. (1989). Multilayer feedforward networks are universal approximators. *Neural Networks, 2*(5), 359–366. doi:10.1016/0893-6080(89)90020-8

Kirkpatrick, S., Gelatt, C. D., & Vecchi, M. P. (1983). Optimization by simulated annealing. *Science, 220*(4598), 671–680. doi:10.1126/science.220.4598.671 PMID:17813860

Pan, W., Schmidt, R., Wickens, J. R., & Hyland, B. I. (2005). Dopamine cells respond to predicted events during classical conditioning: Evidence for eligibility traces in the reward-learning network. *The Journal of Neuroscience, 25*(26), 6235–6242. doi:10.1523/JNEUROSCI.1478-05.2005 PMID:15987953

Robins, A. (1995). Catastrophic forgetting, rehearsal and pseudorehearsal. *Connection Science, 7*(2), 123–146. doi:10.1080/09540099550039318

Rosenblatt, F. (1958). The perceptron: A probabilistic model for information storage and organization in the brain. *Psychological Review, 65*(6), 386–408. doi:10.1037/h0042519 PMID:13602029

Sakarya, O., Armstrong, K. A., Adamska, M., Adamski, M., Wang, I., Tidor, B., & Kosik, K. S. et al. (2007). A post-synaptic scaffold at the origin of the animal kingdom. *PLoS ONE, 2*(6), 506. doi:10.1371/journal.pone.0000506 PMID:17551586

Singh, S. P., Jaakkola, T., & Jordan, M.I. (1994) Learning without state-estimation in partially observable markovian decision processes. *ICML*, 284–292.

Sober, E., & Wilson, D. S. (1999). *Unto others: The evolution and psychology of unselfish behavior*. Harvard University Press.

Sutton, R. S. (1988). Learning to predict by the methods of temporal differences. *Machine Learning, 3*(1), 9–44. doi:10.1007/BF00115009

Valen, L. (1973). A new evolutionary law. *Evolutionary Theory, 1*, 1–30.

Wallin, N. L., & Merker, B. (2001). *The origins of music*. MIT Press.

Chapter 5
Research on Human Cognition for Biologically Inspired Developments:
Human-Robot Interaction by Biomimetic AI

Marko Wehle
Technische Universität Berlin, Germany

Alexandra Weidemann
Technische Universität Berlin, Germany

Ivo Wilhelm Boblan
Technische Universität Berlin, Germany

ABSTRACT

Robotic developments are seen as a next level in technology with intelligent machines, which automate tedious tasks and serve our needs without complaints. But nevertheless, they have to be fair and smart enough to be intuitively of use and safe to handle. But how to implement this kind of intelligence, does it need feelings and emotions, should robots perceive the world as we do as a human role model, how far should the implementation of synthetic consciousness lead and actually, what is needed for consciousness in that context? Additionally in Human-Robot-Interaction research, science mainly makes use of the tool phenomenography, which is exclusively subjective, so how to make it qualify for Artificial Intelligence? These are the heading aspects of this chapter for conducting research in the field of social robotics and suggesting a conscious and cognitive model for smart and intuitive interacting robots, guided by biomimetics.

DOI: 10.4018/978-1-5225-1947-8.ch005

INTRODUCTION

Humans adapted in the former eras of technological progress often to the use of technology, in spite developed by humans, one had to learn how to handle technology via many steps and realise them with caution. Because of technology's pioneering complexity it was not always satisfying the users needs and the premise of safe handling, special training and expert knowledge was often required to a large extend. In the new era control and feedback control systems, also called Cybernetics, take over for handling technology with ease and comfort. The focus on the practical usage of technology shifted in an evolutionary process towards human centred interfaces, e.g. from first computers with command line via mouse input towards touch-screens. For instance, considering people, and even kids, on using touch-screens one can recognise an intuitive usage, familiar and intuitive movements for interactions are easier to accomplish. In addition, sophisticated countries and states have to face the challenge of a demographic transition in their societies, which conditions the vision of service robotics to develop machines to be adaptive in their social behaviour. Meaning, reflecting the environment and being available to different users or user groups and their pleomorphism. A carer or patient interacting with the same device will have perhaps miscellaneous requirements and emphasis for it. Therefore, the research on biological cognitive abilities and confident behaviour, as well machine learning with information seeking aspects, should be considered for developing artificial intelligence (AI) systems. Thus far, it is not a new idea and the subject of mind, consciousness and models of thinking and self-awareness are discussed already since the 16th century, but often in rather philosophical or mathematical semantic ways, because the inside perspective is hard to grasp. Notably the beginning in understanding of mind led to impressive sociological impact, for example by the "Age of Enlightenment". Hence resulting in innovative thinking, which still influences current research and this research is a remaining challenge to science and engineering with impressive progress about the last six decades. Despite the different nature of former scientific contributions, all of the work has one major aspect in common: to achieve the goal of an implementation of artificial thought, mind and consciousness – only an interdisciplinary perspective can provide the necessities and insights from biological role models towards intuitive artificial intelligent systems. With the aim to provide input to the development of intuitive user interfaces and artificial perception, leading to artificial cognition, only joint competence from fields like biology (physiology, cognition), physics/mathematics (cognition, information processing and artificial intelligence), engineering (cybernetics, biomimetics, robotics), sociology (cooperation, synergy of human and technology, as well sociological impact and consequences, ethics), design (materials, aesthetics, appearance), philosophy and arts can identify and display what humans are capable of and what is requested for feasible, useful and intuitive interaction with technology. Research is not aiming only to understand the basic mechanisms of mind by modelling it, also for generating computer models for robot artificial intelligence. So, that machines can interact (Human-Robot-Interaction: HRI) according to the gold standard of intuitive interaction, which is the role model of Human-Human-Interaction (HHI). Thus, empowering the robot with consciousness to be willing to learn, for adaptivity and its gain for autonomy and persistence as a service tool, able to tackle unknown tasks, changes of plans and at least mimicking HHI in HRI.

Reciting that "Biomimetics combines biology and technology with the goal of solving technical problems through the abstraction, transfer, and application of knowledge gained in interdisciplinary co-operation from biological models" (Bionik, 2012), the human could be the quasi-role-model for the robot. This is correct insofar as it is assumed that biological structures have been developed in the course of 3.8 billion years of evolution and are optimised under the given conditions in mutual dependency with the environment. Now synthetic consciousness can be a useful concept for implementing intuitive HRI, despite the term consciousness somehow evades precise definition and the debate about it should be left to others, it is a concept for combining different ideas of modelling AI in robotic systems to gel intuitive and adaptive behaviour in AI. The question that rises therefore beforehand is, how can a human being, due to its biological and cognitive abilities, interact intuitive and modest? Given the biological role-model – the human – and its failsafe operation as an outline for biomimetic developments, it is important to study the processes of subjective perception and their application, to exploit the comfort zone of people for optimal interactions.

Consequently, robot developments are driven by the similarity of how we perceive the world through our senses to solve all the different tasks we are able to accomplish – so robots should receive the same information with their sensors and process it via adaptive artificial intelligence. The sensors absorb signals and transmit them to the robots controller. Sensors are available for a variety of measurements of changes in the environment in a variety of forms. The sensors of the robot can perceive even a wider range than the physiological senses of nature, but robots are limited at seeing the natural environment by their processing. Because the "brain" of the robot would be faced with the complex task to reconstruct images from the jumble of lines, shadows, and flitting spots of colour that are recorded by cameras and giving the input a meaning. The tactile sense as another example is a vast challenge for developing robotic hands which can tackle a variety of tasks as human hands do. The options in technology are more comprehensive as in the physiology of a human, but millions of years of evolution and adaption lead to a filtering process, which would remain to the engineers and programmers for the developments. In addition to give robots the necessary autonomy for operating, planning tasks and mission accomplishment, they have to be aware and their artificial intelligence has to lead to an embodiment for the interest of managing resources and given priorities in tasks. Nevertheless, there is also a catalogue of interests in AI developments for intuitive Human-Robot-Interactions aiming for social robotics, in summary, setting up clear and humble standards for common Robot-Human communication and interaction aspects, which can help to guide future developments. The acceptance of social technology and its impact in society – to be secure, fair and in the favour of most, should be improved by following a biomimetic approach and some basic questions:

- How can a robot act accordingly and adapt to a human being to achieve a simple and convenient interaction?
- What are cognitive capabilities, skills and limits of humans, theoretically, to mimic HHI in HRI?
- How can anticipation, support and help for preventing frustration in HRI?
- What are technical options for sensor fusion, artificial intelligence and perception modelling?
- How can privacy and as well data security be assured?

In order to elaborate these questions, HRI is in research a flourishing field, because the challenge is to overcome certain barriers for intuitive interacting AI by setting humble standards and a baseline for training an AI machine, the rest is, in an ideal case, left to adaptivity. The reasoning behind this is, that programming an open world and complex social behaviour may take infinite time and may never converge due to changes, caused by mutual interaction with the environment. Especially the process of decision making in unknown terrain and in adaptive interaction situations is a progressive problem.

BIOLOGICAL ASPECTS: ROLE MODEL FOR ARTIFICIAL INTELLIGENT HRI

New technologies will to be developed in participative manner, eventually: through intensive HRI research by the advantages of video analyses, as well evaluation of user behaviour and comfort via social cues. Innovative non invasive measurements of physiological aspects, like monitoring skin conductance, gaze tracking and heart rate, blushing, speech analyses and analyses of questionnaires can help in order to establish a baseline. There are manifold biomimetic aspects for artificial intelligence to be considered and phenomenography is a powerful tool to classify most aspects, which will become goals in technology developments. As a starting point to layout an implementation, rather physiological aspects provide key aspects, for instance sensor-fusion and neural network dynamics lead for information integration, pre-requisites for error correcting approaches, conscious information processing and weighting for output, in the end this progresses to decision making and interaction. But in the first instance, the window to our world is provided and in the same time limited by the physiology of our senses. In order to perceive and interact with our environment, we need constant feedback. Humans receive information in the order of magnitude of a 10^9 bit/s through our senses; only $10^1 - 10^2$ bit/s are added and processed consciously. The remaining information will be processed subconsciously or filtered to be not used. Conversely, we generate, for example by speaking and motor information about 10^7 bit/s towards the environment. Figure 1 displays the interconnection between perceiving of and interacting with the environment for an embodied intelligence.

Figure 1. Organisation scheme for AI in operational architectonics mimicking biological paragons

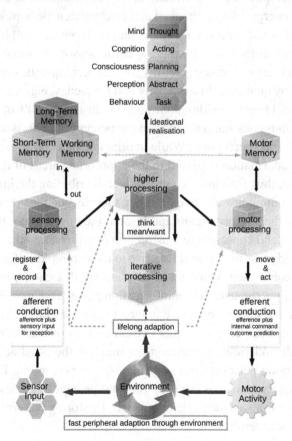

The neurobiological hypothesis behind these schematics in Figure 1 is the model for explanations of higher order mental activities. Assuming that humans perceive their environment and register it via multiple over the organism distributed sensory cells. The sensory processing within the cerebral cortex delivers information to the working memory and as well the long-term memory (LTM). The higher order processing and the motor processing can convert signals in fast movements, while the motor memory is delivering therefore already manifested excitation patterns towards the motor active neurons. Additionally, before higher level processing, contents can be iteratively processed in cycles, for the purpose of temporal extended thought processes. Motor active aiming and thinking corresponds here, with what is considered as will. Intensive, sufficiently long, vehement thinking results in ideational realisation or consciousness. Appropriately induced actions will be recognised as consciously triggered. The actual consciousness will stay without repercussion, in the sense of physical compatibility.

Generally we perceive our world with 5 senses, but for HRI especially the 3 senses for vision, acoustic and tactility are considered to be important, so to be focussed for developments. The stimuli of the environment affect the body in various forms of energy, like mechanical and electromagnetic waves mainly. In the sensory organs, there are specific receptors and each sensory cell has its adequate stimulus which causes for each stimulus a specific sensory impression. Within one sensory modality (vision, acoustic, tactility) the different qualities of a stimulus can be distinguished by quantities like intensity and frequency, e.g. sound or light. For instance, the optical sense provides alone and very fast about 80% of information of the surrounding, thus constitutes the most of our perception. This is accompanied by the acoustic and haptic perception. While in principle perception is indirect, meaning the stimulus information is passed to the appropriate areas of the brain via the thalamus as a hub, thus filtering the amount and distributing the information. The specific regions communicate with each other, they decode the previously encoded information from the sensory organs and discern the information. But of course it is the composition and conscious reconstruction of information that provides us an overall picture and most important gives rise to a meaning for information. Also a human being is confronted with a lot of information that cannot be recorded and processed. Therefore, the selection of information passed is of utter importance and already begins in the sensory organs, e.g. target selection cells in vision, additionally filtering processes occur in further certain regions of the brain. Remarkably, the brain can shift individual perception fractions on the timeline, which in turn assembles perception performances and fills gaps in perception. For continuous, gapless perception the brain has to manipulate our perception of time in the performance. Perception is also a memorising process, by storing patterns of perception, and depends on our attention.

Perception leads to neurobiological consciousness and cognition, the localisation of consciousness is thought to be shown in large cortical areas of the left brain half, additionally support for the consciousness is given by input from the hindbrain, anterior to the cerebellum, seen as the stem of the brain and towards thalamic structures. A signal is retrieved as conscious input by signal propagation time of more then 0.5s and so to say is conversely a processing which is extensively carried out in the human brain, also called cognitive processes (Pfützner, 2014). Nevertheless, a healthy human is always seen as conscious while being not in a coma or deep sleep and therefore consciousness is a central aspect of our life and in interactions as well. Consciousness is fuelled with perceptions and memories giving meanings to our cognitive processing. As several definitions for consciousness arise, they all share the activeness of thought (Koch, 2013):

- Respective to our common sense, consciousness is equal to our inner mental life, consciousness appears if we wake up in the morning and is present till we fall asleep (not dreaming), it is present if we dream and disappears if we are in deep sleep, coma or being under general anaesthetic, death makes it disappear forever.
- On the basis of behaviour is consciousness a checklist of actions or psychology, which rates every organism as conscious that can achieve at least one of them (Glasgow Coma Scale).
- A neuronal definition describes minimal psychological mechanisms, which are necessary for conscious perception, an active and functioning cortico-thalamic (or thalamo-cortical) complex (neocortex and thalamus appended by hippocampus and amygdala, basal ganglia and claustrum).
- In philosophy, the general definition is that consciousness is how it is to be like something. How does an experience feel like if it is perceived by an organism and only this particular organism can know how it feels, if it has this experience (phenomenological consciousness).

In cognitive sciences, consciousness is also linked with information process theories, meaning that information exchange between regions of higher order in the visual cortex and the planning stages of the prefrontal cortex are perceived as conscious. Supported by the model of "global radiation", which states that data in a workspace is available to a number of underlying or subordinate processes (working memory, speech, planning module, etc.) and emanating information makes them conscious. Hereby is also worth noting the consideration that the workspace is rather limited and information is rivalling, so information can get expelled. However, conscious information is therefore accessible as a unity and globally for the whole system. Physiologically this is achieved by weeping pyramidal cells in the prefrontal cortex and from this follows the creation of the global workspace. Information theory is often used in this context as a mathematical formalism, which can quantify the causal interactions of each part of the neuronal system. It describes how much a status of each part influences the status of the other parts and how this influence develops with time. Also, it categorises and characterises therefore the interrelation between all components of the system, which is seen as a unity comprised by its components. Consciousness is not an accumulation of bits, it is not about culmination of data, it is rather the relation between those bits. The architecture of the neuronal system, its inner organisation, is crucial for consciousness. Another refinement of the model is the so called "double aspect theory" retrieved from philosophical monist theories, but still considers a distinction between mental and physical aspects. Which concludes that information of two originated states with inherent and elementary attributes exists divided into extrinsic and intrinsic states, whilst the number of discrete states positively correlates with the repertoire of conscious experiences/apperceptions. Centre point is as well the integration of information, each apperception is especially informative and specially differentiated and conscious states share the attribute of integration of information. Each conscious state is a monad, but it cannot be disassembled into its single components anymore, which could be independently experienced (Tononi, 2004). The quantity of conscious experiences, which is created from any physical system in a certain state, is equal to the amount of integrated information of these states, plus the information generated by its sub-entities. As integrative step, the system has to discriminate between the states within the repertoire of states, acting as a unit – the system cannot split the information into a collection of causal independent parts anymore. For instance, in a split-brain patient live two independent conscious units, each with information independent from the other hemisphere – the integration of information is for the brain as a whole unit unachievable.

Consciousness is assumed to be equal to the content of short-term memory (STM) and long-term memory (LTM) (Thompson, 2010):

- Consciousness plays a key role as necessity for cognition and cogitation.
- Conscious experiences appear as apperception – if attention is paid to the senses.
- Self-consciousness includes the moment/situation.
- Consciousness spreads with perception over time (past) for aspects of experiences and knowledge.
- Memory of knowledge, experience and skills in the long-term memory can be retrieved from the subconscious mind.

Recalling consciousness as a process which is applying numerous feedback loops regarding different parameters (e.g. temperature, space, time and in relation to each other) to create a model of an environment, mainly to attain aims (e.g. procreation, survival, food, etc). Biologically there is a classification of consciousness in its peculiarity (Kaku, 2014):

1. **Stream of Consciousness:**
   a. Mobile organisms with a central nervous system have a so called stage-1-consciousness, because they require a set of parameters to register their changing environment (e.g. reptiles, they possess hundreds or more feed-back loops which regulate their senses of smell, balance, tactility, hearing and vision, blood pressure etc., with individual feed back loops in the specific brain areas as well). The human brain roams sensory information through the brain stem (Truncus encephali), passes the thalamus with pre-processing and filtering, reaching eventually several areas of the cortex for further processing and will be passed to the prefrontal cortex. This processing results in our physical position in space.

2. **Sociological Rooting:**
   a. Organisms which not only possess a model of their location, also a relation to other organisms (social beings with emotions), have an exponential increase of feedback loops with a correlating complexity of behaviour. Therefore, creating a model of a position in a "society", which is depending on the establishment of brain structures in the limbic system, whereas the limbic system consists of the hippocampus (long-term memory), amygdala (centre for emotions) and the thalamus (relay station/hub for sensory input). This system issues new parameters to refine models for the relationship to others. In the human brain, emotions will be created in the limbic system and processed there, in the framework of the stage-2-consciousness the brain is confronted with a constant stream of information from sensory input, but emotion are the fast reaction of the limbic system on a situation, for instance the fastest in emergency situations, which even neglect an authorisation from the prefrontal cortex. The hippocampus is crucial for the contribution and the digestion of memories. Mirror neurons will therefore also play a role for emulation and for empathy and raise the ability not only to mimic complex processes, also to empathise with others.

3. **Simulation of Future/Prediction of Outcome:**
   a. If an organism reaches stage-3-consciousness, the number of feed-back loops is tremendous, so that no supervision is needed for filtering incoming data, in order to simulate future outcomes of situations and actions,

so that predictions can be made in order to make decisions. With this model of the world, simulating future, causalities are connected and form a tree of causalities (or a decision tree). In the human brain, the key aspect of stage-3-consciousness is formed in the dorsolateral prefrontal cortex, which is assumed as the most recently evolved part of the brain, it conveys between the orbitofrontal cortex (decision centre) and nucleus accumbens (centre of desire) and serves as a working space of mind.

Deducing that in order to feel experiences; consciousness and cognition, the presence of information in short-term memory as a workspace and stored information from long-term memory is needed. Because the short-term memory is limited in capacity and memory, the persistence ranges from a few minutes towards 24 hours, new content is extruding older information. The long-term memory is described as a selection of information, which are filtered and consolidated from short-term memory by repetition and learning. Whilst all information, once attained in the long-term memory, are permanent and pattern regular memory trails, so called engrams, which facilitate remembering contents by biochemical connections/processes. Figure 2 summarises how the information storage is classified in the human brain in terms of memory aspects.

The Papez-circuit, see Figure 3, is thought to play a major role for information exchange between short-term memory and long-term memory, since experiments and observations have shown that damage of some of the involved parts can result in memory and language impairment. Repeated passing of the circuit can lead to information transfer from short-term memory to long-term memory, while this is also thought to be a cause of dreaming for long-term memory consolidation.

How the memory consolidation can be depicted in a schematic way is shown in Figure 4. Additionally, the instance of the iconic memory is a mainly visual sensory memory and part of the short-term memory, it is thought to be a domain which quickly records apperceptions from senses, e.g. a face or a scene, and is able to transfer the information more or less directly to the long-term memory.

Some fragments of information still stay in the short-term memory and are available for the working memory. Are these information new or respectively motor skills and they are not practised, only a part is transferred to the long-term memory and most of it will be lost.

Long-term memories are conserved in a formation of groups of neurons, which fire in the same pattern as the original experience was represented. "Complete memories" are divided in components (emotions, sentiments, thoughts, etc.) and in each case distributed to be stored in the competent or relevant areas of the brain. The simultaneous firing or activation of these groups of neurons represents these memories at large (Carter et al., 2010). Attention (t ~ 0.2s) arranges neurons, which

Figure 2. Hypothetical memory organisation scheme in a human brain, different types and aspects of memory (in blue) are connected to their associated brain structures (in green). This organisational scheme depicts the idealisation for interconnections between networks forming network complexes, additionally it shows an idealised hierarchical assumption for the long-term memory (LTM) as a top level memory entity, which is a naturally inspired assumption for supporting a global workspace theory and instantaneous memory access for all processing brain structures. Cross-connections are not drawn but biologically evident. (MTL: medial temporal lobe).

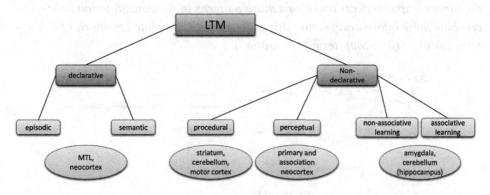

Figure 3. The Papez circuit with information flow in circular manner between the brain entities involved

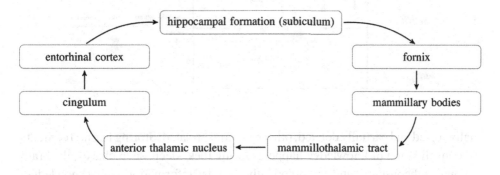

register the event to fire more frequent, this increases the intensity of experiences and in addition increases the probability to memorise this event. The thalamus regulates therefore the brain activity regarding the aim of attention, whereas the frontal lobe filters information to increase the attention span by averting possible diversions. Sentiments or feelings ($t \sim 0.2-0.5$s) are perceived through combination in associative areas. This especially happens within the memory consolidation process in deep sleep (delta-sleep), while information gathered throughout a day are absorbed, assigned and partially presorted, during the sleep phase it will be

Figure 4. Schematic layout for memory consolidation processes, where sensory information, which also includes procedural knowledge (like learned motor activity), is taken up, filtered and moved through parts of the brain stem and kept temporarily for short time with full detail in the working memory (seen as sensory or iconic memory), for processing the information. Further processing and association of a part of these information reaches the short term-memory (STM), for instance by paying attention to it, which gives it importance for the brain after a certain timespan forming spatiotemporal patterns and when these patterns are seen as relevant, the hippocampus repeats and loops those patterns in the consolidation process to combine these information containing patterns with associated memories for long-term storing. (LTP: long-term potentiation).

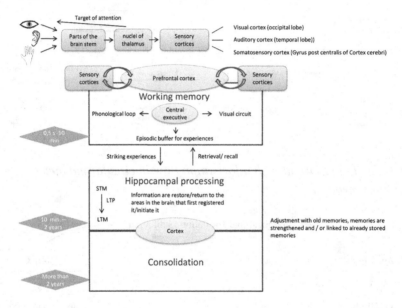

finally sorted and partially deleted, otherwise consolidated. Storing learned contents and consolidation of knowledge happens during these deep sleep phases, the brain combines subconscious and parenthetically recorded information to new knowledge, at the same time learning is conducted, the brain also subconsciously solves problems and combines knowledge to ideas. In the wake phase recorded information will be stored temporarily and is so recalled for long-term memory consolidation. Facts, which are connoted with emotions, remain easier in the memorising process and are known to last longer, because their activation patterns are much stronger. Pre-sorting and filtering of importance of information is thought to be carried out through a process called "tagging", this process can be influenced and emphasised by emotions (Born & Wilhelm, 2012). Important information is tagged through gathering and perception, while standing in a context, these tags support memory consolidation during sleep phases. The paradigm is also seen to be valid for premeditatedly recorded information (motivation aspects), which are correspondingly tagged. Since the brains memory consists out of many different systems, the central hub hippocampus processes information, for instance information is filtered, valued and compared and passed on to the long-term memory in the cerebral cortex. Different kind of memories can be stored in different systems, for instance is in the cerebellum the procedural memory, perceptual memory in the cerebral cortex and factual knowledge is located in the left hemisphere of the brain.

The human brain is subject of massive stimulation in every second being conscious and it can not only rely on filter processes in "bottom-up" approach, this information processing also has to be carried out "top-down", in order to select relevant information from the massive amount of stimuli and experiences. Events can be even predicted from experience, touching, scent, taste, the brain constantly and continuously processes information and makes predictions from this. Consequently, if the predictions become reality, the brain can discard the information processing and dismiss the information, because the implicit knowledge about the event is already present. If the event causes a "better than" signal in perception, learning will be triggered and only this can cause an organism to adapt its behaviour over time for optimisation. Learning is by this means not everything what is perceived, rather what is perceived with positive repercussions (Spitzer, 2002).

Individual perception of self is also a result of a distinction between objectivity and subjectivity. Objective results require review by measurements without human influences like emotions or feelings, whereas subjective results are influenced by involvement and estimates like taste, memories and associations. Objective reality engages with life, how humans perceive reality and with the construal of coalesced personal experience. While subjective perception is different for each individual (senses work different, matching in standing by memories is different etc.), but still comparable, because individuals have comparable apperceptions and use learned expressions from extrinsic input. Consequence is, that an objective reality which is perceived remains objective, apart from the individual independent character, because humans interact with objective reality and explore it as a subjective extract, while this is than subjective reality.

SILICON DEDICATED TO CONSCIOUS HRI

Now, rather than to simulate a brain in order to conduct research on its processing, the aim is to emulate attributes of higher order processing for an implementation in an AI structure. Therefore, not the entirety of physiological and biochemical attributes has to be re-created, but individual aspects of those can be implemented for benefit, e.g. for a reward system for learning or achieving an aim, or even empathy in HRI. Before starting to model any ideas about AI architectures, the division of tasks concerning the aspects of filtering information and processing information on different levels has to be tackled. The term consciousness is here a vehicle to operate with subjective entities to address questions about information processing.

In cognitive sciences and philosophy, the ability to abstract from information and changing the level of representation of information is an alternative way to distinguish between unconscious and conscious states. From hereby inspired modelling attempts are preferably symbolic representations of artificial intelligence and therefore efforts to refer to knowledge representations which are suitable to express human expertise. Whereas in neuronal networks these representations are covered within patterns in the network activity, here the knowledge is depicted in data structures following rules of causality and association, which is emphasising multiple levels of representation in perceptual information processing.

In terms of a better scientific understanding, the questions what is the nature of consciousness and if a machine can be conscious will remain idealistic to be answered and may in present research not even converge to unfeigned machine consciousness. But imitative consciousness and essentially approaching machine autonomy by awareness can be tackled; despite the lacking definition of the terms (Rosenthal, 2009). Therefore, neurobiological findings will serve as a layout and biomimetic inspiration for technological developments. Neurophysiology provides the insights of neural architectures and the operational partitioning thereof, these insights are often obtained by electric field and imaging experiments, which obey an analysis in contrastive manner. The brain activity is monitored as patterns during events in the experiment, a distinction between conscious and unconscious states is possible, for instance given under laboratory conditions making a test person aware and conscious about a briefly seen written word or not, obtaining the outcome that patterns of conscious brain activity are monitored only for subjects perceiving the written input, called the "attentional blink" (Dehaene & Naccache, 2001).

Consciousness may be the product of carefully balanced chaos.

This statement is displayed in the context of a biological study to reveal the importance of "cortical integration" in maintaining consciousness (Tagliazucchi et al., 2015). This means, in the current context of AI modelling, the processing and combination of multiple inputs from different "senses" at once. Whereas the fact if consciousness by itself is subjective or objective is rather philosophical, the division between conscious and unconscious processing can be made, and is even measurable (Tagliazucchi et al., 2015). Most of the experiences for humans are created by the complex intertwining of several sensations like vision, smell, touch and the reminiscence of previous experiences with the same object, for instance of a fruit. For this, the brain is merging all the inputs into a subjective experience at once, whilst consciousness is creating a meaning for the sensory patterns conceived by exploring the spatial patterns in the brain. It has been concluded that, in the brain, a well-balanced and optimised connectivity between neurons creates a large number of possible pathways and within this network of neurons consciousness might appear by exploring the network meticulously. These experimental results agree with the theoretical lead of information process theories, that a physical basis for awareness is achieved in a complex active system with conscious memory, which can be seen only as an integrated and unified system of specialised compartments for processing. In this respect division of labour, distribution of tasks and parallel processing is implemented and complex network dynamics provide an overview for pattern formation, to preserve integrity of procedural information processing as well representation of declarative knowledge. But also like suggested in Information Integration Theory (Tononi, 2004; Koch, 2009), the largest number of pattern forming arrangements is not necessarily implying the maximum connectivity between neurons. Because the signals need to be distinguishable and the cortical circuits also flexible, the arrangement of the patterns is what is thought of as driving consciousness.

Despite facing a line of philosophical implications within consciousness research models and each one driven by different objectives, a categorisation of model systems can be undertaken by some central attributes of concepts. In summary there is a distinction of models with global workspace, or integrated information, or internal model of self, or higher order representation within the abstraction of represented contents, or attention seeking and exploring mechanisms, these fundamental criteria can help to classify different models, as long as the particular criteria is central for the modelling approach. Of course, the listed features can overlap and applying criteria like qualitative-ness, subjectivity, sense and notion of self, unity, etc. and behaviour measurements on humans like the Glasgow-coma-scale, do not necessarily contribute to overcome the problems assigned to machine consciousness (Reggia, 2013). Several attempts to model synthetic consciousness are carried out and they were carefully realised in the context of information processing aspects of functional consciousness, not as any kind of subjective experience. Because the emulated aspects of consciousness within its assumed neuronal correlates are modelled by the help of computational methods, like it is done in many fields, for example enzyme-ligand binding or even activity and reaction transition states and nobody would expect this reaction even to happen in a simulation, as we would not put the substrate into the computer and expect the product of the reaction as physical entity coming out. The expectations are indeed not so high that machines develop phenomenological consciousness to be present, but simulations are evaluated in which sense they can reflect experimental correlates and in particular how they can help to improve artificial intelligent systems in functionality.

Substantial for a consideration in modelling a neurobiological layout are a few ideas, for instance is the biological role model here seen by the raise of global distributed neural activity in the brain via global patterns. Where the brain is seen as organised in a global network of specialised processing units organised in subnetworks like sensory input processing, motion control, learning and mainly working on an unconscious level, but giving raise to consciousness as a unit by the means of a global information processing. This high level of interconnection and cross linking enables spatiotemporal patterns from modules to be spread globally and accessible for any mental state, if conscious (Baars, 2002; Baars et al., 2003; Massimini, 2005). The ideas for those theories are vastly inspirited by the "global workspace theory" of Bernard Baars (Baars, 2002, 2005). Several modelling attempts have been carried out in computational manner, for example with "IDA" (Intelligent Distributed Agent), which is an assembly of Java "codelets", a later version even is able to learn ("LIDA") and given a self-model too (Franklin & Patterson Jr, 2006; Snaider et al., 2011). Rather than a neuronal network, these program fragments are specialised on their tasks and executed in parallel as modules, but communicate via a global workspace. Other models show a stricter structure of neuronal networks, even incorporating biological relevant features like models of spiking neurons and explicit oscillatory behaviour. For instance, the "stoop" task model has been showing to simulate the "attentional blink" (Dehaene et al., 2006; Raffone & Pantani, 2010). Also robotic implementations have been tackled for a global workspace model to control a simulated robot with approximations of the concepts of consciousness, imagination, and emotion (Shanahan, 2006; Shanahan & Baars, 2005). While some of the models are made for simulating consciousness, they all show the significance of a global workspace approach, inspired by and taken from biology, to create instantaneous consciousness based on experience and empirical knowledge. The global workspace processing is collocating the subconscious processing done in specialised parts of the brain where local processes are carried out. To premise up on the global workspace model and additionally getting an idea what the global workspace is, one might assume that consciousness is correlated to the utilisation of information integrated in a system. For instance, realised in the concept of a neurocontroller for simulated robot vision (in order to make it "attracted to positive stimuli"), information integration based predictions about the conscious states of a spiking neural network (Gamez, 2010) were achieved. The evaluation of this trial was carried out by a measure of φ. Information integration theory (IIT), in contrast to others, already enables a quantification or measure for consciousness of a system with its number φ, which can be useful as a concept. Unfortunately, to compute this aspect is prohibitively computational expensive, so that for the experimental implementation only an approximate and more efficient algorithm could be applied (Gamez, 2010; Tononi, 2004, 2008; Tononi & Koch, 2014).

Further progress has been made for a first person perspective with self-awareness, in the frame of an internal self-model. As a necessity of conscious mind, the basis for the first person perspective is a neuronal representation of body properties in the brain, even if somewhat scaled and referred to as cortical homunculus which is a physical representation of the human body and this neural mapping can be even distinguished between a sensory and a motor representation. This aims the so called "body image": a modelled idea of the sensory-motor cortex (Bongard et al., 2006). A self-model in artificial intelligence, or even one step further as self-awareness, is more than helpful for a machine to support its way towards a first person perspective. So the aspect, which is central for a biomimetic approach, is the embodiment and the robots awareness of its extremities, to learn motions and to adopt within executing physical tasks. Moving away from a central controlling system upon which all sensors, actuators and limbs depend, provides the opportunities to outsource computation to the body and the environment in order to help to abstract information for higher integrity and to take advantage of ontologies within AI systems. This so called *morphological computation* is a notion of soft robotics and uses the capabilities of materials to effectively carry out computations and sensorial tasks through their properties of elasticity, viscosity and compliance (e.g. electric sense, magnetic fields, shape change). In physical robots this can be achieved by sensory data processing and morphological computing in the limbs, which can be used to classify the input towards concepts of data and the concepts will be passed on to a higher level of processing in symbolic representations of causality (Chella et al., 2008; Chella & Macaluso, 2009). Additionally, soft robotics actuation and persistent autonomy can pay off together in energy harvest, simplified control, safer HRI and extending the robots endurance (Lane, 2012). While in addition, the use of special distributed neural network architectures helps to minimise computational effort and to ensure maximum efficiency. The virtual representation of a machines physique as approach for embodiment is ingeniously for autonomy and mobility of robots nevertheless and therefore a must have in an artificial intelligent robot.

Other vital functions, for instance plasticity in recovery states of a machine for memory consolidation can be even essential rather than plainly advantageous. A necessity for this idea is the phenomenological abstraction of perception and a hierarchy of operations for spatiotemporal pattern representation, which will also serve the purpose of instantaneous information and memory access. This is quite significant because the implementation of artificial intelligence, and therein contained aspects of perception and memory processing of information should lead to a synthetic knowledge that is useful for the perception of the environment and, accordingly, for integration into it via embodiment. In this respect an implementation does not mean seemingly autonomy by image processing, classification and conversion of observations into coordinates, the aim is to achieve interaction and communication with the user. In addition the technology should be participative to achieve a maximal acceptance, even if a convergence towards 100% is unrealistic. But exploration, guessability and willingness to learn should be integrated into the system, so that the robot adaptively follows the users behaviour. By stages, the exploration and attention of an artificially intelligent system can also be driven intrinsically by conscious awareness to fraction input streams of visual and acoustic data, while filtering of information is mainly thought to happen in subconscious areas of the brain. So, consciousness and attention are not synonym, but definitely linked and highly correlated. A valuable side effect is that, attention mechanisms are useful for exploration and learning in machine behaviour, driven by information gain to base decision making on machine experience, whilst learning can be reinforced due to positive reward, like modelling neurotransmitter distribution etc (Distefano et al., 2015).

In the often studied role model for human cognitive developments, children development, it is observed how an organism can learn to discover its own physical role in the environment, interact with objects and establish social behaviour. These studies show the basic mechanisms of organisation and progressive learning by increasing complexity of processes and interaction, while the connection between brain and physical body is networking with respect to the physical and social environment. Aiming the reproduction of such role models in robotic developments is helping to understand the basic mechanism not only further, also it raises the opportunity to mimic the progressive learning curve for social interaction in application for HRI research (Nguyen & Oudeyer, 2013; Oudeyer, 2013).

The perpetual dialogue between social studies and engineering can build up research to robots which are learning by watching and exploring through curiosity and can make use of their developmental trajectories to self-organise and discover the physical world by their physical attributes, estimate the functionality of an interactive object by visual recognition and as well the ability to communicate. This technology foresight ideally enables AI structures to be primed by limited training for social common sense on an established baseline dataset and afterwards to structure its own learning experiences, creating its own sets of skills, for instance manipulation and handling of objects, by specialised application and depending directly on its environment towards increasing complexity of its sensorimotor capabilities.

Modular Artificial Intelligence on a Pseudo-Biological Layout

In order to link biological input and developments of robotic AI technology in a bottom-up approach, following the course of

Kinematics → Dynamics → Phenomenology (Taketani, 1971)

This course can help to avoid first hand implications by aiming for synthetic consciousness. In the current context this hierarchy of physical principles is motivating to model a structure of causal connected small entities, which will form an AI connected to the physical world in the end. In order to follow the lead of biological role models and applying biomimetic layouts, but not mimicking low-level neurophysiology, the modelling approach is summarised by the guidance of the Operational Architectonics Theory (OA) (Fingelkurts et al., 2012), and it describes the higher level features of machine consciousness in a hierarchical operational framework. In contrast (Fingelkurts et al., 2012), the term operational modules includes in this chapters context, additionally to spatially and temporal organised patterns of brain activity, the organisation of higher level features abstraction of information processing and perception. To start from the bottom, again a fundamental biological fact supports the idea: the brain is divided into functional units (modules) which each developed evolutionary a specialised functional architecture, but it is always to be considered as a "whole" for the preservation of "integrity of procedural information processing". Thus, the revised idea of OA can be extended with modularity in AI aspects by implementing functional units for task distribution and parallel information processing capabilities to aim for autonomy and persistence in robotics. Necessary phenomenological abstraction and a hierarchy of operations are thought to represent spatiotemporal patterns, which ensure the immediate exploration of information for their instantaneous access. This does not only offer new functionality in the processing of sensory data, it is in many ways connected with feedback about changes in the environment and even the impact of actions by the robot itself. In principle, this allows also for predictions of an outcome of an action through internal simulation of action sequences. The basic idea is illustrated in Figure 5 as integrated hierarchy of operational units.

Nevertheless, a neurological or anatomically inspired path still has to be trodden, in order to embed all phenomenological contents in a unified three-dimensional spatial coordinate system. A possible implementation aims consequently for flexibility by using different types of neurons in the network formation, e.g. an opportunity is provided in codelets (Franklin & Patterson Jr, 2006; Snaider et al., 2011), which can form an artificial neural network (ANN) by a bottom-up hierarchy via small recurrent networks organised in microcircuits over local networks of microcircuits (Local Area Networks (LAN)) as intra-cortical layout, which organise functional units and level up towards corticocortical connections as interconnected LAN's forming organisational units.

Specifically, for an implementation, one can consider the small recurrent neuronal circuits inspired by the neocortex, the so called microcircuits, see Figure 6. This

Figure 5. Organisation scheme for implementing an AI following the idea of an operational architectonics hierarchy by mimicking biological paragons

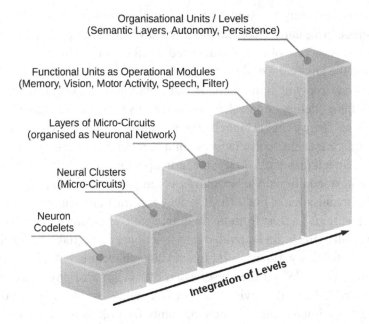

layout is suggested for an implementation, since in the neocortex the encoding for nerve impulses and its circuitry is one of the key aspects for the brains processing capabilities. Basis for the biological computing is the recurrent connectivity and the major aspect of inhibition in the connections, which leads to the formation of dynamical spatial networks already in the smallest scale. Biologically not all the mechanisms in inhibition are well understood, additionally the classification of inhibitory cells follows a non-standard terminology and this is complicating the situation also for modelling these aspects. Because there is no clear distinction between the different types of inhibitory cells and their connective specificity on subregions of their target neurons, most modelling attempts usually use only general inhibitory neurons for their tasks. But what is known can be helpful and used for modelling inhibition in cortical circuits. Of all cerebral cortical neurons about 15% are inhibitory and there exist about a dozen morphological distinct types (Douglas & Martin, 2004). It is inviting to assume the existence of specific spatial grids formed of inhibitory neurons, embedded in the complex lattice of excitatory neurons. But the actual distribution is mainly organised in boutons[1] of inhibitory neurons and is rather dense and local. The lateral axon extension is usually not more than 0.5mm, in comparison the excitatory neurons form less dense local bouton clusters with more exceeding lateral projections (Binzegger et al., 2007; Douglas & Martin, 2009).

Observations for different types of inhibitory neurons forming specific synapses with distinct parts of targeted neurons promote the idea of functional specificity, but unfortunately here biological access and evidence for the mechanisms is rare and simulations show no biophysical effects either, but have shown that inhibition is not acting as a switch, rather that effectiveness of inhibition is graded depending by the firing rate and the arriving excitatory current at the soma of pyramidal cells for example. Taken together, this view supports that some specific inhibitory cells control the output while others rather control the input to neurons (Douglas & Martin, 1990). To summarise the main functions of inhibition by neurons, they moderate excitation of course and they as well inhibit inhibitory cells, in principle to de-allocate circuits from inhibition. A further explanatory thought for the roles of inhibition in cortical circuits, and for instance the generation of non-linearity in linear excitatory projections, is the normalisation by division of the linear firing rate of each neurone by growing input of an aggregation of cortical cells. The dividing process is proposed as a mechanism of "shunting inhibition", which decreases the resistance of target cells proportional to global network activity. Nevertheless, the so called division is indeed rather a subtractive mechanism by changing of firing rates. The excitatory and inhibitory systems together form therefore the algebra of the nervous systems and enable processing by gain control (Douglas & Martin, 2009).

From the observations it seems clear that the reflex effect of concurrent stimulation of excitatory afferent nerve with inhibitory afferent nerve [...] is an algebraic summation of the effects obtainable from the two nerves singly [...]. The net change which results there when the two areas are stimulated concurrently is an algebraic sum of the plus and minus effects producible separately by stimulating singly the two antagonistic nerves. (Sherrington, 1908)

Emphasised is here the spike threshold importance and the fact of neurons being below threshold not contributing to the current circuitry. Inhibitory cells can keep the membrane potential under control and therefore actively shape the dynamical configuration of the circuits.

Considering inhibition as an important flexibility factor in the model, one can assume a dynamic network without explicitly changing the connectivity, but one step further, more flexibility and particularly a high depth of a network can be provided by recurrence, which aims for the so called deep learning. But the biological background is also provided from observations in the cortex. Estimates assume that the human cortex contains $\sim 10^9$ neurons and the architecture is laminar, while the functional diversity of the neurons can be broken down to about 100 different types in two major classes: excitatory and inhibitory neurons.

Figure 6. The definition of a microcircuit model is derived form cortical layers, represented via populations of exciting (triangles and green connections) and inhibiting neurons (circles and red connections). All Layers depicted here receive potential input from other microcircuits and external modules. The input can be seen as thalamocortical projections to corresponding layers, plus output in corti-cothalamic projections as recursion loops.

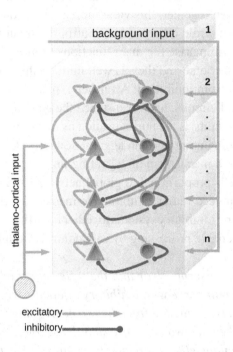

Connections between those neurons are estimated from animal physiological data, mainly visual cortex of cat and monkey, as well from mouse and rat somatic cortex. Riveting circuit properties were revealed with this anatomical data, concerning the physiological connection of neurons in cortex' laminar and inter-laminar structures and as a consequence thereof, providing intriguing insights about fundamental properties of cortical processing. Important as an aspect for modelling is the dominance of local cortical synapses over those afferent to other cortical areas, which can be understood as clustering neurons to local networks and those connect to each other as bundles. The vast majority of cortical excitatory synapses and also most of the inhibitory synapses originate from neurons within local cortical areas. Concluding in afferent projections of cortex from and to thalamus and other individual cortical areas comprise a rather small percentage (5 – 10%) of all excitatory synapses in the target area. In the same way the local neocortical areas are interconnect sparsely as well. Nevertheless, these afferents are sufficient to drive the excitation of the cortex (Douglas & Martin, 2004, 2009). Figure 6 captures these mentioned aspects in forming a microcircuit out of neuron codelets in a model idea. For enabling recurrence already in these small scale model clusters, one can assume that same types of neurons prefer connections with similar types and locally. In fact, superficial layers of the cortex are mainly connected excitatory by pyramidal cells with extensive arborisations about 70% of its own type. Thus, first order recurrent connections between cortical cells are likely between own types, in which a target neuron projects back to its source neuron in a tight positive feedback loop. Meaning, that cortical computation is carried out by positive feedback of relatively small afferent signals, so appearing as selection and re-combination of signals. An additional control parameter is given by spiking, individual neurons operating on small rate modes, because generally lots of input spikes are needed to produce a spike output event of a neuron. Positive feedback potentiation may be adverse for the balance, but the amplification of positive feedback enhanced neuronal activity is stabilised if the sum of excitatory positive current is less than the total of dissipated negative current through membrane leak conductances, action potential and synaptic conductances. This states, that positive feedback is a way to amplify small input signals to stand out of the noise in the cortex. This signal-noise-balancing is crucial for the network circuits, so that magnitudes of causally related signals are always controlled. However, the distinction between noise (spontaneous activity) and small signal input is not clear yet and can't be easily covered in artificial neuronal networks either (Douglas & Martin, 2004). For a better understanding of cortical circuits in research the focus was on models with linear threshold neurons, which comprise continuous positive output. This output is directly proportional to the positive difference between excitation and inhibition those neurons receive, if the difference is not positive or zero they do not contribute to the output. ANNs modelled with these linear threshold neurons (from excitatory and a smaller number of inhibitory types), interestingly, produce non-linear behaviour for the output, despite the amplification of the input is linear. The result of this behaviour is important, because it rises the capability to actively impose interpretations on incomplete or noisy input by restoring basal activity distributions from the connectivity of excitatory pathways in the network. For instance, the weight matrix of synaptic interactions describes the circuitry between various neurons in a network. If a neuron is now inactive, it contributes to the network in a temporary degenerative way and is so decoupled from the circuit, so to say not expressing its interactions. The full weight matrix can be now depicted as a reduced matrix, called the "effective weight matrix", whilst "silent" neurons are zeroed. The changes in network activity due to rise and fall of neurons are directly reflected in the weight matrix, which becomes a timed dynamical entity, the so called "permitted set" of neurons. Specifically, for local recurrent circuitry, the control is illustrating that patterns of thalamic input can be selected and input is mapped therefore also topographically across cortical areas, effectively by recurrent connections being mainly local. These variations in magnitudes of a response due to changes in attention to a cortical stimulus, or simply neuromodulation, can be viewed as changes controlled by external attentional input. The mediation is simplified as an extension of the "permitted set" concept, which expresses the recurrent activity not monosynaptically between local clustering of connected neurons representing members of the cortical maps, single neuronal connections and activity would have to defeat failure as well (versus flexibility). In conclusion, the neuronal cortical computing or processing and organisation is done by local circuits or subcortical nuclei with a proportionate distribution of neuronal interconnections, surely evolutionary driven by limits in connectivity and energy consumption, as well robustness and reliability.

On the assumption that artificial neuronal networks can be seen as spatial memory, e.g. Hopfield networks or bidirectional associative memory networks or self-organising maps, they display stable patterns of activation and can be considered as solution to constraint satisfaction problems approximating complex functions, while reducing the parameter space efficiently. The major restriction or limitation in this case lies in the division between training and reproduction phase, so to state the rigidity of the network organisation after the training period. In order to achieve the best results for flexibility and to implement a type of "intuition" in an ANN, learning and training has to become a process of plasticity. Information seeking and learning through exploration, and driven by curiosity, novelty, surprise and positive reinforcement (plus "emotional tagging"), ensures a steeper learning curve and provides success rating (Baranes et al., 2015). With saturation, the learned and processed information will be owned as an interest and skill. Even thinkable is the possibility to enable mechanisms which can drive persistence in learning (for a selection of skills) which can lead learning to perfection, for instance like in the learning process when acquiring motor skills for playing an instrument. More precisely, robots must be able to act autonomously over longer periods of time, not only within interaction tasks, learning and to achieve goals, also to manage resources and to recover within time constraints. This requires greater flexibility in the way the robot chooses to sense, interact and remember in achieving goals, including an ability to identify when it has not been successful executing an action (Spranger et al., 2010). State of the art autonomous robots seek for human assistance if they recognise that they are in situations beyond their logic or sensing abilities. Typically, this is the case for robots with pre-programmed/planned tasks, this often imposes unwanted operational constraints and is limiting the use cases. Task planning adds sophistication to simple switching of behaviour in traditional autonomous architecture, so to say adaptive planning has to respond to execution conditions and re-plan when failures or opportunities occur. Most recent attempts to process complex decision making resulted in an impressive demonstration of network capabilities, where the ANN was playing "intuitive" in the game "Go" and able to beat a professional human player. The success of "AlphaGo" is based on an efficient combination of machine learning methods to train a pattern recognising deep learning network, plus Monte Carlo tree search to estimate the value of each game state in the production phase (Silver et al., 2016). Here the advantage was played out by the use of several ANN's for the purpose of training each other. This clearly demonstrated the technical feasibility of combined machine learning and reproduction phase, but the shortcomings lie in the tree search and the requirements of dedicated hardware for the sophistication of processing. If this can be improved with efficiency and exploration mechanisms for robots via functional network architectures and synthetic consciousness through a global workspace, a big progress step can be made. For these considered aspects, learning has to provide flexibility and robustness in execution of actions, as well teaching abilities, so that it allows for consideration of spatial and temporal variabilities. Further extensions to reinforcement learning, state-action maps (policies) and noise filtering can be applied as well. Artificial Intelligence offers the prospect of realising cognition desired for persistent autonomy and the control of the robot can be stabilised and tuned to robot motion and contact conditions during task execution, whilst skill learning provides the means to respond to disturbances and errors within behaviour, without a recourse in planning. Intrinsic physical world modelling in AI processes sensor data to maintain a logical description of the environment, while it is used for directing the sensors accordingly to task execution and information seeking. AI status assessment monitors the performance of action execution and uses live sensor data for interpretation of the state of the environment to detect and diagnose failures and success of the task execution. Nevertheless, intelligence is as well devoted to spend time and resources to explore and obtain information, but the intrinsic motivation for such behaviour is not well discovered yet. Developments in machine learning and eye movement behaviour have shown, there is a connection between curiosity and information gain for learning progress mechanism in neuronal aspects (Baranes et al., 2015). A starting point in this research field of curiosity driven learning is the exploration of environment by its observers and actors, while they estimate their own epistemic states and how they specify their own uncertainties in order to find strategies to reduce theses uncertainties. Considerations show that possible motivations, besides gain control in elementary network aspects, can be derived from intrinsic and as well extrinsic factors. For extrinsic motivation the example of monitoring an obstacle while movements, with the goal of successfully moving towards a specific aim. This is a natural behaviour while pursuing a task-related sampling of information seeking, driven by maximising progress towards the goal. More complex is the goal setting of learning complex strategies, like in playing chess, over a long period of time. Intrinsically motivated information seeking in contrast is described as pursuing the goal as a goal in itself, like gathering information on reading for understanding, driven by positive reward mechanisms in the brain itself (Gottlieb et al., 2013). This falls back to the information sampling during solving a task by strategy progression and includes generating informational actions, as well learning. Machine learning approaches tackle this exploration or strategy searching for solving a task as an optimisation problem, where the task is modelled as a cost function and the strategy is simply to minimise this cost function.

Implementations take advantage of reinforced learning, stochastic optimisation, evolutionary algorithms and Bayesian optimisation. Supported is this procedure by division of duties, biological speaking e.g. eye movements and information filtering by target selection via cell activity. The agent monitors the uncertainty or predictability of action consequences and employs this quantity for the deployment of resources, like gaze. Finally, the environment becomes predictable by decreasing the uncertainty of future states through minimising the scattering or maximise the clustering of hidden states in the model. Another factor which can play a role is the trapping in unlearnable situations, because sampling can happen in a very large space. Contrary to the example used above, the real world is full of unsolvable tasks, maybe due to given limitations of the agent or irreducible uncertainty. Attention focus factors can be given by time dependencies for exploration based on heuristics and also task planning has to be constructive – one cannot walk before learning how to stand up. An attractive factor here can be provided by sensory novelty of information and uncertainty, while it is known biologically to enhance neuronal response, so that novelty can act as an intrinsic reward by dopamine release. Contextual novelty, like surprise, can combine sensory novelty with high prediction error and results in high attentional attraction. Additionally, the factor of curiosity is rising with awareness of differences for uncertainty between current state and reference state, as the goal or task. So this deprivation phenomenon is regarded to propel learning oriented tasks, which is driving the agent to fill a gap in knowledge for reward, e.g. minimising uncertainty about the state of the environment (Gottlieb et al., 2013).

These arguments definitely speak again for a modular approach in implementing robotic AI and support as well the approach to combine machine learning with deep learning networks, this leads to a network of networks. Starting with the neuron codelets of specific types forming microcircuits and connecting these microcircuits as LANs can meet this idea, which is depicted in Figure 7. From a network of networks arise further aspects which are advantageous, already simplest network structures coupled via symmetric nearest neighbour connectivity matrices display a rich variety of oscillatory behaviour by applying time delays. These time delays arise from the network topologies where time $t(i-j)$ is a function of distance between nodes $|i-j|$ of network interconnections. While still in small local networks (microcircuits) the time delay for propagation is allowed to be neglected. The implied

Figure 7. Organisation scheme for AI in operational networks. The specific modules are artificial neural networks (ANN) in their own right and organised in Local Area Networks (LAN's), they can posses very different structures from each other, are interchangeable and can posses even specialised modelled neurone types. The overall global organisation is done via the interconnection and cross-linking of these modules, and especially by sharing a common workspace and memory. The connections are timed by distance to achieve spatiotemporal dynamics.

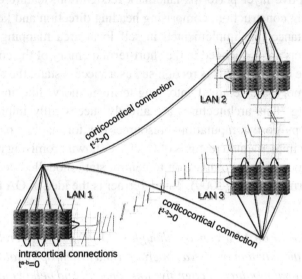

assumption of a homogeneous connection topology in the network, which is symmetric and translational invariant, is fulfilled by the fact that the recursion and inhibition in microcircuits mimics the heterogeneous connectivity observed in the biological structures of the cortex (Jirsa, 2004). The modular structure and the fact that neural information processing is not localised in one small brain area, plus a global workspace idea, the achievement of implementing several network classes and their hierarchy of connections leads beneficially to an interplay between connectivity and spatiotemporal dynamics. This interplay is eventually achieving the connection between time and space via geometry. This network-network connections can be organised in "global weight & connectivity matrices", again these are limited in flexibility, but in "sleep mode" plasticity can be achieved through machine learning from the short-term memory. But more crucial at this point is the reproduction of "parent information processing" by abstraction, for example as semantic events by summation in local "Field Potentials" or potential fields for the production of higher-level patterns of neural activity. Biomimetic modelling, connectivity and functioning of significant parts of the brain to determine an architecture as of a series of nested sensorimotor loops are fundamental for this ideas. The networks have to consist out of tightly coupled layers for behavioural control; respectively the reactive, the adaptive and the contextual layers, and each one increasingly performing more memory dependent mappings from sensory states to action. The reactive layer performs reflex actions, including exploration, collision avoidance, search and homing, using sensory modalities and predefined sensory-motor mappings. The adaptive layer performs landmark recognition, feature extraction and memory segment construction, comprising heading direction and landmark information, for instance like implemented in self local area mapping ideas. These memory segments are sequenced in the short-term memory of the contextual layer until a goal state occurs. If this is recognised as a success state, the contents of the short-term memory are retained into long-term memory, like in hippocampus memory training. This architectures are already successfully implemented with modest general purpose computational resources e.g. for mapless navigation.

Exemplarily implemented features of OA have shown promising results in decision making processes, in comparison to central state modelled decision making algorithms (Burmakin et al., 2009). Taken further is the idea of OA by a stream of

Figure 8. Scheme for an AI stream of "thoughts". This illustration relates neuronal assemblies and their dynamics with an operation and to neurophysiological abstract levels of operational modules, if cognitive phenomenal and behavioural operations coincide in time. Operational modules, as a result of synchronised operations caused by distributed transient neuronal assemblies, can be further synchronised between each other on shifted timescales as well and form so a more abstract and complex operational module, constituting an integrated experience. Consequently, functionally distinct operational modules can co-exist on different timescales.

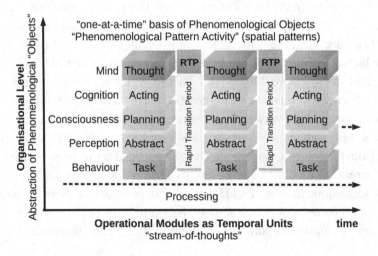

"thoughts" implementation via operational modules in an abstraction level hierarchy, see Figure 8, adapted from (Fingelkurts et al., 2012). Respectively, OA assumes, besides functional layers, the implementation of operational modules as time dependent connected abstractions of network activity. But the rapid transition periods, which basically reset parts of the working memory, are mutually independent between operational modules and coincide with self-organised stability in the network (Fingelkurts et al., 2012). This is to idealise semantic abstraction towards spatio-temporal pattern interpretations, which is an approach for generating sense in phenomenological space and time events. Apart from automatically resulting in a sense of time in artificial intelligence machines, the integration of information as a "stream-of-thoughts" means "spatial operational modules as temporal units", which means a sequential "stream of thought", but at the same time processing has from the global workspace all the information available and therefore unifies into a parallel processing of information, which promises to result in time dependent and predictive "thinking" in robots.

CONCLUSION

In contrast to a central processing unit (CPU), the performance of the human brain is clearly due to it's fundamentally different way of processing and its different state of matter. While computer chips follow mainly the paradigm of precision and fast calculation in sequential manner, the neuronal structures process massively parallel and abstract, while being less precise, but due to abstraction being more efficient and focusing on the real world representation. The global workspace idea gives rise to instantaneous access to contexts of information for processing and unifies the spatial networking and co-existence of time wise shifted functional spatio-temporal patterns. An artificial intelligence model, able to cover the latter aspects, should comprise to be intuitive, self-aware and even synthetically conscious for the means of an interactive robot, taught by biology. Joint aspects from different research disciplines and experiments lead to models of biomimetic approaches for artificial intelligence. To create robots, which should be able to learn, to recognise the environment, and to adjust to the change of situations respectively, research on cognitive abilities and AI is pulling on one string. By the biological role model, biomimetic aspects follow the modular organisation of the human brain as paragon and technologies like machine learning combined with deep learning networks will provide sufficient and efficient platforms to achieve these goals in robots. Therefore, the prediction is clear, that AI is able to mimic intuition and empathy in robots for intuitive user interactions.

REFERENCES

Baars, B. J. (2002, January). The conscious access hypothesis: Origins and recent evidence. *Trends in Cognitive Sciences*, *6*(1), 47–52. doi:10.1016/S1364-6613(00)01819-2 PMID:11849615

Baars, B. J. (2005). Global workspace theory of consciousness: Toward a cognitive neuroscience of human experience. *Progress in Brain Research*, *150*, 45–53. doi:10.1016/S0079-6123(05)50004-9 PMID:16186014

Baars, B. J., Ramsøy, T. Z., & Laureys, S. (2003, December). Brain, conscious experience and the observing self. *Trends in Neurosciences*, *26*(12), 671–675. doi:10.1016/j.tins.2003.09.015 PMID:14624851

Baranes, A., Oudeyer, P. Y., & Gottlieb, J. (2015). Eye movements reveal epistemic curiosity in human observers. *Vision Research*, *117*, 81–90. doi:10.1016/j.visres.2015.10.009 PMID:26518743

Binzegger, T., Douglas, R. J., & Martin, K. A. C. (2007, November). Stereotypical Bouton Clustering of Individual Neurons in Cat Primary Visual Cortex. *The Journal of Neuroscience*, *27*(45), 12242–12254. doi:10.1523/JNEUROSCI.3753-07.2007 PMID:17989290

Bionik, V.-F. (2012). Biomimetics – Conception and strategy – Differences between bio- mimetic and conventional methods/products. *VDI-Handbuch Bionik*, *1*, 1-1. Retrieved from https://www.vdi.de/richtlinie/vdi_6220_blatt_1-bionik_konzeption_und_strategie_abgrenzung_zwischen_bionischen_und_konventionellen/

Bongard, J., Zykov, V., & Lipson, H. (2006, November). Resilient Machines Through Continuous Self- Modeling. *Science*, *314*(5802), 1118–1121. doi:10.1126/science.1133687 PMID:17110570

Born, J., & Wilhelm, I. (2012, March). System consolidation of memory during sleep. *Psychological Research*, *76*(2), 192–203. doi:10.1007/s00426-011-0335-6 PMID:21541757

Burmakin, E., Fingelkurts, A. A., & Fingelkurts, A. A. (2009). Self-organization of dynamic distributed computational systems applying principles of integrative activity of brain neuronal assemblies. *Algorithms*, *2*(1), 247–258. doi:10.3390/a2010247

Carter, R., Aldridge, S., Page, M., Parker, S., Frith, C., & Frith, U. (2010). *Das Gehirn: Anatomie, Sinneswahrnehmung, Gedaechtnis, Bewusstsein, Stoerugen* (K. Hofmann & J. Wissmann, Trans.). Dorling Kindersley.

Chella, A., Frixione, M., & Gaglio, S. (2008, October). A cognitive architecture for robot self-consciousness. *Artificial Intelligence in Medicine, 44*(2), 147–154. doi:10.1016/j.artmed.2008.07.003 PMID:18715770

Chella, A., & Macaluso, I. (2009, January). The perception loop in CiceRobot, a museum guide robot. *Neurocomputing, 72*(4-6), 760–766. doi:10.1016/j.neucom.2008.07.011

Dehaene, S., Changeux, J. P., Naccache, L., Sackur, J., & Sergent, C. (2006). Conscious, preconscious, and subliminal processing: A testable taxonomy. *Trends in Cognitive Sciences, 10*(5), 204–211. doi:10.1016/j.tics.2006.03.007 PMID:16603406

Dehaene, S., & Naccache, L. (2001, April). Towards a cognitive neuroscience of consciousness: Basic evidence and a workspace framework. *Cognition, 79*(1–2), 1–37. doi:10.1016/S0010-0277(00)00123-2 PMID:11164022

Distefano, S., Milano, P., & Mazzara, M. (2015). Neuromodulating Cognitive Architecture.*Conference Paper*.

Douglas, R. J., & Martin, K. A. (2004). Neuronal Circuits of the Neocortex.*Annual Review of Neuroscience, 27*(1), 419–451. doi:10.1146/annurev.neuro.27.070203.144152 PMID:15217339

Douglas, R. J., & Martin, K. A. C. (1990, September). Control of Neuronal Output by Inhibition at the Axon Initial Segment. *Neural Computation, 2*(3), 283–292. doi:10.1162/neco.1990.2.3.283

Douglas, R. J., & Martin, K. A. C. (2009). Inhibition in cortical circuits. *Current Biology, 19*(10), 398–402. doi:10.1016/j.cub.2009.03.003 PMID:19467204

Fingelkurts, A. A., Fingelkurts, A. A., & Neves, C. F. H. (2012). Machine consciousness and artificial thought: An operational architectonics model guided approach. *Brain Research, 1428*, 80–92. doi:10.1016/j.brainres.2010.11.079 PMID:21130079

Franklin, S. & Patterson, F. (2006). The lida architecture: Adding new modes of learning to an intelligent, autonomous, software agent. *pat, 703*, 764–1004.

Gamez, D. (2010). Information integration based predictions about the conscious states of a spiking neural network. *Consciousness and Cognition, 19*(1), 294–310. doi:10.1016/j.concog.2009.11.001 PMID:20018526

Gottlieb, J., Oudeyer, P. Y., Lopes, M., & Baranes, A. (2013). Information-seeking, curiosity, and attention: Computational and neural mechanisms. *Trends in Cognitive Sciences, 17*(11), 585–593. doi:10.1016/j.tics.2013.09.001 PMID:24126129

Jirsa, V. K. (2004). Connectivity and dynamics of neural information processing. *Neuroinformatics*, 2(2), 183–204. doi:10.1385/NI:2:2:183 PMID:15319516

Kaku, M. (2014). *Die Physik des Bewusstseins: Uber die Zukunft des Geistes.* Rowohlt Verlag GmbH.

Koch, C. (2009). *A "Complex" Theory of Consciousness.* Retrieved 2015-10-24, from http://www.scientificamerican.com/article/a-theory-of-consciousness/

Koch, C. (2013). *Bewusstsein.* Berlin: Springer Berlin Heidelberg. doi:10.1007/978-3-642-34771-9

Lane, D. M. (2012). Persistent autonomy artificial intelligence or biomimesis? In Autonomous under-water vehicles (auv), 2012 ieee/oes (pp. 1–8). doi:10.1109/AUV.2012.6380719

Massimini, M. (2005, September). Breakdown of Cortical Effective Connectivity During Sleep. *Science*, 309(5744), 2228–2232. doi:10.1126/science.1117256 PMID:16195466

Nguyen, S. M., & Oudeyer, P.-Y. (2013). Socially guided intrinsic motivation for robot learning of motor skills. *Autonomous Robots*, 36(3), 273–294. doi:10.1007/s10514-013-9339-y

Oudeyer, O. (2013). *Object learning through active exploration.* Hal.Archives-Ouvertes.Fr.

Pfutzner, H. (2014). *Bewusstsein und optimierter Wille.* Berlin: Springer Berlin Heidelberg.

Raffone, A., & Pantani, M. (2010, June). A global workspace model for phenomenal and access consciousness. *Consciousness and Cognition*, 19(2), 580–596. doi:10.1016/j.concog.2010.03.013 PMID:20382038

Reggia, J. A. (2013). The rise of machine consciousness: Studying consciousness with computational models. *Neural Networks*, 44, 112–131. doi:10.1016/j.neunet.2013.03.011 PMID:23597599

Rosenthal, D. (2009). *Concepts and definitions of consciousness. In Encyclopedia of Consciousness.* Amsterdam: Elsevier.

Shanahan, M. (2006). A cognitive architecture that combines internal simulation with a global workspace. *Consciousness and Cognition*, 15(2), 433–449. doi:10.1016/j.concog.2005.11.005 PMID:16384715

Shanahan, M., & Baars, B. (2005, December). Applying global workspace theory to the frame problem. *Cognition, 98*(2), 157–176. doi:10.1016/j.cognition.2004.11.007 PMID:16307957

Sherrington, C. S. (1908). Reciprocal innervation of antagonistic muscles. thirteenth note.-on the antagonism between reflex inhibition and reflex excitation. *Proceedings of the Royal Society of London. Series B, Containing Papers of a Biological Character, 80*(544), 565–578. doi:10.1098/rspb.1908.0053

Silver, D., Huang, A., Maddison, C. J., Guez, A., Sifre, L., van den Driessche, G., & Hassabis, D. (2016, January). Mastering the game of Go with deep neural networks and tree search. *Nature, 529*(7587), 484–489. doi:10.1038/nature16961 PMID:26819042

Snaider, J., McCall, R., & Franklin, S. (2011). The LIDA Framework as a General Tool for AGI. In D. Hutchison et al. (Eds.), *Artificial General Intelligence* (Vol. 6830, pp. 133–142). Berlin: Springer Berlin Heidelberg. doi:10.1007/978-3-642-22887-2_14

Spranger, M., Thiele, C., & Hild, M. (2010). Integrating high-level cognitive systems with sensorimotor control. *Advanced Engineering Informatics, 24*(1), 76–83. doi:10.1016/j.aei.2009.08.008

Tagliazucchi, E., Chialvo, D. R., Siniatchkin, M., Brichant, J.-F., Bonhomme, V., … Laureys, S. (2015, September). *Large-scale signatures of unconsciousness are consistent with a departure from critical dynamics.* arXiv:1509.04304

Taketani, M. (1971). On formation of the Newton Mechanics. *Progress of Theoretical Physics, 50*(Supplement), 53–64. doi:10.1143/PTPS.50.53

Thompson, R. (2010). Das Gehirn: Von der Nervenzelle zur Verhaltenssteuerung (A. Held, Trans.). Spektrum Akademischer Verlag.

Tononi, G. (2004). An information integration theory of consciousness. *BMC Neuroscience, 5*(1), 42. doi:10.1186/1471-2202-5-42 PMID:15522121

Tononi, G. (2008). Consciousness as integrated information: A provisional manifesto. *The Biological Bulletin, 215*(3), 216–242. doi:10.2307/25470707 PMID:19098144

Tononi, G. & Koch, C. (2014). *Consciousness: Here, There but Not Everywhere.* Arxiv, 15.

ENDNOTE

[1] Bouton: Knoblike enlargement at the end of an axon, where it forms a synapse with other neurons.

Chapter 6
The BioDynaMo Project:
Experience Report

Roman Bauer
Newcastle University, UK

Marco Manca
CERN openlab, Switzerland

Lukas Breitwieser
CERN openlab, Switzerland

Manuel Mazzara
Innopolis University, Russia

Alberto Di Meglio
CERN openlab, Switzerland

Fons Rademakers
CERN openlab, Switzerland

Leonard Johard
Innopolis University, Russia

Max Talanov
Kazan Federal University, Russia

Marcus Kaiser
Newcastle University, UK

Alexander Dmitrievich Tchitchigin
Innopolis University, Russia

ABSTRACT

Computer simulations have become a very powerful tool for scientific research. Given the vast complexity that comes with many open scientific questions, a purely analytical or experimental approach is often not viable. For example, biological systems comprise an extremely complex organization and heterogeneous interactions across different spatial and temporal scales. In order to facilitate research on such problems, the BioDynaMo project aims at a general platform for computer simulations for biological research. Since scientific investigations require extensive computer resources, this platform should be executable on hybrid cloud computing systems, allowing for the efficient use of state-of-the-art computing technology.

DOI: 10.4018/978-1-5225-1947-8.ch006

This chapter describes challenges during the early stages of the software development process. In particular, we describe issues regarding the implementation and the highly interdisciplinary as well as international nature of the collaboration. Moreover, we explain the methodologies, the approach, and the lessons learned by the team during these first stages.

INTRODUCTION

Most laboratories in computational biology develop their own custom software to carry out a specific simulation. These applications are monolithic, difficult to extend, and usually do not scale. Consequently, a lot of resources are spent in developing functionality that has already been created elsewhere. The BioDynaMo project has been started to close the gap between very specialized applications and highly scalable systems to give life scientists access to the rapidly growing computational resources.

Our project started as a code modernization initiative based on the simulation software for neuronal development Cx3D (Zubler & Rodney, 2009). Cx3D is a tool that can generate sophisticated structures based on simple rules defined by the computational scientist. Although Cx3D has a very compact code base (15 kLOC), it can perform complex simulations like "cortical lamination". However, the absence of modern software development practices such as automated tests and thus continuous integration, coding standards, and code reviews prohibits a sustainable development process.

The multidisciplinary nature of this initiative requires expertise from different backgrounds. In comparison with other simulation packages, this poses additional challenges in managing diverse collaborators, aligning project members, and defining unique selling propositions.

Aiming at a platform that will be used by a great number of researchers simulating large scale systems, software errors will have a huge impact. Therefore, we give an overview about software verification, different approaches, and why it has great significance for this project.

CODE MODERNIZATION

High performance and high scalability are the prerequisites to address ambitious research questions like modeling epilepsy. Our efforts in code modernization were driven by the goal to remove unnecessary overhead and update the software design to tap the unused potential caused by the paradigm shift to multi- and many-core systems. Prior to 2004, since performance was clock speed driven, buying a processor of the next generation automatically increased application performance without changing a single line of code. Physical limitations forced the CPU vendors to change their strategy to push the edge of the performance envelope (Sutter, 2005). Although this paradigm shift helped to improve theoretical throughput, sequential applications benefit only marginally from new processor generations. This puts additional burden on the application developers who have to refactor existing applications and deal with the increased complexity of parallel programs. As core counts are constantly increasing, the portion of unused computing resources will grow in the future if these changes are not applied. Furthermore, a modern processor offers multiple levels of parallelism that goes beyond the number of cores: it features multiple threads per core, has multiple execution ports able to execute more than one instruction per clock cycle, is pipelined and provides vector instructions also referred to as SIMD (Single Instruction Multiple Data).

Last year's Intel Modern Code Development Challenge was about optimizing sequential C++ brain simulation code provided by the Newcastle University in the UK. The task for participating students was to improve the run-time as much as possible. Using data layout transformations (array of structures AoS to structure of arrays SoA), parallelization with OpenMP, a custom memory allocator and Intel Cilk Plus array notation, the winner was able to improve the run-time by a factor of 320. This reduced the initial execution time on a Intel Xeon Phi Knights Corner Coprocessor with 60 cores from 45 hours down to 8.5 minutes. This clearly shows the economic potential of code modernization efforts. These findings still have to be integrated into the entire code base, since this result has been obtained on a small code sample.

Furthermore, we ported the Java code base to C++. This language is better suited for High Performance Computing as it has fine-grained control over low-level memory allocation and arrangement and provides the right ecosystem for parallelization and optimization. We chose the following iterative porting approach. First, a Java class is selected and replaced by its C++ translation. In the second step, this C++ class is connected to the remaining Java application. Finally, the Java/C++ hybrid is compiled and used to execute a number of tests. If all tests are successfully passed, the developer can proceed with the next iteration by selecting another Java class. This procedure significantly simplifies debugging in case the test simulations are not consistent with the original Java results. The error has to be within the changes since the last iteration. Although this approach is associated with additional development overhead in connecting classes in C++ to Java, it gives the benefit of obtaining a runnable system after each iteration. Without that additional effort, the first time the C++ version would be able to execute these tests, would be at the very end, after all classes have been ported.

MANAGING DIVERSE COLLABORATORS

A complex scientific simulation software is a collaborative effort between possibly quite disjoint areas of expertise. Consequently, a considerable challenge in

BioDynaMo was to arrive at a clear list of specifications that could be understood both by neuroscientists and computer scientists. The challenge does not lie only in communication: we also needed to define an optimal project scope. In such a project, the various impacts of each objective cannot initially be fully understood by all members.

As a single example, the implementation of electrophysiology and certain ephaptic couplings opens the possibility for fast interaction over large distances. The spatial scales, over which we are looking at such interaction entirely decide the feasibility within a cloud computing environment. If the interactions of interest to neuroscientists are highly non-local, it breaks the space partitioning that underlies our parallelization strategy. On the other hand, if the relevant interaction distances of interest are small, this will behave no differently from the other local interactions already allowed by the model. Given that the initial set of specifications simply dictated ephaptic coupling, it took considerable discussion to isolate a balance between the resulting computational cost and the value of performing a range of simulations depending on such interactions.

It follows from the scientific application that the challenge in designing specifications is quite different from the corresponding process in consumer applications. In the actual setting, it might be impossible for the developer to reach a full or even satisfactory understanding of the specific needs of the end user within reasonable time.

Our initial attempt at waterfall approach failed and a proper specification was never produced. The deep reliance on a range of domain experts means that our experience primarily centered around knowledge acquisition, similarly to what has previously been described in scientific software development (Kelly, 2015).

In retrospect, our solution was a gradual transition toward an iterative strategy, somewhat similar to greedy optimization. In our approach, we started with an existing prototype specification. Each group of scientific expertise suggested one or several improvements, which was then passed around for consideration and evaluation. Frequent meetings followed up each feature or parameter in order to evaluate what its impact would be in the product value. All changes better than the current prototype as well as all perspectives taken into consideration were agreed upon.

The advantage of such an iterative approach already in the planning stage is the possibility to exploit collective domain knowledge, even if no single person is able to fully grasp the impacts of each aspect of the specification. In all other regards, our experience in multidisciplinary collaboration was in line with previous findings in the biomedical software field (Kane et al., 2006).

MANAGING DIVERSE COLLABORATORS

A related, but separate, issue was to define the software uniqueness in comparison with other available software tools on the market. To maximize the potential of our software, we decided on two essentially orthogonal development strategies. These led to the possibility to use one of two unique attributes to define our simulator.

The simulator generalization essentially led to the transformation of a simulation dedicated to neuroscience into a cloud-based simulator of biological tissue and, in the extreme, to a local interaction between objects and spaces. This led to considerable discussions between project members as to how define our simulator. Are we designing a neurodevelopment simulator extendable to other areas, or are we actually designing a locality-exploiting physics engine on the cloud with a neurodevelopment library included?

In answering the same question on a more abstract level, are we defined by the technology or by the existing user base? The technological interaction is clearly defined, so what it boils down to is how to maximize the software utility.

In other words, we face a traditional question of marketing. In the project, marketing activities started out with a low priority. The early discussion centered on the feasibility of the technical specifications, while marketing was neither the expertise nor special interest of any partner in the scientific collaboration. In part, this is a consequence of the stakeholder incentives, since network participation in other activities benefits from the academic credit received in a parallel software practice and within the software subfield (Howison & Herbsleb, 2011).

While participants lack incentives for this, the underdevelopment and importance of market research for open-source software in general (Whitmore, Namjoo & Arzrumtsyan, 2015) and scientific software in particular (Howison et al., 2015) are well-known. We believe the initial efficiency of any supportive activities such as these would be improved by clear recognition and task allocation early on in the project. Alternatively, we could search for partners with a wider view of the development process in mind, e.g. involve marketing researchers that could also benefit from academic credit for these activities.

SOFTWARE VERIFICATION FOR LARGE SCIENTIFIC SIMULATIONS

Software plays a pervasive role in the modern world and its development requires particular attention to correctness and resilience. In such a technology-dependent world, software verification is becoming a delicate matter, and is raising interest from both academia and industry. While, however, the effort of software verification was mostly concerned with safety-critical systems in automotive, transportation and aerospace industries (and in general where human lives are at stake) recently attention has moved to more traditional, lower stake and off-the-shelf commercial (or not) software.

Computer simulations are not exempt from risks either, although the concept of catastrophic has not to be seen in terms of direct, immediate life threats. Simulations can run on a single or multiple machines, or in a cloud, and run for a few minutes only or for hours and days. The computational costs, and the financial costs as a consequence can be considerable implying a significant loss in case of errors and need to rerun all or part of the simulation. In particular, small errors can propagate and accumulate into substantial errors later in the simulation. Therefore, techniques that ensure software quality seem necessary.

Need for Verification Tools

There is a common belief in the industry that developing software with a high assurance level is too expensive, therefore not acceptable, especially for non-safety-critical or financially-critical applications. Tools and techniques for the formal development of software have played the key role in demystifying this belief. Complex systems from any domain have a behavior that is difficult to predict and techniques for ensuring correctness can be expensive and laborious; however, fixing bugs after deployment would be even more expensive. Post-deployment faults may even lead to disasters; the literature contains many examples of avoidable faults that had catastrophic consequences. Complex systems also show high level of concurrency, i.e. multiple intertwined threads of executions, often running on different hardware, which need to be synchronized and coordinated, and which must share information, often through different paradigms of communication, and race conditions are often subtle and critical sources of bugs that testers may easily miss. Here is where verification tools are of paramount importance to ensure software quality.

Overview of Major Verification Approaches

Tools for software verification allow the application of theoretical principles in practice, in order to ensure that nothing bad will ever happen (safety). The extra effort required by the use of these tools is certainly not for free and comes with increased development costs (Meyer, 2009). There are several approaches described in the literature, and the list here cannot be exhaustive; for instance abstract interpretation (Cousot & Cousot, 1977) and model checking (Clarke et al., 1999), that seek the automation to formally proving certain conditions of systems. However, these techniques tend to verify simple properties only. On the other end of the spectrum, there are interactive techniques for verification such as theorem provers (Loveland, 1978). These techniques aim at more complex properties, but demand the interaction of users to help the verification. Approaches for finding a good trade-off between these techniques also exist, e.g. auto-active: users are not needed during the verification process (it is automatically performed); they are required instead to provide guidance to the proof using annotations (Khazeev et al., 2016).

Towards a Verification Approach for BioDynaMo

A rigorous development approach is also necessary for the BioDynaMo project if we want to achieve high levels of resilience. Some of the approaches have to be ruled out by the very nature of the project and its own peculiarities, for example the programming languages and the fact that it is born as a code modernization experience; therefore, the software life-cycle followed by the artifact is also nonstandard. In the absence of a total control on the process and the technologies in use, ex-post model checking appears here to be the most viable solution.

DISCUSSION

The field of computational biology covers a wide range of scientific topics, each producing many different scientific models, such as those described by Bauer et al. (2014), Freund (2014) and Izhikevich and Edelman (2008). Hence, a general platform for biological research should be able to meet a number of different requirements. It is crucial that this diversity of the prospective users already be taken into account during the software development process. Incorporating such diversity means that the multidisciplinary project team of BioDynaMo must be able to efficiently interact, and make decisions based on the expertise of each team member.

In addition to these more scientifically-centered aspects, considerable challenges also arise from a computational/technological point of view. Initial steps toward such efficient software implementation have been made in the context of the "Intel Modern Code Developer Challenge" competition. Overall, we believe we have created a collaborative foundation for the efficient continuation of the very ambitious software development project of BioDynaMo.

However, considerable challenges remain to be approached and tackled in the current software development process. The verification and validation of the software is paramount. The recent study of Eklund, Nichols, and Knutsson (2016) demonstrates the extraordinary risks that arise when the correctness and validity of software tools for scientific research are not properly assessed. We have identified this key aspect to require further efforts in parallel to the overall development process.

123

ACKNOWLEDGMENT

M.Mazzara and L.Johard received logistic and financial support by Innopolis University, in particular by the Service Science and Engineering lab (SSE) within the Institute of Technologies and Software Development.

R.Bauer and M.Kaiser were supported by the Human Green Brain Project (www.greenbrainproject.org) through the Engineering and Physical Sciences Research Council (EP/K026992/1). R. Bauer was also supported by the Medical Research Council of the United Kingdom (MR/N015037/1). The funders had no role in study design, data collection and analysis, decision to publish, or preparation of the manuscript.

M.Manca contribution has been supported by SCImPULSE Foundation, a public benefit organization based in The Netherlands.

A.Di Meglio, L.Breitwieser, and M.Manca were supported by CERN, and CERN openlab under the program "Code Modernization", made possible by a cooperation with Intel, to which we extend our thanks.

REFERENCES

Kane, Hohman, Cerami, McCormick, Kuhlmman, & Byrd. (2006). Agile methods in biomedical software development: a multi-site experience report. *BMC Bioinformatics, 7*(1).

Kelly, D. (2015). Scientific Software Development Viewed as Knowledge Acquisition: Towards Understanding the Development of Risk-Averse Scientific Software. *Proceedings of the ACM 2011 conference on Computer supported cooperative work*. ACM.

Howison, J., & Herbsleb, J. D. (2015). Scientific software production: incentives and collaboration. *Proceedings of the ACM 2011 conference on Computer supported cooperative work*. doi:10.1016/j.jss.2015.07.027

Whitmore, A., Choi, N., & Arzrumtsyan, A. (2015). Open source software: The role of marketing in the diffusion of innovation. Information Technology and Control, 38(2).

Howison, J., Deelman, E., McLennan, M. J., da Silva, R. F., & Herbsleb, J. D. (2015). Understanding the scientific software ecosystem and its impact: Current and future measures. *Research Evaluation*.

Zubler, F., & Douglas, R. (2009). A framework for modeling the growth and development of neurons and networks. *Frontiers in Computational Neuroscience, 3.* doi:10.3389/neuro.10.025.2009 PMID:19949465

Sutter, H. (2005). The free lunch is over: A fundamental turn toward concurrency in software. *Dr. Dobbs Journal, 30*(3), 202-210.

Khazeev, M., Rivera, V., & Mazzara, M. (2016). Usability of AutoProof: a case study of static debugging. *The 5th international Conference in Software Engineering for Defense Applications.*

Meyer, B. (2009). *Touch of Class: Learning to Program Well with Objects and Contracts.* Springer Publishing Company, Incorporated. doi:10.1007/978-3-540-92145-5

Cousot, P., & Cousot, R. (1977). Abstract Interpretation: A Unified Lattice Model for Static Analysis of Programs by Construction or Approximation of Fixpoints. *Proceedings of the 4th ACM SIGACT-SIGPLAN Symposium on Principles of Programming Languages.* ACM. doi:10.1145/512950.512973

Clarke, J., Grumberg, O., & Peled, D. A. (1999). Model Checking. MIT Press.

Loveland, D. W. (1978). *Automated Theorem Proving: A Logical Basis (Fundamental Studies in Computer Science).* Elsevier North-Holland.

Bauer, R., Zubler, F., Pfister, S., Hauri, A., Pfeiffer, M., Muir, D. R., & Douglas, R. J. (2014). Developmental self-construction and self-configuration of functional neocortical neuronal networks. *PLoS Computational Biology, 10*(12), e1003994. doi:10.1371/journal.pcbi.1003994 PMID:25474693

Freund. (2014). Numerical simulation of flowing blood cells. *Annual Review of Fluid Mechanics.*

Izhikevich & Edelman. (2008). Large-scale model of mammalian thalamocortical systems.*Proceedings of the national academy of sciences.*

Eklund, Nichols, & Knutsson. (2016). Cluster failure: Why fmri inferences for spatial extent have inflated false-positive rates. *Proceedings of the National Academy of Sciences.*

Chapter 7
Software Development Crisis:
Human–Related Factors' Influence on Enterprise Agility

Sergey Zykov
National Research University Higher School of Economics, Russia

ABSTRACT

Software development is critically dependent on a number of factors. These factors include techno-logical and anthropic-oriented ones. Software production is a multiple party process; it includes customer and developer parties. Due to different expectations and goals of each side, the human factors become mission-critical. Misconceptions in the expectations of each side may lead to misbalanced production; the product that the developers produce may significantly differ from what the customers expect. This misbalanced vision of the software product may result in a software de-livery crisis. To manage this crisis, the authors recommend using software engineering methods. Software engineering is a discipline which emerged from the so-called "software crisis" in the 1960s: it combines technical and anthropic-oriented "soft" skills. To conquer the crisis, this chapter discusses general architecture patterns for software and hardware systems; it provides instances of particular industries, such as oil and gas and nuclear power production.

DOI: 10.4018/978-1-5225-1947-8.ch007

INTRODUCTION

This chapter focuses on human factor-related project lifecycle estimation and optimization, which are based on software engineering methods and tools.

Enterprise systems are usually large-scale and complex; they combine hardware and software. Managing development of large and complex software systems is a key problem in software engineering discipline. In the 1960s, this discipline emerged as a result of the so-called "software crisis". This term originated from the critical development complexity, which happened due to the rapid growth of computational power. The challenge was so dramatic that the NATO had to arrange an invitation-only conference, which brought together leading researchers and practitioners from the US and Europe to search for a remedy. The conference was held in 1967 in Germany; its key participants were such famous computer science professors and Turing Award winners as Alan Perlis from the USA, Edsger Dijkstra from Holland, Friedrich Bauer from Germany, and Peter Naur from Denmark. Many of these researchers were also the NATO Science Committee representatives of their countries. At that time, the computing power of the machines (including the IBM B-5000) became so overwhelming that a number of software development projects were late, over budget or totally unsuccessful. Irrespective of human efforts, the complexity of the hardware and software systems was hard to cope with by means of the old methods and techniques. At the same time, the term "crisis" was coined by F.Bauer; later on E.Dijkstra also used it in his Turing Award lecture.

However, not only did the participants recognize the crisis state of software production management, but they also announced a remedy. This was software engineering. The term was suggested by the same F. Bauer, and the idea was that software developers could apply the engineering methods used in material production to the emerging domain of large-scale software systems in order to make the software projects more measurable, predictable and less uncertain. It appeared that this software engineering approach was feasible, though the methods and practices used had to differ substantially from those used in large-scale and complex material production. The fundamental difference between large-scale software and material production was the distribution of time and cost by the development lifecycle phases. In the case of software, maintenance was the most time and cost consuming activity; it often exceeded 60% of the expenses for the entire project (Schach, 2011). This is why the new software engineering discipline was in need of new methodologies, techniques and tools.

Another distinct feature of software product development was that it involved a number of parties with clearly different goals and expectations. These were end users or customers, developers and their management. Due to multiple sides' participation in the development of the software products, these sides usually lacked common understanding of the resulting product: the customers often used business terms, while the developers preferred technological jargon.

Currently, this same lack of common vision complicates the development processes; it is a possible source of a local production crisis in terms of a certain software project. To deal with this kind of vision incompatibility crisis, software engineers should add to their purely technical abilities a very special kind of skillset also known as "soft" skills. These are teamwork, communications, negotiations, and basics of risk management, to name a few. Thus, in order to address the crisis, which has a human factor-related root cause, a high quality software engineer should possess a carefully selected blend of technical and managerial skills.

BACKGROUND

Issues related to software and hardware system development, often referred to as systems of systems, tend to become even more essential and critical in the enterprise context. One positive solution is creating uniform architectural patterns for such complex systems. To verify the patterns, specific instances are required for particular industries, such as oil and gas and nuclear power production.

The general principles of describing the architecture, i.e. key components and relationships of the software system (for instance, in terms of components and connectors), commonly used in software engineering (Lattanze, 2008), are generally applicable for enterprise system engineering. Therewith, top level architectural design is critical; it determines the key concepts and interfaces for software and hardware subsystems of large-scale and complex objects of system engineering. At this level, an adequate and practically applicable approach is based on high-level patterns, which describe the interfaces for the software and hardware system components. The foundations of this approach have been laid by E. Gamma (Gamma, Helm, Johnson, & Vlissides, 1998); they were applied later to enterprise software systems, where the models for pattern representation and means of pattern management are given sufficient coverage (Fowler, 2002; Freeman, Bates, Sierra, & Robson, 2004; Zykov, 2009).

However, each instance of the patterns is essentially dependent not only upon the problem domain of the enterprise application, but also upon the nature of the end user. That is why in addition to patterns which refer to the technological aspect of system architecture, the authors suggest considering certain anthropic-oriented issues of the mission-critical systems. This is the other component which critically influences large-scale software development, and which may easily result in a software production crisis in the case of undisciplined development or communication problems.

The models of communication between the customer and developer, which may be distorted by different understanding of the product goals and expectations, are often based on Shannon's communication model (Shannon, & Weaver, 1949). One of such applied models is the informing science framework (Cohen, 1999); it includes a sender and a receiver, each of which is an informing system as well (Gill, Bhattacherjee, 2007).

In the case of human factor-dependent software development, the communication model should be more complex; the authors propose certain improvements later in this chapter.

THE HUMAN FACTORS: LESSONS LEARNED FROM CRISIS

The recent global economy crisis taught us a number of lessons. An important part of these lessons is that the so-called "human factor errors", which result from critical uncertainties and anarchic, undisciplined lifecycle management, often dramatically influence the product quality and the project outcomes. The authors' systematic approach to the impact of these human-related factors on large-scale systems development, in terms of architecture, has at least three perspectives. These are: (i) business process perspective, (ii) data flow perspective, and (iii) system interface perspective.

For each of the perspectives, or architectural views (dynamic, static and system views respectively), the authors identify a certain number of business management levels, such as everyday management, short-term planning and strategic decision-making. The combination of these architectural perspectives (or views) and the business management levels results in the enterprise engineering matrix, which determines enterprise agility (Figure 1).

The enterprise agility matrix allows the identification of a number of human factor-related mission critical dependencies for the systemic properties of large-scale systems. These critical dependencies can be derived from certain relationships between the values in the cells of the enterprise agility matrix. Based on this, it is possible to suggest a set of constraints which guard the system development process from potential human-related errors. This set of constraints can also warn the system architect of potential problems, challenges or risks in their architectural decisions. Such risks are represented in terms of contradicting relationships between the business processes, data flows and system interfaces. The matrix allows for human factor-based agility estimation in terms of process management, data integrity and interface quality.

In addition to the enterprise agility matrix, the authors present an adaptive methodology of software system development lifecycle, which allows the mitiga-

Figure 1. The enterprise agility matrix

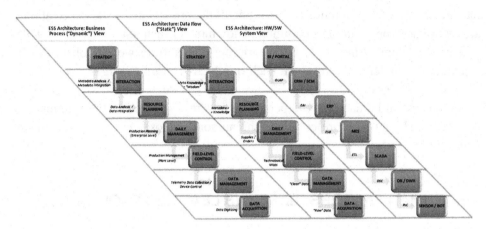

tion of development crises of particular software projects, specifically on mass and large-scale products.

The methodology is based on extracting common enterprise software patterns of module level and applying them to a series of heterogeneous implementations. The approach includes an extension of the standard spiral lifecycle by means of formal models for data representation and management, and by supporting CASE tools based on domain specific languages. The methodology has a number of enterprise-scale implementations as a series of portal-based enterprise systems (Zykov, 2010). The implementation industries include oil and gas resource planning, an airline dispatching and a nuclear power plant construction support.

Let us discuss the reasons for the 1960s crisis in software development in more detail. At that time, the software industry had just started moving towards disci-plined product development; the software production lifecycle was anarchic in many ways, since no systematic approach existed. Therewith, software development did not allow for adequate planning and managing of such global project parameters as project duration and budget. Often, the software products of this period were unique masterpieces; they used a build-and-fix approach as the core "methodology". To overcome the crisis, a systematic approach to product lifecycle management was required. This approach was to include technical and managerial aspects, such as adequate architecture choice and transparent client-to-developer communication, respectively.

During the following decade, the software development process gradually became a science rather than an art; however, due to imperfect technologies it did not become a serial production. Large-scale software research and development centers appeared, such as the Software Engineering Institute of the Carnegie Mellon University (http://

www.sei.cmu.edu). The value of software, as compared to hardware, increased dramatically. Mission-critical software systems appeared on a mass scale, such as military and life-support applications. However, the crisis in software engineering lasted longer and was deeper than that in material manufacturing. The absence of a "silver bullet", or a universal methodology for software development, explicitly indicates that the crisis is not over. Optimization of the software product lifecycle is required to conquer the crisis; this should address technological and managerial aspects. For this optimization, software engineering methods are useful, as they systematically approach both aspects of software development.

The focus of software engineering discipline is "serial" production of large-scale, complex and high quality software systems. The software product quality is measurable by a number of attributes, such as performance in terms of latency and throughput, reliability, security, fault tolerance, ergonomics, strategic reusability and maintainability.

To address the human-related factors, which influence the software production processes, the authors suggest adding a mission-critical crisis quality attribute such as agility. The crisis agility can be interpreted and measured in terms of portability, maintainability, adaptability, or a similar quality attribute. In order to make a software system crisis-agile by design, architects should plan it to be decomposable to smaller subsystems in order to be assembled later using the bottom-up approach; from the lower hierarchy levels up to the higher ones.

Complex and mission-critical enterprise architectures usually focus on multiple perspectives, such as process, data and high-level structure (Lattanze, 2008). Single-perspective architecting limited, for instance, to software product structure only, is clearly insufficient for crisis agility. The present-day crisis manifests itself in high turbulence and fluctuating customer demand. The inefficient enterprises with excessive resource consumption and overheads usually end up with severely downsized profits. In a crisis, the enterprise architecture should extend beyond traditional software engineering boundaries and reach the system engineering scope. Agile methodologies can assist in overcoming the current crisis of enterprise software engineering.

Another possible source of human-related crisis is the heterogeneous nature of enterprise systems which usually embrace versatile architectures, databases and data warehouses, and which include strong and weak structured data. The authors analyze the application of software engineering models, methods and tools for the enterprise domain in order to achieve better software product quality; they discuss a few examples of human factor-based implementations of large-scale software systems.

MODELING COMMUNICATION: INFORMING FRAMEWORK

Communication is often mission-critical for large-scale software development. A miscommunication between the client and the developer may easily result in a distorted common vision, and in a local crisis of software production. To avoid this, an adequate model is required; this model is based on an informing science framework (Cohen, 1999), which uses Shannon's communication model (Shannon, & Weaver, 1949). The initial informing framework usually includes a transmitting side, a receiving side and an environment. In our case, the transmitting side is the client, the receiving side is the developer, and the environment includes the entire set of hardware and software systems installed at the client's and the developer's sites. In this case, the model for the basic informing system is a plain LC oscillating circuit which contains a capacitor and an inductive coupling. In order to oscillate, the circuit usually needs a feedback loop.

However, in the case of software development the actual model should be more complex. One important observation is that both the sending side and the receiving side are informing systems by themselves (Gill, Bhattacherjee, 2007). Another addendum to the initial model is a mechanism for a resonant communication. To provide this, the informing circuit requires a feedback controller. Since the informing circuit should model bidirectional feedback control, it needs positive and negative feedback loops.

Typically, a LC circuit has two clearly distinct kinds of feedback, positive and negative. The positive feedback increases the amplifier gain, and the negative one reduces it. Uncontrolled positive feedback may cause unwanted spontaneous oscillations, which may produce an output with no input, and even destroy the circuit; this is a model of a situation when the resonance does no longer promote communication. Uncontrolled negative feedback decreases the gain so that the output value is critically low for communication to happen.

The authors suggest a number of enhancements to the informing circuit, which provide controlled resonance and model adequate communication between the client and the developer side in the oscillating environment that models crisis uncertainties in product requirements. To provide controlled resonance, the model requires two controlled feedback loops: one for positive, and the other for negative feedback. Each of the communicating sides, the client and the developer, requires a dedicated pair of feedback loops.

To maintain controlled feedback oscillation, the circuit model requires positive and negative feedback compensators which turn on when the informing signal input or output value becomes excessively high or extremely low. These feedback compensators assist in avoiding unwanted, spontaneous resonance, which models communication problems and other crisis-related uncertainties. After the informing circuit has been designed and implemented, it requires thorough testing in order to ensure that the compensators work as designed. Concerning the circuit testing metrics, both positive and negative feedback should remain within their prescribed value ranges. Not only does the positive feedback assist in a resonant communication with a high signal value, it also helps to compensate the informing noise, which is a possible source of a miscommunication and, consequently, a reason for crisis. Possible sources of noise include both the client and the developer sides.

To model crisis, the authors suggest using noise and unwanted resonance. To provide controlled communication, the enhanced oscillating circuit should use a carefully designed and calibrated bidirectional feedback circuit, which keeps the informing signal within the prescribed operating range of lower and upper thresholds.

HUMAN FACTOR-DRIVEN KNOWLEDGE TRANSFER PRACTICES

After faculty training in software engineering at Carnegie Mellon University, the authors discovered a family of key practices that influence the knowledge transfer between the client and the developer. Some of these knowledge transfer practices are also known as "seven principles"; they assist the "informed" communications between the client and the developer (Ambrose, Bridges, DiPietro, Lovett, & Norman, 2010). The authors suggest using these practices as an enhancement to the above informing model.

The authors found that in crisis the critical knowledge transfer practices include prior knowledge, knowledge organization, mastery, feedback, course climate and motivation. The practices are deeply interrelated; however, they influence the knowledge transfer differently.

Concerning prior knowledge, its role in the software engineering education is not straightforward. Usually, the students and the faculty relate what they learn to what they have known previously, and they interpret their new knowledge in terms of their prior knowledge (National Research Council, 2000). The students tend to connect their prior knowledge to their new knowledge; however, this previously acquired knowledge is often incomplete or inappropriate (Alvermann, Smith, & Readence, 1985; Resnick, 1983). The authors found that the gap between the prior knowledge and the new knowledge could be bridged by means of self-reflection and case-based reasoning. Mentoring the students through analogical reasoning helps them to focus on deeper conceptual relationships rather than on surface similarities, which often lead to wrong decisions (Gentner, Loewenstein, & Thompson, 2003). After a number of case studies, the students' knowledgebase improves, and their learning efficiency increases (Schwartz, & Bransford, 1998).

Self-motivation is another critical human-related factor; however, we should separate the subjective value from the personal expectancies (Ames, 1990; Wigfield, & Eccles, 2000). The authors also found that the students with clear learning goals often use more complex strategies for deeper mastering the curricula and coping with communication crises (Barron, & Harackiewicz, 2001).

To progress in software engineering, the students should acquire component-based skills, practically integrate and apply these skills to hands-on realistic tasks, paying attention to the applicability constraints, such as stakeholder priorities.

One more critical human-related factor is mastery; it improves from novice to expert level and includes competence and consciousness (Sprague, & Stuart, 2000). In the case of software engineering, the students seldom manage to apply their skills to a different context; however, creative mentoring is a way to build up their mastery (Cognition and Technology Group at Vanderbilt, 1994; Gick, & Holyoak, 1980).

Feedback is interrelated with practice; they both yield to a professional-level balance of theoretical knowledge and practical skills. In order to make knowledge transfer more resonant, the authors recommend to focus practice and feedback on the same learning objectives (Ambrose, Bridges, DiPietro, Lovett, & Norman, 2010). In crisis, the feedback should be prompt and frequent; therewith, even a short feedback if it follows immediately often results in a successful knowledge transfer (Hattie, & Timperley, 2007). Feedback, if supported by individual mentoring, often helps to promote knowledge transfer (Anderson, Corbett, Koedinger, & Pelletier, 1995).

Self-directed learning, as a critical factor, requires an efficient personal metacognitive cycle; this includes self-evaluation of knowledge and skills, self-management and self-adjustment (Pascarella, & Terenzini, 2005). In crisis, the metacognitive skills are mission-critical; for software engineering curriculum, the authors recommend to use self-reflection, team-based concept mapping and brainstorming techniques (Novak, 1998; Zimmerman, 2001).

Other recommendations for the crisis conditions include clear-cut ground rules and transparent policies; cognitive load reduction to minimum; fast, frequent, specific and goal-directed feedback; open, warm, and friendly knowledge transfer environment (Ambrose, Bridges, DiPietro, Lovett, & Norman, 2010; Gill, & Bhattacherjee, 2007).

THE ARCHITECTURAL OUTLINE FOR AN ENTERPRISE SYSTEM

Most of the complex and mission-critical enterprise-level software systems include a number of subsystems of different levels. Subsystems of the higher levels assist in long-term planning and decision-making; the lower levels support the hardware devices for data acquisition, such as sensors or robots. Therewith, the enterprise architectural design often reaches out of the software engineering scope, and relates to system engineering. Additionally, enterprise software components are usually anthropic-oriented, since they often serve information requests of quite different groups of users, such as top and middle management, analysts and designers, to name a few.

The authors embed the pattern-based approach to enterprise software systems representation (Gamma, Helm, Johnson, & Vlissides, 1998; Fowler, 2002) into the system engineering, and extend the approach in order to embrace both hardware and software systems. Due to the scale of the problem domain, a rigorous proof of the approach adequacy is beyond the scope of this chapter. Instead, the authors' focus is the general pattern, which describes the high-level architecture of the hardware and software system. The authors will illustrate the pattern by a set of practical examples, which demonstrate applicability of their approach. Once the high-level architectural pattern is identified and described, it becomes possible to instantiate it with a family of domain-specific implementations. The domains for the hardware and software systems include oil and gas industry and nuclear power production. These domain-specific examples clearly indicate that their architectural foundations have very much in common. Therewith, the suggested high-level architectural pattern allows for a more unified approach towards building enterprise systems of systems. Pattern-based development provides a more efficient cloning of systems of systems in terms of time and cost.

Table 1 shows a general outline of the high-level pattern, which describes enterprise hardware and software system architecture.

The top Level A of the Table 1 represents the software tools for strategic data analysis by the enterprise top management. It is the "dashboard", which allows monitoring dynamics of the key performance indicators. Level A aggregates the data from the software systems, which plan the enterprise resources, such as human resources, financials and time, to name a few. An enterprise internet portal or a similar tool integrates and visualizes high-level reports; it provides a flexible, reliable and secure online data access by means of a user-friendly interface of a dashboard type.

The Level B informs the end-user employees of the critical updates in their standard business processes, such as document approval, communication with clients and suppliers, and target email messaging. Every two adjacent levels are interrelated. For instance, Level A aggregates and consolidates the data of Level B in order to provide a more strategic view of the key performance indicators. Therewith, Level B represents the software system, which monitors relationships between the key organizational units and individual enterprise employees with their clients

Table 1. Architecture outline of the enterprise hardware and software systems

Portal "Dashboard" of Key Performance Indicators						Level A: Strategy
Supply Chain Management	Channel Management	CRM	Marketing Campaigns	Marketing Plans		Level B: Relations
Accounts Payable	Accounts Receivable	General Ledger	Manufacturing	HR	PLM	Level C: Resource Management
Warehouse		Payroll		Inventory		Level D: Accounting
SCADA			CAD	CAM	CAE	Level E: "Drivers"
Databases / Data warehouses						Level F: Data
Hardware			Units / Parts			Level G: Hardware

and partners. Level B is functionally similar to a customer relations management (CRM) system. The essential anthropic-oriented functional features of Level B are:

- Managing the channels of interaction with the clients: email, fax and IP telephony;
- Planning and managing events: special offers and sales;
- Managing the data on enterprise partners and clients: custom clients, marketing campaigns and preferred communication methods.

The Level C is linked to the adjacent ones; it represents the Enterprise Resource Planning (ERP) software systems. Again, Level B consolidates the data from Level C to get a more strategic representation of the key performance indicators. Level C includes the ERP components, which assist end users in management and planning of such types of resources as fixed assets, payables or supplies, receivables or orders, production and services, human resources, financials and documentation.

The Level D contains more operational, lower level software systems as compared to the previous Levels A, B and C. Therewith, the previous Level C is a more "analytical" one than the Level D, as Level C allows monitoring and forecasting dynamics of the key production indicators, such as revenues, profits, overheads, expenditures and personnel defections. Level D is linked to the two adjacent levels: Level C and Level E; it embraces the software systems for accounting, warehousing and inventory management.

The levels of data aggregation and system utility for strategic analysis and decision-making are growing bottom-up, so that Level A is the top of the strategic ones, and Level G is the bottom of the operational ones.

Level E contains the software systems with the "drivers", which are the interfaces between the software and the hardware components of the enterprise system of systems. Level E contains the systems for the end users, who develop and manage design documentation (CAD/CAM/CAE), and who interact with field-based devices and sensors (supervisory control and data acquisition, SCADA), which perform plant operations, such as assembly-line production. Similarly, Level E communicates with the neighboring Level D and Level F.

The Level F is a dedicated data level; it represents databases and data warehouses. The family of software systems for this level includes DBMS with data mining plug-ins, analytical and online transaction processing (OLAP/OLTP), middleware, and the anthropic-oriented tools for enterprise content management (ECM). Essential features of Level F are large size, high availability, and heterogeneity of the data. The heterogeneity is subdivided into architectural and structural. Architectural heterogeneity examples include non-normalized and legacy systems data. Structural heterogeneity examples include weak-structured audio and video data streams, and scanned documentation.

Below the Level E for "drivers" and the Level F for data, there is one more level, which is the hardware Level G. Level G includes such devices as robots, programming logic controllers and sensors, to name a few. Level G handles analog data; it supplies the data to the Level E, which digitizes, aggregates, stores and uses it for the enterprise applications.

INSTANCE ONE: OIL AND GAS ENTERPRISE

This section instantiates the above architectural pattern by an example of the system of systems used in the production and distribution businesses of an oil and gas enterprise. Therewith, the focus is the anthropic-oriented activities of a vertically integrated enterprise, which does exploration, production, processing, transportation, delivery and distribution of oil and gas products.

In this case, the Level A instance is a software toolkit, which integrates the strategic data views for the enterprise management. This toolkit monitors and displays dynamics of the key performance indicators by means of an enterprise internet portal; this is the "dashboard" of the top managers. The enterprise portal aggregates the data acquired from the lower system levels and visually represents it in terms of high-level reports. It provides data access for the anthropic-oriented activities; typically, these are business-oriented queries of the enterprise top and middle management. The portal predominantly aggregates data from the software enterprise resource planning systems, including general-purpose and domain-specific ones. The general-purpose enterprise resource planning systems manage human resources, financials and time. Reports of the domain-specific enterprise resource planning systems include gas balances, oil and gas upstream and downstream dynamics, visualized seismic exploration data and the like.

The Level B instance supports interaction of the key departments and employees of the oil and gas enterprise with their clients and partners. The basic functional features of this level include informing the employees of the urgent updates of the standard business processes, such as anthropic-oriented activities regarding oil and gas shipment contracts and other documents approval, communication with oil and gas distributors and other kinds of clients, interaction with gas pipeline producers and other kinds of suppliers. The Level B instance also supports such anthropic-oriented activities as target email messaging of the product articles, price lists for the produced and processed items. This level is functionally similar to a CRM system. The Level B instance manages the employee interaction channels, such as gas communication, email, fax, intelligent IP telephony and the others. This level also manages the distribution networks and partners' and clients' data, including regular customers, VIP clients, and a number of other types of data.

The Level C instance is linked to the adjacent Level B and Level D; it represents the software systems for resource planning and management. This level includes the ERP modules and subsystems, which assist in management and planning of the oil and gas products including fixed assets, facility supplies for deposit construction and oil and gas processing, human and financial resources, and document management.

The Level D instance contains the operational software systems, which are involved in such anthropic-oriented activities as payroll and product supply management. Specifically for the oil and gas enterprise, product supply management includes such activities as monitoring oil and gas transportation by pipelines, rail, sea, and the like.

The Level E instance contains the software systems for developers and managers of the design documentation including exploration and seismic data maps, and the systems interacting with the devices and sensors, which perform plant operations, such as exploration wells drilling, and oil and gas production.

The Level F instance for an oil and gas enterprise represents databases and data warehouses. The family of software systems for this level includes database management systems with data mining plug-ins, anthropic-oriented activities for analytical and online transaction processing, and content management tools. For an oil and gas enterprise, reliable and fault-tolerant Oracle DBMS-based solutions are common. Typically, these are integrated with domain-specific enterprise resource planning applications for upstream and downstream management, and with online data visualization tools. Other reasons for Oracle-based implementations are big data size and high availability. In the case of oil and gas enterprise, the data is heterogeneous in both architectural and structural aspects (Zykov, 2015).

The hardware Level G instance is located below the data level. It includes such devices as programming logic controllers and sensors used for exploratory drilling, and oil and gas production. Level G typically operates with the analog data.

INSTANCE TWO: NUCLEAR POWER INDUSTRY

This section illustrates the above architectural pattern by an example of the system of systems used in the production and distribution businesses of a nuclear power enterprise. Therewith, the focus will be on the anthropic-oriented activities of design and construction of reaction units for nuclear power plants (NPP).

In this case, the Level A instance is a software toolkit, which integrates the strategic data views for the enterprise management. This toolkit monitors and displays dynamics of the key performance indicators by means of an enterprise internet portal; this is the "dashboard" of the top managers of a nuclear holding company. The enterprise portal aggregates the data acquired from the lower system levels and visually represents it in terms of high-level reports. It provides data access for the anthropic-oriented activities; typically, these are top and middle management business-oriented queries. The portal predominantly aggregates data from the software enterprise resource planning systems, including general-purpose and domain-specific ones. The general-purpose enterprise resource planning systems manage human resources, financials and time. Reports of the domain-specific enterprise resource planning system include assembly maps, technical documentation, NPP monitoring data down to reaction units and their parts, production and distribution of the electricity, nuclear fuel supplies and waste utilization, and the like.

The Level B instance supports interaction of the key departments and employees of the NPP with their clients and partners. The basic functional features of this level include informing the employees of the urgent updates of standard business processes, such as anthropic-oriented activities regarding NPP design documentation, contracts and other documents approval, communication with reaction unit customers and other kinds of clients, interaction with NPP unit producers and other kinds of suppliers. The Level B instance also supports such anthropic-oriented activities as target email messaging of the product articles, price lists for the produced and processed NPP units. This level is functionally similar to a customer relations management system. The Level B instance manages employee interaction channels, such as NPP-specific communication, email, fax, VoIP telephony and the others. Distribution networks planning and management is less essential in terms of anthropic-oriented approach as compared to the oil and gas enterprise.

The Level C instance of the NPP enterprise hardware and software system is linked to the adjacent Level B and Level D; it represents the software systems for anthropic-oriented ERP and production lifecycle management (PLM).

The Level C instance includes the ERP modules and subsystems, which assist in management and planning of the NPP reaction units and their components production; it manages fixed assets, supplies for the NPP unit construction and electricity processing, human and financial resources, and documents. Design documents are mission-critical for the NPP construction. Possible instances of this level for the NPP industry include Siemens and Catie software products (Zykov, 2015).

The Level D instance of the NPP contains the operational software systems, which are involved in such anthropic-oriented activities as payroll and product supply management. Specifically, for the NPP enterprise, product supply management includes such activities as monitoring reaction unit construction, shipment and assembly, reaction unit assembly maps and technical conditions, and the like.

The Level E instance of the NPP contains the software systems for developers and managers of the design documentation; these include NPP unit assembly maps, technical conditions, and the anthropic-oriented systems interacting with devices and sensors, which perform plant operations such as heat generation and reaction unit temperature/pressure control.

The Level F instance of the NPP enterprise represents databases and data warehouses. The family of software systems for this level includes database management systems with data mining and OLAP, and anthropic-oriented enterprise content management tools. For an NPP enterprise, reliable and fault-tolerant Oracle DBMS-based solutions are common. Typically, these are integrated with domain-specific PLM and ERP applications for the NPP design and production lifecycle management, electricity production and distribution, and with the online 6D modeling and data visualization tools. The 6D models include 3D visualization of the units to be designed, and domain-specific models for the resources required to design and construct NPP, such as time, human and financial resources. The authors discussed the other reasons for Oracle-based implementations choice in the previous section.

The hardware Level G instance is located below the data level. It includes such devices as the NPP programming logic controllers and sensors. This level typically operates with the analog data.

THE ENTERPRISE AGILITY MATRIX REVISITED

A crisis-agile system of systems architecture should be scalable, which means that the system of systems should be easily decomposable to smaller components of multiple levels for possible subsequent reengineering. Typically, the focus of complex and mission-critical enterprise architectures has three perspectives. The first perspective is dynamics, or process-related components and connections. The second perspective is statics, or data-related components and connections. The second perspective is hardware/software-specific arrangement of the components and connections (Lattanze, 2008).

Any architectural design, which does not consider the relationships of the above three perspectives, is clearly insufficient to provide crisis agility. Critical dependencies between the dynamic, static and hardware/software perspectives should be detected, analyzed and monitored during the system lifecycle; it is mission-critical to address these dependencies at the architectural design stage of each individual system development. In crisis, the enterprise architecture should include not only software engineering, but also system engineering; it should rely on the experience of the Agile methodologies.

Further, the authors discuss the ways to achieve such an agility through a specific integration environment augmented with a knowledge base, which contains formal specifications of the business and technology constraints for the process, system and data artifacts. The idea is to detect the critical factors for terms and costs reduction of the software products in order to identify the best applicable combination of the architectural patterns for enterprise software. In crisis, software lifecycle agility, in terms of adjustment for the project size and scope, becomes mission-critical.

Let us revisit the general pattern of the enterprise system architecture, the enterprise agility matrix, which consists of processes, data and systems (Figure 1). (Zykov, Shapkin, Kazantsev, & Roslovtsev, 2015). The first perspective shows the dynamics of architecture; it contains a decomposition of the strategic goals into certain stages of business processes and their smaller parts, such as actions and tasks. The second perspective reflects the decomposed data objects that the business processes use. The third perspective embraces the enterprise hardware and software systems, which operate these data.

DYNAMIC PROCESS MANAGEMENT FOR CRISIS AGILITY

The agility of enterprise architecture incorporates the ideas of flexibility, adaptability and a number of other quality attributes (Lattanze, 2008). Enterprise architecture includes coordination costs required for communication between the process participants, the client and the developer, and the services, which integrate and orchestrate the data, processes and applications. These activities require a resonant communication between the client and the developer in order to support their collaborative business processes (Zykov, 2015).

Long-term monitoring of the enterprise performance reveals the intangible components, which define the enterprise strategies. Two examples of these components are enterprise learning and enterprise knowledgebase. After the 2000s, the knowledge management was often limited to static database structures; these stored such enterprise knowledge assets as blogs, wikis and heterogeneous content. Currently, the enterprise content includes data and metadata, which is knowledge. State-of-the-art semantic-based technologies are capable to enhance the performance, usability and availability of the enterprise content. The enterprise content can be stored and retrieved. Thereafter, the aggregated and integrated content is presented to a number of employee categories, who work on multiple level problems ranging from daily management to strategic decision-making.

The outline of the general high-level pattern (Fowler, 2002; Freeman, Bates, Sierra, & Robson, 2004; Hohpe, & Woolf, 2004) has the form of a matrix for processes, data and systems; it describes the enterprise conceptual framework for system of systems (Figure 1). Data aggregation degree and system utility for strategic analysis and decision-making grow bottom-up across the level hierarchy. Each level communicates directly with the adjacent ones; it is the consumer for the lower level and the provider for the higher level.

The top, "strategic" level, which corresponds to Level A of the Table 1, represents decision-making and business intelligence. In terms of software systems, it integrates strategic data snapshots for the enterprise management and presents the dashboard for monitoring the dynamics of key performance indicators of the enterprise. Level A aggregates and analyses data from the software systems for planning enterprise resources; these systems include general-purpose and domain-specific subsystems. An enterprise internet portal or a similar tool integrates and visualizes high-level reports; it provides flexible, reliable and secure online access for the managers by means of a dashboard-like interface. Typical examples of the domain-specific reports generated by the portal and the business intelligence systems for oil and gas and NPP enterprises are the same as above.

The next, "interactive" level, which corresponds to Level B of the Table 1, represents the data, processes, and software systems for interaction of the key enterprise organizational units and individual employees with their clients and partners. Level B propagates the enterprise knowledge to the Level A, which is using it as a source of meta-knowledge, or wisdom, for strategic analysis and decision-making. A possible provider of the knowledge and data analyzer is a tool for online analytical processing (OLAP). The "interactive" Level B is functionally similar to a customer relations management system. Typical examples of the domain-specific reports generated by the CRM subsystems for oil and gas and NPP enterprises are the same as above.

The next, "resource" level, which corresponds to Level C of the Table 1, represents the enterprise resource planning software systems, and the respective data and processes. Level C consolidates the "accounting" level data from the lower Level D in order to form a more strategic representation of the key performance indicators. A tool for enterprise application integration (EAI) is a possible provider of the metadata, or knowledge, and the metadata integrator. The "resource" Level C is functionally similar to an enterprise resource planning system. Typical examples of the domain-specific reports generated by the ERP subsystems for oil and gas and NPP enterprises are the same as above.

The next, "accounting" level, which corresponds to Level D of the Table 1, contains lower-level software systems as compared to the previous levels. The previous Level C is more analytical; it focuses on forecasting dynamics of key production indexes, such as revenues, profits, overheads, personnel defections and expenditures. The Level D is more operational; it includes software systems for accounting, warehousing, inventory management and the like. Typical examples of the functions and domain-specific reports generated by the daily management subsystems of Level D for oil and gas and NPP enterprises are the same as above.

The next, "supervisory" level, which corresponds to Level E of the Table 1, contains the software systems that incorporate the "drivers", i.e. the interfaces between software and hardware components. This level contains the SCADA systems for the end users who interact with the field-based devices and sensors, which perform plant operations, such as assembly-line production. In oil and gas, Level E deals with exploration and seismic data maps, and the systems that interact with the devices and sensors, which perform plant operations, such as drilling exploration wells, and producing oil and gas. In NPP, Level E deals with unit assembly maps, technical conditions and the anthropic-oriented systems interacting with the devices and sensors, which perform plant operations, such as heat generation, and reaction unit temperature and pressure control.

The next, "data" level, which corresponds to Level F of the Table 1, represents databases and data warehouses. Level F includes DBMS with data mining plug-ins, OLAP and online transaction processing OLTP subsystems, middleware, and enterprise anthropic-oriented content management tools. The key features of Level F are big data size, high availability and data heterogeneity. At Level F, data heterogeneity can be subdivided into architectural and structural heterogeneity. The architectural heterogeneity examples are non-normalized data and legacy systems data. The structural heterogeneity instances are weak-structured audio and video data, and scanned documentation. In NPP, Level F includes the data of custom-integrated domain-specific PLM and ERP applications for design and production management, electricity production and distribution, and the online 6D modeling and data visualization tools; the latter ones include 3D visualization of the units. In NPP, Level F heterogeneity, as usual, is both architectural and structural (Zykov, 2015).

Below the Level F, there is the bottom level, which corresponds to Level G of the Table 1; this is the hardware level. Level G includes hardware devices and human-machine interfaces. Level G operates in terms of analog data. Level F aggregates these analog data, digitizes and processes them for the enterprise applications of the upper levels.

FUTURE RESEARCH DIRECTIONS

The future of the software development is critically dependent on human-related factors. The authors analyzed a number of these factors and presented certain models for them. These factors were prioritized, and the critical relationships between them were identified. One instance of such closely related factors is the tandem of practice and feedback. The suggested communication model, which is based on bidirectional feedback, assists in establishing and maintaining resonant interaction between the client and the developer of the software product. In order to increase crisis agility, the authors recommend improving personal metacognitive cycle and implementing the enterprise agility matrix, which contains certain constraints for critical dependencies between data, processes and system components. However, finding out more about the dependencies between the human-related factors and between the above-mentioned models is a matter of future research.

CONCLUSION

The authors analyzed the nature and root causes of the software development crisis, which started in the 1960s and, as some researchers argue, is still present in the industry. The crisis resulted from a number of factors, which included technological ones and anthropic-oriented ones.

Since software production is a multiple side process, and the sides often have clearly different expectations and goals, efficient managing of these anthropic-oriented factors is mission-critical. Misconceptions in the communication between the software production sides may easily lead to a misbalanced vision and, consequently, the software that the developers produce may significantly differ from what the clients expect. This misbalanced vision may result in a software delivery crisis. To manage the crisis, the authors recommend using software engineering methods, which combine technical and anthropic-oriented "soft" skills. To deal with the crisis, the authors suggest using architecture patterns for hardware and software systems; they also provide instances of oil and gas and nuclear power production industries. This approach can be extended for systems of systems, which include complex and multiple level hardware and software components.

An architectural pattern for such systems of systems was suggested, which included five application levels, a data level and a hardware level. The application levels ranged from the key components for strategic decision-making down to the "driver" components. The data level included the "processed" digital and the "raw" analog data. The architectural pattern was instantiated by the functional outlines for systems of systems in oil and gas and nuclear power industries. The authors identified and discussed the anthropic-oriented fragments of these mission-critical components of the enterprise systems, which, if architected systemically, may essentially help to cope with the software production crisis.

REFERENCES

Alvermann, D.E., Smith, L.C., & Readence, J.E. (1985). Prior knowledge activation and the comprehension of compatible and incompatible text. *Reading Research Quarterly, 20*(4), 420-436.

Ambrose, S. A., Bridges, M. W., DiPietro, M., Lovett, M. C., & Norman, M. K. (2010). *How Learning Works. Seven Research-Based Principles for Smart Teaching*. John Wiley & Sons.

Ames, C. (1990). Motivation: What teachers need to know. *Teachers College Record, 91*, 409–472.

Anderson, J. R., Corbett, A. T., Koedinger, K. R., & Pelletier, R. (1995). Cognitive tutors: Lessons learned. *Journal of the Learning Sciences, 4*(2), 167–207. doi:10.1207/s15327809jls0402_2

Barron, K., & Harackiewicz, J. (2001). Achievement goals and optimal motivation: Testing multiple goal models. *Journal of Personality and Social Psychology, 80*(5), 706–722. doi:10.1037/0022-3514.80.5.706 PMID:11374744

Bass, L., Clements, P., & Kazman, R. (2012). Software Architecture in Practice (3rd ed.). Addison-Wesley.

CMMI Product Team CMMI for Development. (2006). Retrieved November 25, 2015, from http://www.sei.cmu.edu/pub/documents/06.reports/pdf/06tr008.pdf

Cognition and Technology Group at Vanderbilt. (1994). From visual word problems to learning communities: Changing conceptions of cognitive research. In K. McGilly (Ed.), *Classroom lessons: Integrating cognitive theory and classroom practice* (pp. 157–200). Cambridge, MA: MIT Press/Bradford Books.

Cohen, E. B. (1999). Reconceptualizing Information Systems as a Field of the Transdiscipline Informing Science: From Ugly Duckling to Swan. *Journal of Computing and Information Technology*, *7*(3), 213–219. Retrieved from http://elicohen.info/uglyduckling.pdf

Fowler, M. (2002). *Patterns of Enterprise Application Architecture*. Addison-Wesley.

Freeman, E., Bates, B., Sierra, K., & Robson, E. (2004). *Head First Design Patterns*. O'Reilly.

Gamma, E., Helm, R., Johnson, R., & Vlissides, J. (1998). *Design Patterns CD: Elements of Reusable Object-Oriented Software*. Addison-Wesley.

Gentner, D., Loewenstein, J., & Thompson, L. (2003). Learning and transfer: A general role for analogical encoding. *Journal of Educational Psychology*, *95*(2), 393–405. doi:10.1037/0022-0663.95.2.393

Gick, M. L., & Holyoak, K. J. (1980). Analogical problem solving. *Cognitive Psychology*, *12*(3), 306–355. doi:10.1016/0010-0285(80)90013-4

Gill, G., & Bhattacherjee, A. (2007). The Informing Sciences at a crossroads: The role of the Client. *Informing Science Journal*, *10*, 17–39.

Hattie, J., & Timperley, H. (2007). The power of feedback. *Review of Educational Research*, *77*(1), 81–112. doi:10.3102/003465430298487

Hohpe, G., & Woolf, B. (2004). *Enterprise Integration Patterns: Designing, Building, and Deploying Messaging Solutions*. Addison-Wesley.

Innopolis University Presentation. (2014). Retrieved November 25, 2015, from http://innopolis.ru/files/docs/uni/innopolis_university.pdf

Kondratiev, D., Tormasov, A., Stanko, T., Jones, R., & Taran, G. (2013). Innopolis University – a new IT resource for Russia. *Proceedings of the International Conference on Interactive Collaborative Learning (ICL)*. doi:10.1109/ICL.2013.6644718

Kuchins, A. C., Beavin, A., & Bryndza, A. (2008). *Russia's 2020 Strategic Economic Goals and the Role of International Integration*. Washington, DC: Center for Strategic and International Studies.

Lattanze, A. (2008). *Architecting Software Intensive Systems: A Practitioner's Guide*. Auerbach. doi:10.1201/9781420045703

National Research Council. (2000). *How people learn: Brain, mind, experience, and school*. Washington, DC: National Academy Press.

Novak, J. (1998). *Learning, creating, and using knowledge: Concept maps as facilitative tools in schools and corporations*. Mahwah, NJ: Erlbaum.

Pascarella, E., & Terenzini, P. (2005). *How college affects students: A third decade of research*. San Francisco: Jossey-Bass.

Resnick, L.B. (1983). Article. *Mathematics and Science Learning, 220,* 477-478.

Schach, S. R. (2011). *Object-Oriented and Classical Software Engineering* (8th ed.). New York, NY: McGraw-Hill.

Schwartz, D. L., & Bransford, J. D. (1998). A time for telling. *Cognition and Instruction, 16*(4), 475–522. doi:10.1207/s1532690xci1604_4

Shannon, C. E., & Weaver, W. (1949). *The mathematical theory of communication*. Urbana, IL: University of Illinois Press.

Sprague, J., & Stuart, D. (2000). *The speaker's handbook*. Fort Worth, TX: Harcourt College Publishers.

Wigfield, A., & Eccles, J. (2000). Expectancy-value theory of achievement motivation. *Contemporary Educational Psychology, 25*(1), 68–81. doi:10.1006/ceps.1999.1015 PMID:10620382

Zimmerman, B. J. (2001). Theories of self-regulated learning and academic achievement: An overview and analysis. In B. J. Zimmerman & D. H. Schunk (Eds.), *Self-regulated learning and academic achievement* (2nd ed.; pp. 1–3). Hillsdale, NJ: Erlbaum.

Zykov, S. (2009). Designing patterns to support heterogeneous enterprise systems lifecycle. In *Proceedings of the 5th Central and Eastern European Software Engineering Conference in Russia (CEE-SECR)*. doi:10.1109/CEE-SECR.2009.5501184

Zykov, S. (2010). Pattern Development Technology for Heterogeneous Enterprise Software Systems. *Journal of Communication and Computer, 7*(4), 56–61.

Zykov, S. (2015). Enterprise Applications as Anthropic-Oriented Systems: Patterns and Instances. In *Proceedings of the 9th KES Conference on Agent and Multi-Agent Systems: Technologies and Applications*, (pp. 275-283). Springer. doi:10.1007/978-3-319-19728-9_23

Zykov, S. (2015). Human-Related Factors in Knowledge Transfer: A Case Study. In *Proceedings of 9th KES Conference on Agent and Multi-Agent Systems: Technologies and Applications (KES-AMSTA-2015)*, (pp. 263-274). Springer. doi:10.1007/978-3-319-19728-9_22

Zykov, S., Shapkin, P., Kazantsev, N., & Roslovtsev, V. (2015). Agile Enterprise Process and Data Engineering via Type-Theory Methods. In *Proceedings of the 5th International Symposium ISKO-Maghreb*.

KEY TERMS AND DEFINITIONS

Agility: Ability to adapt to uncertainties and changes of environment.

Crisis: Misbalanced production and realization of a surplus value, the root cause of which is separation between the producers and the means of production.

Enterprise Agility Matrix: Matrix, the columns of which correspond to processes, data and systems, and the rows of which contain enterprise system levels. Used to detect and predict local crises of software production.

Human-Related Factor: A factor originating from human nature, which influences requirements elicitation, and, consequently, software development.

Oscillator Circuit: An electric circuit, which consists of capacitor and inductive coupling. Uses feedback for oscillation.

Quality Attribute: A systemic property of a software product, which critically influences its quality.

Software Engineering: A set of tasks, methods, tools and technologies used to design and implement complex, replicable and high-quality software systems, which include a database.

Chapter 8
Predictive Regulation in Affective and Adaptive Behaviour:
An Allostatic–Cybernetics Perspective

Robert Lowe
University of Gothenburg, Sweden & University of Skövde, Sweden

Gordana Dodig-Crnkovic
University of Gothenburg, Sweden

Alexander Almer
University of Gothenburg, Sweden

ABSTRACT

In this chapter, different notions of allostasis (the process of achieving stability through change) as they apply to adaptive behavior are presented. The authors discuss how notions of allostasis can be usefully applied to Cybernetics-based homeostatic systems. Particular emphasis is placed upon affective states – motivational and emotional – and, above all, the notion of 'predictive' regulation, as distinct from forms of 'reactive' regulation, in homeostatic systems. The authors focus here on Ashby's ultrastability concept that entails behavior change for correcting homeostatic errors (deviations from the healthy range of essential, physiological, variables). The

DOI: 10.4018/978-1-5225-1947-8.ch008

authors consider how the ultrastability concept can be broadened to incorporate allostatic mechanisms and how they may enhance adaptive physiological and behavioral activity. Finally, this chapter references different Cybernetics frameworks that incorporate the notion of allostasis. The article then attempts to untangle how the given perspectives fit into the 'allostatic ultrastable systems' framework postulated.

INTRODUCTION

Mid-twentieth century ('first-wave') Cybernetics led by Ashby (1952) has had, at its core, the concept of adaptive behavior serving homeostatic control. Cybernetics has been considered a forerunner for modern Cognitive Science (cf. Pickering 2010, Staddon 2014) and has also provided strong input to the domain of Systems Biology (Froese & Stewart 2010). In this chapter, we will discuss the role of an emerging perspective of (second order) homeostasis known as 'allostasis' and how it may fit within a Cybernetics approach as it concerns adaptive behavior.

Ashby (1952), as a chief exponent of first-wave cybernetics, coined the term *ultrastability*, which refers to the requirement of multiple (at least two) feedback loops – behavioural and internal ('physiological') – in order to achieve equilibrium between an organism and its environment. This perspective has, ever since, been a source of inspiration for many artificial systems, and theoretical, conceptions of adaptive behavior. Such work has focused on the role of essential variable (or homeostatic) errors that signal the need for behavioural change in order to maintain an organism-environment equilibrium. Essential variables are those variables *most critical* to the viable functioning of the (biological or artificial) organism. Approaches that have emphasized the existence of double feedback loops have manifested in studies of activity cycles of both behavioural and internal states (e.g. McFarland & Spier 1997; Di Paolo 2000, 2003; McFarland 2008). According to these approaches, homeostatic processes typically amount to *reactive* (corrective) responses that are purely behavioural including those mediated by a proximal action selection process. In more recent years, Cybernetics- and Artificial Intelligence-based perspectives on homeostasis (and ultrastability) have considered the role of *prediction* in regulating organisms' behavioural and internal needs (Muntean & Wright 2007, Lowe & Ziemke 2011, Seth 2014).

While allostasis has many definitions (for example, McEwen and Wingfield 2003; Berridge 2004; Sterling 2004, 2012; Schulkin 2011), a common thread among them is a focus on the predictive regulatory nature of biological organisms (particularly humans). Homeostasis, by comparison, is more typically conceived as a reactive process. However, a number of commentators have pointed out that this perspective emanates from a misconception of Cannon's (1929) original detailing of homeostasis (cf. Day 2005, Craig 2015). It is therefore, contentious, as to whether given notions of allostasis amount to i) *complementary* versus *substitutive* positions with respect to homeostasis, ii) definitions that provide *illuminating* versus *confusing* emphases on aspects of homeostatic regulation. Furthermore, in relation to ii), it may be illuminating to consider the relation between notions of homeostasis-allostasis and those (mis)applied to Cybernetics approaches. We will consider these aspects in the section "Allostasis and Emotion in Cybernetics".

At the heart of the predictive regulation emphasis of allostasis is the need for biological / artificial organisms to be imbued with adaptive global states that are, nevertheless, not divorced from local homeostatic needs (cf. Damasio 2003). In such a manner, organisms can overcome perceived environmental challenges that place great demands on the organism's physiological and behavioural capabilities. Such demands may be transient (cf. Wingfield 2004) – do not have long-term effects on local homeostatic regulation – or long-lasting (cf. Sterling 2004, 2012) – modulate long-term sensitivities to expected physiological demands preparatory to adaptive behaviour. In either case, these demands require the mechanistic means to differentially suppress (or augment) the signaling influence of local homeostatic variables in the service of the whole organism, its ability to survive, and its ability to reproduce (or achieve a particular designer-specified task). This *predictive regulation* provides the essence of the allostasis-cybernetics perspective on adaptive behavior that we will consider here.

A core consideration for biological or artificial organisms (and organism-environment systems) is how local homeostatic ('motivational') requirements are embedded within higher order (including emotional) allostatic processes. This chapter will attempt to explain how allostasis and ('classical') homeostasis should be considered, and complemented, within an extended (i.e. allostatic) ultrastable framework. It will also look at specific examples and theoretical frameworks that make use of the allostasis term and discuss how they may be related to *allostatic ultrastable systems*.

The remainder of this chapter breaks down as follows. In the next section "Homeostasis and Cognition in Cybernetics", we will discuss the commonly used notion of homeostasis and its popular use in Cybernetics- and robotics-based applications, specifically in relation to the work of Ashby (1952, 1960) and his *ultrastable system*. Following this, in the section "Allostasis and Emotions in Cybernetics", we will look at different perspectives on allostasis, as they relate to homeostasis, from both the viewpoints of biologists and cyberneticians (or roboticists). In the section thereafter "Allostasis in Cognitive-Affective Cybernetics Theory", we will discuss the use of the term allostasis in particular Cybernetics-relevant theories of cognition and emotion. Finally, we will end with a "Conclusion" section summarizing the content of the chapter.

HOMEOSTASIS AND COGNITION IN CYBERNETICS

The notion of homeostasis has gone hand in hand with Cybernetics since the pioneering work of Ashby (1952). Ashby, considered by many as the leader of the Cybernetics movement outside the US (cf. Seth 2014), manifested a control theoretic understanding of homeostasis in terms of the *ultrastability* principle as utilized in his homeostat artefact. The ultrastable system consists of an organism and an environment. The organism's homeostatic regulatory processes are governed by signals from monitors of one or more essential variables (EVs). These EVs are so-called because their values, operating within rigid boundaries, determine whether the organism-environment system is in equilibrium (inside boundaries) or not (outside boundaries). If the system is in equilibrium, the organism is said to be exhibiting adaptive behavior and if not its behavior is not considered adaptive. When the value of the essential variable(s) falls outside its rigid limits, random changes to the organism's parameter set that affect its mode of interaction with its environment are enacted. These random changes are continued until such a point where a new parameter set is found that enables an organism-environment interaction that satisfies the homeostasis of the organism's essential variable(s), i.e. the value of the essential variable(s) falls within the limits.

To summarize, the ultrastable system consists of:

1. An Environment,
2. An Organism that consists of:
    a. **Viability Indicators:** One or more Essential Variables
    b. **Re-Parameterization to Meet Present Demands:** Random changes to the organism's behavioural parameter set
    c. **Sensor-Motor morphology:** Interactive interface mapped to the behavioural parameter set.

The essential variable (EV) term was first coined by Cannon (1929) in relation to biological organisms whose viability depends on the maintenance within tight operational limits of a few such variables. Examples of these EVs include glucose, water, and pH levels in the blood. Ashby's analogy to the perceived Cannonian view on homeostasis has been considered to draw from a control theoretic tradition within Cybernetics (cf. Froese & Stewart 2010). The Ashbyan ultrastable system is schematized in Figure 1 (right) and flanked, for comparison, by a diagram of a standard control theoretic loop. Both perform a form of reactive homeostatic control insofar as outputs from controlled variables consist of errors from set points and are minimized using an *effector* (sub-)system. In the case of the ultrastable system this effector sub-system consists of the sensor-motor mappings (parameters) whose

Figure 1. Left. Control theoretic loop. Summed errors sensed as deviations from the ideal state(s) of the controlled variable(s) induce effectors to promote error-reducing activity. Right. Ashby's ultrastable system. The ultrastable system consists of an external environment (Env), and an organism (Org) that is depicted inside the dashed polygon. The organism's effector consists of S (parameterizations of sensor-motor mappings) and R (physical actuators) and is comprised of the sensorimotor ('nervous') system that, via Env, provides the first-order feedback loop of the organism-environment system. The controlled variable for the ultrastable system is the organism's essential variable (EV) whose activity (thick line) when falling outside fixed limits (thin lines) generates an error signal. This sensed signal then drives the effector by way of changing the sensor-motor mappings at S – a transfer function, which modifies the organism-environment interaction.

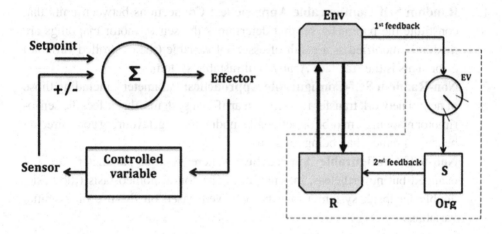

settings determine the mode of organism-environment interaction affecting the controlled variable. The ultrastable system consists of a double feedback system: The first concerning feedback from the organism-environment interaction as it affects essential variable homeostasis; the second concerning the feedback given by the essential (controlled) variable that modulates the organism-environment coupling.

From the perspective of artificial systems, ultrastability offers an approach to understanding adaptive behavior without recourse to strong design. It does this by exploiting random processes that, given enough time, permit (re-) establishment of organism-environment equilibrium. The simplicity of the ultrastable system is a strength thereby, i.e. that behavior is adaptive if the organism-environment system is in equilibrium, and not otherwise. Ultrastable systems, including Ashby's exemplar, the homeostat, though simple, are nevertheless not immune to the effects of design decisions. These design decisions may constrain the adaptivity and flexibility of the organism, particularly in regard to changing or incompletely known (by the designer) environments. For the homeostat, design concerns the setting of the internal homeostatic ranges that provide the source of negative-feedback operation errors. For Ashby-inspired artificial systems, e.g. robotic agents, imbued with ultrastability, the design typically concerns the setting of ranges (set points) within which essential variables (e.g., battery level) are "comfortable" (cf. Di Paolo 2003; Avila-Garcìa & Cañamero 2005; Pitonakova 2013).

Applying the ultrastability notion to adaptive artificial ('cybernetic') systems has often involved compromising on some aspects of the canonical description so as to promote behavior adaptive to the given task. Design decisions for ultrastable-like artificial systems may thus be categorized according to their strictness of adherence to the notion of ultrastability (see Lowe 2013):

1. **Random Self-Configurable Approaches:** Connections between units that constitute the parameter set that determines the sensor-motor mappings are randomly modified as a result of essential variable (the controlled variable) error. This is the standard Ashbyan ultrastable system.

2. **Non-Random Self-Configurable Approaches:** Parameters, including those of neural network transfer functions in artificial systems, that affect the sensorimotor mappings, may be directionally modulated (e.g. favouring goal-directed behavior) rather than being random.

3. **Non-Self-Configurable Approaches:** Where internal parameters are not changed but nevertheless, internal and behavioural homeostasis (the basic, double feedback systems) may be achieved based on the use of essential variables.

Furthermore, as examples of artificial systems-based applications, ultrastable-like robotics approaches may be classified into those that use one essential variable type, e.g., energy or neural (network) activity, and those that use two or more essential variable types, e.g., fuel and temperature levels. The use of multiple essential variables creates an action selection problem where sensor-motor mappings are required to be differentiated in order to adaptively satisfy multiple homeostatic needs.

The above-mentioned relaxations of the original specification of Ashyban ultrastability permit greater scope for applications that maintain the core concept of a double feedback loop. One such important modification concerns the notion of adaptive behavior and whether Ashbyan ultrastable systems are really imbued with this property (cf. Pickering 2010). Of the ultrastable types listed above, we will in turn provide specific examples of each as they have been applied to robot (or simulated robotics), as an example of an artificial organism, scenarios. We will then consider the extent to which they imbue the artificial organisms with adaptive behavior.

In the case of 1., *random self-configurable approaches*, Di Paolo (2003) provides a fitting example (also see Di Paolo 2000, Pitonakova 2013). Di Paolo's simulated phototactic robot, that uses simple light sensors and motors to interact with its environment, is required to maintain its battery level (essential variable) homeostatically while moving in its simple environment. When the robot's essential variable is out of bounds – battery level is too high or too low – random changes in the sensor-motor mapping parameters (that provide transfer functions for light sensor activity onto motor activity) ensues. Only when parameters are found that permit the re-establishment of organism-environment interactive equilibrium (behavioural stability, cf. McFarland & Bösser 1993) is ultrastability achieved.

Whilst the above provides an apparently faithful instantiation of Ashbyan ultrastability, it also highlights limitations with the application of this notion to artificial and biological organisms. The robot in Di Paolo's (2003) example arrives at an equilibrium state only through a drawn out trial-and-error interactive process. It has been pointed out that such trial-and-error behaviours, even those that chance upon an equi- librium (re-)establishing behaviour, cannot be considered adaptive as small changes in the environment may render the particular behaviour insufficient to maintain equilibrium (cf. Pickering 2010). The problem with trial-and-error processes is not just their inefficiency and non-adaptivity in the context of a mobile biological or artificial organism (cf. Manicka & Di Paolo 2009, though also see Pitonakova 2013). Rather, in a complex, dynamic and hazardous environment, purely trial-and-error driven behaviour is *non-viable* – the organism risks encountering damage or even destruction if it repeatedly tries out the "wrong" behaviour. Usefully incorporating the ultrastable system concept in designing for complex organism-environment systems, thus, requires compromising on the purity of the Ashbyan vision whilst acknowledging the need to minimize the extent of design of the equilibrium (re-)establishing process.

In the case of 2., *non-random self-configurable approaches*, Lowe et al. (2010) provide a representative case study. Here, the robot's task was to survive, as long as possible, via selecting, over a number of trials between two resources that replenished different essential variables. In this case, an evolutionary robotics approach was used in order to 'ground' artificial metabolic processes in an artificial neural network controller for a simulated (e-puck) robot.

The robot-environment could be compared to an ultrastable system:

1. **Essential Variables:** Values were given by the level of "energy" and "water" within a simulated microbial fuel cell (cf. Melhuish et al. 2006).
2. **Fixed Homeostatic Limits:** Thresholds, set by the genetic algorithm (GA), determined essential variable monitor nodes' homeostatic limits/regime.

3.   **Parameter Modulation:** Chemical node activation of the network adapted the gain of nodes' electrical activity output, a function that directly altered the robot's sensorimotor activity interaction with its environment. This concerns the S component of the organism (see Figure 1).

   This approach was *non-random* since the GA determined the *direction* of the modulation of the output function slope. However, the directedness (affecting action selection mediation) of the ultrastable behaviour was not explicitly designed. It emerged from the evolutionarily designing for satisficing (via a fitness function of 'time of survival'). Nevertheless, the directed activity of the modulator nodes allowed for motors to be activated in particular directions as a response to sensory (camera) inputs. This promoted adaptive solutions to an action selection problem based on a particular type of ultrastable system by eliminating the random nature of re-parameterizations (at S, Figure 1 right).

   Finally, in relation to 3., *non self-configurable approaches*, much work has been done using the ultrastability-inspired approach of satisfying two feedback loops (for internal and behavioural homeostasis) in order to provide stable dynamics. McFarland and Spier (1997), Avila-Garcìa and Cañamero (2005), and also Kiryazov et al. (2013) have utilized variables that are provisioned with homeostatic limits, where activity outside these limits comprises "physiological drive" errors. They are essential variables. Adaptive behavior consists of achieving stable activity cycles where multiple essential variables are homeostatically maintained according to error reducing behaviours (e.g. remaining stationary at a recharger zone when battery level is low). In these works, there is a basic sense in which essential variables non-randomly influence motivated decision-making. The example of Lowe et al. (2010) above, in a sense, provides an evolutionarily grounded version of such *non self-configurable approaches* where parameter values that affect organism-environment interactions are modulated as a result of essential variable 'errors'. In the case of the *non self-configurable approaches*, however, the networks do not structurally reconfigure, i.e. the sensor-motor transfer functions do not change. In this sense, sensorimotor re-paramerization to meet current demand, is not included. Instead, the strength of errors from specific variables modulates the tendency to choose one action over another.

   The *non-random self-configurable approaches* and *non self-configurable approaches* arguably require more design decisions than the pure Ashbyan ultrastability interpretation (category 1). They can, nevertheless, be considered ultrastable-like. Importantly, these approaches that use non-random (sensorimotor) re-parameterizations to meet current demand, are equipped to deal with action selection problems. Firstly, they arrive at the equilibrium states more quickly with a lower likelihood of incurring highly maladaptive re-parameterizations (e.g. that happen to cause collisions). Furthermore, these design decisions partially deal with two major problems of action selection – *opportunism* and *persistence* – where organisms have multiple essential variables (EVs) and thus, needs to be satisfied. Simply, opportunism requires organisms to be flexible in their action selection when an opportunity to satisfy a non-dominant need arises. For example, the organism may most urgently need to replenish a battery level deficit, but senses a proximal heat source that can reduce a thermal deficit (of being too cold). Under some circumstances, it is adaptive to be opportunistic in this way – though not always., e.g. it may lead to the phenomenon of 'dithering', moving back and forth between motivated actions to the point of exhaustion. Persistence, alternatively, entails the sustained performing of an action that best satisfies the most urgent need. This may occur even in the presence of an opportunity to act upon an easier target concerning a less urgent need.

Notwithstanding the provided solutions to the limitations in adaptive-behaviour of the Ashbyan ultrastability notion, critical limitations still pertain. Fundamentally, the adaptive capability of organisms within ultrastable systems is compromised by the fact they are heteronomous (influenced by forces outside the organism) as opposed to being autonomous (Franchi 2013). Organisms, in order to have autonomous, adaptive, control, are required to have regulative capabilities from within, e.g. of a predictive nature. Such predictive regulatory control allows for organisms to *persist*, and yet be flexibly *opportunistic*, in their goal-directed behaviour. They also allow organisms to meet demands in changing environmental contexts. This type of control allows 'ultrastable' systems to address three important shortcomings noted by Ashby (1954) of the ultrastability concept that are of biological relevance (cf. Vernon 2013), namely: i) inability to adapt gradually[1], i.e. re-parameterization is not directed in relation to meeting (predicted) demands; ii) inability to conserve previous contextual adaptations, i.e. there is no (predictive) prior knowledge; iii) the trial and error re-parameterizations require an arbitrary time length to 'hit upon' the adaptive solution. Above all ii) cannot be met by the ultrastable-like systems mentioned in this section. In the following section, we will further discuss the importance of *non-reactive* means of provisioning systems with opportunistic and persistence capabilities in relation to adaptive and predictive behavior that also helps deal with some of the shortcomings of the reactive ultrastable system.

ALLOSTASIS AND EMOTION IN CYBERNETICS

What is Allostasis?

The notion of allostasis has, in recent years, been put forward variably as a substitute for, or as a complement to, homeostasis in regards to adaptive behavior. For Sterling

(2004, 2012), for example, the 'classical' homeostasis model is wrong. On this account allostasis is about *prediction* whereas homeostasis is about *reaction*. Alternatively, Wingfield (2004) on the other hand, views allostasis as imbuing organisms with emergency mechanisms that facilitate long-term homeostasis. Allostasis, generally, concerns (physiological and sensorimotor) re-parameterizations for meeting demand not just for short-term homeostasis (or equilibrium) but for predicted longer-term adaptive gain. Thus, notwithstanding the different definitions and foci, unifying the perspectives on allostasis, whether it concern short-term or longer-term adaptation, is the notion of *predictive regulation*.

The term allostasis has further been applied to the social domain (Schulkin 2011), as well as to the workings of artificial (cybernetic) systems (Munteaun and Wright 2007, Lowe and Kiryazov 2013, Vernon et al. 2015). Moreover, allostasis has recently found specific application to Ashby-ultrastable systems (Gu et al. 2014, Seth 2014, also see Lowe 2016).

Controversies exist in the use of the allostasis term, not least because of the different definitions used. Day (2005), has suggested that allostasis is a redundant term and adds little (perhaps only confusion) to the understanding of what Cannon (1929) meant by homeostasis. Allostasis, like Cannonian homeostasis, has considered prediction as a key means by which nervous systems can avoid potential irrecoverable deficits (cf. Day 2005). Allostasis has also been viewed (McEwen & Wingfield 2003, McEwen 2004) as a means for achieving homeostasis of essential variables where *essential* concerns variables for which viable bounds are particularly rigid (e.g. for blood glucose and water levels and pH levels). Other variables, including stress levels and blood pressure are considered somewhat less essential, though, are also required to be maintained within certain 'healthy' ranges. Irrespective of the controversies that exist, we feel the notion of allostasis as it concerns responses to anticipated threats to ongoing viability (maintenance of homeostasis of essential variables) has utility. Further, as Sterling (2004, 2012) describes it: "[t]here are solid scientific reasons [for its use as a term]: the allostasis model connects easily with modern concepts in sensory physiology, neural computation, and optimal design" (Sterling 2004, p.22). Of particular interest here is the role allostasis can bring to bear to cybernetic, including neural computational, understanding of adaptive behavior.

Allostatic Ultrastability

The ultrastability notion has been criticized on the grounds of its painting a picture of life as passive-contingent (Froese & Stewart 2010; Franchi 2013, 2015). Artificial (or hypothetical biological) organisms imbued purely with ultrastability processes are externally driven (heteronomous) and in the absence of such external perturbations (environmental changes), will do nothing. At least one obvious problem with this notion is that environmental dynamics, particularly as they confront organisms with nervous systems of the complexity of humans, are ever-changing and perturb organisms on a variety of time scales. Nervous systems, themselves, exhibit spontaneous activity in the absence of external perturbations, and are required to produce responses in the absence of, e.g. prior to, changes that may 'break' the organisms, i.e. lead to irrecoverable deficits (cf. McFarland & Bösser 1993).

Similar to the previous section, we now wish to categorize different types of conceptions of allostasis in an attempt to clarify the properties of the most popular perspectives on homeostatic – allostatic regulation (see also Lowe 2016).

1. **Reactive Homeostatic Regulation:** Ashbyan homeostasis, essential variable errors (via first-order feedback) produce signals that lead to behavioural corrective measures (second-order feedback). The essential variables are "immediately affected by the environment only" (Ashby 1960, p.81). Thus, re-parameterizations affect only sensorimotor, and current, demand.
2. **Predictive Transient Regulation:** Satisfaction of goals has the effect of facilitating long-term homeostatic equilibrium. The reactive process (Position 1) is embedded within this allostatic process. Second-order feedback involves behavioural corrective mechanisms. Third-order feedback involves transient re-setting of local homeostatic bounds to meet predicted demand.
3. **Predictive Non-Transient Regulation:** Survival and reproduction (as well as goals) require neurophysiological states to deal with predicted demands. Second-order feedback involves behaviour suited to meet predicted demands. Third-order feedback involves modulation of local homeostatic activity. Demands are ever-changing throughout daily and seasonal cycles; thereby, no 'resetting' exists.

Position 1 was covered in the previous section and will thus not be re-visited here. It suffices to say that ultrastability provides somewhat adaptive behavior. This 'adaptive' behavior is limited by a lack of (goal) directedness and prior knowledge requisite to flexible opportunistic and persistent sequential behavior.

In regard to case 2, it might be considered that the examples of Avila-Garcìa and Cañamero (2005) and Lowe et al. (2010) conform to *transient regulation*, at least insofar as motivated behavior may persist in the face of non-related essential variable needs. In these cases, corrective behaviours were instigated as a function of homeostatic errors, i.e. adaptive behavior is reactively driven. These examples are very much borderline cases, however. The sense in which allostasis is normally considered is in terms of *predictive regulation*. Here, *prior* knowledge, based on sensed environmental contingencies, may bring to bear in a top-down fashion on local homeostatic (essential) variables. In control theoretic terms, we can compare the classic ('homeostatic') control loop from Figure 1 (left), to that of Figure 2 (left) – a predictive 'allostatic' controller (Sterling 2004). Prior knowledge allows for a prediction of the (peripheral) physiological requirements (cf. Schulkin 2004) of the organism in relation to environmental contingencies. This can manifest both in terms of the actions required, and the physiological cost of persisting in these actions until the threat is averted (or goal state achieved). This means that errors signaling certain homeostatic deficits / surfeits may be transiently suppressed, e.g. via shifting thresholds or gain parameters on the output signals (Sterling 2004). Furthermore, S (in Figure 1, right; Figure 2, right) should be seen as providing peripheral changes that constitute re-parameterizations *both* of sensor-motor couplings *and* of peripheral physiological activations (stress levels, blood pressure) that meet the predicted demand of the situation. The effector of the control loop (Figure 2, left) must be considered to consist of corrective responses to predicted challenges that concern behavioural activity (2nd feedback loop) and autonomic (peripheral physiological) activity (the 3rd feedback loop that we suggest is necessary). Naturally, further feedback loops may be necessary to engender biological organisms with the necessary flexibility to deal with even transient challenges to homeostatically realized equilibrium states. We can, for example, imagine a 4th (autonomic) feedback loop between 'S' and the EVs that signal internal changes to EV values (glucose mobilization) according to perceived demand. We might further expect 'S' to not consist of purely non-directional (i.e. random) changes to parameters but changes directed according to deficits or surfeits in the level of the essential variable. This is also in accordance with research done on the effects of neurons in the hypothalamus sensitive to surfeits and deficits in blood glucose and oxygen levels (cf. Canabal et al. 2007).

In goal-directed behaviours, unlike in the *non-random self-configurable* and *non self-configurable ultrastable systems described in the previous section*, an organism typically needs to produce *sequences* of actions in order to arrive at the state satisfying the essential variables. This requires prior knowledge of the length of the sequence, proximity to goal as well as an ability to deal with obstacles that may predictably occur during the goal-directed behavior. The above-mentioned *reactive* artificial organisms are only equipped to persist in relation to persistent (exteroceptive) sensory stimulation. More adaptive organisms should be able to persist according to prior knowledge and predictive regulation. Figure 3, depicts an ultrastable system with multiple essential variables. In a predictive regulatory system, such as that of Figure 2 (right), the organism's controller may differentially suppress / increase the effects of homeostatic errors by modulating the gains / thresholds of the error-sensing function. In this way predicted demand for ongoing goal-directed behavior can be adjusted so as to enhance the prospects of achieving the goal, which may include an *essential variable satisfying state*.

Figure 2. Left. Predictive (allostatic) control loop. Unlike for the classical 'homeo-static' control loop, prior knowledge of the controller provides a top-down predictive control, which entails re-setting of homeostatic bounds or otherwise suppressing / increasing of the effects of homeostatic errors on the effector. Right. Allostatic ultrastable system. Depicted is the classic ultrastable system with additional dashed arrows superimposed. In this case, prior knowledge is given by the sensorimotor activity at R which constitutes the nervous system (cf. Froese & Stewart 2010). This provides a third feedback loop, which modulates the homeostatic regime (set points) according to predicted demand. In this way the artificial organism has two means by which to achieve homeostasis when 1st feedback produces an error signal: i) behaviourally (via 2nd feedback), ii) autonomically (via 3rd feedback). Autonomic changes also consider 2nd feedback, i.e. the predicted demand of producing par-ticular behaviours.

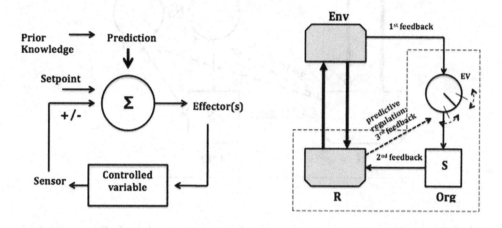

The above predictive (allostatic) form of regulation for single or multiple es-sential variable based ultrastable systems might be viewed according to either case 2, *predictive transient regulation* or case 3, *predictive non-transient regulation*, as described above. The former ultrastable system, however, requires re-setting of homeostatic bounds to 'ideal' values following the transient episode. These 'ideal' values could be set by evolution (in biological organisms) by an evolutionary algo-rithm (in artificial organisms) or by a designer (see previous section for discussion). Furthermore, particularly in case 3, variables such as blood pressure and stress levels might also be considered (lesser) essential variables whose outputs effect physiological re-parameterizations (preparedness for particular actions). A distinc-tion between the monitored and signaled levels of the (*greater* or *lesser*) essential variables and the effects they have on preparing the organism for specific respons-es (in 'S') may be made in this respect. Note, this also applies to the greater essen-

Figure 3. Allostatic ultrastable system with multiple essential variables (EVs). In this version of the allostatic ultrastable system (depicted in Figure 2, right), there are multiple essential variables (EV1, EV2). The influence of these EVs on the S (effector) that modulates sensorimotor parameterization may be differentially weighted according to prior experience of the demand required to carry out the action requisite to survival / goal-directed needs. These EVs may also be differentially weighted according to the particular action needed.

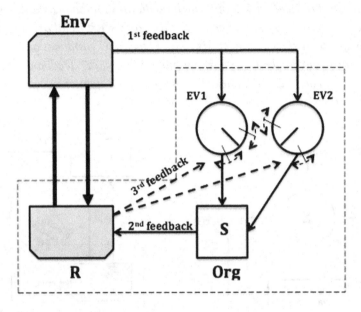

tial variables (e.g. blood glucose levels) whose levels are to be a) monitored, and b) effect action preparedness.

To reiterate, *predictive transient regulation*, the predictive (3rd feedback) loop *transiently* modifies the error sensing parameters of the essential variable(s) over the duration of the goal-directed behavioural episode. This may happen, above all, in cases where motivational homeostatic needs are deprioritized in favour of basic survival needs, e.g. life-threatening situations, mating opportunities, long-sequence goal-directed behaviour (Sterling 2004). Such cases typically involve emotional states that are stimulated by external sensory signals (rather than purely internal sensory signals). Predictive regulation (based on nervous system activity) thereby modulates the homeostatic parameters either to suppress or augment their effects on sensorimotor parameterization (via the effector) in the service of behavioural *persistence*. As an example, blood glucose levels and blood pressure may rise beyond their nominal homeostatic upper limit in order to sufficiently energize the organism over a goal-directed episode. The organism thus engages in an emotional episode that culminates in achievement or not of a goal state. Critically, from the (*predictive*) *transient regulation* perspective, following the achievement of this state, the 'ideal' homeostatic regimen (non-emergency critical limits) is again adhered to. This *predictive transient regulation* perspective is consistent with Wingfield (2004) who suggests allostasis, compared to reactive homeostasis, provides greater flexibility of the organism-environment coupled system as a whole and entails "emergency adjustments of physiology and behaviour to maintain homeostasis in the face of challenges" (Wingfield 2004, p.312). It is also consistent with Gu and Fitzgerald (2014) who assume that allostasis is "the process of achieving homeostasis" (p.1). Emergency adjustments to cognitive and physiological processes have been previously put forward as providing a major function of emotions (e.g. Simon 1967; Oatley & Johnson-Laird 1987, 1996; Sloman 2001). Naturally, however, flexibility entails non-rigidity in relation to behavioural persistence. The organism must still allow for *opportunistic* behavior given sufficiently beneficial opportunities. Such opportunism, however, must be weighed against, not simply proximity of stimulus (as for the reactive homeostatic approaches), but in relation to the proximity of the alternative goal-directed behavior achievement, as well as time and energy invested in that alternative behavior. Such prior knowledge (of the properties of the behavioural sequence) guard against 'dithering' caused by an abundance of opportunities for satisfying one essential variable.

Contrary to the above *transient* perspective of allostasis (predictive regulation), Sterling's (2004, 2012) position concerning allostasis is that it is best conceived *not as a form of homeostasis*. Sterling has advocated that the reactive model centred on local homeostasis is wrong. Allostatic processes do not merely sub-serve homeostatic local states; neither are allostatic processes merely "emergency systems superimposed on the homeostatic model" (Sterling 2012, p.2). The standard model of homeostasis, that typically concerns local homeostatic defending of set points is considered misguided. Allostasis, rather, is viewed as a top-down interactive-constitutive process that recruits resources from many (local) physiological systems to meet predicted current demand. But this demand should not be considered transient or in the service of long-term realization of ideal homesostatic states. Sterling (2004, 2012) suggests that there are no ideal states, mean values of essential variables "need not imply a setpoint but rather the most frequent demand" (Sterling 2004, p.23). Perceived demand is set by external sources, e.g., social norms, in relation to the organism's objectives. This exerts a pressure, both in terms of survival and reproduction. Adaptive behavior, in this view, is constrained, rather than set, by homeostatic needs. Moreover, the ideal physiological state for the organism – in terms of self-maintenance – is not static. Sterling uses the example of blood pressure, which fluctuates throughout the day as a consequence of daily rhythms and may be elevated for prolonged periods according to perceived external (e.g. work pressure) demands – high blood pressure can be of adaptive advantage. For Sterling (2012), a healthy system should be defined as one of "optimal predictive fluctuation" (Sterling 2012, p.9). The organism is continuously in a non-equilibrium state (or in a precarious state, cf. Froese & Stewart 2010), something which, in complex environments, Ashby would expect of a given ultrastable system. However, the organism is not passive-contingent, it is predictive, in part creating its own demands to survive and reproduce in the world and its dynamic homeostatic regulation of essential variables reflects this.

In the next part of this article, we will discuss the aforementioned notions of predictive regulation (allostasis) in relation to cybernetics-compatible views on cognition and adaptive behavior and attempt to illuminate to what extent such views fit into the above-mentioned allostasis descriptions.

ALLOSTASIS IN COGNITIVE-AFFECTIVE CYBERNETICS THEORY

Allostats and Adaptive Behaviour

Munteaun and Wright (2007) suggest that Artificial Intelligence approaches to the study of autonomy and agency need to account for the phenomenon of allostasis. They put forward an example of how artificial agents might have built-in allostats that override set points of homeostats under certain conditions. The example homeostat given is a mobile 'space rover' that is designed to have homeostatic set-points determine which inclines it attempts to negotiate based on perceived steepness. Through allostatic mechanisms the space rover 'allostat' may override such set-points according to expectancies based on prior knowledge. Effectively, the allostatically regulated space rover is able to modify pre-designed set- points according to the experience of the demands of the situation; thus, the local homeostatic mechanism becomes subsumed in the global allostatic process resembling the allostatic ultrastable systems depicted in Figures 2 (right) and 3. Through re-setting homeostatic limits back to the ideal state having met a particular demand, the allostat provides an example of a *predictive transient regulating* organism. This less conservative (than a reactive homeostat) artificial agent thereby has greater flexibility in its behaviour being less constrained by initial implementation design. Such behavioral dynamics rooted in allostatic regulation need not be inconsistent with the type of emergent homeostatic behavioral dynamics noted by Di Paolo (2000, 2003) but rather, can be viewed as extending behavioral flexibility in order to meet the demands of an organism in a changing and challenging environment. In such artificial allostats, the 'S' component of the organism (Figure 2 and 3) need concern primarily sensor-motor re-parameterization rather than physiological analogues. An organism's battery level, for example, might be allowed to run down to dangerously low levels in order for a sequential goal-directed behavior to be achieved. On the other hand, by analogy, 'physiological' re-parameterizations might manifest in terms of speed of movement (somewhat analogous to stress levels) that further run down the allostat's battery but allow it to deal with predicted demand.

Predictive Processing, Cybernetics and Emotions

Seth (2013, 2014) provides a predictive processing (PP) account of cognition, extending earlier PP accounts that were focused on exteroceptive (sensory) and proprioceptive (motoric) inference (cf. Friston 2010, 2013). Seth posits that intero-ceptive processing, a term used also by Damasio (2010) and Craig (2013, 2015) in relation to biological homeostasis and affective feelings, can also fit within an inferential (predictive modeling) perspective. It is also suggested by Seth (2015) that his interoceptive inference account fits naturally into a cybernetics, specifically Ashbyan ultrastability, framework. This is further said to "lead to … a new view of emotion as active inference" (Seth 2015, p.1), where active inference is defined as "selective sampling of sensory signals so as to improve perceptual predictions" (p.3).

Drawing from Gu et al. (2014), Seth (2014) refers to the 2nd feedback loop of Ashby's as being allostatic and that allostasis is "[t]he process of achieving ho-meostasis" (p.2). This would put Seth's (2014) and Gu et al.'s (2014) predictive processing account of allostasis in category 2., of the previous section, i.e. *predic-tive transient regulation*, where 'ideal' regulative states are realizable. Further Seth (2014) suggests: "On this theory of interoceptive inference … emotional states (i.e., subjective feeling states) arise from top-down predictive inference of the causes of interoceptive sensory signals" (p.9). This particular view has similarities to Lowe and Ziemke (2011), who have suggested that emotional feeling states have a pre-dictive regulatory (top-down) role on likely bodily changes as a result of perceived external (exteroceptive) signals – a form of interoceptive inference.

The Lowe and Ziemke (2011) position, however, is considered more in line with category 3 – *predictive non-transient regulation*. Figure 4 depicts an interpreta-tion of the theory conceived as compatible with a predictive processing account. In Figure 4 (left) is shown Sterling's (2004) account of prior predicted allostatic loads – expected demands - as a function of perceived context, e.g. in relation to the perception of an appraised emotion-inducing stimulus. This load is transduced into a non-linear (i.e. sigmoid) response function. In Figure 4 (right), this is conceived as exteroceptive signals (at 'R') eliciting predicted prior (allostatic) loads/demands. These are interoceptive predictions of the probable bodily states (EV settings). Output responses are sensitive to the signaled level of EVs and parameterize the body (in

2.1.) accordingly. This has the function of preparing the organism for an appropriate action response. If such action preparation (2.2) is insufficient, for example, hormone or glucose mobilization in the circulatory system is insufficient to prepare a viable action, an interoceptive error is signaled and the organism shifts its predicted allostatic loads (Figure 4, left). Thereby, responsivity to the EVs, e.g. blood pressure level, blood glucose level, is suppressed or augmented (differentially over EVs), leading to a re-parameterization at 'S'. The organism is now physiologically, and sensor-motorically, modified to meet a newly predicted demand, in turn preparing for a new, or modified, action. Essentially, the organism predicts its bodily changes (that prepare action) and simultaneously induces them through this prediction. The prediction is then confirmed/disconfirmed as a result of bodily feedback, which sets in motion a modified prediction whose error the organism seeks to minimize within the ultrastable system. There are no ideal states (set ranges) but rather the EV ranges are more or less in flux depending on expected demand and how rigid are their genetically set critical limits. Predictive regulation here is adaptive to the extent that it promotes survival to reproduce or otherwise achieve certain short- and long-term tasks/goals. Adaptive behavior is not specifically for homeostasis in this view.

ALLOSTATIC ULTRASTABILITY AND THE BAYESIAN BRAIN

In relation to Ashby's *ultrastable system*, Seth (2014) identifies three means by which interoceptive prediction errors can be minimized:

1. "Updating predictive models (perception, corresponding to new emotional contents);
2. Changing interoceptive signals through engaging autonomic reflexes (autonomic control or active inference);
3. Performing behavior so as to alter external conditions that impact on internal homeostasis (allostasis)" (p.9/10).

In relation to Figure 3, we might view i. as entailing differential strengthening of the multiple 3rd feedback connections to autonomic reflexes, the activity of which (ii.) may then lead to modifications in the interoceptive (error) signals produced. In this way, the organism is differentially behaviourally prepared (for enacting iii.) according to the particular (emotional) demands of the situation. This would provide a type of embodied appraisal (Prinz 2004) comprising perceived correspondence between exteroceptive signals and interoceptive signals as a function of experience. It could also be linked to Damasio's (1994, 2010) perspective on somatic markers (and interoceptive processing) wherein perception / prediction of different physiological

Figure 4. Interoceptive inference in an Allostat. Left. Predicted probability distributions of allostatic loads (top); response sensivity to predicted loads (bottom) – from Sterling (2004). Right. Allostatic ultrastable system (from Figure 3) with functional description. In R, the organism receives exteroceptive (and proprioceptive) inputs that signal expected demand (requirements for action), (3). EVs transduce a range of inputs (prior probability distribution) into a range of outputs (e.g via a sigmoid function), in (2.1). The range of activation of EVs is differentiated according to a) rigidity (genetic), b) expected demand (learning). The most essential variables are the most rigid in relation to expected range of inputs and output signaling sensitivity. The response is stronger or weaker as a function of the input signal and the monitoring response function (sigmoid parameters). This, in turn, parameterizes i) sensorimotor, ii) physiological states (stress hormones, blood pressure, etc.), according to the expected demand for preparing the organism for action (2.2). This internal loop is continuous in relation to ever-changing perceived environmental conditions and internal capabilities to cope with such conditions.

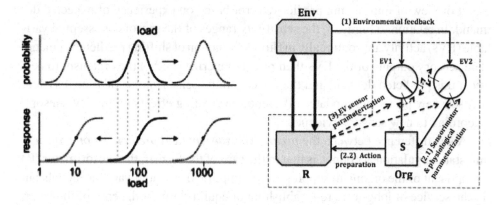

'markers' differentially prepares the organism for action and constrains action selection to options compatible with the physiological state (see also Lowe & Ziemke 2011). Finally, iii. standardly instantiates Ashby's 2nd feedback loop. However, the reference to allostasis here is not entirely representative of Sterling's (2004, 2012) allostasis conception[2]. In fact, i. and ii. are also part of the allostatic process for Sterling (see Figure 2, left). Prior expectations of physiological requirements to meet perceived physical demand entailing changes in autonomic processes (mobilization of metabolic resources) is at the core of Sterling's allostasis account. Nevertheless, Sterling's position on allostasis appears to fit quite well with the predictive processing standpoint. Sterling, for example, consistent with predictive processing models (cf. Seth 2013, Hohwy 2014), refers to allostatic loads being Bayesian by nature. Essential variable sensors are sensitive to signals as a function of a prior (Gaussian) distribution, which constitutes ranges of probable essential variable (physiological) values relevant to meeting a given (exteroceptively perceived) demand. The posterior is computed based on new sensory evidence such that a shift in the sensitivity range may result. Following Figure 4 (left), Figure 5 visualizes this effect in relation to physiological change (e.g. the output of an 'essential' variable such as blood pressure) whose prior probabilistic range constitutes an expected demand (upon the system for sustaining adaptive behavior). This distribution, in a healthy system (Figure 5, A) is able to rapidly shift to a new distribution (posterior distribution) when demand changes. The unhealthy system (Figure 5, B) lacks such *optimal predictive fluctuation* as a result of prolonged exposure to high demand. According to Sterling (2004), though unhealthy, this latter system shouldn't be considered maladaptive since it is adapted to expect, and respond to, previous (prolonged) demand according to (prior) probabilities based on sensory evidence.

The allostatic organism is adaptive, in this view, less from the point of view of achieving homeostasis (according to a notion of fixed set points) and more from the point of view of minimizing predictive error based on experience of expected demand. In relation to Figure 3, the sensitivity ranges of the sensors of essential variable (EVs) activity are continually in flux as a function of shifting predicted demand. The sensory outputs of the EVs then re-parameterize (in 'S') the organism to best meet this predicted demand and the effects on the sensorimotor (nervous) system (R) sets new posteriors (updates differential weighting effects on the EV sensors) according to new sensory evidence.

A key difference between the *predictive transient*, and *predictive non-transient* allostatic regulation accounts, is that in the case of the former, the sensorimotor (R) component of the organism suppresses (or amplifies) essential variable signals but in the service of long-term re-establishing of equilibrium. In the case of the latter, the achievement of equilibrium states is less clear since essential variable signal sensitivity ranges shift not just according to ever-changing environmental demands but also according to daily, seasonal cycles as adapted by evolutionary pressures (Sterling 2004).

An Allostatic Cognitive-Affective Architectural Framework

Ziemke and Lowe (2009), Lowe and Kiryazov (2014) and Vernon et al. (2015) have offered perspectives on cognitive-affective architectural development that adopt a Sterling (2004, 2012) inspired allostatic viewpoint. Here the focus is on the 'higher level of organization' (Vernon et al. 2015, p.7), coordinating local (homeostatic) processes to serve adaptive behavior. Based on Damasio's (2003) nested hierarchy of homeostatic regulation, the architectural approach, nevertheless, emphasizes the top-down regulatory role of emotional feelings on its constitutive (e.g. reflexes,

Figure 5. A. 'Healthy system'. Here the (prior) probability distribution based on statistical sampling of homeostatic ('essential variable') states shifts according to a demand. This permits responses sensitive within the new expected range of sensor inputs. It exhibits 'optimal predictive fluctuation' by virtue of its rapidly shifting from low to high to low demand based on updated predictions (posteriors). B. 'Unhealthy system'. Here, as a result of prolonged high demand, response sensitivity may be relatively resistant to shifting demand. The system expects high demand, and does not flexibly respond to sudden and brief low demand. The system thus sustains the same potentially high-cost physiological response. From Sterling (2004).

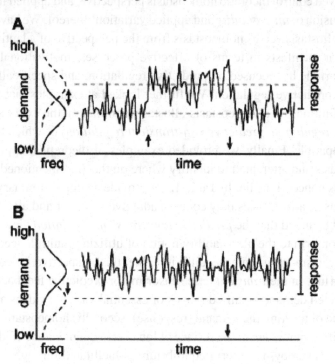

drives, motivations) processes. This could be seen as a type of interoceptive (predictive) processing. The architecture also emphasizes the integrative role of sensory (exteroceptive) and motoric (proprioceptive) states within this allostatic regulatory framework. The schema could apply to both *predictive transient regulation* and *predictive non-transient regulation*. In either case, adaptive behavior would require design of 'desirable' homeostatic bounds from which (interoceptive prediction) errors can be signaled. As alluded to previously in this article, an evolutionary robotics approach, in principle, could allow for context-sensitive or life-time relevant homeostatic bounds to be established as a statistical measure of organismic success. Any such "optimal predictive fluctuation" (Sterling 2012, p.12) would be sensitive to instability of the system as a whole. A trade-off, thus, must be sought between the inflexibility of the ultrastable system that imbues *reactive homeostatic regulation* and one that imbues *predictive transient* or *predictive non-transient regulation*.

CONCLUSION

In this article, we have discussed the notion of allostasis, in relation to the classically conceived control theoretic homeostasis perspective, and applied it to Ashby's cybernetic vision of *ultrastability* and applied variations thereof. We have attempted to evaluate allostasis versus homeostasis from the perspective of adaptive behavior and how that manifests in terms of affective processes, motivational, and emotional. The article has focused on predictive regulation, and specifically allostatic accounts of predictive regulation. We further looked at examples that fit different possible definitions on a homeostasis-allostasis continuum, the extremes (*reactive homeostatic regulation*, *predictive non-transient regulation*) of which being seemingly incompatible. Finally, we provided examples of theoretical approaches that enlist allostasis and attempted to identify where on the aforementioned continuum the allostasis conceptions lie. In Table 1, we provide a simple summary of the different aspects of allostasis as they concern adaptive behavior and affective states.

It should be noted that the *predictive non-transient regulation* view does not so obviously conform to the ultrastability notion of utilizing multiple feedback to establish an organism-environment equilibrium since this perspective, instead, concerns a continual flux. In the *transient* case sensorimotor predictive feedback concerns: firstly, expected demand – shifted ranges of essential variable values are tolerated in the service of meeting the demand (response); secondly, homeostatic needs – the transient shifted ranges are in the service of long-term maintenance of ideal homeostatic ranges. Thereby, long-term equilibrium is facilitated through the allostatic process, which is *thereby* adaptive. In the *non-transient* case, no such equilibrium state obviously exists. Shifting demands are adaptive insofar as the organism is able to sustain a viable coupling to the environment in the service, ultimately, of evolutionary exigencies (i.e. reproduction). Nevertheless, as previously alluded to, some variables are *more* essential than others (Day 2005). Even in the non-transient case it is imperative to respect the limited phase space of viable states of certain essential

Table 1. Properties of homeostatic-allostatic ultrastable systems

	Reactive Homeostasis	Transient Allostasis	Non-transient Allostasis
Trigger	• Interoceptive signals (i.e. of homeostatic / essential variable errors)	• Exteroceptive predictive signals (perceived threat to goal-directed behavior) • Interoceptive predictive signals (predicted homeostatic errors)	• Exteroceptive predictive signals (perceived threat to goal-directed behavior) • Interoceptive predictive signals (predicted homeostatic errors)
Effects	• Errors signaled until behavioural change re-establishes homeostasis • No structural change (to homeostatic error sensing)	• Exteroceptive/ Interoceptive errors signaled until behavioural change re-establishes goal-directed behavior • Local homeostatic errors suppressed / augmented • No structural change (to 'ideal' homeostatic error sensing)	• Exteroceptive/ Interoceptive errors signaled until behavioural change re-establishes goal-directed behavior • Local homeostatic activity suppressed / augmented • Structural changes occur (to homeostatic activity sensing) that reflect life-time experience.
Adaptive Behavior	Cognition for homeostasis	Cognition for homeostasis	Cognition for reproduction / specified tasks (in artificial systems)
Affective State	Motivational / Drive-based	• Motivational / Drive-based • Emotions (for facilitating motivated goal-directed behavior)	• Motivational / Drive-based • Emotions (for facilitating motivated goal-directed behavior)

variables (e.g. pH levels). On this basis, the organism-environment coupling is still constrained to a type of equilibrium that obeys the demands of the most *essential* variables. To some extent, therefore, the difference between *predictive transient* and *predictive non-transient* regulatory perspectives on allostasis may concern the emphasis that the former places on the role of the most essential variables with respect to the latter, in which case both types of allostasis may be considered within an adapted ultrastability framework.

REFERENCES

Ashby, W. R. (1952). *Design for a brain* (1st ed.). New York: John Wiley & Sons.

Ashby, W. R. (1954). Design for a brain. John Wiley & Sons. doi:10.5962/bhl.title.6969

Ashby, W. R. (1960). *Design for a brain* (2nd ed.). New York: John Wiley & Sons. doi:10.1007/978-94-015-1320-3

Avila-Garcìa, O., & Cañamero, L. (2005). Hormonal modulation of perception in motivation-based action selection architectures. In *Proceedings of the symposium Agents that Want and Like: Motivational and Emotional roots of Cognition and Action* (pp. 9–17). University of Hertfordshire.

Berridge, K. C. (2004). Motivation concepts in behavioral neuroscience. *Physiology & Behavior, 81*(2), 179–209. doi:10.1016/j.physbeh.2004.02.004 PMID:15159167

Canabal, D. D., Song, Z., Potian, J. G., Beuve, A., McArdle, J. J., & Routh, V. H. (2007). Glucose, insulin, and leptin signaling pathways modulate nitric oxide synthesis in glucose-inhibited neurons in the ventromedial hypothalamus. *American Journal of Physiology. Regulatory, Integrative and Comparative Physiology, 292*(4), 1418–1428. doi:10.1152/ajpregu.00216.2006 PMID:17170237

Cannon, W. B. (1929). Organization for physiological homeostasis. *Physiological Reviews, 9*, 399–31.

Craig, A. D. (2013). An interoceptive neuroanatomical perspective on feelings, energy, and effort. *Behavioral and Brain Sciences, 36*(06), 685–686. doi:10.1017/S0140525X13001489 PMID:24304783

Craig, A. D. (2015). *How do you feel? An interoceptive moment with your neurobiological self*. Princeton University Press. doi:10.1515/9781400852727

Damasio, A. R. (1994). *Descartes' Error: Emotion, Reason, and the Human Brain*. New York: GP Putnam's Sons.

Damasio, A. R. (2003). *Looking for Spinoza: Joy, Sorrow, and the Feeling Brain*. Harcourt.

Damasio, A. R. (2010). *Self Comes to Mind: Constructing the Conscious Brain*. New York: Pantheon Books.

Day, T. A. (2005). Defining stress as a prelude to mapping its neurocircuitry: No help from allostasis. *Progress in Neuro-Psychopharmacology & Biological Psychiatry, 29*(8), 1195–1200. doi:10.1016/j.pnpbp.2005.08.005 PMID:16213079

Di Paolo, E. A. (2000). Homeostatic adaptation to inversion of the visual field and other sensorimotor disruptions. In J-A. Meyer, A. Berthoz, D. Floreano, H. Roitblat & S W. Wilson (Eds.), *From Animals to Animats,Proc. of the Sixth International Conference on the Simulation of Adaptive Behavior*. MIT Press.

Di Paolo, E. A. (2003). Organismically-inspired robotics: Homeostatic adaptation and natural teleology beyond the closed sensorimotor loop. In K. Murase & T. Asakura (Eds.), *Dynamical Systems Approach to Embodiment and Sociality*. Adelaide, Australia: Advanced Knowledge International.

Franchi, S. (2013). Homeostats for the 21st Century? Simulating Ashby Simulating the Brain. *Constructivist Foundations, 9*(1), 93–101.

Franchi, S. (2015). Ashbian Homeostasis as non-Autonomous Adaptation. *SASO 2015 Ninth IEEE International Conference on Self-Adaptive and Self-Organizing Systems*.

Friston, K., Schwartenbeck, P., FitzGerald, T., Moutoussis, M., Behrens, T., & Dolan, R. J. (2013). The anatomy of choice: Active inference and agency. *Frontiers in Human Neuroscience, 7*, 1–18. doi:10.3389/fnhum.2013.00598 PMID:24093015

Friston, K. J. (2010). The free-energy principle: A unified brain theory? *Nature Reviews. Neuroscience, 11*(2), 127–138. doi:10.1038/nrn2787 PMID:20068583

Froese, T., & Stewart, J. (2010). Life after Ashby: Ultrastability and the autopoietic foundations of biological individuality. *Cybernetics & Human Knowing, 17*(4), 83–106.

Gu, X., & FitzGerald, T. H. (2014). Interoceptive inference: Homeostasis and decision-making. *Trends in Cognitive Sciences, 18*(6), 269–270. doi:10.1016/j. tics.2014.02.001 PMID:24582825

Hohwy, J. (2014). The neural organ explains the mind. In *Open MIND*. Frankfurt am Main, Germany: MIND Group.

Kiryazov, K., Lowe, R., Becker-Asano, C., & Randazzo, M. (2013). The role of arousal in two-resource problem tasks for humanoid service robots. In RO-MAN, 2013 IEEE (pp. 62-69). IEEE. doi:10.1109/ROMAN.2013.6628532

Lowe, R. (2013). Designing for Emergent Ultrastable Behaviour in Complex Artificial Systems – The Quest for Minimizing Heteronomous Constraints. *Constructivist Foundations, 9*(1), 105–107.

Lowe, R. (2016). The Role of Allostasis in Sense-Making: A Better Fit for Interactivity than Cybernetic-Enactivism? *Constructivist Foundations, 11*(2), 251–254.

Lowe, R., & Kiryazov, K. (2014). Utilizing Emotions in Autonomous Robots: An Enactive Approach. In Emotion Modeling (pp. 76-98). Springer International Publishing.

Lowe, R., Montebelli, A., Ieropoulos, I., Greenman, J., Melhuish, C., & Ziemke, T. (2010). Grounding motivation in energy autonomy: a study of artificial metabolism constrained robot dynamics. In ALIFE (pp. 725–732). Odense: The MIT Press.

Lowe, R., & Ziemke, T. (2011). The feeling of action tendencies: On emotional regulation of goal-directed behaviour. *Frontiers in Psychology*, *346*(2), 1–24. PMID:22207854

Manicka, S., & Di Paolo, E. A. (2009). Local ultrastability in a real system based on programmable springs. In *Advances in artificial life.Proceedings of the tenth European Conference on Artificial Life (ECAL09)*. Berlin: Springer.

McEwen, B. S. (2004). Protective and Damaging Effects of the Mediators of Stress and Adaptation: Allostasis and Allostatic Load. In J. Schulkin (Ed.), *Allostasis, Homeostasis, and the Costs of Adaptation*. Cambridge University Press. doi:10.1017/CBO9781316257081.005

McEwen, B. S., & Wingfield, J. C. (2003). The concept of allostasis in biology and biomedicine. *Hormones and Behavior*, *43*(1), 2–15. doi:10.1016/S0018-506X(02)00024-7 PMID:12614627

McFarland, D. (2008). *Guilty Robots, Happy Dogs*. New York: Oxford University Press.

McFarland, D., & Bösser, T. (1993). *Intelligent Behavior in Animals and Robots*. The MIT Press.

McFarland, D., & Spier, E. (1997). Basic cycles, utility and opportunism in self-sufficient robots. *Robotics and Autonomous Systems*, *20*(2-4), 179–190. doi:10.1016/S0921-8890(96)00069-3

Melhuish, C., Ieropoulos, I., Greenman, J., & Horsfield, I. (2006). Energetically autonomous robots: Food for thought. *Autonomous Robots*, *21*(3), 187–198. doi:10.1007/s10514-006-6574-5

Muntean, I., & Wright, C. D. (2007). Autonomous agency, AI, and allostasis. *Pragmatics & Cognition*, *15*(3), 485–513. doi:10.1075/pc.15.3.07mun

Oatley, K., & Johnson-Laird, P. N. (1987). Towards a Cognitive Theory of Emotions. *Cognition and Emotion*, *1*(1), 29–50. doi:10.1080/02699938708408362

Oatley, K., & Johnson-Laird, P. N. (1996). The communicative theory of emotions: Empirical tests, mental models, and implications for social interaction. In L. L. Martin & A. Tesser (Eds.), *Striving and feeling: Interactions among goals, affect, and self-regulation*. Hillsdale, NJ: Erlbaum.

Pickering, A. (2010). *The cybernetic brain: Sketches of another future*. Chicago, IL: University of Chicago Press. doi:10.7208/chicago/9780226667928.001.0001

Pitonakova, L. (2013). Ultrastable neuroendocrine robot controller. *Adaptive Behavior, 21*(1), 47–63. doi:10.1177/1059712312462249

Prinz, J. J. (2004). *Gut Reactions: A Perceptual Theory of Emotion*. Oxford University Press.

Schulkin, J. (2004). *Allostasis, homeostasis, and the costs of physiological adaptation*. Cambridge University Press. doi:10.1017/CBO9781316257081

Schulkin, J. (2011). *Adaptation and well-being: Social allostasis*. Cambridge University Press. doi:10.1017/CBO9780511973666

Seth, A. K. (2013). Interoceptive inference, emotion, and the embodied self. *Trends in Cognitive Sciences, 17*(11), 565–573. doi:10.1016/j.tics.2013.09.007 PMID:24126130

Seth, A. K. (2014). The Cybernetic Bayesian Brain. In *Open MIND*. Frankfurt am Main, Germany: MIND Group.

Simon, H. A. (1967). Motivational and emotional controls of cognition. *Psychological Review, 74*(1), 29–39. doi:10.1037/h0024127 PMID:5341441

Sloman, A. (2001). Beyond shallow models of emotion. *Cognitive Processing, 2*(1), 177–198.

Staddon, J. (2014). *The new behaviorism*. Psychology Press.

Sterling, P. (2004). Principles of allostasis: optimal design, predictive regulation, pathophysiology and rational therapeutics. In J. Schulkin (Ed.), *Allostasis, Homeostasis, and the Costs of Adaptation*. Cambridge University Press. doi:10.1017/CBO9781316257081.004

Sterling, P. (2012). Allostasis: A model of predictive regulation. *Physiology & Behavior, 106*(1), 5–15. doi:10.1016/j.physbeh.2011.06.004 PMID:21684297

Vernon, D. (2013). Interpreting Ashby–But which One? *Constructivist Foundations, 9*(1), 111–113.

Vernon, D., Lowe, R., Thill, S., & Ziemke, T. (2015). Embodied cognition and circular causality: On the role of constitutive autonomy in the reciprocal coupling of perception and action. *Frontiers in Psychology*, 6. PMID:26579043

Wingfield, J. C. (2004). Allostatic Load and Life Cycles: Implications for Neuroendo-crine Control Mechanisms. In J. Schulkin (Ed.), *Allostasis, Homeostasis, and the Costs of Adaptation*. Cambridge University Press. doi:10.1017/CBO9781316257081.011

Ziemke, T., & Lowe, R. (2009). On the Role of Emotion in Embodied Cognitive Architectures: From Organisms to Robots. *Cognitive Computation*, *1*(1), 104–117. doi:10.1007/s12559-009-9012-0

KEY TERMS AND DEFINITIONS

Adaptive Behavior: Behaviour which promotes individual well-being, survival, reproductive advantage or task-specific/goal-directed achievement.

Affective States: Umbrella term for value-based states including feelings, moods, emotions, motivations and drives.

Allostasis: Top-down predictive regulation of local homeostatic variables.

Allostatic Ultrastable Systems: Predictive regulating organism that, through multiple feedback loops, strives for equilibrium with the environment in accordance with the maintenance of its (most) essential variables.

Emotional States: Physiological preparatory states to action.

Homeostasis: Maintenance of organismic essential variables within critical bounds.

Motivational States: Physiological states that reflect sub-optimal maintenance of essential variables.

Predictive Regulation: A physiological and sensorimotor process that entails re-parameterization of the organism to suit predicted action-based demand.

ENDNOTES

[1]   The organism is either adaptive or not depending on whether the essential variables are within the critical bounds.

[2]   It can be noted that Gu et al. (2014) directly reference Sterling (2004) in relation to their notion of "allostasis is the means for achieving homeostasis", though it is not clear that this is consistent with Sterling's position.

Chapter 9
Mathematical Models of Desire, Need, Attention, and Will Effort

Alexander J. Ovsich
Boston College, USA

ABSTRACT

According to Spinoza, "Love is nothing else but pleasure accompanied by the idea of an external cause". Author proposes that desire is nothing else but a change of pleasure accompanied by the idea of its cause, that terms 'desire', 'want' and their cognates describe change of the pleasantness of the state of a subject (PSS in short) associated with X, that if change of PSS is positive/negative, then X is called desirable/undesirable correspondingly. Both positive and negative desires can be strong, so strength of desire characterizes its magnitude. Need of X is defined here as a cyclical desire of X that gets stronger/weaker with dissatisfaction/satisfaction of its need. Author also explores an idea that the stronger is desire of X by a subject, the more attention this subject pays to X. Distribution of attention and influence on it by the will effort are analyzed in this paper.

DOI: 10.4018/978-1-5225-1947-8.ch009

INTRODUCTION

The main objective of this chapter is to present new, closely linked mathematical models of desire, need, and attention. According to Spinoza (1674/1955), "*Love* is nothing else but *pleasure accompanied by the idea of an external cause: Hate* is nothing else but *pain accompanied by the idea of an external cause*" (p. 140). The author posits that desire is nothing else, but a *change* of pleasure accompanied by the idea of its cause. These definitions are so close, because loving/liking and desiring are two facets of the same process that author calls "Hedonic Recognition"[1] – the terms 'desire', 'want' and their cognates are used to describe *change* of the pleasantness of the state of a subject[2] associated with X, while the terms 'love'/'like' and their cognates are used to describe the hedonic *end result of this change*. If X causes a positive/negative change, then X is called "desirable"/"undesirable" correspondingly.

Some support for this view on desire can be found in the classical literature, for example, in the writings of Aristotle and Locke; it also has some experimental backing (Ovsich & Cabanac, 2012). The author finds verification of this idea in the analysis of the process of needs satisfaction that has a typical pattern: dissatisfaction of a need for X creates desire for X by *lowering* current pleasantness of the state of a subject (pangs of hunger, pain of the withdrawal from a drug, etc.) while, at the same time, usually *raising* pleasantness of perceiving or even imagining X. These two simultaneous processes make X to be a factor of maximization of pleasantness, make X desirable. In other words, this creates the positive hedonic gap between the pleasantness of a state of a subject *with* and *without* X and this gap is called "desire for X". The magnitude of the hedonic gap of desire is the measure of X's desirability or desire strength; it increases with growth of dissatisfaction of the need for X, that in the terminology of this theory means that *desire for X gets stronger*. The exact opposite happens with the satisfaction of a need.

Desires attract attention of a subject to their objects. For example, objects of a dissatisfied need come to the attention of a subject more and more persistently with the growth of this need's dissatisfaction. If a need is grossly dissatisfied, then objects and activities of satisfaction of this need can dominate the center of attention of a subject, consume attention. In the first approximation, the stronger the desire is for X, the more attention X gets and this proportionality is explored in this chapter. Voluntary attention is driven by the will effort that can suppress or support competing desires. This mechanism is addressed here in the framework consistent with William James's (1927) approach.

BACKGROUND

The author presents here closely linked mathematical models of desire, need, and attention. Need and attention models are built upon the model of desire. Hence, desire is the pivotal entity of this inquiry and its first topic. There are many ways (Marks, 1986) and faces (Schroeder, 2004) of desire, but, first of all, there is one fundamental question about the meaning and definition of desire.

There is not much of a consensus about the notion of desire. The quite common understanding of desire as a propositional attitude was highly criticized by Bence Nanay (2013). "A number of philosophers have drawn attention to an ambiguity in the word 'desire' " (De Sousa, 2011, p. 227). Schueler (1995, p. 6), who "... focused on contemporary philosophers...", noted that "... the views I am criticizing suffer from a deep ambiguity in terms such as 'desire', 'want' and their cognates". Frankfurt (2004, p.10) called the notion of desire "rampantly ubiquitous" and wrote:

Moreover, its various meanings are rarely distinguished; nor is there much effort to clarify how they are related. These matters are generally left carelessly undefined in the blunt usages of common sense and ordinary speech.

The level of ambiguity in understanding desire is such that the validity of the notion of desire itself is sometimes questioned or even denied outright. For example, DeLancey (2002, p. ix) wrote:

Since my concern in this book is with basic emotions and other motivational states, I will on several occasions discuss the inappropriateness of the philosopher's notion of desire; it is hard to overestimate the harm that this notion has done to moral psychology, action theory, and other aspects of philosophy of mind.
... (for example, there are many kinds of motivational states, but no generic one corresponding to the philosophical notion of desire)....

However, as Marks (1986, p. 10) carefully noted:

...it may well be the case, as I believe, that there remains a single, significant, psychological phenomenon appropriately named "desire." If so, then it is this – desire proper – which, ultimately, constitutes the subject matter of the theory of desire.

His belief is shared by the author of this paper.

There is not much clarity in understanding need, attention, will effort, and their relation to desire. According to Douglas and Peters (1979), "...attention was a neglected topic within psychology for many years" and there was "Confusion Caused by Definitions of Attention" (p. 178). The history of philosophy presents a substantial collection of notions on will. Bourke (1964) thought there to be "... eight distinctive views" of these notions "taken by Western thinkers" (p. 8).

MATHEMATICAL MODEL OF DESIRE

Hedonistic Approach to Desire

Schroeder (2004, pp. 27-31) identified three types of the desire theories. Two of them are represented by motivational and hedonistic theories of desire[3]. Schroeder considered hedonistic theories of desire to be superior to the motivational. Indeed, the hedonistic approach to desire has a very long and impressive history. Aristotle (2004, I, 11, 1370b) directly defined desire through pleasure: "Everything, too, is pleasant for which we have the desire within us, since desire is the craving for pleasure". The same can be said about Spinoza (1674/1955, Proposition XXXVII) and Mill (1861/1957, p. 49), who wrote: "...desiring a thing and finding it pleasant, aversion to it and thinking of it as painful, are phenomena entirely inseparable or, rather, two parts of the same phenomenon". Schroeder (2004, p. 27), referring to this Mill's opinion, wrote "Mill is not the only distinguished historical figure to have considered such a view." Schroeder further elaborated: "Hobbes, Hume, and Kant apparently had similar thoughts, though interpretation of these thinkers is difficult" (2004, p. 185). Arpaly and Schroeder (2014) think that "Thus, intrinsic desires are not made desires by their relations to action or pleasure" (p. 125), though they see some connection between pleasure and desire satisfaction.

Aristotle (2004, I, 11, 1370b), in line with his clearly hedonistic definition of desire as "the craving for pleasure" quoted above, not only defines anger as a desire for revenge (Konstan, 2006, p. 41; Kenny, 1963, p. 193) or retaliation (Tailor, 1986, p. 231), but also provides rather detailed descriptions of what it means at the hedonic level (Aristotle, 2004, 1.11, 1371a): "Revenge, too, is pleasant; it is pleasant to get anything that it is painful to fail to get, and angry people suffer extreme pain when they fail to get their revenge; but they enjoy the prospect of getting it" (also see 2.2, 1378b). It is important here to note that Aristotle's desire for revenge (anger) involves a *positive hedonic change*, transition from the hedonically negative to the hedonically positive state experienced even while imagining "the prospect of getting it".

Aristotle's hedonistic approach to desire was echoed by Locke who defined desire as follows: "The uneasiness a man finds in himself upon the absence of anything whose present enjoyment carries the idea of delight with it, is that we call desire" (1690/1824, Book II, Chapter 20, Section 6). Desire for Locke is also about the *hedonic gap* between the more negative hedonic level ("uneasiness") of the state of the desiring subject without an object of desire and the more positive hedonic level ("enjoyment") with it. As for Aristotle, Locke's interpretation of desire is also about the *positive hedonic change* associated with the desired phenomenon.

The vital fact of the matter here is that such a hedonic gap, which is a hedonic change associated with the object of desire, is a regular property of the subjective experience of desire. This is true for the "low" physiological desires as well as for the "high" psychological desires. This sameness allows one to express desire for an action, power or sex, metaphorically, as being "power hungry", "hungry for the loved one."

Definition and Model of Desire

The model of desire discussed here (and in Ovsich 1998a, 1998b, 2012; Ovsich & Cabanac, 2012) is based upon the dynamic interpretation of the Hedonistic Principle, declaring that animals and humans alike are motivated/driven to maximize pleasantness of their internal state (Pleasantness of the State of a Subject or PSS[4] here). The direct inference from the Hedonistic Principle is that one of the most important characteristics of any phenomenon (X) for a subject (S) driven to maximize her PSS should be *how much* X maximizes (or minimizes) the PSS as measured by the PSS change by X ($\Delta PSS_{s,x}$). For the human subject it should also mean that words and expressions describing the PSS changes ought to be notable and widely used.

The author proposes that terms such as 'desire,' 'want,' and their cognates describe the PSS change (ΔPSS) associated with (caused by) a phenomenon (object, activity, etc.):

- X associated with positive $\Delta PSS_{s,x}$ is called "desirable", "wanted";
- X associated with negative $\Delta PSS_{s,x}$ is called "undesirable", "unwanted";
- X associated with zero $\Delta PSS_{s,x}$ is called "indifferent", though sometimes it is called "undesirable" in the sense of the *lack* of any desire.

The common feature in the last two cases above is a non-positive (zero or negative) change of the PSS ($\Delta PSS_{s,x} <= 0$) or an absence of the positive change of the PSS by X. It indicates, that:

- A subject reports a presence or absence of desire for a phenomenon depending upon the presence or absence of the positive change of the PSS associated with that phenomenon;
- What is usually called 'desire' of X is a positive change of the PSS associated with X;
- An object of desire is a factor of the PSS maximization.

From the hedonistic viewpoint, it is quite clear why a positive rather than a negative or zero change of the PSS is used as the bases for terms 'desire' and 'want' describing PSS alteration. According to the Hedonistic Principle, a subject is looking for *maximization* of the PSS that is represented by a *positive* PSS change, $\Delta PSS_{s,x} >$ 0. The use of the negative prefix to describe something as undesirable, unwanted, usually points to the opposite of the positive PSS change that subjects are seeking or, sometimes, to the absence of the positive PSS change.

If we interpret desire as an algebraic variable that can be positive or negative (where the desirable X is an object of the positive desire and undesirable X is an object of the negative desire), then we can define the desire of X in general as a term describing a change of the PSS ($\Delta PSS_{s,x}$) associated with X. Here is the definition of a desire: *a subject's (S) desire for X is a word to describe a change of the Pleasantness of the State of this Subject ($\Delta PSS_{s,x}$) associated with ('caused' by) X, where X can be an object or an activity, perceived, remembered, or imagined. Desirability of X for S is an ability of X to maximize/minimize the PSS.*

Below is the formula of desire that incorporates all three types of the ΔPSS, where S is a subject experiencing desire, X is an object of desire, ΔPSS is the change of the Pleasantness of the State of the Subject:

$$DESIRE_{s,x} = \Delta PSS_{s,x} \tag{1}$$

If $\Delta PSS_{s,x} > 0$, then x is called "desirable".
If $\Delta PSS_{s,x} < 0$, then x is called "undesirable".

The above definition and formula of desire are consistent both with hedonistic/ utilitarian approach to desire and with the contemporary point of view, that "… the primary linkage of the notion of desire to a notion other than itself is to the notion of affect – pleasure or displeasure in the widest sense" (Strawson, 2010, p. 284). Experimental support of this model of desire is demonstrated in Ovsich & Cabanac, 2012.

Desire Strength

A desire is often characterized or measured by its *strength*. Both positive and negative desire can be experienced as strong or weak. This means that the strength of desire is a sign-independent characteristic of desire. Therefore, a mathematical sign of the magnitude or an absolute value (|value|) should be applied to express strength of the subject's (S) desire for X ($\Delta PSS_{s,x}$):

$$\text{Strength of S desire for } X = |DESIRE_{s,x}| = |\Delta PSS_{s,x}| \qquad (2)$$

Desiring and Liking as Facets of the Hedonic Recognition

According to Spinoza (1674/1955), "Love is nothing else but pleasure accompanied by the idea of an external cause" (p. 140). The author proposes that desire is nothing else but a *change* of pleasure accompanied by the idea of its cause. These definitions are so close because loving/liking and desiring are two different aspects of the same process. Indeed, Spinoza's level of "pleasure accompanied by" X is reached as a result of the PSS change triggered by X, i.e., as a consequence of desiring X. The author posits that the terms 'desire' and 'want' are used to describe *change of the PSS* generated by X while terms 'love'/'like', etc. are used to describe the hedonic *end result of this change* - the end level of ΔPSS.

In the process of the Object Recognition an Object is not only recognized and categorized as a banana, a chair, John, etc., but also recognized hedonically as pleasant/unpleasant (P/U), liked/disliked, desirable/undesirable. The author calls the latter form of recognition "Hedonic Recognition". The fact of the matter is that in the process of the Object Recognition that includes Hedonic Recognition, the PSS of the subject changes from the antecedent, preceding perception/imagination of the object level PSS_1 to the end result level PSS_2. This hedonic transition creates a PSS change: $\Delta PSS = PSS_2 - PSS_1 = PSS_{end} - PSS_{bgn}$. The author posits that P/U, or liking/disliking of X, is determined by the end level PSS_2, while desirability of X is determined by the PSS change (ΔPSS). In other words, liking is determined by the position PSS_{end} on the hedonic axes while desiring is determined by the hedonic change depending not only on PSS_{end}, but also on the preceding level PSS_{bgn}. This means that though X can be equally liked in two different situations by the same subject, it can be desirable in one of them and undesirable in another, depending on whether the end level PSS_2 was reached by:

1. *Raising* the PSS from the *lower* preceding/beginning level PSS_1, creating positive ΔPSS, making X desirable, or by
2. *Lowering* the PSS from the *higher* preceding level PSS_1, creating negative ΔPSS, making X undesirable.

There are many possible combinations of liking and desiring, depending on where on the P/U continuum the hedonic change of desire begins and ends. Five cases of these combinations are analyzed below.

1. X is liked/pleasant ($PSS_{s,x} > 0$) and desirable ($\Delta PSS_{s,x} > 0$).

X can be represented in this case by food for a hungry S, entertainment for a bored one, etc. Two different types of this case are represented graphically below - one with negative PSS in the beginning (PSS_1 or PSS_{bgn}) and another one with positive PSS_1. In both cases 1a and 1b,

$$DESIRE_{s,x} = PSS_{s,x} - PSS_{s,y} > 0.$$

Case 1a:

```
        y                 x
    ---.------|--------.------------> PSS


        bgn        0      end
        PSS₁              PSS₂
```

Case 1b:

```
                        y       x
    ----------|----.----------.----> PSS
              0    bgn        end
                   PSS₁       PSS₂
```

There is nothing painful about the kind of desire that is represented by the last graph above (Case 1b) - its 'beginning' and 'end' are both in the area of positive P. This case supports Edwards (1979) critique of "… the false claim of Schopenhauer's pessimism that all pleasures result from the satisfaction of painful desire" (p. 95).

2.   X is liked/pleasant ($PSS_{s,x} > 0$) and undesirable ($\Delta PSS_{s,x} < 0$).

```
              x              y
--------|--.----------.----> PSS
        0  end        bgn
           PSS₂       PSS₁
```

In this case, X may be offered/available when S is in possession of Y, or doing Y that is more pleasant than X. X minimizes the PSS here, i.e. X is undesirable, though X is pleasant in and of itself, and is liked by S.

X does not have to be unpleasant/disliked/aversive/associated with a negative PSS in order to be categorized as undesirable - it just has to be *less pleasant* than Y available at the same time. This point of view is in disagreement with Arpaly & Schroeder's (2014) description of the negative desirability ("intrinsic aversion" in their terminology) when they equate it with "…desiring that things not be the case because we have an aversion to them in themselves" (p. 128).

Here is an example for this case (2): S is eating S's favorite dish Y. When dish X is offered S declines it and says that s/he doesn't want it. This does not necessarily mean that S has an aversion to X in itself or does not like it, but only that S likes Y *more* than X. When X is offered, S experiences negative $\Delta PSS_{s,x}$ and, therefore, categorizes X as undesirable to S at the moment.

3.   X is disliked/unpleasant ($PSS_{s,x} < 0$) and undesirable ($\Delta PSS_{s,x} < 0$).

In this case both desire and attitude toward their object (x) are negative: a subject does not want something unpleasant in and of itself - bad smell, view, event, news, etc.

```
      x                   y
---.------------|-------.----------> PSS
   end          0       bgn


      x       y
--.--------.-----|-----------------> PSS
   end     bgn   0
```

4.   X is disliked/unpleasant ($PSS_{s,x} < 0$) and desirable ($\Delta PSS_{s,x} > 0$):

```
      y        x
--.--------.-----|----> PSS
   bgn        end    0
```

This case corresponds to the so called "choice of the lesser of two evils" and will be discussed more below.

5. X is indifferent ($\text{PSS}_{s,x} = 0$) and desirable ($\Delta\text{PSS}_{s,x} > 0$).

```
      y            x
   --.-------.|----> PSS
                0
     bgn        end
```

This case corresponds to acts of bodily evacuation, use of painkillers, use of drugs by an advanced addict that does not enjoy the drug anymore, etc. It will be discussed below in more detail.

Case 1 corresponds to what Don Locke (1982) called a "genuine" desire, while cases 4 and 5 correlate to his "formal" desire. There are endless instances of cases 4 and 5. For example, one can very much want to go to the bathroom without liking it, not taking any pleasure in the act of evacuation. The same is true for taking a pain-killer (even it does not eliminate pain completely), for taking literal or metaphorical "bitter medicine", etc.. Mary eats an apple that is good enough for her, but that she doesn't really want (Marks, 1986). A young philosopher accepts an offer to teach at a community college that he doesn't really like, but accepts because it is the best offer he has at the time. Women may submit to sex under a threat (Staude, 1986, pp. 134, 177, 178-179). A terminally ill patient wants to commit suicide, preferring death to suffering. De Sousa (2011, p. 242) describes unpleasant or indifferent cases, that are nevertheless desirable as follows:

A smoker may desire to smoke, yet not enjoy it. To be sure, her desire might focus on relief from the pain of not smoking. In true addicts, perhaps the pain of withdrawal may seem to be the only source of the desire.

These are situations in which the subject is sometimes hesitant to use the terms 'desire' and 'want' to describe experiences of positive ΔPSS. Instead, one would say that it was (or will be) done because s/he had to, or ought to do it. Otherwise, one might declare that s/he didn't (does not) have a choice' (apparently implying a hedonically sound choice), or that these actions were (are) in response to a sense of duty or obligation. Still, these cases are often self-described as desirable, as something a subject wanted, though it can be expressed with a degree of reservation. After all, at times people will say that they 'want to have surgery' or 'want to die'. One can have a 'death wish' and it can be a literally correct description of how one actually feels.

What is common and notable about cases 4 and 5 is that they describe desires with no end pleasure - the hedonic end result of desire is not positive (it's negative or zero) while the PSS change experienced by the subject is positive. An object of such desire is still a factor of the PSS maximization, but satisfaction of such desire doesn't bring the PSS into the area of positive PSS, or into the domain of happiness. In the author's opinion, this 'hedonic incompleteness' of desire is the source of that reluctance to use the terms 'desire', 'want' and their cognates in these cases.

It seems that Aristotle's understanding of desire as "craving for pleasure", as well as Mill's one (see quotes in the paragraph "Hedonistic Approach to Desire") are too narrow, because they do not cover cases of desire with no end pleasure. On the contrary, a proposed understanding of desire as craving for pleasure *increase* (or displeasure *decrease*) covers a lot more, if not all, of the ground - in all the above cases, there is a PSS *change* associated with the object of positive or negative desire.

Desire, Motivation, and Pleasure

There is a question about the "disconnection between desire, motivation and pleasure" (De Sousa, 2011, p. 242; Corns, 2014) associated with the above discussion. It seems to be based upon the narrow understanding of desire as craving for pleasure[5], and/or the static, fragmented interpretation of the Hedonistic Principle, where pleasure is the source of a positive motivation and displeasure/pain is the source of a negative one. These views on desire present a contradiction in understanding of cases 4 and 5 above as having positive motivation of desire without end pleasure. The dynamic interpretation of the Hedonistic Principle exercised here, where the source of positive motivation is not pleasure, but *pleasure maximization,* eliminates this contradiction. The point here is that it is not pleasure *per se*, but a *change* of pleasure that is a necessary and often sufficient condition of the hedonic experience called desire.

It is especially clear from the point of view of the strong form of the Hedonistic Principle, declaring that a subject is motivated by pleasure maximization *and only by it*. If only pleasure maximization motivates, then there is no motivation without it and only the PSS *change* of desire carries what was called a "motivational oomph" in Robinson & Berridge (2015), Corns (2014). According to Berridge (2004, p. 194):

'Liking' is essentially hedonic impact - the brain reaction underlying sensory pleasure-triggered by immediate receipt of reward such as a sweet taste (unconditioned 'liking'). ... 'Wanting', or incentive salience, is the motivational incentive value of the same reward. ... But incentive 'wanting' is not a sensory pleasure. 'Wanting' is purely the incentive motivational value of a stimulus, not its hedonic impact.

A good illustrative analogy with liking and wanting, subscribing motivational power to the latter rather than to the former, is through the comparison of them with an electrical potential and voltage respectively. Any point of the conductor can have an electric potential, but it takes *difference* of potentials (voltage) between two points to move electrons between them, to "motivate" them into action. Similarly, every phenomenon has its pleasantness/unpleasantness for a subject (including zero level), but it takes a *change* of pleasantness, a *difference* in the pleasantness level (desire in the author's theory) to motivate and move a subject. In real life, your answer to the question "Do you *like* tuna sandwiches?" does not describe your current motivation toward them, while your answer to the question "Do you *want* tuna sandwich?" does; there is no principal inconsistency or contradiction if the former answer is "yes" and the latter is "no", or *vice versa*.

The best proof and illustration of the presented view on desire is provided by the following analysis of the process of strengthening and weakening of desires generated by needs during the process of their satisfaction.

NEED AS A PERIODIC DESIRE

Definition of a Need

As Audi (1993, p. 29) wrote, "Human needs are innate and quickly give rise to desires". Rubinshteòin (1957) has declared that *"desire is a concrete form of the need's existence"*[6]. Experiencing a need means feeling the corresponding desire. If a subject experiences a desire for X repeatedly or regularly it is usually said that the subject *needs* X. This is clearly demonstrated by the needs that emerge and cease to exist with age or during changing circumstances, for example, the needs for sex, smoking, or drugs. The origination/disappearance of such needs is acknowledged when the corresponding desire begins/stops being recurring, cyclical, periodic. One can properly say that s/he occasionally wants X, but does not need it (anymore).

Need is defined here as a term used for a periodic or cyclical desire. This is true for all kinds of needs. A need is characterized by the strength and frequency of its desire. Need, being a cyclical process is like a 'wave' of desire.

Satisfaction and Dissatisfaction of a Need and its Desire

According to the Hedonistic Principle, animals and humans alike are motivated/driven by the hedonic strive to maximize their PSS. Therefore, a major tool of their orientation is hedonic 'pricing' through attaching a factor of pleasantness/unpleasantness (P/U) to a phenomenon in order to establish it as a positive or negative factor of the PSS maximization, and determine its likability and desirability. By using variants of reward and punishment, like the carrot and stick scenario, both nature and society affix hedonic sticker-prices of P/U and set values of good and bad. Alteration of this P/U or hedonic 'pricing' is the most significant instrument of adjustment of animal and human orientation and choice. This process has been experimentally studied by Cabanac (1971, p. 1105) who called it "alliesthesia":

In order to avoid using a whole sentence saying that a given external stimulus can be perceived either as pleasant or unpleasant depending upon signals coming from inside the body, it may be useful to use a single word to describe this phenomenon. I hereby propose the word alliesthesia coming from esthesia (meaning sensation) and allios (meaning changed).

Modification of the hedonic values of objects and activities by alliesthesia, which depends on the level of satisfaction of a subject's needs, is very important for understanding the mechanism of needs satisfaction through desire generation. Most needs have two definable features:

- The dissatisfaction of any need of a subject negatively affects the PSS, the PSS level *goes down* with time;
- At the same time, the pleasantness of perceived or imagined objects/activities related to this need's satisfaction *goes up* for the subject.

These two aspects are easily recognizable in the following description of Bertrand Russell (1921, p. 67):

...it seems clear that what, with us, sets a behavior-cycle in motion is some sensation of the sort which we call disagreeable. Take the case of hunger: we have first an uncomfortable feeling inside, producing a disinclination to sit still, a sensitiveness to savory smells, and an attraction towards any food that there may be in our neighborhood.

This means that the hedonic gap between the PSS *without* the object(s) of a need satisfaction and the PSS *with it* grows. *This gap is a desire and its magnitude is its strength that grows.*

Satisfaction of any need of a subject produces exactly opposite effects:

- The PSS becomes more positive, goes up as a result of satisfaction of a need;
- The P (pleasantness) of the objects of this need's satisfaction goes down.

As the hedonic gap of desire gets smaller, desire gets weaker, all the way down to the satiation point when ΔPSS of desire becomes equal to zero – desire is satisfied, it "disappears". At this time, the opposite side of the desire cycle starts again.

The needs satisfaction process clearly shows that motivation, or motivational 'oomph', grows and diminishes together with desire, and not with liking. Indeed, though the pleasantness-likability of food increases together with dissatisfaction of the need for food due to alliesthesia, one still generally likes food after one has eaten, though one does not want to eat anymore, and is not motivated to eat. One likes what s/he put in their refrigerator, but is motivated to open it only when hungry. On the other hand, one who is extremely hungry ($\Delta PSS_{s,food} \gg 0$) may be motivated to eat things that s/he dislikes ($PSS_{s,this\ food} < 0$). Aren't these patterns tried-and-true with regard to the entire smörgåsbord of life?

MATHEMATICAL MODEL OF ATTENTION

Attention and Hedonistic Principle

Desires catch attention, and the stronger the desires are, the more attention they and their objects get. This statement can be presented as an empirical observation. It can be also deduced from the Hedonistic Principle: if it is true that subjects are motivated/driven to maximize the pleasantness of their internal state (PSS), then the more a phenomenon influences the process of the PSS maximization, the more attention should be paid to it. The magnitude of the influence of X on the process of the PSS maximization is measured by the magnitude of the PSS change ($|\Delta PSS_{s,x}|$) associated with X, or, said another way, the magnitude of the influence of X is determined by the strength of the desire of S for X. In the first approximation, attention of a subject S toward a phenomenon X can be considered to be proportional to the strength of desire for it:

$$ATT_{s,x} = k|(\Delta PSS_{s,x}| = k|DESIRE_{s,x}|, \tag{3}$$

where k is a positive coefficient of proportionality.

Attention to a Single Phenomenon

Let's analyze the formula of attention to a single phenomenon (3) to see if it describes the reality of attention correctly.

Case 1: $\Delta PSS_{s,x} > 0$ or $DESIRE_{s,x} > 0$.

In this case X is a factor of PSS *maximization*, meaning that the subject wants X.

If $\Delta PSS_{s,x} > 0$, $DESIRE_{s,x} > 0$ then $ATT_{s,x} > 0$.

According to Equation (Eq.) 3, $ATT_{s,x}$ increases/decreases if the positive $DESIRE_{s,x}$ increases/decreases. The greater the desire for X by a subject S, the more attention is paid by S to X.

Case 2: $\Delta PSS_{s,x} < 0$ or $DESIRE_{s,x} < 0$.

In this case, X is a factor of PSS *minimization,* meaning that the subject does not want X.

If $\Delta PSS_{s,x} < 0$, $DESIRE_{s,x} < 0$ then $ATT_{s,x} > 0$.

The formula $ATT_{s,x} = k|DESIRE_{s,x}|$ illustrates that the stronger the negative desire for X - the more bothersome, painful, and undesirable X is – the more attention is paid to it.

Cases #1 and #2 show that, according to Eq. 3, a subject pays attention to both desirable and undesirable phenomena; the stronger (more desirable or undesirable) it is, the more attention will be paid to it. The substance of this matter is that eliminating the sources of the PSS minimization is just as important for the hedonistic process as acquiring the sources of the PSS maximization because of the integrative character of the PSS. A subject's concentration on the sources of a positive ΔPSS for their hedonic *exploitation* as well as concentration on the sources of a negative ΔPSS for their *elimination* is equally important for this process of the PSS maximization. Attention paid to X doesn't depend on the *sign* of ΔPSS_x or a desire for X, but only on the *magnitude* of the PSS change that is the strength of desire for X. In summary, attention paid to X is *sign-independent* of whether X is desirable or undesirable, but depends only on the *strength* of desirability/undesirability of X. Attention is "blind" to the sign of desire; attention depends only on its strength.

Case 3: $\Delta PSS_{s,x} = 0$ or $DESIRE_{s,x} = 0$.

If $\Delta PSS_{s,x} = 0$, $DESIRE_{s,x} = 0$ then $ATT_{s,x} = 0$.

If X doesn't affect the PSS maximization, if X is neither desirable nor undesirable, then a subject does not pay attention to X. It does not mean that X is hedonically indifferent, or is not liked or disliked. One likes what s/he put in the refrigerator, but does not pay attention to it, is not motivated to eat until getting hungry, experiencing the desire to eat.

The above analysis of the formula (3) for attention shows that this formula gives an accurate basic description of some fundamental features of attention. It correctly illustrates the fact that both positive and negative influences on a subject's PSS get attention, and that the degree of attention to a phenomenon is proportional to the magnitude of its desirability. It is fair to say that at least in some measure this formula applies.

A graphic representation for attention to a single phenomenon as a function of desire in the first approximation looks like a letter "V", with its point at the zero of the crossing of the vertical axis of attention and the horizontal axis of positive/negative desire:

Hedonistic Resolution of the Frame Problem

Though Case #3 above is the least important hedonically, it is the most important statistically. At any given moment, animals and humans alike do not pay attention to the great majority of phenomena accessible to them, because they are hedonically indifferent to them, the phenomena do not affect their PSS. This allows them to concentrate on the small percentage of the world's phenomena that are important for their well-being. Zero desire gets zero attention, and this works as a powerful hedonic filter facilitating efficient utilization of the finite resources of a limited

Figure 1. Attention to a single phenomenon as a function of desire (first approximation)

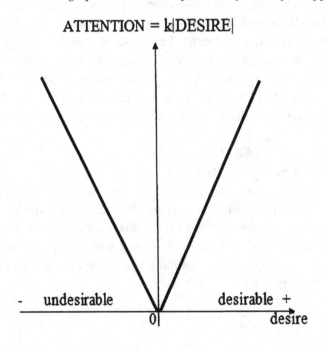

ATTENTION = k|DESIRE|

creature facing an infinite Universe. This is the essence of "… the human talent for *ignoring* what should be ignored, while staying alert to relevant recalcitrance when it occurs" (Dennett, 1990, p. 162).

The author would suggest that imitation of this hedonic mechanism is the key to resolution of one of the fundamental problems of Artificial Intelligence, called "the qualification problem" by McCarthy (1968), though usually called a "frame problem", and described by Dennett (1990, p. 161) as follows:

What is needed is a system that genuinely ignores most of what it knows, and operates with a well-chosen portion of its knowledge at any moment. Well chosen, but not chosen by exhaustive consideration. How, though, can you give a system rules for ignoring - or better, since explicit rule-following is not the problem, how can you design a system that reliably ignores what it ought to ignore under a wide variety of different circumstances in a complex action environment?

The author agrees with McFarland's (2008, p. 156) point of view:

It is worth noting that animals do not suffer from the frame problem, and this may be because they have a value system (see Chapter 8), the cost and risks involved in their decision-making acting as constraints on their behavior.

Attention to Multiple Phenomena

The model of attention to a 'single' phenomenon above is very much an abstraction, because in reality a subject always perceives multiple phenomena. This model, however, represents an approximation of a real situation, where the subject concentrates mainly on one phenomenon in the center of attention. The higher the percentage of total attention paid to the phenomenon in the center of attention, the closer this model comes to reality.

There are certain situations when a phenomenon is singled out and placed in the center of attention. This occurs in a process of choice making when the elements of choice are appraised by a subject one by one: when a 'new' phenomenon catches the attention of a subject and is appraised, or perhaps an 'old' phenomenon is re-appraised. This also happens when a phenomenon becomes 'the chosen one', catching the center of attention while competing phenomena are pushed to the periphery of attention.

The fact of the matter is that at any given moment the attention of a subject is *distributed* between multitudes of simultaneously perceived phenomena[7]. The author proposes that the total volume of attention of a subject perceiving n phenomena at the moment t ($ATTtotal_{s,t}$) can be described as the sum of attention paid to each of them:

$$\text{ATTtotal}_{s,t} = \text{ATT}_{s,t,1} + \text{ATT}_{s,t,2} + \ldots + \text{ATT}_{s,t,n} \tag{4}$$

Now, let's merge two last formulas by replacing every component of the right part of Eq. 4, representing attention to one of the n phenomena, with its expression from Eq. 3:

$$\text{ATTtotal}_{s,t} = k|\Delta\text{PSS}_{s,t,1}| + \ldots + k|\Delta\text{PSS}_{s,t,n}| =$$

$$= k|\text{DESIRE}_{s,t,1}| + \ldots + k|\text{DESIRE}_{s,t,n}| \tag{5}$$

This formula of attention describes distribution of attention between n simultaneously perceived phenomena in proportion with their desire's strength[8].

Center of Attention

Attention has its periphery, and most focused, or 'brightest' area, which is called the 'center of attention'. Let's assign numbers in Eq. 5 to perceived phenomena from 1 to n *in descending order*, in accordance with the volume of attention paid by a subject to each of them, so that:

$$\text{ATT}_{s,t,1} > \text{ATT}_{s,t,2} > \ldots > \text{ATT}_{s,t,n} \tag{6}$$

Thus, the number one ($\text{ATT}_{s,t,1}$) will be assigned from now on to the phenomenon having the most attention, or being at the center of attention - the phenomenon associated with the largest positive or negative PSS change, the one that is most desirable or undesirable, i.e., corresponding to the *strongest desire*:

$$|\Delta\text{PSS}_{s,t,1}| > \ldots > |\Delta\text{PSS}_{s,t,n}| \tag{7}$$

or

$$|\text{DESIRE}_{s,t,1}| > \ldots > |\text{DESIRE}_{s,t,n}| \tag{8}$$

General Formula of Attention

There is another general feature of attention that has to be taken in consideration: attention has an upper limit. In the words of Csikszentmihalyi (1978, p. 337): "The main assumption I shall be making is that attention is a form of a psychic energy needed to control the stream of consciousness, and that attention is a limited psychic resource". This means that at any moment (t) there is a maximum or an upper limit ($ATTmax_{s,t}$) for the attention of a subject (S) and that at any moment (t) this maximum is not greater than the total attention of a subject:

$$ATTmax_{s,t} >= ATTtotal_{s,t} =$$

$$= k|\Delta PSS_{s,t,1}|+...+k|\Delta PSS_{s,t,n}| =$$

$$=| DESIRE_{s,t,1}|+...+k|DESIRE_{s,t,n}| \qquad (9)$$

It is important that this *general formula of attention* includes within itself the formula for attention to a single phenomenon (Eq. 3) as a particular case, corresponding to the situation when n = 1, when one phenomenon consumes all attention (see Eq. 13).

$$ATTmax_{s,t} = ATTtotal_{s,t} = k|DESIRE_{s,t,1}| \qquad (10)$$

Let's find out how the general formula of attention works with some combinations of values of its variables/parameters, and how the formula's implications reflect reality.

Change of Desirability and Redistribution of Attention

Here we will consider what happens with distribution of attention if desirability of one of the n simultaneously perceived phenomena changes.

Case 1: Change of *positive* desirability of the phenomenon X; $DESIRE_{s,x} > 0$.

If positive desire grows, then its magnitude or strength ($|DESIRE_{s,x}|$) gets larger. According to Eq. 3 ($ATT_{s,x} = k|DESIRE_{s,x}|$), attention towards the phenomenon grows together with the *strength of the desire* for it.

With the additional attention paid to one of the n phenomena, this particular one will move up in the 'attention hierarchy'; it will get an *attention 'promotion'*. This phenomenon would rise in the hierarchy of the attention levels corresponding to n different phenomena perceived at the same time (t).

$$ATTs,t,1 > ATTs,t,2 > ... > ATTs,t,n \qquad (11)$$

Its position will move from right to left in Eq. 11 and its number (n) will *decrease* until it becomes the *number one* (n=1) phenomenon – one in the center of attention. The reverse process of an *attention 'demotion'* occurs when the strength of desirability of the phenomenon decreases.

Attention 'promotion' and 'demotion', as prescribed by Eq. 9, do take place in reality. A good illustration of such a promotion is provided by taking note of a growing desire corresponding to an ongoing unsatisfied need. Such a desire strengthens until it gets into the center of attention of a subject, together with the objects and ways of its satisfaction. In the course of satisfaction of a need, the reverse process takes place. Desire gets weaker, and the attention paid to the objects and actions of satisfaction for this desire decreases, and as such, these objects and acts move out from the center of the subject's attention to its periphery, and finally completely out of the attention's range. The center of attention gets overtaken by the phenomenon that is next in the desire strength hierarchy.

Case 2: Change of *negative* desirability (undesirability) of X: $DESIRE_{s,x} < 0$.

If negative desire grows, the magnitude of its undesirability ($|DESIRE_x|$) gets larger. Eq. 3 shows that attention towards the phenomenon grows together with the strength or magnitude of its *undesirability*. As in Case #1, with the additional attention paid to one of the n phenomena, that particular one will move up in the attention hierarchy, and will earn an attention promotion. A good illustration of the cases where attention grows toward *undesirables* is provided by any kind of the increase of unpleasantness, discomfort or pain. The more unpleasant and undesirable something becomes to a subject, the more attention is drawn thereto.

Comment about Cases 1 and 2: The similarity in changes of attention in the above Cases 1 and 2 illustrates the independence of attention paid to a phenomenon from the positive or negative sign of its desirability. Attention to X is "blind" to the sign of X's desirability, and it is so for a good reason - animals and humans alike should pay attention to both pleasures of life and its pitfalls in order to act upon them.

Hedonic 'Pricing' and Redistribution of Attention

Let us suppose that a subject perceives the same n phenomena for a given time when $ATTmax_{s,t} = ATTtotal_{s,t}$, but the attention that is required for one of n phenomena grows.

$$ATTmax_{s,t} = ATTtotal_{s,t} =$$

$$= ATT_{s,t,1} + ... + ATT_{s,t,n} =$$

$$= k|DESIRE_{s,t,1}| + ... + k|DESIRE_{s,t,n}| \qquad (12)$$

This formula shows that as one of the n phenomena (number x <= n) gathers more attention, then the other (n-1) phenomena will have less attention left to them. If the maximum of available attention ($ATTmax_{s,t}$) is not used up ($ATTmax_{s,t}$ < $ATTtotal_{s,t}$), then the total disbursed attention ($ATTtotal_{s,t}$) can be increased up to the level of $ATTmax_{s,t}$. Conversely, if the maximum of available attention is already used up ($ATTmax_{s,t} = ATTtotal_{s,t}$), then the total of available attention ($ATTtotal_{s,t}$) must be redistributed. If the remainder of attention is not enough for the rest (n-1) of the evident phenomena, then some of them will receive no attention at all. Hence, a reduction of the number (n) of the perceived phenomena takes place. At this point, attention becomes more focused or narrowed. If attention to X grows so much that it requires *all* of the available attention of a subject, then all of it has to be spent on X only:

$$ATTmax_{s,t} = ATTtotal_{s,t} = ATT_{s,t,x} \tag{13}$$

It may be that an adult deeply concentrated on inner thoughts, or a child running after a ball, may not pay enough attention to that oncoming car. The more concentrated a subject is on something, the more difficult it will be for anything else to catch one's attention. And conversely, if the concentration of attention for a subject is low, then any new phenomena can easily get to the center of attention. For example, a bored child in the classroom is just looking for anything new to switch attention to.

A good example of the narrowing down of attention is the case when a need of a subject has not been satisfied for a long period of time. (A 'long' period of time can be probably defined as a multiple of the regular or average period of time between satisfactions of this need). In this case, objects and activities associated with satisfaction of the subject's need usually become both more pleasant and desirable (due to alliesthesia), and demand more and more attention. They gradually push everything out of the center of the subject's attention to the periphery. Eventually the objects and activities of this need's satisfaction become 'super-values' for that moment.

This converges with one of the basic postulates of Ethology, as described by Cabanac (2000, p. 1): "One basic postulate of Ethology is that behavior tends to satisfy the most urgent need of the behaving subject (Tinbergen, 1950; Baerends, 1956)", because the strongest desire corresponds to the 'most urgent need' of this postulate. As James (1927) said: "What holds attention determines action" (p. 448).

If James is right, then the 'division of labor' between desiring and liking in regard to choice and action seems to be as follows: desire (strength) determines *what* gets in the center of attention, holds it and is acted upon, while liking/disliking defines the *type of an action* as positive/negative, accepting/rejecting, consuming/destroying, assimilation/fight-or-flight correspondingly.

Change of the Objects of Attention

At any moment, new phenomenon can appear and make demands on a subject's attention. The following redistribution of attention can result in possible promotion of a hedonically important new phenomenon to the center of attention. This can be as sudden and unpredictable as its appearance.

The stage of the attention distribution described by Eq. 13 can be reached at once in the case of a hedonically significant new phenomenon, like an unforeseen extreme danger or excitement. For example, while walking down the street one perceives numerous objects but pays little attention to most of them. A subject can see many cars on the street and pay little or no attention to them. However, the distribution of a subject's attention changes right away with the recognition of a friend inside a car, or when it seems that one of these cars is going to hit the subject.

Maslow's Pyramid of Needs in Real Time as a Table of the Current Desires

It is generally accepted that animals and humans alike are driven by satisfaction of their needs and that the composition of the human needs is represented by Maslow's pyramid of needs. Let's transform Maslow's pyramid of needs into a table of desires generated by these needs, and sort them by their current strength in descending order. This way the strongest desire will be represented by the element number one on the top of this table. Let's also include in this table all other desires experienced by a subject at the moment. This would include unique, occasional, discrete desires of a subject (versus repetitious, cyclical desires of needs).

Such a table can be very informative in describing the motivational state of a subject, her/his preferences at the moment, especially if this table is constantly re-sorted by the desire's strength. It is important because the stronger desire is the more attention it gets. The strongest desire, its objects and associated with it activities have the highest probability to get in the center of attention of a subject, to stay in it, and to be acted upon.

Voluntary Attention

By a certain age humans become able to somewhat control their attention. This ability is called voluntary attention and is considered to be attention driven by will or will effort. The question is - how do attention and will connect and interact?

Voluntary Attention and Will Effort

The history of philosophy presents a substantial collection of notions on will. According to Bourke (1964), there are "... eight distinctive views" of these notions "taken by Western thinkers" (p. 8). The point of view on will effort discussed here has a lot in common with some of these meanings, i.e., understandings of will as an "intelligent preference", a "rational appetite", a "dynamic power" (Bourke, 1964, pp. 9-13).

Locke (1690/1824) asserted, that "...the will in truth signifies nothing but a power, or ability, to prefer or choose..." (p. 229, Book 2, § 17, Edit 12). It would be, probably, better to say that will signifies nothing but a power, or ability of a subject, to *influence* one's own preference or choice. The difference is significant because choice does not employ will at all times. A lot of common choices are 'will-effortless', do not involve will. Desires are often quite sufficient for determining choice. Animals and human infants can be said *not* to possess will, but they certainly have needs and desires, display preferences and choose. As Vilunas (1976) has noted[9], "Will effort is necessary while one has to act either without an immediate emotional impulse or against it, when, for example, one has to restrain anger, interrupt an exciting activity, or ignore physical pain, etc." (p. 51).

There is an important difference between choice made with and without the involvement of will. Without the will's participation, elements of choice are usually (1) first evaluated by a subject and then (2) a choice of one of these elements is made based upon the balance of their desirablities. This algorithm is *reversed* in the case when a choice is made with participation of the will: choice is made first (1), often by a rational decision and then (2) is enforced by the will effort that re-estimates and outright adjusts desirabilities of the elements of choice in order to support the predetermined preference. Such an 'unnatural' algorithm of choice made by will is the main reason why this voluntary type of choice needs the reinforcement of the will effort. Will always fights off other choices that might have otherwise prevailed.

Hedonistic Choice and Will Effort

The above exercised approach to attention suggests that for a phenomenon to be in the center of attention of a subject, to be chosen, it must have the dominant hedonic importance for that subject at that time, i.e., it must be 'the number one phenomenon' - the one with the greatest strength/magnitude of desirability (see Eq. 8). The essence of the will effort is in shifting desirability balance in favor of a predetermined phenomenon. According to Eq. 8, this shift can be implemented by one of these two following ways or by both of them applied together:

1. By maximizing the hedonic importance or magnitude of desirability for the pre-chosen phenomenon (will's end) by stimulating a corresponding hedonic association with it, such as thinking of or imagining an associated P/U, hedonic reward/punishment;
2. By minimizing the magnitude of desirability of phenomena competing with a pre-chosen one.

Let's consider a simple case of a choice between just two phenomena, A and B, with corresponding desires DES_a and DES_b.

Phenomenon A is chosen, is in the center of attention of a subject if,

$$|DES_a| > |DES_b|. \tag{14}$$

Buridan's ass case corresponds to:

$$|DES_a| = |DES_b|. \tag{15}$$

Phenomenon A is *not* chosen if,

$$|DES_a| < |DES_b|. \tag{16}$$

Let's consider the last case (Eq. 16) when phenomenon A is not chosen at the moment, but the subject has made a conscious, rational decision to choose A over B that requires what is described by Eq. 14. To accomplish this s/he has to apply will effort (WE in short) strong enough to shift the balance of desirabilities from the situation described by Eq. 16 to Eq. 14. Mathematically speaking this means that:

$$|DES_a + WE| > |DES_b| \tag{17}$$

or

$$|DES_a| > |DES_b - WE| \tag{18}$$

Equations 14 - 18 are similar to the formulas offered by William James (1927, p. 444) who spoke about a subject conquering and overcoming impulses and temptations in the chapter 'Will' of his book:

The facts can be most briefly symbolized thus, P standing for propensity, I for ideal impulse, and E for the effort:

I per se < P.

I + E > P.

In other words, if E adds itself to I, P immediately offers the least resistance, and motion occurs in spite of it.

What is presented as will effort ("WE") in Equations 17 and 18 has to be a variable of the same nature as other members of the equation in order to be added to them. The other two elements are desires or changes of the PSS. Therefore, what is coded as WE must also be a change of the PSS (ΔPSS) or desire created by the will effort, desire being a function of will: $WE = \Delta PSS_{we}$. As Kant (1785/1983, p. 11) wrote, "The faculty of desire whose internal ground of determination and, consequently, even whose liking [das Belieben) is found in reason of the subject is called the will".

Accordingly, Eq. 17 can be rewritten as follows:

$$|DES_a + \Delta PSS_{we}| > |DES_b| \tag{19a}$$

or

$$|DES_a + DES_{we}| > |DES_b|. \tag{19b}$$

Will effort can be also applied to a *competing* element of choice in order to reduce its desirability:

$$|DES_a| > |DES_b - DES_{we}|, \tag{19c}$$

Of course, will effort (ΔPSS_{we}) may not be strong enough to change the choice, to suppress the dominating desire. This case seems to correspond to the case of *akrasia,* or weakness of will.

Will Effort as Effort of Attention

There is another question about will that needs to be answered: how can a subject voluntarily, by using will effort, change a hedonic value of an element of choice, an attitude or desire toward it? William James (1927) wrote: "Volitional effort is effort of attention" (p. 450), "Effort of attention is thus the essential phenomenon of the will" (p. 452). But what does an "effort of attention" get done and how? According to James (1927, p. 452):

The strong-willed man, however, is the man who hears the still small voice unflinchingly, and who, when the death-bringing consideration comes, looks at its face, consents to its presence, clings to it, affirms it, and holds it fast, in spite of the host of exciting mental images which rise in revolt against it and would expel it from the mind. Sustained in this way by a resolute effort of attention, the difficult object erelong begins to call its own congeners and associates and ends by changing the disposition of the man's consciousness altogether.

The dialectical approach, as well as common sense, tells us that any phenomenon has its good and bad aspects for a subject, with positive and negative sides. Evaluating a phenomenon involves estimating these sides and coming up with their total in a way that helps determine an attitude toward it. Hedonic integration[10] facilitates the summation of this total. The more attention is paid to one side of a phenomenon the more influence it has on the total hedonic value of the phenomenon as a whole.

Just by controlling one's attention, by applying voluntary attention, one can concentrate more on the positive sides of a phenomenon and turn a blind eye to negative sides, thus shifting the balance of positivity or negativity of this phenomenon by one's own volition. Concentrating more on the fullness or emptiness of that 50% measured bottle, one can adjust one's perception of it, to be half full or half empty. The downside of this is that our attitudes can be somewhat off the mark or one-sided. The upside of this process is that it gives humans their summary attitudes and some measure of will power.

The control of attention or the usage of voluntary attention is the essence of will, as James has asserted, because attention is the will's executor. A level of mastery of this control determines the scope of freedom for a subject's will. Damasio wrote (1994, p. 175):

Willpower draws on the evaluation of a prospect, and that evaluation may not take place if attention is not properly driven to both the immediate trouble and the future payoff, to both the suffering now and the future gratification. Remove the latter and you remove the lift from under your willpower's wings. Willpower is just another name for the idea of choosing according to long-term outcomes rather than short-term ones.

Affective (Arnold, 1970) or hedonic memories can be retrieved by remembering or imagining something emotionally/hedonically charged, and this is exactly what will effort accomplishes. Will effort deliberately activates emotional/hedonic memories of a subject by insistently reminding a subject about certain features or consequences of choice and/or making a subject imagine these consequences. Will effort directs the attention of a subject toward those features of the elements of choice that change their desirabilities, and, therefore, their balance, in ways advantageous for the will's goal. Suppression of the leading desire can, of course, be produced by weakening it by closure of the hedonic gap of this desire, i.e., by lowering the anticipated or experienced pleasantness of the desired object ("poisoning" it for a subject), or by minimizing unpleasantness of the undesired one.

Will influences the subject's choice from the inside in the same way that other people, and society at large, do it from the outside - by reminding a subject about the consequences of these choices, and the external and internal rewards and punishments associated therewith. When imposed by will, however, these rewards and punishments are self-inflicted and self-determined which apparently qualifies such a will effort to be categorized as "free", and will's guidance of attention as being voluntary.

While willing oneself, a subject often talks to him- or herself internally or even externally – s/he recalls propositional attitudes of beliefs, deliberates, argues, shames him- or herself, etc. This verbalization may hold the key to understanding mechanism of the will effort. It is proven that words and propositions are emotionally, and therefore, hedonically charged. Humans, and only humans, possess this way to influence their own and others' PSS through language. Only normal and mature enough humans with the command of language possess will power, because only they can discuss with themselves the pros and cons of X and Y, and talk themselves into one behavior and against another.

FUTURE RESEARCH DIRECTIONS

Formalization of any process in mathematical terms paves the way for creation of its computer model. The author believes that proposed models of desire, need, attention, and will effort can be computerized and implemented by Artificial Intelligence. These models need to be developed further in greater detail. They also need experimental verification, though the model of desire presented here has experimental support (Ovsich & Cabanac, 2012).

One of the questions to be pursued further is about the relationship between desire and attitude. Desire is understood here as a kind of a relative attitude that depends on the relative positions of two points on the hedonic continuum, versus, so to speak, an "absolute" attitude of liking that is determined by only one such point. This view does not directly contradict the currently common, though contested (Nanay, 2013), categorization of desire as a propositional attitude. However, it should be taken into consideration that, "Despite its central place in explaining human behavior (Allport, 1935), there is no universally agreed upon definition of what precisely is represented by an attitude" (O'Reilly, Roche & Cartwright, 2015, p. 162).

CONCLUSION

The author has presented here new, closely linked mathematical models of desire, need and attention (including voluntary attention driven by the will effort) based upon the Hedonistic Principle. According to the Hedonistic Principle, subjects are motivated/driven to maximize pleasantness of their internal state (Pleasantness of the State of the Subject (PSS)). Hence:

1. The (most) important characteristic of any phenomenon (X) for such a subject (S) should be how much X influences the process of the PSS maximization that is measured by the PSS change associated with X ($\Delta PSS_{s,x}$). The author proposes that the terms 'desire', 'want' and their cognates describe the PSS change associated with (caused by) X:

$$DESIRE_{s,x} = \Delta PSS_{s,x}$$

If $\Delta PSS_{s,x} > 0$, then x is called "desirable".
If $\Delta PSS_{s,x} < 0$, then x is called "undesirable".

The magnitude of the PSS change is what is called the "strength of desire":

Strength of S desire for X = $|DESIRE_{s,x}|$ =
= $|\Delta PSS_{s,x}|$

The author posits that the desirability of X is determined by the PSS change (ΔPSS) while the liking/disliking of X is determined by the end level of this PSS change.

Experiencing a need means feeling the corresponding desire. If a subject experiences a desire for X repeatedly or regularly, it is usually said that the subject needs X. Need for X is defined here as a recurring, periodic desire of X.

2. The more X affects the process of the PSS maximization, the more attention a subject should pay to it:

$$ATTENTION_{s,x} \sim |\Delta PSS_{s,x}| \sim |DESIRE_{s,x}| = k|DESIRE_{s,x}|$$

According to this formula, attention is "blind" to the sign of desire, depends only on its strength. Zero desire gets zero attention, and this works as a powerful hedonic filter facilitating efficient utilization of the finite resources of animals and humans alike.

Considering that attention has an upper limit ($ATTmax_{s,t}$), and that the overall attention ($ATTtotal_{s,t}$) of a subject (S) at any moment (t) is distributed between a number (n) of phenomena in proportion with their desirability strength, the following formula is proposed:

$$ATTmax_{s,t} >= ATTtotal_{s,t} =$$

$$= k|\Delta PSS_{s,t,1}| + \ldots + k|\Delta PSS_{s,t,n}| =$$

$$= |DESIRE_{s,t,1}| + \ldots + k|DESIRE_{s,t,n}|$$

The phenomenon with strongest desirability/undesirability gets to the center of attention.

It is generally accepted that animals and humans alike are driven by satisfaction of their needs, and that the basic composition of human needs is represented by Maslow's pyramid. The author's definition of a need as a periodic desire, combined with a mathematical model of desire, allows for the creation of the real time representation of Maslow's pyramid of needs in action. The author suggests transforming Maslow's pyramid of needs into a table of desires generated by these needs. Elements of this table should be sorted by the current strength of desires in descending order. This way the strongest desire will be represented by the number one element on the "top" of this table. This table should also incorporate occasional, discrete desires of a subject in addition to repetitious, cyclical desires of needs.

Such a table can be informative in describing the motivational state of a subject, and the subject's preferences at the moment.[11] The strongest desire, along with its associated objects and activities, have the highest probability of getting to the center of attention of a subject, and of being acted upon. For humans, possible influence of the will effort in suppressing or supporting desires should be taken into consideration. The essence of the will effort is in shifting desirability balance and, therefore, distribution of attention in favor of a predetermined phenomenon.

REFERENCES

Aristotle, . (2004). *Rhetoric* (T. W. Rhys, Trans.). Dover Publications.

Arnold, M. B. (1970). Perennial Problems in the Field of Emotion. In *Feelings and Emotion* (pp. 169–185). New York: Academic Press.

Arpaly, N., & Schroeder, T. (2014). *In Praise of Desire*. Oxford, UK: Oxford University Press.

Audi, R. (1993). *Action, Intention, and Reason*. Ithaca, NY: Cornell University Press.

Barrett, L. F. (2006). Valence is a basic building block of emotional life. *Journal of Research in Personality*, *40*(1), 35–55. doi:10.1016/j.jrp.2005.08.006

Berridge, K. (2004). Motivation concepts in behavioral neuroscience. *Physiology & Behavior*, *81*(2), 179–209. doi:10.1016/j.physbeh.2004.02.004 PMID:15159167

Bourke, V. J. (1964). *Will in Western thought*. New York: Sheed and Ward.

Cabanac, M. (1971). Physiological role of pleasure. *Science*, *173*(4002), 1103–1107. doi:10.1126/science.173.4002.1103 PMID:5098954

Cabanac, M. (1992). Pleasure: The common currency. *Journal of Theoretical Biology*, *155*(2), 173–200. doi:10.1016/S0022-5193(05)80594-6 PMID:12240693

Cabanac, M. (2000). Pleasure, the prerational intelligence. In H. Ritter, H. Cruse, & J. Dean (Eds.), *Prerational Intelligence: Adaptive Behavior and Intelligent Systems Without Symbols and Logic* (pp. 201–213). Dordrecht: Kluwer Academis Publishers.

Cabanac, M. (2010). The Fifth Influence. The Dialectics of Pleasure. iUniverse Books.

Corns, J. (2014). Unpleasantness, motivational oomph, and painfulness. *Mind and Language*, *29*(2), 238-254.

Csikszentmihalyi, M. (1978). Attention and the Holistic Approach to Behavior. In The Stream of consciousness: scientific investigations into the flow of human experience (pp. 335-358). New York: Plenum Press.

Damasio A. R. (1994). *Descartes' Error: Emotion, Reason, and the Human Brain*. Bard, an Avon Book.

De Sousa, R. (2011). *Emotional Truth*. New York: Oxford University Press, Inc.

DeLancey, C. (2002). *Passionate Engines: What Emotions Reveal About Mind and Artificial Intelligence*. Oxford, UK: Oxford University Press. doi:10.1093/0195142713.001.0001

Dennett, D. C. (1990). Cognitive Wheels: The Frame Problem of AI. In M. E. Boden (Ed.), *The philosophy of artificial intelligence* (pp. 147–171). Oxford, UK: Oxford University Press.

Douglas, V. I., & Peters, K. G. (1979). Clearer Definition of Attentional Deficit. In G. A. Hale & M. Lewis (Eds.), *Attention and cognitive development*. New York: Plenum Press. doi:10.1007/978-1-4613-2985-5_8

Edwards, R. B. (1979). *Pleasures and Pains*. Ithaca, London: Cornell University Press.

Frankfurt, H. G. (2004). *The reasons of love*. Princeton, N.J.: Princeton University Press.

James, W. (1927). *Psychology*. New York: Henry Holt and Company.

Johnston, V. (1999). *Why We Feel. The Science of Human Emotions*. Reading, MA: Perseus Books.

Kahneman, D., Diener, E., & Schwartz, N. (1999). *Well-Being: The Foundations of Hedonic Psychology*. New York: Russel Sage Foundation.

Kant, I. (1798). Anthropology from a pragmatic point of view (M. J. Gregor, Trans.). The Hague, The Netherlands: Martinus Nijhoff.

Kant, I. (1929). Selections (T. M. Greene, Ed.). New York: Charles Scribner's Sons.

Kant, I. (1983). *Ethical Philosophy the complete texts of GROUNDINGS for the METAPHYSICS of MORALS and METAPHYSICAL PRINCIPLES OF VIRTUE (Part II of the Metaphysics of Morals)* (J. W. Ellington, Trans.). Hackett Publishing Co.(Original work published 1785)

Katz, L. D. (2005). Three Faces of Desire. *Philosophical Reviews, University of Notre Dame*. Retrieved 14 September 2015 from http://ndpr.nd.edu/review.cfm?id=3861

Kenny, A. (1963). *Action, Emotion, and Will*. London: Routledge and Kegan Paul.

Konstan, D. (2006). *The Emotions of the Ancient Greeks: Studies in Aristotle and Classical Literature (Robson Classical Lectures)*. Toronto: University of Toronto Press. doi:10.3138/9781442674370

Locke, D. (1982). Beliefs, Desires and Reasons for Actions. *American Philosophical Quarterly*, *19*, 241–249.

Locke, J. (1690/1824). An Essay Concerning Human Understanding. London: Baldwin. doi:10.1093/oseo/instance.00018020

Marks, J. (Ed.). (1986). The Ways of Desire: New Essays in Philosophical Psychology on the Concept of Wanting. Chicago: Precedent Publishing.

McCarthy, J. (1968). Programs with Common Sense Proceedings of the Teddington Conference on the Mechanization of Thought Processes. In M. Minsky (Ed.), *Semantic Information Processing* (pp. 403-418). Cambridge, MA: MIT Press.

McFarland, D. (2008). *Guilty Robots, Happy Dogs: The Question of Alien Minds*. Oxford, UK: Oxford University Press.

Mill, J. S. (1957). *Utilitarianism* (O. Priest, Ed.). New York: Macmillan. (Original work published 1861)

Nanay, B. (2013). *Between Perception and Action*. Oxford, UK: Oxford University Press. doi:10.1093/acprof:oso/9780199695379.001.0001

O'Reilly, A. G., Roche, B., & Cartwright, A. (2015). Function over Form: A Behavioral Approach to Implicit Attitudes. In Z. Jin (Ed.), *Exploring Implicit Cognition: Learning, Memory, and Social Cognitive Processes*. IGI Global. doi:10.4018/978-1-4666-6599-6.ch008

Ovsich, A., & Cabanac, M. (2012). Experimental Support of the Mathematical Model of Desire. *International Journal of Psychological Studies.*, *4*(1), 66–75. doi:10.5539/ijps.v4n1p66

Ovsich, A. J. (1998a). Outlines of the Theory of Choice: Attitude, Desire, Attention, Will. *Intelligent Control (ISIC), 1998. Held jointly with IEEE International Symposium on Computational Intelligence in Robotics and Automation (CIRA), Intelligent Systems and Semiotics (ISAS), Proceedings* (pp. 503-510). doi.org/doi:<ALIGNMENT.qj></ALIGNMENT>10.1109/ISIC.1998.713713

Ovsich, A. J. (1998b). Outlines of the Theory of Choice: Attitude, Desire, Attention, Will. *Proceedings of the 1998 Twentieth World Congress of Philosophy*. Retrieved 14 September 2015 from http://www.bu.edu/wcp/Papers/Acti/ActiOvsi.htm

Ovsich, A. J. (2012). Mathematical Models of Desire, Need and Attention. In *Proceedings of AISB/IACAP World Congress 2012*. Retrieved from http://events.cs.bham.ac.uk/turing12/proceedings/03.pdf

Plutchik, R. (1980). *Emotion. A psychoevolutionary Synthesis*. New York: Harper & Row.

Rado, S. (1964). Hedonic Self-Regulation of the Organism. In R. G. Heath (Ed.), *The Role of Pleasure in Behavior* (pp. 257–264). New York: Harper & Row.

Robinson & Berridge. (2015). *Wanting vs Needing* (2nd ed.). International Encyclopedia of the Social & Behavioral Sciences. doi:10.1016/B978-0-08-097086-8.26091-1

Rubinshteòin, S. L. (1957). *Bytie I soznanie; o meste psikhicheskogo vo vseobshcheòi vzaimosvþiÆazi þiÆavleniòi materialñnogo mira.* Moskva: Izd-vo Akademii nauk SSSR.

Russell, B. (1921). *The Analysis of Mind.* London: G. Allen & Unwin, Ltd.

Russell, J. A. (2003). Core affect and the psychological construction of emotion. *Psychological Review, 110*(1), 145–172. doi:10.1037/0033-295X.110.1.145 PMID:12529060

Schroeder, T. (2004). *Three Faces of Desire.* Oxford, UK: Oxford University Press. doi:10.1093/acprof:oso/9780195172379.001.0001

Schueler, G. F. (1995). Desire. Its Role in Practical Reason and the Explanation of Action. Cambridge, MA: MIT Press.

Spinoza, B. (1955). *On the Improvement of the Understanding. The Ethics. Correspondence.* New York: Dover Publications, Inc.(Original work published 1674)

Staude, M. (1986). Wanting, Desiring and Valuing: The Case against Conativism. In J. Marks (Ed.), *The Ways of Desire: New Essays in Philosophical Psychology on the Concept of Wanting* (pp. 175–198). Chicago: Precedent Publishing, Inc.

Strawson, G. (2010). Mental Reality. Cambridge, MA: MIT Press.

Tailor, C. C. W. (1986). Emotions and Wants. In J. Marks (Ed.), *The Ways of Desire: New Essays in Philosophical Psychology on the Concept of Wanting* (pp. 217–231). Chicago: Precedent Publishing.

Vilunas, V. K. (1976). Psychology of the Emotional Phenomena. Moscow: Moscow University.

Young, P. T. (1961). *Motivation and Emotion.* New York: John Wiley & Sons, Inc.

ADDITIONAL READING

Frankfurt, H. G. (1999). *Necessity, Volition, and Love*. Cambridge University Press.

Pugh, G.E. *The Biological Origin of Human Values*. New York: Basic Books, Inc., Publishers.

Searle, J. R. (1997). *The Mystery of Consciousness*. New York: The New York Review of Books.

KEY TERMS AND DEFINITIONS

Attention: At any given moment, the activity of a subject's perception, called 'attention', is distributed between multitudes of simultaneously perceived phenomena. The author proposes that the total volume of attention ($ATTtotal_{s,t}$) for a subject (S) perceiving n phenomena at the moment (t) has an upper limit ($ATTmax_{s,t}$) and can be described as the sum of attention paid to each phenomenon: $ATTmax_{s,t} >= ATTtotal_{s,t} == k|\Delta PSS_{s,t,1}| + ... + k|\Delta PSS_{s,t,n}| = |DESIRE_{s,t,1}| + ... + k|DESIRE_{s,t,n}|$ This formula describes the distribution of attention between n simultaneously perceived phenomena in proportion with their desire's strength. According to this formula, the largest portion of attention is allocated to the phenomenon causing (associated with) the largest positive or negative PSS change - one that is most desirable or undesirable, and corresponds to the *strongest desire*. This situation is usually described as the phenomenon being in the center of attention. Distribution of attention can be influenced by the will effort.

Desire: The author posits that the subject's (S) desire for X is a word used to describe a change of the Pleasantness of the State of this Subject ($\Delta PSS_{s,x}$) associated with X, where X can be an object or an activity, perceived, remembered, or imagined. Desirability/undesirability of X for S is an ability of X to maximize/minimize the PSS. $DESIRE_{s,x} = \Delta PSS_{s,x}$. If $\Delta PSS_{s,x} > 0$, then x is called "desirable". If $\Delta PSS_{s,x} < 0$, then x is called "undesirable". Strength of S desire for $X = |DESIRE_{s,x}| = |\Delta PSS_{s,x}|$.

Happiness: Maximization of the PSS has an upper limit; this limit, representing the most pleasant internal state possible, is called "happiness". In other words, the state of happiness is an upper limit of the PSS maximization.

Hedonic Recognition: In the process of the Object Recognition, an Object is not only recognized and categorized as a banana, a chair, John, etc., but also recognized hedonically as pleasant/unpleasant (P/U), liked/disliked, desirable/undesirable. The author calls the latter form of recognition "Hedonic Recognition", that is, recognition of the hedonic properties of a phenomenon. In the process of the Object Recognition, that includes Hedonic Recognition, the PSS of the subject changes from the antecedent level PSS_1 to the end result level PSS_2. This hedonic transition creates a PSS change: $\Delta PSS = PSS_2 - PSS_1$. The author posits that the desirability of X is determined by the PSS change (ΔPSS), while the liking/disliking of X is defined by the end level of this change (PSS_2).

Hedonistic Principle: Animals and humans alike are motivated/driven to maximize the pleasantness of their internal state called here the Pleasantness of the State of the Subject (PSS).

Need: Experiencing a need means feeling the corresponding desire. A need is characterized by the strength and frequency of its desire. If a subject experiences a desire for X repeatedly, periodically, it is usually said that the subject *needs* X. This is clearly demonstrated by the needs that emerge and cease to exist with age or during changing circumstances, for example, the needs for sex, smoking, or drugs. The origination/disappearance of such needs is acknowledged when the corresponding desire begins/stops being recurrent. *Need is defined here as a term used for a periodic or cyclical desire.* This is true for all kinds of needs - physiological, psychological, pathological needs of addictions, etc.

Pleasantness/Unpleasantness (P/U): P/U is one of many antagonistic pairs of expressions commonly used to describe positive/negative orientation to a phenomenon. A subject experiences orientation to the perceived phenomena - positive, negative or indifferent that is categorized by that human subject as P, U or indifferent. The only attribute that is common to all the numerous P/U phenomena is the +/- orientation of the subject toward it. This attribute, or quality of phenomena, is usually labeled as 'pleasantness' and 'unpleasantness'. This is the *meaning of P/U*. As Kant (1798, p. 99) has asserted: "Enjoyment is pleasure through the senses, and what delights the senses is called agreeable. Pain is displeasure through the senses, and what produces it is disagreeable. ... We can also describe these feelings in terms of the effect that the sensation of our state produces on our mind. What directly (by the senses) prompts me to leave my state (to go out of it) is disagreeable to me - it pains me. What directly prompts me to maintain this state (to remain in it) is agreeable to me - it delights me." Referring to pleasure, Edwards (1979, p. 95) wrote: "Rather it means "the set of all feelings for which we have a psychic tension or attraction," and no circularity is involved. Similarly, "pain" in the generic sense means "the set of all feelings against which we have a psychic tension or aversion." The disposition to continue or to interrupt the current experience, to approach or avoid an action, or the tendency to go on or to stop, are the common features of pleasant or unpleasant experiences. A similar position is taken by Kahneman (1999, pp. 5, 8) in his definition of pleasantness/utility/Good-Bad dimension. In some primal form, the mechanism of a positive/negative orientation exists in the most primitive of organisms, because any life form, regardless of its level of complexity, has to be involved in a selective exchange with its environment, i.e. choice or orientation (see Rado, 1964, p. 260; Johnston, 1999, pp. 66 - 67). "Pleasantness" and "unpleasant-ness" are considered in this work to be the most common terms used to describe an intentional, orientational quality of attractiveness/repulsiveness, which are the two existing types of orientation. *The acceptability or P/U of a phenomenon to a subject are terms indicating a +/- orientation of a subject toward the phenomenon.* Other feasible terms would be "agreeableness" (Kant, 1929, p. 290), or "agreability" (Edwards, 1979, p. 43), because *the meaning of P/U of x is the positive/negative acceptability, agreeableness, or agreability of x.* P/U are labels for the tendencies of the attraction/repulsion felt by a subject toward the phenomenon. They describe a vector of orientation so they are in turn vectors themselves. Their magnitude de-scribes the degree or 'strength' of orientation. Their positive or negative designation describes the direction of orientation - toward or away from the object.

Pleasantness of the State of a Subject (PSS): There are at least seven compo-nents of the stream of consciousness which possess their own, intrinsic P/U that are usually experienced in the organ of the sensation: algic (pain), emotional[12], gustatory, olfactory, spatial, tactile, thermal sensations. A subject can experience all of them at once, or any number of them at the same time. This is one good reason to look for more precision and clarity while referring to pleasure and pain in order to clarify which one or ones are referred to. This is why it makes sense to utilize an inclusive characteristic, or a measurement, of the combined or total P of the state of a subject that includes *all* P/U components of a subject's state. The author calls their combina-tion or aggregate a 'Pleasantness of the State of a Subject' (PSS in short). The PSS at the moment (t) is a sum of all P/U components of the stream of consciousness experienced at t: $PSS_t = P_{algic} + P_{emotion} + P_{gustatory} + P_{olfactory} + + P_{spatial} + P_{tactile} + P_{thermal}$. Dif-ferent types of P can be totaled in the formula above, because the same quality of pleasantness is added up and because P "summate algebraically" (Plutchick, 1980, p. 115; Kahneman 1999, p. 5).[13] The PSS is a sum of the P/U of all components of the stream of consciousness. In accordance with this definition, the PSS combines all the P/U, orientational or vectorial components of the stream of consciousness. Therefore, any influence on orientation ought to work through the PSS.

Will Effort: The essence of the will effort is to adjust the desirability balance in favor of a predetermined phenomenon. This can be done by strengthening the "favorite" desire or/and by weakening its competition. Will effort directs the atten-tion of a subject toward those features of the elements of choice that change their desirabilities and, therefore, their balance in ways advantageous for the will's goal. Will effort activates emotional/hedonic memories of a subject by insistently remind-ing a subject about certain features or consequences of the choice and/or making a subject imagine these consequences.

ENDNOTES

[1] See "Key Terms and Definitions".

[2] See "Key Terms and Definitions".

[3] Schroeder presented in his book "the third face of desire", his own reward and punishment theory of desire. For review of the theory see Katz (2005); for references to objections to it see Arpaly & Schroeder (2014, p. 127).

[4] See "Key Terms and Definitions".

[5] See Aristotle's quote in the paragraph "Hedonistic Approach to Desire".

[6] Translated by Ovsich.

[7] See, for example, Damasio, 1994, p. 199.

[8] The author suggests that in the first approximation, k is the same for all the simultaneous objects of attention.

[9] Translated by Ovsich.

[10] According to Plutchick (1980), "hedonic process summates algebraically" (p. 115). Also, see Cabanac (1992, p.182), Kahneman (1999, p. 5).

[11] Such a table can serve as a core of the hedonistic choice engine of an autonomous system, of a robot.

[12] Young (1961) describes experienced location of emotions as "thoracical" (p. 149).

[13] A PSS is quite close to what is called a Valence of the Core Affect in Russell (2003), Barrett (2006).

Compilation of References

To continue our tradition of advancing medicine, healthcare, and life sciences research, we have compiled a list of recommended IGI Global readings. These references will provide additional information and guidance to further enrich your knowledge and assist you with your own research and future publications.

Abu-Faraj, Z. O. (2012). Bioengineering/biomedical engineering education. In Z. Abu-Faraj (Ed.), *Handbook of research on biomedical engineering education and advanced bioengineering learning: Interdisciplinary concepts* (pp. 1–59). Hershey, PA: Medical Information Science Reference. doi:10.4018/978-1-4666-0122-2.ch001

Achehboune, A., & Driouchi, A. (2014). Potential skilled labor migration, internationalization of education with focus on medical education: The case of Arab countries. In A. Driouchi (Ed.), *Labor and health economics in the Mediterranean region: Migration and mobility of medical doctors* (pp. 83–122). Hershey, PA: Medical Information Science Reference. doi:10.4018/978-1-4666-4723-7.ch004

Adomi, E. E., Egbaivwie, E., & Ogugua, J. C. (2013). Use of the internet by medical practitioners in private hospitals in Warri, Delta State, Nigeria. In A. Cartelli (Ed.), *Fostering 21st century digital literacy and technical competency* (pp. 213–221). Hershey, PA: Information Science Reference. doi:10.4018/978-1-4666-2943-1.ch015

Afolabi, M. O., Babalola, O. O., & Ola-Olorun, O. J. (2012). Counselling in pharmacy practice: Exploring the use of online counselling interactions to improve medicine use among people living with HIV/AIDS (PLWHA). In B. Popoola & O. Adebowale (Eds.), *Online guidance and counseling: Toward effectively applying technology* (pp. 91–103). Hershey, PA: Information Science Reference. doi:10.4018/978-1-61350-204-4.ch007

Ahmad, Y. J., Raghavan, V. V., & Martz, W. B. Jr. (2011). Adoption of electronic health records. In *Clinical technologies: Concepts, methodologies, tools and applications* (pp. 132–146). Hershey, PA: Medical Information Science Reference. doi:10.4018/978-1-60960-561-2.ch109

Al-Dossary, S., Al-Dulaijan, N., Al-Mansour, S., Al-Zahrani, S., Al-Fridan, M., & Househ, M. (2013). Organ donation and transplantation: Processes, registries, consent, and restrictions in Saudi Arabia. In M. Cruz-Cunha, I. Miranda, & P. Gonçalves (Eds.), *Handbook of research on ICTs for human-centered healthcare and social care services* (pp. 511–528). Hershey, PA: Medical Information Science Reference. doi:10.4018/978-1-4666-3986-7.ch027

Al-Khudairy, S. (2014). Caring for our aging population: Using CPOE and tele-homecare systems as a response to health policy concerns. In C. El Morr (Ed.), *Research perspectives on the role of informatics in health policy and management* (pp. 153–166). Hershey, PA: Medical Information Science Reference. doi:10.4018/978-1-4666-4321-5.ch010

Albert, A., Serrano, A. J., Soria, E., & Jiménez, N. V. (2010). Clinical decision support system to prevent toxicity in patients treated with Digoxin. In A. Shukla & R. Tiwari (Eds.), *Intelligent medical technologies and biomedical engineering: Tools and applications* (pp. 1–21). Hershey, PA: Medical Information Science Reference. doi:10.4018/978-1-61520-977-4.ch001

Alexandrou, D. A., & Pardalis, K. V. (2014). SEMantic PATHways: Modeling, executing, and monitoring intra-organizational healthcare business processes towards personalized treatment. In *Software design and development: Concepts, methodologies, tools, and applications* (pp. 1036–1062). Hershey, PA: Information Science Reference. doi:10.4018/978-1-4666-4301-7.ch050

Alhaqbani, B., & Fidge, C. (2013). A medical data trustworthiness assessment model. In *User-driven healthcare: Concepts, methodologies, tools, and applications* (pp. 1425–1445). Hershey, PA: Medical Information Science Reference. doi:10.4018/978-1-4666-2770-3.ch071

Ali, S., Abbadeni, N., & Batouche, M. (2012). *Multidisciplinary computational intelligence techniques: Applications in business, engineering, and medicine* (pp. 1–365). Hershey, PA: IGI Global. doi:10.4018/978-1-4666-1830-5

Alonso, J. M., Castiello, C., Lucarelli, M., & Mencar, C. (2013). Modeling interpretable fuzzy rule-based classifiers for medical decision support. In *Data mining: Concepts, methodologies, tools, and applications* (pp. 1064–1081). Hershey, PA: Information Science Reference. doi:10.4018/978-1-4666-2455-9.ch054

Alonso-Barba, J. I., Nielsen, J. D., de la Ossa, L., & Puerta, J. M. (2012). Learning probabilistic graphical models: A review of techniques and applications in medicine. In R. Magdalena-Benedito, E. Soria-Olivas, J. Martínez, J. Gómez-Sanchis, & A. Serrano-López (Eds.), *Medical applications of intelligent data analysis: Research advancements* (pp. 223–236). Hershey, PA: Information Science Reference. doi:10.4018/978-1-4666-1803-9.ch015

Anderson, J. G. (2010). Improving patient safety with information technology. In K. Khoumbati, Y. Dwivedi, A. Srivastava, & B. Lal (Eds.), *Handbook of research on advances in health informatics and electronic healthcare applications: Global adoption and impact of information communication technologies* (pp. 144–152). Hershey, PA: Medical Information Science Reference. doi:10.4018/978-1-60566-030-1.ch009

Anderson, J. G. (2011). Regional patient safety initiatives. In *Clinical technologies: Concepts, methodologies, tools and applications* (pp. 1491–1503). Hershey, PA: Medical Information Science Reference. doi:10.4018/978-1-60960-561-2.ch506

Andonegui, J., Serrano, L., & Eguzkiza, A. (2010). E-health applications in ophthalmic diseases: Ongoing developments. In M. Cruz-Cunha, A. Tavares, & R. Simoes (Eds.), *Handbook of research on developments in e-health and telemedicine: Technological and social perspectives* (pp. 1088–1115). Hershey, PA: Medical Information Science Reference. doi:10.4018/978-1-61520-670-4.ch052

Andrés, A. R. (2014). Understanding the migration of medical doctors in the context of Europe. In A. Driouchi (Ed.), *Labor and health economics in the Mediterranean region: Migration and mobility of medical doctors* (pp. 139–157). Hershey, PA: Medical Information Science Reference. doi:10.4018/978-1-4666-4723-7.ch006

Ann, O. C., & Theng, L. B. (2014). A facial expression mediated natural user interface communication model for children with motor impairments. In G. Kouroupetroglou (Ed.), *Assistive technologies and computer access for motor disabilities* (pp. 254–284). Hershey, PA: Medical Information Science Reference. doi:10.4018/978-1-4666-4438-0.ch009

Anselma, L., Bottrighi, A., Molino, G., Montani, S., Terenziani, P., & Torchio, M. (2011). Supporting knowledge-based decision making in the medical context: The GLARE approach. *International Journal of Knowledge-Based Organizations, 1*(1), 42–60. doi:10.4018/ijkbo.2011010103

Apostolakis, I., Valsamos, P., & Varlamis, I. (2011). Quality assurance in evidence-based medicine. In A. Moumtzoglou & A. Kastania (Eds.), *E-health systems quality and reliability: Models and standards* (pp. 86–99). Hershey, PA: Medical Information Science Reference. doi:10.4018/978-1-61692-843-8.ch008

Archibald, D., MacDonald, C. J., Hogue, R., & Mercer, J. (2013). Accessing knowledge from the bedside: Introducing the tablet computer to clinical teaching. In C. Rückemann (Ed.), *Integrated information and computing systems for natural, spatial, and social sciences* (pp. 96–109). Hershey, PA: Information Science Reference. doi:10.4018/978-1-4666-2190-9.ch005

Aspradaki, A. A. (2013). Deliberative democracy and nanotechnologies in health. *International Journal of Technoethics*, *4*(2), 1–14. doi:10.4018/jte.2013070101

Assis-Hassid, S., Reychav, I., Pliskin, J. S., & Heart, T. H. (2013). The effects of electronic medical record (EMR) use in primary care on the physician-patient relationship. In M. Cruz-Cunha, I. Miranda, & P. Gonçalves (Eds.), *Handbook of research on ICTs for human-centered healthcare and social care services* (pp. 130–150). Hershey, PA: Medical Information Science Reference. doi:10.4018/978-1-4666-3986-7.ch007

Atanasov, A. (2011). Quality and reliability aspects in evidence based e-medicine. In A. Moumtzoglou & A. Kastania (Eds.), *E-health systems quality and reliability: Models and standards* (pp. 100–117). Hershey, PA: Medical Information Science Reference. doi:10.4018/978-1-61692-843-8.ch009

Attalla, D. S. (2011). Health hazards of mobile information communication technologies. In A. Abdel-Wahab & A. El-Masry (Eds.), *Mobile information communication technologies adoption in developing countries: Effects and implications* (pp. 237–251). Hershey, PA: Information Science Reference. doi:10.4018/978-1-61692-818-6.ch016

Au, S., & Gupta, A. (2011). Gastrointestinal motility online educational endeavor. In A. Moumtzoglou & A. Kastania (Eds.), *E-health systems quality and reliability: Models and standards* (pp. 163–182). Hershey, PA: Medical Information Science Reference. doi:10.4018/978-1-61692-843-8.ch014

Azar, A. T. (2013). Overview of biomedical engineering. In Bioinformatics: Concepts, methodologies, tools, and applications (pp. 1-28). Hershey, PA: Medical Information Science Reference. doi:10.4018/978-1-4666-3604-0.ch001

Azar, A. T., & Eljamel, M. S. (2014). Medical robotics. In Robotics: Concepts, methodologies, tools, and applications (pp. 1116-1147). Hershey, PA: Information Science Reference. doi:10.4018/978-1-4666-4607-0.ch054

Bagheri, F. B. (2013). eSelf or computerized self network: A tool for individual empowerment & implementation of optimal healthcare. *International Journal of User-Driven Healthcare, 3*(2), 20–32. doi:10.4018/ijudh.2013040103

Baharadwaj, N., Wadhwa, S., Goel, P., Sethi, I., Arora, C. S., Goel, A., & Parthasarathy, H. et al. (2014). De-noising, clustering, classification, and representation of microarray data for disease diagnostics. In R. Srivastava, S. Singh, & K. Shukla (Eds.), *Research developments in computer vision and image processing: Methodologies and applications* (pp. 149–174). Hershey, PA: Information Science Reference. doi:10.4018/978-1-4666-4558-5.ch009

Baijou, A. (2014). A descriptive overview of the emigration of medical doctors from MENA to EU. In A. Driouchi (Ed.), *Labor and health economics in the Mediterranean region: Migration and mobility of medical doctors* (pp. 192–218). Hershey, PA: Medical Information Science Reference. doi:10.4018/978-1-4666-4723-7.ch008

Bauer, K. (2010). Healthcare ethics in the information age. In J. Rodrigues (Ed.), *Health information systems: Concepts, methodologies, tools, and applications* (pp. 1761–1776). Hershey, PA: Medical Information Science Reference. doi:10.4018/978-1-60566-988-5.ch114

Bauer, K. A. (2013). Caught in the web: The internet and the demise of medical privacy. In *User-driven healthcare: Concepts, methodologies, tools, and applications* (pp. 1252–1272). Hershey, PA: Medical Information Science Reference. doi:10.4018/978-1-4666-2770-3.ch063

Bayona, S., Espadero, J. M., Fernández, J. M., Pastor, L., & Rodríguez, Á. (2011). Implementing virtual reality in the healthcare sector. In N. Rao (Ed.), *Virtual technologies for business and industrial applications: Innovative and synergistic approaches* (pp. 138–163). Hershey, PA: Business Science Reference. doi:10.4018/978-1-61520-631-5.ch009

Begg, M., Dewhurst, D., & Ross, M. (2010). Game informed virtual patients: Catalysts for online learning communities and professional development of medical teachers. In J. Lindberg & A. Olofsson (Eds.), *Online learning communities and teacher professional development: Methods for improved education delivery* (pp. 190–208). Hershey, PA: Information Science Reference. doi:10.4018/978-1-60566-780-5.ch011

Bennett, E. E., Blanchard, R. D., & Fernandez, G. L. (2012). Knowledge sharing in academic medical centers: Examining the nexus of higher education and workforce development. In V. Wang (Ed.), *Encyclopedia of e-leadership, counseling and training* (pp. 212–232). Hershey, PA: Information Science Reference. doi:10.4018/978-1-61350-068-2.ch016

Bera, T. K., & Nagaraju, J. (2014). Electrical impedance tomography (EIT): A harmless medical imaging modality. In R. Srivastava, S. Singh, & K. Shukla (Eds.), *Research developments in computer vision and image processing: Methodologies and applications* (pp. 235–273). Hershey, PA: Information Science Reference. doi:10.4018/978-1-4666-4558-5.ch013

Berler, A., & Apostolakis, I. (2014). Normalizing cross-border healthcare in europe via new e-prescription paradigms. In C. El Morr (Ed.), *Research perspectives on the role of informatics in health policy and management* (pp. 168–208). Hershey, PA: Medical Information Science Reference. doi:10.4018/978-1-4666-4321-5.ch011

Beswetherick, J. (2012). Health care information systems and the risk of privacy issues for the disabled. In *Cyber crime: Concepts, methodologies, tools and applications* (pp. 870–890). Hershey, PA: Information Science Reference. doi:10.4018/978-1-61350-323-2.ch411

Bhattacharya, P., Asanga, A. P., & Biswas, R. (2011). Stomodeum to proctodeum: Email narratives on clinical problem solving in gastroenterology. In R. Biswas & C. Martin (Eds.), *User-driven healthcare and narrative medicine: Utilizing collaborative social networks and technologies* (pp. 34–53). Hershey, PA: Medical Information Science Reference. doi:10.4018/978-1-60960-097-6.ch003

Biswas, R., & Martin, C. M. (2011). *User-driven healthcare and narrative medicine: Utilizing collaborative social networks and technologies*. Hershey, PA: IGI Global. doi:10.4018/978-1-60960-097-6

Biswas, R., Martin, C. M., Sturmberg, J., Mukherji, K., Lee, E. W., & Umakanth, S. (2011). Social cognitive ontology and user driven healthcare. In *Clinical technologies: Concepts, methodologies, tools and applications* (pp. 1996–2012). Hershey, PA: Medical Information Science Reference. doi:10.4018/978-1-60960-561-2.ch710

Biswas, R., Sturmberg, J., Martin, C. M., Ganesh, A. U., Umakanth, S., & Lee, E. W. (2011). Persistent clinical encounters in user driven e-health care. In *Clinical technologies: Concepts, methodologies, tools and applications* (pp. 1030–1046). Hershey, PA: Medical Information Science Reference. doi:10.4018/978-1-60960-561-2.ch403

Black, N. P., Fromme, H. B., Maniscalco, J., Ferrell, C., Myers, J., & Augustine, E. … Blankenburg, R. (2013). Innovation in patient care and medical resident education: Using blended instruction to transform nighttime patient care from a service model into an educational model. In A. Ritzhaupt, & S. Kumar (Eds.), Cases on educational technology implementation for facilitating learning (pp. 161-176). Hershey, PA: Information Science Reference. doi:10.4018/978-1-4666-3676-7.ch010

Blatt, A. J. (2013). Geospatial applications in disease surveillance: Solutions for the future.*International Journal of Applied Geospatial Research, 4*(2), 1–8. doi:10.4018/jagr.2013040101

Boaduo, N. A., & Boaduo, N. K. (2012). ICTs for enhanced use of indigenous medicinal plants by the Ashante speaking people of Ghana. In R. Lekoko & L. Semali (Eds.), *Cases on developing countries and ICT integration: Rural community development* (pp. 16–24). Hershey, PA: Information Science Reference. doi:10.4018/978-1-60960-117-1.ch002

Boboc, C., & Titan, E. (2014). Inputs from the new economics of migration of medical doctors in eastern and central Europe. In A. Driouchi (Ed.), *Labor and health economics in the Mediterranean region: Migration and mobility of medical doctors* (pp. 241–266). Hershey, PA: Medical Information Science Reference. doi:10.4018/978-1-4666-4723-7.ch010

Boboc, C., & Țițan, E. (2014). Migration of medical doctors, health, medical education, and employment in eastern and central Europe. In A. Driouchi (Ed.), *Labor and health economics in the Mediterranean region: Migration and mobility of medical doctors* (pp. 158–191). Hershey, PA: Medical Information Science Reference. doi:10.4018/978-1-4666-4723-7.ch007

Bolsin, S., & Colson, M. (2010). IT benefits in healthcare performance and safety. In J. Rodrigues (Ed.), *Health information systems: Concepts, methodologies, tools, and applications* (pp. 71–88). Hershey, PA: Medical Information Science Reference. doi:10.4018/978-1-60566-988-5.ch006

Bongers, B., & Smith, S. (2014). Interactivating rehabilitation through active multimodal feedback and guidance. In *Assistive technologies: Concepts, methodologies, tools, and applications* (pp. 1650–1674). Hershey, PA: Information Science Reference. doi:10.4018/978-1-4666-4422-9.ch087

Borges, A. P., & Laranjeira, E. (2013). Why and how did health economics appear? Who were the main authors? What is the role of ITCs in its development? In M. Cruz-Cunha, I. Miranda, & P. Gonçalves (Eds.), *Handbook of research on ICTs and management systems for improving efficiency in healthcare and social care* (pp. 971–987). Hershey, PA: Medical Information Science Reference. doi:10.4018/978-1-4666-3990-4.ch051

Bourgeois, S., & Yaylacicegi, U. (2012). Electronic health records: Improving patient safety and quality of care in Texas acute care hospitals. In J. Tan (Ed.), *Advancing technologies and intelligence in healthcare and clinical environments breakthroughs* (pp. 18–32). Hershey, PA: Medical Information Science Reference. doi:10.4018/978-1-4666-1755-1.ch002

Brandt, R., & Rice, R. (2012). Dermatological telemedicine diagnoses and andragogical training using web 2.0 mobile medicine video conferencing. In V. Dennen & J. Myers (Eds.), *Virtual professional development and informal learning via social networks* (pp. 276–293). Hershey, PA: Information Science Reference. doi:10.4018/978-1-4666-1815-2.ch016

Brzezinski, J., Kosiedowski, M., Mazurek, C., Slowinski, K., Slowinski, R., Stroinski, M., & Weglarz, J. (2013). Towards telemedical centers: Digitization of inter-professional communication in healthcare. In M. Cruz-Cunha, I. Miranda, & P. Gonçalves (Eds.), *Handbook of research on ICTs and management systems for improving efficiency in healthcare and social care* (pp. 805–829). Hershey, PA: Medical Information Science Reference. doi:10.4018/978-1-4666-3990-4.ch042

Carlén, U., & Lindström, B. (2012). Informed design of educational activities in online learning communities. In A. Olofsson & J. Lindberg (Eds.), *Informed design of educational technologies in higher education: Enhanced learning and teaching* (pp. 118–134). Hershey, PA: Information Science Reference. doi:10.4018/978-1-61350-080-4.ch007

Carrigan, E., Ugaz, A., Moberly, H. K., Page, J., Alpi, K. M., & Vreeland, C. (2013). Veterinary medicine: All collections great and small. In S. Holder (Ed.), *Library collection development for professional programs: Trends and best practices* (pp. 248–268). Hershey, PA: Information Science Reference. doi:10.4018/978-1-4666-1897-8.ch015

Caruana, C. J. (2012). The ongoing crisis in medical device education for healthcare professionals: Breaking the vicious circle through online learning. *International Journal of Reliable and Quality E-Healthcare*, *1*(2), 29–40. doi:10.4018/ijrqeh.2012040103

Catapano, G., & Verkerke, G. J. (2012). Artificial organs. In Z. Abu-Faraj (Ed.), *Handbook of research on biomedical engineering education and advanced bioengineering learning: Interdisciplinary concepts* (pp. 60–95). Hershey, PA: Medical Information Science Reference. doi:10.4018/978-1-4666-0122-2.ch002

Chandra, S., Shah, N. K., & Sriganesh, V. (2011). The cochrane students journal club and creating a secondary learning resource for gathering and appraising evidence: An example of rational use of medicines to prevent malaria relapse. *International Journal of User-Driven Healthcare, 1*(4), 31–41. doi:10.4018/ijudh.2011100103

Chang, A. Y., Littman-Quinn, R., Ketshogileng, D., Chandra, A., Rijken, T., Ghose, S., & Kovarik, C. L. et al. (2012). Smartphone-based mobile learning with physician trainees in Botswana. *International Journal of Mobile and Blended Learning, 4*(2), 1–14. doi:10.4018/jmbl.2012040101

Charissis, G., Melas, C., Moustakis, V., & Zampetakis, L. (2010). Organizational implementation of healthcare information systems. In M. Cruz-Cunha, A. Tavares, & R. Simoes (Eds.), *Handbook of research on developments in e-health and telemedicine: Technological and social perspectives* (pp. 419–450). Hershey, PA: Medical Information Science Reference. doi:10.4018/978-1-61520-670-4.ch020

Chaudhuri, A., Young, J., Martin, C. M., Sturmberg, J. P., & Biswas, R. (2011). Hematology: The river within. In R. Biswas & C. Martin (Eds.), *User-driven healthcare and narrative medicine: Utilizing collaborative social networks and technologies* (pp. 16–33). Hershey, PA: Medical Information Science Reference. doi:10.4018/978-1-60960-097-6.ch002

Chen, J. Y., Xu, H., Shi, P., Culbertson, A., & Meslin, E. M. (2013). Ethics and privacy considerations for systems biology applications in predictive and personalized medicine. In Bioinformatics: Concepts, methodologies, tools, and applications (pp. 1378-1404). Hershey, PA: Medical Information Science Reference. doi:10.4018/978-1-4666-3604-0.ch071

Cherian, E. J., & Ryan, T. W. (2014). Incongruent needs: Why differences in the iron-triangle of priorities make health information technology adoption and use difficult. In C. El Morr (Ed.), *Research perspectives on the role of informatics in health policy and management* (pp. 209–221). Hershey, PA: Medical Information Science Reference. doi:10.4018/978-1-4666-4321-5.ch012

Chetioui, Y. (2014). Perception by Moroccan physicians of factors affecting their migration decisions. In A. Driouchi (Ed.), *Labor and health economics in the mediterranean region: Migration and mobility of medical doctors* (pp. 337–375). Hershey, PA: Medical Information Science Reference. doi:10.4018/978-1-4666-4723-7.ch014

Chorbev, I., & Joksimoski, B. (2011). An integrated system for e-medicine (e-health, telemedicine and medical expert systems). In *Clinical technologies: Concepts, methodologies, tools and applications* (pp. 486–507). Hershey, PA: Medical Information Science Reference. doi:10.4018/978-1-60960-561-2.ch218

Ciufudean, C., Ciufudean, O., & Filote, C. (2013). New models for ICT-based medical diagnosis. In M. Cruz-Cunha, I. Miranda, & P. Gonçalves (Eds.), *Handbook of research on ICTs and management systems for improving efficiency in healthcare and social care* (pp. 892–911). Hershey, PA: Medical Information Science Reference. doi:10.4018/978-1-4666-3990-4.ch046

Clark, J. M. (2014). Implementation of electronic records in a medical practice setting. In J. Krueger (Ed.), *Cases on electronic records and resource management implementation in diverse environments* (pp. 211–225). Hershey, PA: Information Science Reference. doi:10.4018/978-1-4666-4466-3.ch013

Clark, T. (2011). Health and health care grid services and delivery integrating eHealth and telemedicine. In E. Kldiashvili (Ed.), *Grid technologies for e-health: Applications for telemedicine services and delivery* (pp. 36–64). Hershey, PA: Medical Information Science Reference. doi:10.4018/978-1-61692-010-4.ch003

Claster, W., Ghotbi, N., & Shanmuganathan, S. (2010). Data-mining techniques for an analysis of non-conventional methodologies: Deciphering of alternative medicine. In W. Pease, M. Cooper, & R. Gururajan (Eds.), *Biomedical knowledge management: Infrastructures and processes for e-health systems* (pp. 82–91). Hershey, PA: Medical Information Science Reference. doi:10.4018/978-1-60566-266-4.ch006

Condaris, C. (2012). Scales to scalpels: Doctors who practice the healing arts of music and medicine. *International Journal of User-Driven Healthcare, 2*(3), 84–84. doi:10.4018/ijudh.2012070109

Corrigan, D., Hederman, L., Khan, H., Taweel, A., Kostopoulou, O., & Delaney, B. (2013). An ontology-driven approach to clinical evidence modelling implementing clinical prediction rules. In A. Moumtzoglou & A. Kastania (Eds.), *E-health technologies and improving patient safety: Exploring organizational factors* (pp. 257–284). Hershey, PA: Medical Information Science Reference. doi:10.4018/978-1-4666-2657-7.ch016

Crisóstomo-Acevedo, M. J., & Aurelio Medina-Garrido, J. (2010). Difficulties in accepting telemedicine. In J. Rodrigues (Ed.), *Health information systems: Concepts, methodologies, tools, and applications* (pp. 1628–1639). Hershey, PA: Medical Information Science Reference. doi:10.4018/978-1-60566-988-5.ch104

Danforth, D. R. (2010). Development of an interactive virtual 3-D model of the human testis using the second life platform. *International Journal of Virtual and Personal Learning Environments, 1*(2), 45–58. doi:10.4018/jvple.2010040104

Daniel, V. M. (2011). Genomics and genetic engineering: Playing god? In S. Hongladarom (Ed.), *Genomics and bioethics: Interdisciplinary perspectives, technologies and advancements* (pp. 111–129). Hershey, PA: Medical Information Science Reference. doi:10.4018/978-1-61692-883-4.ch008

Daskalaki, A. (2010). *Informatics in oral medicine: Advanced techniques in clinical and diagnostic technologies*. Hershey, PA: IGI Global. doi:10.4018/978-1-60566-733-1

Davis, S. A. (2013). Global telemedicine and eHealth: Advances for future healthcare – Using a systems approach to integrate healthcare functions. In V. Gulla, A. Mori, F. Gabbrielli, & P. Lanzafame (Eds.), *Telehealth networks for hospital services: New methodologies* (pp. 15–32). Hershey, PA: Medical Information Science Reference. doi:10.4018/978-1-4666-2979-0.ch002

de Leeuw, E. (2012). The politics of medical curriculum accreditation: Thoughts, not facts? *International Journal of User-Driven Healthcare*, *2*(1), 53–69. doi:10.4018/ijudh.2012010108

De Luca, S., & Memo, E. (2010). Better knowledge for better health services: Discovering guideline compliance. In J. Rodrigues (Ed.), *Health information systems: Concepts, methodologies, tools, and applications* (pp. 233–255). Hershey, PA: Medical Information Science Reference. doi:10.4018/978-1-60566-988-5.ch017

DeSimio, T., & Chrisagis, X. (2012). Medical e-reference: A benchmark for e-reference publishing in other disciplines. In S. Polanka (Ed.), *E-reference context and discoverability in libraries: Issues and concepts* (pp. 116–125). Hershey, PA: Information Science Reference. doi:10.4018/978-1-61350-308-9.ch011

Dhakal, B., & Ross, S. D. (2011). Medical student perspectives: Journey through different worlds. In R. Biswas & C. Martin (Eds.), *User-driven healthcare and narrative medicine: Utilizing collaborative social networks and technologies* (pp. 125–133). Hershey, PA: Medical Information Science Reference. doi:10.4018/978-1-60960-097-6.ch009

Dong, Y., Lu, H., Gajic, O., & Pickering, B. (2012). Intensive care unit operational modeling and analysis. In A. Kolker & P. Story (Eds.), *Management engineering for effective healthcare delivery: Principles and applications* (pp. 132–147). Hershey, PA: Medical Information Science Reference. doi:10.4018/978-1-60960-872-9.ch006

Doyle, D. (2011). E-medical education: An overview. In A. Shukla & R. Tiwari (Eds.), *Biomedical engineering and information systems: Technologies, tools and applications* (pp. 219–238). Hershey, PA: Medical Information Science Reference. doi:10.4018/978-1-61692-004-3.ch012

Driouchi, A. (2014). Introduction to labor and health economics: Mobility of medical doctors in the Mediterranean region. In A. Driouchi (Ed.), *Labor and health economics in the Mediterranean region: Migration and mobility of medical doctors* (pp. 1–22). Hershey, PA: Medical Information Science Reference. doi:10.4018/978-1-4666-4723-7.ch001

Driouchi, A. (2014). Medical knowledge, north-south cooperation, and mobility of medical doctors. In A. Driouchi (Ed.), *Labor and health economics in the Mediterranean region: Migration and mobility of medical doctors* (pp. 376–395). Hershey, PA: Medical Information Science Reference. doi:10.4018/978-1-4666-4723-7.ch015

Duan, X., Wang, X., & Huang, Q. (2014). Medical manipulators for surgical applications. In Robotics: Concepts, methodologies, tools, and applications (pp. 608-618). Hershey, PA: Information Science Reference. doi:10.4018/978-1-4666-4607-0.ch030

Dyro, J. F. (2012). Clinical engineering. In Z. Abu-Faraj (Ed.), *Handbook of research on biomedical engineering education and advanced bioengineering learning: Interdisciplinary concepts* (pp. 521–576). Hershey, PA: Medical Information Science Reference. doi:10.4018/978-1-4666-0122-2.ch012

El Morr, C., & Subercaze, J. (2010). Knowledge management in healthcare. In M. Cruz-Cunha, A. Tavares, & R. Simoes (Eds.), *Handbook of research on developments in e-health and telemedicine: Technological and social perspectives* (pp. 490–510). Hershey, PA: Medical Information Science Reference. doi:10.4018/978-1-61520-670-4.ch023

Eleni, A., & Maglogiannis, I. (2010). Adoption of wearable systems in modern patient telemonitoring systems. In M. Cruz-Cunha, A. Tavares, & R. Simoes (Eds.), *Handbook of research on developments in e-health and telemedicine: Technological and social perspectives* (pp. 1004–1023). Hershey, PA: Medical Information Science Reference. doi:10.4018/978-1-61520-670-4.ch048

Epstein, J. H., Goldberg, A., Krol, M., & Levine, A. (2013). Virtual tools in medical education. In Y. Kats (Ed.), *Learning management systems and instructional design: Best practices in online education* (pp. 364–380). Hershey, PA: Information Science Reference. doi:10.4018/978-1-4666-3930-0.ch019

Eskeland, S., & Oleshchuk, V. (2010). Information security and privacy in medical application scenario. In K. Khoumbati, Y. Dwivedi, A. Srivastava, & B. Lal (Eds.), *Handbook of research on advances in health informatics and electronic healthcare applications: Global adoption and impact of information communication technologies* (pp. 274–287). Hershey, PA: Medical Information Science Reference. doi:10.4018/978-1-60566-030-1.ch017

Esposito, A. (2013). The impact of social media on scholarly practices in higher education: Online engagement and ICTs appropriation in senior, young, and doctoral researchers. In B. Pătruţ, M. Pătruţ, & C. Cmeciu (Eds.), *Social media and the new academic environment: Pedagogical challenges* (pp. 342–367). Hershey, PA: Information Science Reference. doi:10.4018/978-1-4666-2851-9.ch017

Facelli, J. C., Hurdle, J. F., & Mitchell, J. A. (2012). Medical informatics and bioinformatics. In Z. Abu-Faraj (Ed.), *Handbook of research on biomedical engineering education and advanced bioengineering learning: Interdisciplinary concepts* (pp. 577–604). Hershey, PA: Medical Information Science Reference. doi:10.4018/978-1-4666-0122-2.ch013

Fairchild, K. D., & Moorman, J. R. (2012). Heart rate characteristics monitoring in the NICU: A new tool for clinical care and research. In W. Chen, S. Oetomo, & L. Feijs (Eds.), *Neonatal monitoring technologies: Design for integrated solutions* (pp. 175–200). Hershey, PA: Medical Information Science Reference. doi:10.4018/978-1-4666-0975-4.ch008

Fakhar, A. (2014). Beyond brain drain: A case study of the benefits of cooperation on medical immigration. In A. Driouchi (Ed.), *Labor and health economics in the Mediterranean region: Migration and mobility of medical doctors* (pp. 294–313). Hershey, PA: Medical Information Science Reference. doi:10.4018/978-1-4666-4723-7.ch012

Farrell, M. (2011). Use of handheld computers in nursing education. In *Clinical technologies: Concepts, methodologies, tools and applications* (pp. 1504–1517). Hershey, PA: Medical Information Science Reference. doi:10.4018/978-1-60960-561-2.ch507

Ferrer-Roca, O. (2011). Standards in telemedicine. In A. Moumtzoglou & A. Kastania (Eds.), *E-health systems quality and reliability: Models and standards* (pp. 220–243). Hershey, PA: Medical Information Science Reference. doi:10.4018/978-1-61692-843-8.ch017

Fiaidhi, J., Mohammed, S., & Wei, Y. (2010). Implications of web 2.0 technology on healthcare: A biomedical semantic blog case study. In S. Kabene (Ed.), *Healthcare and the effect of technology: Developments, challenges and advancements* (pp. 269–289). Hershey, PA: Medical Information Science Reference. doi:10.4018/978-1-61520-733-6.ch016

Fialho, A. S., Cismondi, F., Vieira, S. M., Reti, S. R., Sousa, J. M., & Finkelstein, S. N. (2013). Challenges and opportunities of soft computing tools in health care delivery. In M. Cruz-Cunha, I. Miranda, & P. Gonçalves (Eds.), *Handbook of research on ICTs and management systems for improving efficiency in healthcare and social care* (pp. 321–340). Hershey, PA: Medical Information Science Reference. doi:10.4018/978-1-4666-3990-4.ch016

Freitas, A., Brazdil, P., & Costa-Pereira, A. (2012). Cost-sensitive learning in medicine. In *Machine learning: Concepts, methodologies, tools and applications* (pp. 1625–1641). Hershey, PA: Information Science Reference. doi:10.4018/978-1-60960-818-7.ch607

Freitas, A., & Costa-Pereira, A. (2010). Learning cost-sensitive decision trees to support medical diagnosis. In T. Nguyen (Ed.), *Complex data warehousing and knowledge discovery for advanced retrieval development: Innovative methods and applications* (pp. 287–307). Hershey, PA: Information Science Reference. doi:10.4018/978-1-60566-748-5.ch013

Freitas, L., Pereira, R. T., Pereira, H. G., Martini, R., Mozzaquatro, B. A., Kasper, J., & Librelotto, G. (2013). Ontological representation and an architecture for homecare pervasive systems. In R. Martinho, R. Rijo, M. Cruz-Cunha, & J. Varajão (Eds.), *Information systems and technologies for enhancing health and social care* (pp. 215–234). Hershey, PA: Medical Information Science Reference. doi:10.4018/978-1-4666-3667-5.ch015

Frigo, C. A., & Pavan, E. E. (2014). Prosthetic and orthotic devices. In *Assistive technologies: Concepts, methodologies, tools, and applications* (pp. 549–613). Hershey, PA: Information Science Reference. doi:10.4018/978-1-4666-4422-9.ch028

Frunza, O., & Inkpen, D. (2012). Natural language processing and machine learning techniques help achieve a better medical practice. In R. Magdalena-Benedito, E. Soria-Olivas, J. Martínez, J. Gómez-Sanchis, & A. Serrano-López (Eds.), *Medical applications of intelligent data analysis: Research advancements* (pp. 237–254). Hershey, PA: Information Science Reference. doi:10.4018/978-1-4666-1803-9.ch016

Fung-Kee-Fung, M., Morash, R., & Goubanova, E. (2011). Evaluating CoPs in cancer surgery. In O. Hernáez & E. Bueno Campos (Eds.), *Handbook of research on communities of practice for organizational management and networking: Methodologies for competitive advantage* (pp. 456–466). Hershey, PA: Information Science Reference. doi:10.4018/978-1-60566-802-4.ch025

Gabbrielli, F. (2013). Telemedicine R&D influencing incoming strategies and organization models. In V. Gulla, A. Mori, F. Gabbrielli, & P. Lanzafame (Eds.), *Telehealth networks for hospital services: New methodologies* (pp. 250–264). Hershey, PA: Medical Information Science Reference. doi:10.4018/978-1-4666-2979-0.ch017

Ganz, A., Schafer, J., Yu, X., Lord, G., Burstein, J., & Ciottone, G. R. (2013). Real-time scalable resource tracking framework (DIORAMA) for mass casualty incidents. *International Journal of E-Health and Medical Communications*, *4*(2), 34–49. doi:10.4018/jehmc.2013040103

Gao, X. W., Loomes, M., & Comley, R. (2012). Bridging the abridged: The diffusion of telemedicine in Europe and China. In J. Rodrigues, I. de la Torre Díez, & B. Sainz de Abajo (Eds.), *Telemedicine and e-health services, policies, and applications: Advancements and developments* (pp. 451–495). Hershey, PA: Medical Information Science Reference. doi:10.4018/978-1-4666-0888-7.ch017

Gavgani, V. Z. (2011). Ubiquitous information therapy service through social networking libraries: An operational web 2.0 service model. In R. Biswas & C. Martin (Eds.), *User-driven healthcare and narrative medicine: Utilizing collaborative social networks and technologies* (pp. 446–461). Hershey, PA: Medical Information Science Reference. doi:10.4018/978-1-60960-097-6.ch030

Germaine-McDaniel, N. S. (2013). The emerging hispanic use of online health information in the United States: Cultural convergence or dissociation? In *User-driven healthcare: Concepts, methodologies, tools, and applications* (pp. 1607–1621). Hershey, PA: Medical Information Science Reference. doi:10.4018/978-1-4666-2770-3.ch079

Ghalib, N. (2014). The design and implementation of paperless medical system (PMS) for offshore operating company: A structured approach. In Software design and development: Concepts, methodologies, tools, and applications (pp. 1064-1072). Hershey, PA: Information Science Reference. doi:10.4018/978-1-4666-4301-7.ch051

Gill, S., & Paranjape, R. (2010). A review of recent contribution in agent-based health care modeling. In J. Rodrigues (Ed.), *Health information systems: Concepts, methodologies, tools, and applications* (pp. 356–373). Hershey, PA: Medical Information Science Reference. doi:10.4018/978-1-60566-988-5.ch024

Gilligan, J., & Smith, P. (2014). A formal representation system for modelling assistive technology systems. In G. Kouroupetroglou (Ed.), *Disability informatics and web accessibility for motor limitations* (pp. 1–42). Hershey, PA: Medical Information Science Reference. doi:10.4018/978-1-4666-4442-7.ch001

Goldberg, E. M. (2014). Business continuity and disaster recovery considerations for healthcare technology. In *Crisis management: Concepts, methodologies, tools and applications* (pp. 1455–1462). Hershey, PA: Information Science Reference. doi:10.4018/978-1-4666-4707-7.ch073

Gonçalves, F., & David, G. (2013). Definition of a retrospective health information policy based on (re)use study. In M. Cruz-Cunha, I. Miranda, & P. Gonçalves (Eds.), *Handbook of research on ICTs and management systems for improving efficiency in healthcare and social care* (pp. 1130–1155). Hershey, PA: Medical Information Science Reference. doi:10.4018/978-1-4666-3990-4.ch059

Gopalakrishnan, R., & Mugler, D. H. (2010). The evolution of hermite transform in biomedical applications. In A. Shukla & R. Tiwari (Eds.), *Intelligent medical technologies and biomedical engineering: Tools and applications* (pp. 260–278). Hershey, PA: Medical Information Science Reference. doi:10.4018/978-1-61520-977-4.ch013

Goyal, R. K., O'Neill, M., Agostinelli, N., & Wyer, P. (2011). Critical illness and the emergency room. In R. Biswas & C. Martin (Eds.), *User-driven healthcare and narrative medicine: Utilizing collaborative social networks and technologies* (pp. 63–74). Hershey, PA: Medical Information Science Reference. doi:10.4018/978-1-60960-097-6.ch005

Graham, I. W. (2011). The nature of nursing work. In A. Cashin & R. Cook (Eds.), *Evidence-based practice in nursing informatics: Concepts and applications* (pp. 51–63). Hershey, PA: Medical Information Science Reference. doi:10.4018/978-1-60960-034-1.ch005

Greenshields, I., & El-Sayed, G. (2012). Aspects of visualization and the grid in a biomedical context. In *Grid and cloud computing: Concepts, methodologies, tools and applications* (pp. 1686–1701). Hershey, PA: Information Science Reference. doi:10.4018/978-1-4666-0879-5.ch710

Grimnes, S., & Høgetveit, J. O. (2012). Biomedical sensors. In Z. Abu-Faraj (Ed.), *Handbook of research on biomedical engineering education and advanced bioengineering learning: Interdisciplinary concepts* (pp. 356–436). Hershey, PA: Medical Information Science Reference. doi:10.4018/978-1-4666-0122-2.ch009

Guedouar, R., & Zarrad, B. (2012). Forward projection for use with iterative reconstruction. In A. Malik, T. Choi, & H. Nisar (Eds.), *Depth map and 3D imaging applications: Algorithms and technologies* (pp. 27–55). Hershey, PA: Information Science Reference. doi:10.4018/978-1-61350-326-3.ch003

Gullà, V. (2013). Leading the technological innovation in healthcare systems: The telematic medicine approach. In V. Gulla, A. Mori, F. Gabbrielli, & P. Lanzafame (Eds.), *Telehealth networks for hospital services: New methodologies* (pp. 134–153). Hershey, PA: Medical Information Science Reference. doi:10.4018/978-1-4666-2979-0.ch009

Guo, R., Wang, Y., Yan, H., Li, F., Yan, J., & Xu, Z. (2011). Pulse wave analysis of traditional chinese medicine based on hemodynamics principles. In L. Liu, D. Wei, & Y. Li (Eds.), *Interdisciplinary research and applications in bioinformatics, computational biology, and environmental sciences* (pp. 194–203). Hershey, PA: Medical Information Science Reference. doi:10.4018/978-1-60960-064-8.ch017

Gupta, A., Goyal, R. K., Joiner, K. A., & Saini, S. (2010). Outsourcing in the healthcare industry: Information technology, intellectual property, and allied aspects. In M. Khosrow-Pour (Ed.), *Global, social, and organizational implications of emerging information resources management: Concepts and applications* (pp. 18–44). Hershey, PA: Information Science Reference. doi:10.4018/978-1-60566-962-5.ch002

Gupta, S., Mukherjee, S., & Roy, S. S. (2013). Modernization of healthcare and medical diagnosis system using multi agent system (MAS): A comparative study. In S. Bhattacharyya & P. Dutta (Eds.), *Handbook of research on computational intelligence for engineering, science, and business* (pp. 592–622). Hershey, PA: Information Science Reference. doi:10.4018/978-1-4666-2518-1.ch023

Ha, S. H. (2011). Medical domain knowledge and associative classification rules in diagnosis. *International Journal of Knowledge Discovery in Bioinformatics, 2*(1), 60–73. doi:10.4018/jkdb.2011010104

Haheim, L. L., & Morland, B. (2010). Health technology assessment: Development and future. In J. Rodrigues (Ed.), *Health information systems: Concepts, methodologies, tools, and applications* (pp. 26–41). Hershey, PA: Medical Information Science Reference. doi:10.4018/978-1-60566-988-5.ch003

Hai-Jew, S. (2010). An elusive formula: The IT role in behavior change in public health. In T. Yuzer & G. Kurubacak (Eds.), *Transformative learning and online education: Aesthetics, dimensions and concepts* (pp. 347–373). Hershey, PA: Information Science Reference. doi:10.4018/978-1-61520-985-9.ch022

Haida, M. (2013). Implications of NIRS brain signals. In J. Wu (Ed.), *Biomedical engineering and cognitive neuroscience for healthcare: Interdisciplinary applications* (pp. 120–128). Hershey, PA: Medical Information Science Reference. doi:10.4018/978-1-4666-2113-8.ch013

Haidegger, T. (2012). Surgical robots: System development, assessment, and clearance. In T. Sobh & X. Xiong (Eds.), *Prototyping of robotic systems: Applications of design and implementation* (pp. 288–326). Hershey, PA: Information Science Reference. doi:10.4018/978-1-4666-0176-5.ch010

Hajiheydari, N., Khakbaz, S. B., & Farhadi, H. (2013). Proposing a business model in healthcare industry: E-diagnosis. *International Journal of Healthcare Information Systems and Informatics*, 8(2), 41–57. doi:10.4018/jhisi.2013040104

Hanada, E. (2013). Effective use of RFID in medicine and general healthcare. In T. Issa, P. Isaías, & P. Kommers (Eds.), *Information systems and technology for organizations in a networked society* (pp. 335–352). Hershey, PA: Business Science Reference. doi:10.4018/978-1-4666-4062-7.ch018

Hara, H. (2013). Women and health in Japan: The rise and obstacles of gender and sex-specific medicine. In M. Merviö (Ed.), *Healthcare management and economics: Perspectives on public and private administration* (pp. 203–207). Hershey, PA: Medical Information Science Reference. doi:10.4018/978-1-4666-3982-9.ch016

Harnett, B. (2013). Patient centered medicine and technology adaptation. In *User-driven healthcare: Concepts, methodologies, tools, and applications* (pp. 77–98). Hershey, PA: Medical Information Science Reference. doi:10.4018/978-1-4666-2770-3.ch005

Hatton, J. D., Schmidt, T. M., & Jelen, J. (2013). Adoption of electronic health care records: Physician heuristics and hesitancy. In R. Martinho, R. Rijo, M. Cruz-Cunha, & J. Varajão (Eds.), *Information systems and technologies for enhancing health and social care* (pp. 148–165). Hershey, PA: Medical Information Science Reference. doi:10.4018/978-1-4666-3667-5.ch010

Heaberg, G. (2011). Case study: Research matchmaker, an advanced nursing practice informatics application. In A. Cashin & R. Cook (Eds.), *Evidence-based practice in nursing informatics: Concepts and applications* (pp. 217–236). Hershey, PA: Medical Information Science Reference. doi:10.4018/978-1-60960-034-1.ch017

Hegde, B. (2011). Learning medicine: A personal view. In R. Biswas & C. Martin (Eds.), *User-driven healthcare and narrative medicine: Utilizing collaborative social networks and technologies* (pp. 184–190). Hershey, PA: Medical Information Science Reference. doi:10.4018/978-1-60960-097-6.ch014

Heilman, J. (2012). Creating awareness for using a wiki to promote collaborative health professional education. *International Journal of User-Driven Healthcare*, 2(1), 86–87. doi:10.4018/ijudh.2012010113

Heinzel, A., Fechete, R., Söllner, J., Perco, P., Heinze, G., Oberbauer, R., & Mayer, B. et al. (2012). Data graphs for linking clinical phenotype and molecular feature space. *International Journal of Systems Biology and Biomedical Technologies, 1*(1), 11–25. doi:10.4018/ijsbbt.2012010102

Hernández-Chan, G. S., Rodríguez-González, A., & Colomo-Palacios, R. (2013). Using social networks to obtain medical diagnosis. In M. Cruz-Cunha, I. Miranda, & P. Gonçalves (Eds.), *Handbook of research on ICTs and management systems for improving efficiency in healthcare and social care* (pp. 306–320). Hershey, PA: Medical Information Science Reference. doi:10.4018/978-1-4666-3990-4.ch015

Hine, M. J., Farion, K. J., Michalowski, W., & Wilk, S. (2011). Decision making by emergency room physicians and residents: Implications for the design of clinical decision support systems. In J. Tan (Ed.), *New technologies for advancing healthcare and clinical practices* (pp. 131–148). Hershey, PA: Medical Information Science Reference. doi:10.4018/978-1-60960-780-7.ch008

Hoonakker, P., McGuire, K., & Carayon, P. (2011). Sociotechnical issues of tele-ICU technology. In D. Haftor & A. Mirijamdotter (Eds.), *Information and communication technologies, society and human beings: Theory and framework (festschrift in honor of Gunilla Bradley)* (pp. 225–240). Hershey, PA: Information Science Reference. doi:10.4018/978-1-60960-057-0.ch018

Hopper, K. B., & Johns, C. L. (2012). Educational technology in the medical industry. In *Wireless technologies: Concepts, methodologies, tools and applications* (pp. 1306–1322). Hershey, PA: Information Science Reference. doi:10.4018/978-1-61350-101-6.ch511

Hsu, P., Tsai, W., & Tsai, C. (2013). Patient safety concerns among emergency medical staff and patients. *International Journal of Privacy and Health Information Management, 1*(1), 29–52. doi:10.4018/ijphim.2013010103

Huang, K., Geller, J., Halper, M., Elhanan, G., & Perl, Y. (2011). Scalability of piecewise synonym identification in integration of SNOMED into the UMLS. *International Journal of Computational Models and Algorithms in Medicine, 2*(3), 26–45. doi:10.4018/jcmam.2011070103

Hughes, B. (2012). Managing e-health in the age of web 2.0: The impact on e-health evaluation. In E-marketing: Concepts, methodologies, tools, and applications (pp. 1268-1288). Hershey, PA: Business Science Reference. doi:10.4018/978-1-4666-1598-4.ch074

Hyde, A., Nee, J., Butler, M., Drennan, J., & Howlett, E. (2011). Preferred types of menopause service delivery: A qualitative study of menopausal womens perceptions. *International Journal of Healthcare Delivery Reform Initiatives*, *3*(1), 1–12. doi:10.4018/jhdri.2011010101

Ilie, V., Van Slyke, C., Courtney, J. F., & Styne, P. (2011). Challenges associated with physicians' usage of electronic medical records. In J. Tan (Ed.), *New technologies for advancing healthcare and clinical practices* (pp. 234–251). Hershey, PA: Medical Information Science Reference. doi:10.4018/978-1-60960-780-7.ch014

Inomata, C., & Nitta, S. (2013). Nursing in integrative medicine and nurses' engagement in caring-healing: A discussion based on the practice and study of music therapy and nursing care for patients with neurodegenerative disorders. In J. Wu (Ed.), *Technological advancements in biomedicine for healthcare applications* (pp. 235–239). Hershey, PA: Medical Information Science Reference. doi:10.4018/978-1-4666-2196-1.ch025

Inthiran, A., Alhashmi, S. M., & Ahmed, P. K. (2012). Medical information retrieval strategies: An exploratory study on the information retrieval behaviors of non-medical professionals. *International Journal of Healthcare Information Systems and Informatics*, *7*(1), 31–45. doi:10.4018/jhisi.2012010103

Isern, D., & Moreno, A. (2010). HeCaSe2: A multi-agent system that automates the application of clinical guidelines. In R. Paranjape & A. Sadanand (Eds.), *Multi-agent systems for healthcare simulation and modeling: Applications for system improvement* (pp. 113–136). Hershey, PA: Medical Information Science Reference. doi:10.4018/978-1-60566-772-0.ch007

Ishaq, G. M., Hussain, P. T., Iqbal, M. J., & Mushtaq, M. B. (2013). Risk-benefit analysis of combination vs. unopposed HRT in post-menopausal women. In Bioinformatics: Concepts, methodologies, tools, and applications (pp. 1424-1440). Hershey, PA: Medical Information Science Reference. doi:10.4018/978-1-4666-3604-0.ch073

Iwaki, S. (2013). Multimodal neuroimaging to visualize human visual processing. In J. Wu (Ed.), *Biomedical engineering and cognitive neuroscience for healthcare: Interdisciplinary applications* (pp. 274–282). Hershey, PA: Medical Information Science Reference. doi:10.4018/978-1-4666-2113-8.ch028

James, R. (2011). Practical pointers in medicine over seven decades: Reflections of an individual physician. In R. Biswas & C. Martin (Eds.), *User-driven healthcare and narrative medicine: Utilizing collaborative social networks and technologies* (pp. 173–183). Hershey, PA: Medical Information Science Reference. doi:10.4018/978-1-60960-097-6.ch013

Janczewski, M. (2010). Healthcare transformation in a net-centric environment. In S. Ghosh (Ed.), *Net centricity and technological interoperability in organizations: Perspectives and strategies* (pp. 99–114). Hershey, PA: Information Science Reference. doi:10.4018/978-1-60566-854-3.ch007

Jesus, Â., & Gomes, M. J. (2013). Web 2.0 tools in biomedical education: Limitations and possibilities. In Y. Kats (Ed.), *Learning management systems and instructional design: Best practices in online education* (pp. 208–231). Hershey, PA: Information Science Reference. doi:10.4018/978-1-4666-3930-0.ch011

Ji, Z., Sugi, T., Goto, S., Wang, X., & Nakamura, M. (2013). Multi-channel template extraction for automatic EEG spike detection. In J. Wu (Ed.), *Biomedical engineering and cognitive neuroscience for healthcare: Interdisciplinary applications* (pp. 255–265). Hershey, PA: Medical Information Science Reference. doi:10.4018/978-1-4666-2113-8.ch026

Jifa, G., Wuqi, S., Zhengxiang, Z., Rui, G., & Yijun, L. (2012). Expert mining and traditional Chinese medicine knowledge. In W. Lee (Ed.), *Systems approaches to knowledge management, transfer, and resource development* (pp. 239–251). Hershey, PA: Information Science Reference. doi:10.4018/978-1-4666-1782-7.ch016

Johnson, D. E. (2012). Electronic medical records (EMR): Issues and implementation perspectives. In A. Kolker & P. Story (Eds.), *Management engineering for effective healthcare delivery: Principles and applications* (pp. 333–351). Hershey, PA: Medical Information Science Reference. doi:10.4018/978-1-60960-872-9.ch016

Johnson, K., & Tashiro, J. (2013). Interprofessional care and health care complexity: Factors shaping human resources effectiveness in health information management. In *User-driven healthcare: Concepts, methodologies, tools, and applications* (pp. 1273–1302). Hershey, PA: Medical Information Science Reference. doi:10.4018/978-1-4666-2770-3.ch064

Jose, J. (2012). Pharmacovigilance: Basic concepts and applications of pharmacoinformatics. In T. Gasmelseid (Ed.), *Pharmacoinformatics and drug discovery technologies: Theories and applications* (pp. 322–343). Hershey, PA: Medical Information Science Reference. doi:10.4018/978-1-4666-0309-7.ch020

Juzoji, H. (2012). Legal bases for medical supervision via mobile telecommunications in Japan. *International Journal of E-Health and Medical Communications*, *3*(1), 33–45. doi:10.4018/jehmc.2012010103

Juzwishin, D. W. (2010). Enabling technologies and challenges for the future of ubiquitous health the interoperability framework. In S. Mohammed & J. Fiaidhi (Eds.), *Ubiquitous health and medical informatics: The ubiquity 2.0 trend and beyond* (pp. 596–622). Hershey, PA: Medical Information Science Reference. doi:10.4018/978-1-61520-777-0.ch028

Kabene, S., & Wolfe, M. (2011). Risks and benefits of technology in health care. In *Clinical technologies: Concepts, methodologies, tools and applications* (pp. 13–24). Hershey, PA: Medical Information Science Reference. doi:10.4018/978-1-60960-561-2.ch102

Kabene, S. M., King, L., & Gibson, C. J. (2010). Technology and human resources management in health care. In S. Mohammed, & J. Fiaidhi (Eds.) Ubiquitous health and medical informatics: The ubiquity 2.0 trend and beyond (pp. 574-595). Hershey, PA: Medical Information Science Reference. doi:10.4018/978-1-61520-777-0.ch027

Kabene, S. M., Wolfe, M., & Leduc, R. (2012). Recruitment and retention of health-care professionals for the changing demographics, culture, and access in Canada. In *Human resources management: Concepts, methodologies, tools, and applications* (pp. 276–290). Hershey, PA: Business Science Reference. doi:10.4018/978-1-4666-1601-1.ch017

Kadiri, M., & Zouag, N. (2014). The new economics of skilled labor migration: The case of medical doctors in MENA. In A. Driouchi (Ed.), *Labor and health economics in the Mediterranean region: Migration and mobility of medical doctors* (pp. 267–292). Hershey, PA: Medical Information Science Reference. doi:10.4018/978-1-4666-4723-7.ch011

Kalantri, S. P. (2012). On being a patient. *International Journal of User-Driven Healthcare*, 2(4), 1–4. doi:10.4018/ijudh.2012100101

Kaldoudi, E., Konstantinidis, S., & Bamidis, P. D. (2010). Web 2.0 approaches for active, collaborative learning in medicine and health. In S. Mohammed & J. Fiaidhi (Eds.), *Ubiquitous health and medical informatics: The ubiquity 2.0 trend and beyond* (pp. 127–149). Hershey, PA: Medical Information Science Reference. doi:10.4018/978-1-61520-777-0.ch007

Kannry, J. L. (2011). Operationalizing the science. In *Clinical technologies: Concepts, methodologies, tools and applications* (pp. 1600–1622). Hershey, PA: Medical Information Science Reference. doi:10.4018/978-1-60960-561-2.ch601

Karayanni, D. (2010). A cluster analysis of physicians values, prescribing behaviour and attitudes towards firms marketing communications. *International Journal of Customer Relationship Marketing and Management, 1*(4), 62–79. doi:10.4018/jcrmm.2010100104

Kastania, A., & Moumtzoglou, A. (2012). Quality implications of the medical applications for 4G mobile phones. *International Journal of Reliable and Quality E-Healthcare, 1*(1), 58–67. doi:10.4018/ijrqeh.2012010106

Kastania, A. N. (2013). Evaluation considerations for e-health systems. In *User-driven healthcare: Concepts, methodologies, tools, and applications* (pp. 1126–1140). Hershey, PA: Medical Information Science Reference. doi:10.4018/978-1-4666-2770-3.ch057

Kaufman, D. (2010). Simulation in health professional education. In D. Kaufman & L. Sauvé (Eds.), *Educational gameplay and simulation environments: Case studies and lessons learned* (pp. 51–67). Hershey, PA: Information Science Reference. doi:10.4018/978-1-61520-731-2.ch003

Kazandjian, V. A. (2013). Learning to accept uncertainty as a quality of care dimension. In A. Moumtzoglou & A. Kastania (Eds.), *E-health technologies and improving patient safety: Exploring organizational factors* (pp. 1–12). Hershey, PA: Medical Information Science Reference. doi:10.4018/978-1-4666-2657-7.ch001

Kearns, W. D., Fozard, J. L., & Lamm, R. S. (2011). How knowing who, where and when can change health care delivery. In C. Röcker & M. Ziefle (Eds.), *E-health, assistive technologies and applications for assisted living: Challenges and solutions* (pp. 139–160). Hershey, PA: Medical Information Science Reference. doi:10.4018/978-1-60960-469-1.ch007

Khan, T. (2013). Transformation of a reluctant patient to a proactive health advocate. *International Journal of User-Driven Healthcare, 3*(1), 71–74. doi:10.4018/ijudh.2013010109

Khetarpal, A., & Singh, S. (2012). Disability studies in medical education. *International Journal of User-Driven Healthcare, 2*(2), 44–51. doi:10.4018/ijudh.2012040105

Kim, J. (2011). The development and implementation of patient safety information systems (PSIS). In Clinical technologies: Concepts, methodologies, tools and applications (pp. 2054-2072). Hershey, PA: Medical Information Science Reference. doi:10.4018/978-1-60960-561-2.ch804

Kldiashvili, E. (2011). The application of virtual organization technology for eHealth. In E. Kldiashvili (Ed.), *Grid technologies for e-health: Applications for telemedicine services and delivery* (pp. 1–17). Hershey, PA: Medical Information Science Reference. doi:10.4018/978-1-61692-010-4.ch001

Kldiashvili, E. (2012). The cloud computing as the tool for implementation of virtual organization technology for eHealth. *Journal of Information Technology Research*, 5(1), 18–34. doi:10.4018/jitr.2012010102

Kldiashvili, E. (2013). Implementation of telecytology in Georgia. In V. Gulla, A. Mori, F. Gabbrielli, & P. Lanzafame (Eds.), *Telehealth networks for hospital services: New methodologies* (pp. 341–361). Hershey, PA: Medical Information Science Reference. doi:10.4018/978-1-4666-2979-0.ch022

Klemer, D. P. (2010). Advances in biosensors for in vitro diagnostics. In A. Lazakidou (Ed.), *Biocomputation and biomedical informatics: Case studies and applications* (pp. 178–186). Hershey, PA: Medical Information Science Reference. doi:10.4018/978-1-60566-768-3.ch011

Kotwani, A. (2013). Transparency and accountability in public procurement of essential medicines in developing countries. In *Supply chain management: Concepts, methodologies, tools, and applications* (pp. 1437–1452). Hershey, PA: Business Science Reference. doi:10.4018/978-1-4666-2625-6.ch085

Kuehler, M., Schimke, N., & Hale, J. (2012). Privacy considerations for electronic health records. In G. Yee (Ed.), *Privacy protection measures and technologies in business organizations: Aspects and standards* (pp. 210–226). Hershey, PA: Information Science Reference. doi:10.4018/978-1-61350-501-4.ch008

Kukar, M., Kononenko, I., & Grošelj, C. (2013). Automated diagnostics of coronary artery disease: Long-term results and recent advancements. In *Data mining: Concepts, methodologies, tools, and applications* (pp. 1043–1063). Hershey, PA: Information Science Reference. doi:10.4018/978-1-4666-2455-9.ch053

Kumalasari, C. D., Caplow, J. A., & Fearing, N. (2013). Simulation followed by a reflection and feedback session in medical education. In L. Tomei (Ed.), *Learning tools and teaching approaches through ICT advancements* (pp. 68–81). Hershey, PA: Information Science Reference. doi:10.4018/978-1-4666-2017-9.ch007

Kumar, R., & Srivastava, R. (2014). Detection of cancer from microscopic biopsy images using image processing tools. In R. Srivastava, S. Singh, & K. Shukla (Eds.), *Research developments in computer vision and image processing: Methodologies and applications* (pp. 175–194). Hershey, PA: Information Science Reference. doi:10.4018/978-1-4666-4558-5.ch010

Kuruvilla, A., & Alexander, S. M. (2010). Predicting ambulance diverson. *International Journal of Information Systems in the Service Sector, 2*(1), 1–10. doi:10.4018/jisss.2010093001

Kyriazis, D., Menychtas, A., Tserpes, K., Athanaileas, T., & Varvarigou, T. (2010). High performance computing in biomedicine. In A. Lazakidou (Ed.), *Biocomputation and biomedical informatics: Case studies and applications* (pp. 106–118). Hershey, PA: Medical Information Science Reference. doi:10.4018/978-1-60566-768-3.ch006

LaBrunda, M., & LaBrunda, A. (2010). Fuzzy logic in medicine. In M. Khosrow-Pour (Ed.), *Breakthrough discoveries in information technology research: Advancing trends* (pp. 218–224). Hershey, PA: Information Science Reference. doi:10.4018/978-1-60566-966-3.ch017

Lagares-Lemos, Á. M., Lagares-Lemos, M., Colomo-Palacios, R., García-Crespo, Á., & Gómez-Berbís, J. M. (2011). DISMON. In *Clinical technologies: Concepts, methodologies, tools and applications* (pp. 995–1007). Hershey, PA: Medical Information Science Reference. doi:10.4018/978-1-60960-561-2.ch324

Lagares-Lemos, Á. M., Lagares-Lemos, M., Colomo-Palacios, R., García-Crespo, Á., & Gómez-Berbís, J. M. (2013). DISMON: Using social web and semantic technologies to monitor diseases in limited environments. In M. Khosrow-Pour (Ed.), *Interdisciplinary advances in information technology research* (pp. 48–59). Hershey, PA: Information Science Reference. doi:10.4018/978-1-4666-3625-5.ch004

Lappas, K. (2014). Functional assessment of persons with motor limitations: Methods and tools. In G. Kouroupetroglou (Ed.), *Disability informatics and web accessibility for motor limitations* (pp. 43–74). Hershey, PA: Medical Information Science Reference. doi:10.4018/978-1-4666-4442-7.ch002

Lazakidou, A., & Daskalaki, A. (2012). *Quality assurance in healthcare service delivery, nursing and personalized medicine: Technologies and processes.* Hershey, PA: IGI Global. doi:10.4018/978-1-61350-120-7

Leal, S., Suarez, C., Framinan, J. M., Parra, C. L., & Gómez, T. (2010). Virtual reality for supporting surgical planning. In M. Cruz-Cunha, A. Tavares, & R. Simoes (Eds.), *Handbook of research on developments in e-health and telemedicine: Technological and social perspectives* (pp. 614–635). Hershey, PA: Medical Information Science Reference. doi:10.4018/978-1-61520-670-4.ch029

Lemma, F., Denko, M. K., Tan, J. K., & Kassegne, S. K. (2011). Envisioning a national e-medicine network architecture in a developing country: A case study. In J. Tan (Ed.), *Developments in healthcare information systems and technologies: Models and methods* (pp. 35–53). Hershey, PA: Medical Information Science Reference. doi:10.4018/978-1-61692-002-9.ch003

Li, G., You, M., Xu, L., & Huang, S. (2012). Personalized experience sharing of Cai's TCM gynecology. In A. Lazakidou & A. Daskalaki (Eds.), *Quality assurance in healthcare service delivery, nursing and personalized medicine: Technologies and processes* (pp. 26–47). Hershey, PA: Medical Information Science Reference. doi:10.4018/978-1-61350-120-7.ch002

Lim, V. K. (2012). The process of medical curriculum development in Malaysia. *International Journal of User-Driven Healthcare*, 2(1), 33–39. doi:10.4018/ijudh.2012010105

Lin, H. (2013). Cultivating chan as proactive therapy for social wellness. In M. Cruz-Cunha, I. Miranda, & P. Gonçalves (Eds.), *Handbook of research on ICTs for human-centered healthcare and social care services* (pp. 151–170). Hershey, PA: Medical Information Science Reference. doi:10.4018/978-1-4666-3986-7.ch008

Liu, Q., Poon, C. C., & Zhang, Y. T. (2012). Wearable technologies for neonatal monitoring. In W. Chen, S. Oetomo, & L. Feijs (Eds.), *Neonatal monitoring technologies: Design for integrated solutions* (pp. 12–40). Hershey, PA: Medical Information Science Reference. doi:10.4018/978-1-4666-0975-4.ch002

Llobet, H., Llobet, P., & LaBrunda, M. (2011). Imaging advances of the cardiopulmonary system. In *Clinical technologies: Concepts, methodologies, tools and applications* (pp. 2183–2190). Hershey, PA: Medical Information Science Reference. doi:10.4018/978-1-60960-561-2.ch812

Logeswaran, R. (2010). Neural networks in medicine: improving difficult automated detection of cancer in the bile ducts. In R. Chiong (Ed.), *Nature-inspired informatics for intelligent applications and knowledge discovery: Implications in business, science, and engineering* (pp. 144–165). Hershey, PA: Information Science Reference. doi:10.4018/978-1-60566-705-8.ch006

Logeswaran, R. (2011). Neural networks in medicine. In *Clinical technologies: Concepts, methodologies, tools and applications* (pp. 744–765). Hershey, PA: Medical Information Science Reference. doi:10.4018/978-1-60960-561-2.ch308

Long, L. R., Antani, S., Thoma, G. R., & Deserno, T. M. (2011). Content-based image retrieval for advancing medical diagnostics, treatment and education. In J. Tan (Ed.), *New technologies for advancing healthcare and clinical practices* (pp. 1–17). Hershey, PA: Medical Information Science Reference. doi:10.4018/978-1-60960-780-7.ch001

Lueth, T. C., D'Angelo, L. T., & Czabke, A. (2010). TUM-AgeTech: A new framework for pervasive medical devices. In A. Coronato & G. De Pietro (Eds.), *Pervasive and smart technologies for healthcare: Ubiquitous methodologies and tools* (pp. 295–321). Hershey, PA: Medical Information Science Reference. doi:10.4018/978-1-61520-765-7.ch014

Lui, K. (2013). The health informatics professional. In *User-driven healthcare: Concepts, methodologies, tools, and applications* (pp. 120–141). Hershey, PA: Medical Information Science Reference. doi:10.4018/978-1-4666-2770-3.ch007

Lui, T., & Goel, L. (2012). A framework for conceptualizing the current role and future trends of information systems in medical training. *International Journal of Healthcare Information Systems and Informatics*, 7(1), 1–12. doi:10.4018/jhisi.2012010101

MacDonald, C. J., McKeen, M., Leith-Gudbranson, D., Montpetit, M., Archibald, D., Rivet, C., … Hirsh, M. (2013). University of Ottawa department of family medicine faculty development curriculum framework. In K. Patel, & S. Vij (Eds.), *Enterprise resource planning models for the education sector: Applications and methodologies* (pp. 197-215). Hershey, PA: Information Science Reference. doi:10.4018/978-1-4666-2193-0.ch014

MacGregor, R. C., Hyland, P. N., & Harvie, C. (2010). Associations between driving forces to adopt ICT and benefits derived from that adoption in medical practices in Australia. In M. Cruz-Cunha, A. Tavares, & R. Simoes (Eds.), *Handbook of research on developments in e-health and telemedicine: Technological and social perspectives* (pp. 652–668). Hershey, PA: Medical Information Science Reference. doi:10.4018/978-1-61520-670-4.ch031

Mackert, M., Whitten, P., & Holtz, B. (2010). Health infonomics: Intelligent applications of information technology. In J. Rodrigues (Ed.), *Health information systems: Concepts, methodologies, tools, and applications* (pp. 117–132). Hershey, PA: Medical Information Science Reference. doi:10.4018/978-1-60566-988-5.ch008

Malik, A. S., & Malik, R. H. (2012). Adolescent medicine curriculum at faculty of medicine, Universiti Teknologi MARA, Malaysia. *International Journal of User-Driven Healthcare*, 2(1), 40–48. doi:10.4018/ijudh.2012010106

Martin, C. M., Biswas, R., Sturmberg, J. P., Topps, D., Ellaway, R., & Smith, K. (2011). Patient journey record systems (PaJR) for preventing ambulatory care sensitive conditions: A developmental framework. In R. Biswas & C. Martin (Eds.), *User-driven healthcare and narrative medicine: Utilizing collaborative social networks and technologies* (pp. 93–112). Hershey, PA: Medical Information Science Reference. doi:10.4018/978-1-60960-097-6.ch007

Masayuki, K., Eiji, K., Tetsuo, T., & Nozomu, M. (2013). Evaluation of olfactory impairment in Parkinson's disease using near-infrared spectroscopy. In J. Wu (Ed.), *Biomedical engineering and cognitive neuroscience for healthcare: Interdisciplinary applications* (pp. 293–302). Hershey, PA: Medical Information Science Reference. doi:10.4018/978-1-4666-2113-8.ch030

Mazzanti, I., Maolo, A., & Antonicelli, R. (2014). E-health and telemedicine in the elderly: State of the art. In *Assistive technologies: Concepts, methodologies, tools, and applications* (pp. 693–704). Hershey, PA: Information Science Reference. doi:10.4018/978-1-4666-4422-9.ch034

Medhekar, A., Wong, H. Y., & Hall, J. (2014). Innovation in medical tourism service marketing: A case of India. In A. Goyal (Ed.), *Innovations in services marketing and management: Strategies for emerging economies* (pp. 49–66). Hershey, PA: Business Science Reference. doi:10.4018/978-1-4666-4671-1.ch003

Medhekar, A., Wong, H. Y., & Hall, J. (2014). Medical tourism: A conceptual framework for an innovation in global healthcare provision. In A. Goyal (Ed.), *Innovations in services marketing and management: Strategies for emerging economies* (pp. 148–169). Hershey, PA: Business Science Reference. doi:10.4018/978-1-4666-4671-1.ch009

Memmola, M., Palumbo, G., & Rossini, M. (2010). Web & RFID technology: New frontiers in costing and process management for rehabilitation medicine. In J. Symonds (Ed.), *Ubiquitous and pervasive computing: Concepts, methodologies, tools, and applications* (pp. 623–647). Hershey, PA: Information Science Reference. doi:10.4018/978-1-60566-960-1.ch039

Menciassi, A., & Laschi, C. (2014). Biorobotics. In *Robotics: Concepts, methodologies, tools, and applications* (pp. 1613-1643). Hershey, PA: Information Science Reference. doi:10.4018/978-1-4666-4607-0.ch079

Mika, K. (2010). Cybermedicine, telemedicine, and data protection in the United States. In J. Rodrigues (Ed.), *Health information systems: Concepts, methodologies, tools, and applications* (pp. 274–296). Hershey, PA: Medical Information Science Reference. doi:10.4018/978-1-60566-988-5.ch019

Mirbagheri, A., Baniasad, M. A., Farahmand, F., Behzadipour, S., & Ahmadian, A. (2013). Medical robotics: State-of-the-art applications and research challenges. *International Journal of Healthcare Information Systems and Informatics*, 8(2), 1–14. doi:10.4018/jhisi.2013040101

Miscione, G. (2013). Telemedicine and development: Situating information technologies in the Amazon. In J. Abdelnour-Nocera (Ed.), *Knowledge and technological development effects on organizational and social structures* (pp. 132–145). Hershey, PA: Information Science Reference. doi:10.4018/978-1-4666-2151-0.ch009

Mobasheri, A. (2013). Regeneration of articular cartilage: Opportunities, challenges, and perspectives. In A. Daskalaki (Ed.), *Medical advancements in aging and regenerative technologies: Clinical tools and applications* (pp. 137–168). Hershey, PA: Medical Information Science Reference. doi:10.4018/978-1-4666-2506-8.ch007

Monzon, J. E. (2012). Bioethics. In Z. Abu-Faraj (Ed.), *Handbook of research on biomedical engineering education and advanced bioengineering learning: Interdisciplinary concepts* (pp. 198–237). Hershey, PA: Medical Information Science Reference. doi:10.4018/978-1-4666-0122-2.ch005

Morais da Costa, G. J., Araújo da Silva Nuno, M., & Alves da Silva Nuno, S. (2010). The human centred approach to bionanotechnology in telemedicine: Ethical considerations. In M. Cruz-Cunha, A. Tavares, & R. Simoes (Eds.), *Handbook of research on developments in e-health and telemedicine: Technological and social perspectives* (pp. 311–335). Hershey, PA: Medical Information Science Reference. doi:10.4018/978-1-61520-670-4.ch015

Morgade, A. T., Martínez-Romero, M., Vázquez-Naya, J. M., Loureiro, M. P., Albo, Á. G., & Loureiro, J. P. (2011). Development of a knowledge based system for an intensive care environment using ontologies. *Journal of Information Technology Research*, 4(1), 21–33. doi:10.4018/jitr.2011010102

Morita, A. (2013). The quantitative EEG change in Parkinson's disease. In J. Wu (Ed.), *Biomedical engineering and cognitive neuroscience for healthcare: Interdisciplinary applications* (pp. 225–234). Hershey, PA: Medical Information Science Reference. doi:10.4018/978-1-4666-2113-8.ch023

Moumtzoglou, A. (2011). E-health as the realm of healthcare quality: A mental image of the future. In A. Moumtzoglou & A. Kastania (Eds.), *E-health systems quality and reliability: Models and standards* (pp. 291–310). Hershey, PA: Medical Information Science Reference. doi:10.4018/978-1-61692-843-8.ch022

Moumtzoglou, A. (2011). E-health as the realm of healthcare quality. In *Clinical technologies: Concepts, methodologies, tools and applications* (pp. 73–92). Hershey, PA: Medical Information Science Reference. doi:10.4018/978-1-60960-561-2.ch105

Moumtzoglou, A. (2011). E-health: A bridge to people-centered health care. In A. Moumtzoglou & A. Kastania (Eds.), *E-health systems quality and reliability: Models and standards* (pp. 47–63). Hershey, PA: Medical Information Science Reference. doi:10.4018/978-1-61692-843-8.ch005

Moumtzoglou, A. (2013). Health 2.0 and medicine 2.0: Safety, ownership and privacy issues. In User-driven healthcare: Concepts, methodologies, tools, and applications (pp. 1508-1522). Hershey, PA: Medical Information Science Reference. doi:10.4018/978-1-4666-2770-3.ch075

Moumtzoglou, A. (2013). Risk perception as a patient safety dimension. In A. Moumtzoglou & A. Kastania (Eds.), *E-health technologies and improving patient safety: Exploring organizational factors* (pp. 285–299). Hershey, PA: Medical Information Science Reference. doi:10.4018/978-1-4666-2657-7.ch017

Mourtzikou, A., Stamouli, M., & Athanasiadi, E. (2013). Improvement of clinical laboratory services through quality. *International Journal of Reliable and Quality E-Healthcare*, 2(2), 38–46. doi:10.4018/ijrqeh.2013040103

Muriithi, M. K., & Mwabu, G. (2014). Demand for health care in Kenya: The effects of information about quality. In P. Schaeffer & E. Kouassi (Eds.), *Econometric methods for analyzing economic development* (pp. 102–110). Hershey, PA: Business Science Reference. doi:10.4018/978-1-4666-4329-1.ch007

Murugan, B. O., & Sornam, S. A. (2013). Internet and online medical journal access skills of the medical practitioners of Tamilnadu: A study. In S. Thanuskodi (Ed.), *Challenges of academic library management in developing countries* (pp. 75–82). Hershey, PA: Information Science Reference. doi:10.4018/978-1-4666-4070-2.ch006

Nadathur, S. G. (2010). Bayesian networks in the health domain. In A. Ali & Y. Xiang (Eds.), *Dynamic and advanced data mining for progressing technological development: Innovations and systemic approaches* (pp. 342–376). Hershey, PA: Information Science Reference. doi:10.4018/978-1-60566-908-3.ch014

Naidoo, V., & Naidoo, Y. (2014). Home telecare, medical implant, and mobile technology: Evolutions in geriatric care. In C. El Morr (Ed.), *Research Perspectives on the role of informatics in health policy and management* (pp. 222–237). Hershey, PA: Medical Information Science Reference. doi:10.4018/978-1-4666-4321-5.ch013

Najarian, S., & Afshari, E. (2010). Applications of robots in surgery. In A. Shukla & R. Tiwari (Eds.), *Intelligent medical technologies and biomedical engineering: Tools and applications* (pp. 241–259). Hershey, PA: Medical Information Science Reference. doi:10.4018/978-1-61520-977-4.ch012

Nakajima, I. (2012). Cross-border medical care and telemedicine. *International Journal of E-Health and Medical Communications*, *3*(1), 46–61. doi:10.4018/jehmc.2012010104

Nakayasu, K., & Sato, C. (2012). Liability for telemedicine. *International Journal of E-Health and Medical Communications*, *3*(1), 1–21. doi:10.4018/jehmc.2012010101

Narasimhalu, D. (2010). Redefining medical tourism. In S. Becker & R. Niebuhr (Eds.), *Cases on technology innovation: Entrepreneurial successes and pitfalls* (pp. 267–285). Hershey, PA: Business Science Reference. doi:10.4018/978-1-61520-609-4.ch014

Naulaers, G., Caicedo, A., & Van Huffel, S. (2012). Use of near-infrared spectroscopy in the neonatal intensive care unit. In W. Chen, S. Oetomo, & L. Feijs (Eds.), *Neonatal monitoring technologies: Design for integrated solutions* (pp. 56–83). Hershey, PA: Medical Information Science Reference. doi:10.4018/978-1-4666-0975-4.ch004

Nokata, M. (2014). Small medical robot. In I. Management Association (Ed.), Robotics: Concepts, methodologies, tools, and applications (pp. 638-646). Hershey, PA: Information Science Reference. doi:10.4018/978-1-4666-4607-0.ch032

Noteboom, C. (2013). Physician interaction with EHR: The importance of stakeholder identification and change management. In S. Sarnikar, D. Bennett, & M. Gaynor (Eds.), *Cases on healthcare information technology for patient care management* (pp. 95–112). Hershey, PA: Medical Information Science Reference. doi:10.4018/978-1-4666-2671-3.ch005

Noury, N., Bourquard, K., Bergognon, D., & Schroeder, J. (2013). Regulations initiatives in France for the interoperability of communicating medical devices. *International Journal of E-Health and Medical Communications*, *4*(2), 50–64. doi:10.4018/jehmc.2013040104

O'Hanlon, S. (2013). Avoiding adverse consequences of e-health. In A. Moumtzoglou & A. Kastania (Eds.), *E-health technologies and improving patient safety: Exploring organizational factors* (pp. 13–26). Hershey, PA: Medical Information Science Reference. doi:10.4018/978-1-4666-2657-7.ch002

O'Leary, D. E. (2012). An activity theory analysis of RFID in hospitals. In Z. Luo (Ed.), *Innovations in logistics and supply chain management technologies for dynamic economies* (pp. 148–166). Hershey, PA: Business Science Reference. doi:10.4018/978-1-4666-0267-0.ch010

O'Neill, L., Talbert, J., & Klepack, W. (2010). Physician characteristics associated with early adoption of electronic medical records in smaller group practices. In J. Rodrigues (Ed.), *Health information systems: Concepts, methodologies, tools, and applications* (pp. 1503–1512). Hershey, PA: Medical Information Science Reference. doi:10.4018/978-1-60566-988-5.ch096

Ogawa, T., Ikeda, M., Suzuki, M., & Araki, K. (2014). Medical practical knowledge circulation based on purpose-oriented service modeling. In M. Kosaka & K. Shirahada (Eds.), *Progressive trends in knowledge and system-based science for service innovation* (pp. 400–424). Hershey, PA: Business Science Reference. doi:10.4018/978-1-4666-4663-6.ch022

Oliveira, T. C., Oliveira, M. D., & Peña, T. (2013). Towards a post-implementation evaluation framework of outpatient electronic drug prescribing. In M. Cruz-Cunha, I. Miranda, & P. Gonçalves (Eds.), *Handbook of research on ICTs and management systems for improving efficiency in healthcare and social care* (pp. 133–155). Hershey, PA: Medical Information Science Reference. doi:10.4018/978-1-4666-3990-4.ch007

Orizio, G., & Gelatti, U. (2012). Human behaviors in online pharmacies. In Z. Yan (Ed.), *Encyclopedia of cyber behavior* (pp. 661–670). Hershey, PA: Information Science Reference. doi:10.4018/978-1-4666-0315-8.ch056

Otero, A., Félix, P., & Barro, S. (2010). Current state of critical patient monitoring and outstanding challenges. In M. Cruz-Cunha, A. Tavares, & R. Simoes (Eds.), *Handbook of research on developments in e-health and telemedicine: Technological and social perspectives* (pp. 981–1003). Hershey, PA: Medical Information Science Reference. doi:10.4018/978-1-61520-670-4.ch047

Ozturk, Y., & Sharma, J. (2013). mVITAL: A standards compliant vital sign monitor. In IT policy and ethics: Concepts, methodologies, tools, and applications (pp. 515-538). Hershey, PA: Information Science Reference. doi:10.4018/978-1-4666-2919-6.ch024

Pal, K., Ghosh, G., & Bhattacharya, M. (2014). Biomedical watermarking: An emerging and secure tool for data security and better tele-diagnosis in modern health care system. In R. Srivastava, S. Singh, & K. Shukla (Eds.), *Research developments in computer vision and image processing: Methodologies and applications* (pp. 208–234). Hershey, PA: Information Science Reference. doi:10.4018/978-1-4666-4558-5.ch012

Paolucci, F., Ergas, H., Hannan, T., & Aarts, J. (2011). The effectiveness of health informatics. In *Clinical technologies: Concepts, methodologies, tools and applications* (pp. 25–49). Hershey, PA: Medical Information Science Reference. doi:10.4018/978-1-60960-561-2.ch103

Parasher, A., Goldschmidt-Clermont, P. J., & Tien, J. M. (2012). Healthcare delivery as a service system: Barriers to co-production and implications of healthcare reform. In A. Kolker & P. Story (Eds.), *Management engineering for effective healthcare delivery: Principles and applications* (pp. 191–214). Hershey, PA: Medical Information Science Reference. doi:10.4018/978-1-60960-872-9.ch009

Parry, D. (2010). Coding and messaging systems for women's health informatics. In J. Rodrigues (Ed.), *Health information systems: Concepts, methodologies, tools, and applications* (pp. 2192–2205). Hershey, PA: Medical Information Science Reference. doi:10.4018/978-1-60566-988-5.ch139

Parry, D. (2012). Computerised decision support for women's health informatics. In *Machine learning: Concepts, methodologies, tools and applications* (pp. 1404–1416). Hershey, PA: Information Science Reference. doi:10.4018/978-1-60960-818-7.ch513

Payne, G. W. (2011). The role of blended learning in 21st century medical education: Current trends and future directions. In A. Kitchenham (Ed.), *Blended learning across disciplines: Models for implementation* (pp. 132–146). Hershey, PA: Information Science Reference. doi:10.4018/978-1-60960-479-0.ch008

Penchovsky, R. (2013). Engineering gene control circuits with allosteric ribozymes in human cells as a medicine of the future. In Bioinformatics: Concepts, methodologies, tools, and applications (pp. 860-883). Hershey, PA: Medical Information Science Reference. doi:10.4018/978-1-4666-3604-0.ch047

Pestana, O. (2014). Information value and quality for the health sector: A case study of search strategies for optimal information retrieval. In G. Jamil, A. Malheiro, & F. Ribeiro (Eds.), *Rethinking the conceptual base for new practical applications in information value and quality* (pp. 116–133). Hershey, PA: Information Science Reference. doi:10.4018/978-1-4666-4562-2.ch006

Peterson, C., & Willis, E. (2011). Social construction of chronic disease: Narratives on the experience of chronic illness. In R. Biswas & C. Martin (Eds.), *User-driven healthcare and narrative medicine: Utilizing collaborative social networks and technologies* (pp. 395–409). Hershey, PA: Medical Information Science Reference. doi:10.4018/978-1-60960-097-6.ch027

Petoukhov, S., & He, M. (2010). Biological evolution of dialects of the genetic code. In S. Petoukhov & M. He (Eds.), *Symmetrical analysis techniques for genetic systems and bioinformatics: Advanced patterns and applications* (pp. 50–64). Hershey, PA: Medical Information Science Reference. doi:10.4018/978-1-60566-124-7.ch003

Petty, G. C., & Joyner, D. H. (2012). The efficacy of continuing education technology for public health physicians practicing in remote areas. In V. Wang (Ed.), *Encyclopedia of e-leadership, counseling and training* (pp. 453–467). Hershey, PA: Information Science Reference. doi:10.4018/978-1-61350-068-2.ch033

Phua, C., Roy, P. C., Aloulou, H., Biswas, J., Tolstikov, A., Foo, V. S., ... Xu, D. (2014). State-of-the-art assistive technology for people with dementia. In *Assistive technologies: Concepts, methodologies, tools, and applications* (pp. 1606-1625). Hershey, PA: Information Science Reference. doi:10.4018/978-1-4666-4422-9.ch085

Portela, F., Cabral, A., Abelha, A., Salazar, M., Quintas, C., Machado, J., ... Santos, M. F. (2013). Knowledge acquisition process for intelligent decision support in critical health care. In R. Martinho, R. Rijo, M. Cruz-Cunha, & J. Varajão (Eds.), *Information systems and technologies for enhancing health and social care* (pp. 55-68). Hershey, PA: Medical Information Science Reference. doi:10.4018/978-1-4666-3667-5.ch004

Postolache, O., Girão, P., & Postolache, G. (2013). Seismocardiogram and ballistocardiogram sensing. In A. Lay-Ekuakille (Ed.), *Advanced instrument engineering: Measurement, calibration, and design* (pp. 223–246). Hershey, PA: Engineering Science Reference. doi:10.4018/978-1-4666-4165-5.ch017

Premkumar, K. (2011). Mobile learning in medicine. In A. Kitchenham (Ed.), *Models for interdisciplinary mobile learning: Delivering information to students* (pp. 137–153). Hershey, PA: Information Science Reference. doi:10.4018/978-1-60960-511-7.ch008

Price, M. (2011). A bio-psycho-social review of usability methods and their applications in healthcare. In *Clinical technologies: Concepts, methodologies, tools and applications* (pp. 1874–1899). Hershey, PA: Medical Information Science Reference. doi:10.4018/978-1-60960-561-2.ch704

Prigione, A. (2012). Stem cell-based personalized medicine: From disease modeling to clinical applications. In *Computer engineering: Concepts, methodologies, tools and applications* (pp. 1855–1866). Hershey, PA: Engineering Science Reference. doi:10.4018/978-1-61350-456-7.ch803

Quinaz, F., Fazendeiro, P., Castelo-Branco, M., & Araújo, P. (2013). Soft methods for automatic drug infusion in medical care environment. In M. Cruz-Cunha, I. Miranda, & P. Gonçalves (Eds.), *Handbook of research on ICTs and management systems for improving efficiency in healthcare and social care* (pp. 830–854). Hershey, PA: Medical Information Science Reference. doi:10.4018/978-1-4666-3990-4.ch043

Quoniam, L., & Lima de Magalhães, J. (2014). Perception of the information value for public health: A case study for neglected diseases. In G. Jamil, A. Malheiro, & F. Ribeiro (Eds.), *Rethinking the conceptual base for new practical applications in information value and quality* (pp. 211–232). Hershey, PA: Information Science Reference. doi:10.4018/978-1-4666-4562-2.ch009

Raghupathi, W. (2010). Designing clinical decision support systems in health care: A systemic view. In M. Hunter (Ed.), *Strategic information systems: Concepts, methodologies, tools, and applications* (pp. 652–661). Hershey, PA: Information Science Reference. doi:10.4018/978-1-60566-677-8.ch043

Raghupathi, W., & Nerur, S. (2012). The intellectual structure of health and medical informatics. In J. Tan (Ed.), *Advancing technologies and intelligence in healthcare and clinical environments breakthroughs* (pp. 1–16). Hershey, PA: Medical Information Science Reference. doi:10.4018/978-1-4666-1755-1.ch001

Räisänen, T., Oinas-Kukkonen, H., Leiviskä, K., Seppänen, M., & Kallio, M. (2010). Managing mobile healthcare knowledge: Physicians' perceptions on knowledge creation and reuse. In J. Rodrigues (Ed.), *Health information systems: Concepts, methodologies, tools, and applications* (pp. 733–749). Hershey, PA: Medical Information Science Reference. doi:10.4018/978-1-60566-988-5.ch046

Raval, M. S. (2011). Data hiding in digitized medical images: From concepts to applications. In A. Daskalaki (Ed.), *Digital forensics for the health sciences: Applications in practice and research* (pp. 29–47). Hershey, PA: Medical Information Science Reference. doi:10.4018/978-1-60960-483-7.ch003

Ravka, N. (2014). Informatics and health services: The potential benefits and challenges of electronic health records and personal electronic health records in patient care, cost control, and health research – An overview. In C. El Morr (Ed.), *Research perspectives on the role of informatics in health policy and management* (pp. 89–114). Hershey, PA: Medical Information Science Reference. doi:10.4018/978-1-4666-4321-5.ch007

Reyes Álamo, J. M., Yang, H., Babbitt, R., & Wong, J. (2010). Support for medication safety and compliance in smart home environments. In J. Rodrigues (Ed.), *Health information systems: Concepts, methodologies, tools, and applications* (pp. 2091–2110). Hershey, PA: Medical Information Science Reference. doi:10.4018/978-1-60566-988-5.ch133

Ribeiro, C., Monteiro, M., Corredoura, S., Candeias, F., & Pereira, J. (2013). Games in higher education: Opportunities, expectations, challenges, and results in medical education. In S. de Freitas, M. Ott, M. Popescu, & I. Stanescu (Eds.), *New pedagogical approaches in game enhanced learning: Curriculum integration* (pp. 228–247). Hershey, PA: Information Science Reference. doi:10.4018/978-1-4666-3950-8.ch012

Rocci, L. (2010). Biomedical technoethics. In R. Luppicini (Ed.), *Technoethics and the evolving knowledge society: Ethical issues in technological design, research, development, and innovation* (pp. 128–145). Hershey, PA: Information Science Reference. doi:10.4018/978-1-60566-952-6.ch007

Rockland, R., Kimmel, H., Carpinelli, J., Hirsch, L. S., & Burr-Alexander, L. (2014). Medical robotics in k-12 education. In Robotics: Concepts, methodologies, tools, and applications (pp. 1096-1115). Hershey, PA: Information Science Reference. doi:10.4018/978-1-4666-4607-0.ch053

Rodrigues, J. J. (2012). *Emerging communication technologies for e-health and medicine*. Hershey, PA: IGI Global. doi:10.4018/978-1-4666-0909-9

Rodrigues, J. J. (2013). *Digital advances in medicine, e-health, and communication technologies*. Hershey, PA: IGI Global. doi:10.4018/978-1-4666-2794-9

Rodrigues, J. J. (2014). *Advancing medical practice through technology: Applications for healthcare delivery, management, and quality*. Hershey, PA: IGI Global. doi:10.4018/978-1-4666-4619-3

Rodríguez-González, A., García-Crespo, Á., Colomo-Palacios, R., Gómez-Berbís, J. M., & Jiménez-Domingo, E. (2013). Using ontologies in drug prescription: The SemMed approach. In J. Wang (Ed.), *Intelligence methods and systems advancements for knowledge-based business* (pp. 247–261). Hershey, PA: Information Science Reference. doi:10.4018/978-1-4666-1873-2.ch014

Rojo, M. G., & Daniel, C. (2011). Digital pathology and virtual microscopy integration in e-health records. In *Clinical technologies: Concepts, methodologies, tools and applications* (pp. 1235–1262). Hershey, PA: Medical Information Science Reference. doi:10.4018/978-1-60960-561-2.ch415

Rompas, A., Tsirmpas, C., Anastasiou, A., Iliopoulou, D., & Koutsouris, D. (2013). Statistical power and sample size in personalized medicine. *International Journal of Systems Biology and Biomedical Technologies*, 2(2), 72–88. doi:10.4018/ijs-bbt.2013040105

Rosiek, A. B., & Leksowski, K. (2011). Quality assurance and evaluation of health-care reform initiatives: Strategy for improving the quality of health care services in public health care units, management model that allows the providing of high quality health care and efficient brand-building. *International Journal of Healthcare Delivery Reform Initiatives*, 3(3), 42–53. doi:10.4018/jhdri.2011070104

Ross, S. (2011). A lexicon for user driven healthcare. *International Journal of User-Driven Healthcare*, 1(1), 50–54. doi:10.4018/ijudh.2011010107

Ross, S. D. (2011). Multiple paths in health care. In R. Biswas & C. Martin (Eds.), *User-driven healthcare and narrative medicine: Utilizing collaborative social networks and technologies* (pp. 113–124). Hershey, PA: Medical Information Science Reference. doi:10.4018/978-1-60960-097-6.ch008

Rosu, S. M., & Dragoi, G. (2014). E-health sites development using open source software and OMT methodology as support for family doctors' activities: A Romanian case study. In M. Cruz-Cunha, F. Moreira, & J. Varajão (Eds.), *Handbook of research on enterprise 2.0: Technological, social, and organizational dimensions* (pp. 72–88). Hershey, PA: Business Science Reference. doi:10.4018/978-1-4666-4373-4.ch004

Ruiz-Fernandez, D., & Soriano-Paya, A. (2011). A distributed approach of a clinical decision support system based on cooperation. In *Clinical technologies: Concepts, methodologies, tools and applications* (pp. 1782–1799). Hershey, PA: Medical Information Science Reference. doi:10.4018/978-1-60960-561-2.ch612

Ryan, P. (2012). Paying for performance: Key design features and the bigger picture. *International Journal of Public and Private Healthcare Management and Economics*, 2(2), 1–16. doi:10.4018/ijpphme.2012040101

Sainz de Abajo, B., & Ballestero, A. L. (2012). Overview of the most important open source software: Analysis of the benefits of OpenMRS, OpenEMR, and VistA. In J. Rodrigues, I. de la Torre Díez, & B. Sainz de Abajo (Eds.), *Telemedicine and e-health services, policies, and applications: Advancements and developments* (pp. 315–346). Hershey, PA: Medical Information Science Reference. doi:10.4018/978-1-4666-0888-7.ch012

Salcido, G. J., & Delgado, E. C. (2013). Intelligent agent to identify rheumatic diseases. In M. Cruz-Cunha, I. Miranda, & P. Gonçalves (Eds.), *Handbook of research on ICTs and management systems for improving efficiency in healthcare and social care* (pp. 451–473). Hershey, PA: Medical Information Science Reference. doi:10.4018/978-1-4666-3990-4.ch023

Schallenberg, S., Petzold, C., Riewaldt, J., & Kretschmer, K. (2013). Regulatory T cell-based immunotherapy: Prospects of antigen-specific tolerance induction. In A. Daskalaki (Ed.), *Medical advancements in aging and regenerative technologies: Clinical tools and applications* (pp. 112–136). Hershey, PA: Medical Information Science Reference. doi:10.4018/978-1-4666-2506-8.ch006

Scheepers-Hoeks, A., Klijn, F., van der Linden, C., Grouls, R., Ackerman, E., Minderman, N., ... Korsten, E. (2013). Clinical decision support systems for 'making it easy to do it right. In Data mining: Concepts, methodologies, tools, and applications (pp. 1461-1471). Hershey, PA: Information Science Reference. doi:10.4018/978-1-4666-2455-9.ch076

Seçkin, G. (2012). Cyber behaviors of self health care management. In Z. Yan (Ed.), *Encyclopedia of cyber behavior* (pp. 722–734). Hershey, PA: Information Science Reference. doi:10.4018/978-1-4666-0315-8.ch061

Serrano, M., Elmisery, A., Foghlú, M. Ó., Donnelly, W., Storni, C., & Fernström, M. (2013). Pervasive computing support in the transition towards personalised health systems. In J. Rodrigues (Ed.), *Digital advances in medicine, e-health, and communication technologies* (pp. 49–64). Hershey, PA: Medical Information Science Reference. doi:10.4018/978-1-4666-2794-9.ch003

Shachak, A., & Reis, S. (2010). The computer-assisted patient consultation: Promises and challenges. In S. Kabene (Ed.), *Healthcare and the effect of technology: Developments, challenges and advancements* (pp. 72–83). Hershey, PA: Medical Information Science Reference. doi:10.4018/978-1-61520-733-6.ch005

Shachak, A., & Reis, S. (2011). The computer-assisted patient consultation. In *Clinical technologies: Concepts, methodologies, tools and applications* (pp. 160–171). Hershey, PA: Medical Information Science Reference. doi:10.4018/978-1-60960-561-2.ch111

Shankar, P. R. (2011). Medical Humanities. In R. Biswas & C. Martin (Eds.), *User-driven healthcare and narrative medicine: Utilizing collaborative social networks and technologies* (pp. 210–227). Hershey, PA: Medical Information Science Reference. doi:10.4018/978-1-60960-097-6.ch016

Shanmuganathan, S. (2010). A stroke information system (SIS): Critical issues and solutions. In W. Pease, M. Cooper, & R. Gururajan (Eds.), *Biomedical knowledge management: Infrastructures and processes for e-health systems* (pp. 177–191). Hershey, PA: Medical Information Science Reference. doi:10.4018/978-1-60566-266-4.ch012

Shegog, R. (2010). Application of behavioral theory in computer game design for health behavior change. In J. Cannon-Bowers & C. Bowers (Eds.), *Serious game design and development: Technologies for training and learning* (pp. 196–232). Hershey, PA: Information Science Reference. doi:10.4018/978-1-61520-739-8.ch011

Shendge, S., Deka, B., & Kotwani, A. (2012). A cross-sectional evaluation of illness perception about asthma among asthma patients at a referral tertiary care public chest hospital in Delhi, India. *International Journal of User-Driven Healthcare*, 2(3), 32–43. doi:10.4018/ijudh.2012070104

Shimoyama, I., Shimada, H., & Ninchoji, T. (2013). Kanji perception and brain function. In J. Wu (Ed.), *Biomedical engineering and cognitive neuroscience for healthcare: Interdisciplinary applications* (pp. 266–273). Hershey, PA: Medical Information Science Reference. doi:10.4018/978-1-4666-2113-8.ch027

Shrestha, S. (2013). Clinical decision support system for diabetes prevention: An illustrative case. In S. Sarnikar, D. Bennett, & M. Gaynor (Eds.), *Cases on healthcare information technology for patient care management* (pp. 308–329). Hershey, PA: Medical Information Science Reference. doi:10.4018/978-1-4666-2671-3.ch017

Shukla, A., Tiwari, R., & Rathore, C. P. (2011). Intelligent biometric system using soft computing tools. In A. Shukla & R. Tiwari (Eds.), *Biomedical engineering and information systems: Technologies, tools and applications* (pp. 259–276). Hershey, PA: Medical Information Science Reference. doi:10.4018/978-1-61692-004-3.ch014

Sibinga, C. T., & Oladejo, M. A. (2013). Bridging the knowledge gap in management and operations of transfusion medicine: Planning, policy and leadership issues. *Journal of Cases on Information Technology*, *15*(1), 69–82. doi:10.4018/jcit.2013010105

Slavens, B., & Harris, G. F. (2012). Biomechanics. In Z. Abu-Faraj (Ed.), *Handbook of research on biomedical engineering education and advanced bioengineering learning: Interdisciplinary concepts* (pp. 284–338). Hershey, PA: Medical Information Science Reference. doi:10.4018/978-1-4666-0122-2.ch007

Sliedrecht, S., & Kotzé, E. (2013). Patients with a spinal cord injury inform and co-construct services at a spinal cord rehabilitation unit. In *User-driven healthcare: Concepts, methodologies, tools, and applications* (pp. 1054–1072). Hershey, PA: Medical Information Science Reference. doi:10.4018/978-1-4666-2770-3.ch053

Sood, R., & Ananthakrishnan, N. (2012). Reforming medical curriculum in India in recent years: Conflicts of political, regulator, educationist and professional natures and strategies for their resolution. *International Journal of User-Driven Healthcare*, *2*(1), 1–13. doi:10.4018/ijudh.2012010101

Springer, J. A., Beever, J., Morar, N., Sprague, J. E., & Kane, M. D. (2011). Ethics, Privacy, and the future of genetic information in healthcare information assurance and security. In M. Dark (Ed.), *Information assurance and security ethics in complex systems: Interdisciplinary perspectives* (pp. 186–205). Hershey, PA: Information Science Reference. doi:10.4018/978-1-61692-245-0.ch009

Srivastava, S. (2011). Medical transcription a pioneer in the healthcare informatics. In A. Shukla & R. Tiwari (Eds.), *Biomedical engineering and information systems: Technologies, tools and applications* (pp. 239–258). Hershey, PA: Medical Information Science Reference. doi:10.4018/978-1-61692-004-3.ch013

Srivastava, S., Sharma, N., & Singh, S. (2014). Image analysis and understanding techniques for breast cancer detection from digital mammograms. In R. Srivastava, S. Singh, & K. Shukla (Eds.), *Research developments in computer vision and image processing: Methodologies and applications* (pp. 123–148). Hershey, PA: Information Science Reference. doi:10.4018/978-1-4666-4558-5.ch008

Stanescu, L., & Burdescu, D. D. (2010). Medical hybrid learning tools. In F. Wang, J. Fong, & R. Kwan (Eds.), *Handbook of research on hybrid learning models: Advanced tools, technologies, and applications* (pp. 355–370). Hershey, PA: Information Science Reference. doi:10.4018/978-1-60566-380-7.ch022

Staudinger, B., Ostermann, H., & Staudinger, R. (2011). IT-based virtual medical centres and structures. In *Clinical technologies: Concepts, methodologies, tools and applications* (pp. 2035–2046). Hershey, PA: Medical Information Science Reference. doi:10.4018/978-1-60960-561-2.ch802

Stefaniak, J. E. (2013). Resuscitating team roles within Wayburn health system. In A. Ritzhaupt & S. Kumar (Eds.), *Cases on educational technology implementation for facilitating learning* (pp. 130–145). Hershey, PA: Information Science Reference. doi:10.4018/978-1-4666-3676-7.ch008

Stein, R. A. (2012). Direct-to-consumer genetic testing: Interdisciplinary crossroads. *Journal of Information Technology Research*, 5(1), 35–67. doi:10.4018/jitr.2012010103

Stergachis, A., Keene, D., & Somani, S. (2013). Informatics for medicines management systems in resource-limited settings. In *Supply chain management: Concepts, methodologies, tools, and applications* (pp. 634–645). Hershey, PA: Business Science Reference. doi:10.4018/978-1-4666-2625-6.ch037

Stevens, D., & Kitchenham, A. (2011). An analysis of mobile learning in education, business, and medicine. In A. Kitchenham (Ed.), *Models for interdisciplinary mobile learning: Delivering information to students* (pp. 1–25). Hershey, PA: Information Science Reference. doi:10.4018/978-1-60960-511-7.ch001

Stolba, N., Nguyen, T. M., & Tjoa, A. M. (2010). Data warehouse facilitating evidence-based medicine. In T. Nguyen (Ed.), *Complex data warehousing and knowledge discovery for advanced retrieval development: Innovative methods and applications* (pp. 174–207). Hershey, PA: Information Science Reference. doi:10.4018/978-1-60566-748-5.ch008

Sugaretty, D. (2014). Risk management in a pandemic crisis at a global non profit health care organization. In *Crisis management: Concepts, methodologies, tools and applications* (pp. 1253–1270). Hershey, PA: Information Science Reference. doi:10.4018/978-1-4666-4707-7.ch063

Sugi, T., Goto, K., Goto, S., Goto, Y., Yamasaki, T., & Tobimatsu, S. (2013). Topography estimation of visual evoked potentials using a combination of mathematical models. In J. Wu (Ed.), *Biomedical engineering and cognitive neuroscience for healthcare: Interdisciplinary applications* (pp. 129–141). Hershey, PA: Medical Information Science Reference. doi:10.4018/978-1-4666-2113-8.ch014

Sujan, H., Borrero, S., & Cranage, D. (2014). Good treats: Eating out not just for joy but also for well-being. In A. Goyal (Ed.), *Innovations in services marketing and management: Strategies for emerging economies* (pp. 118–135). Hershey, PA: Business Science Reference. doi:10.4018/978-1-4666-4671-1.ch007

Swennen, M. H. (2011). The gap between what is knowable and what we do in clinical practice. In R. Biswas & C. Martin (Eds.), *User-driven healthcare and narrative medicine: Utilizing collaborative social networks and technologies* (pp. 335–356). Hershey, PA: Medical Information Science Reference. doi:10.4018/978-1-60960-097-6.ch024

Szewczak, E. J., & Snodgrass, C. R. (2011). Business associates in the national health information network: Implications for medical information privacy. In I. Lee (Ed.), *E-business applications for product development and competitive growth: Emerging technologies* (pp. 186–198). Hershey, PA: Business Science Reference. doi:10.4018/978-1-60960-132-4.ch009

Tabrizi, N. T., Torabi, Z., Bastani, P., Mokhtarkhani, M., Madani, N., Parnian, N., & Hajebrahimi, S. (2013). Assessing the perception of pain and distress of female patients undergoing routine urethral catheterization in cesarean delivery. *International Journal of User-Driven Healthcare*, *3*(2), 78–84. doi:10.4018/ijudh.2013040109

Tanaka, H., & Furutani, M. (2013). Sleep management promotes healthy lifestyle, mental health, QOL, and a healthy brain. In J. Wu (Ed.), *Biomedical engineering and cognitive neuroscience for healthcare: Interdisciplinary applications* (pp. 211–224). Hershey, PA: Medical Information Science Reference. doi:10.4018/978-1-4666-2113-8.ch022

Tang, X., Gao, Y., Yang, W., Zhang, M., & Wu, J. (2013). Audiovisual integration of natural auditory and visual stimuli in the real-world situation. In J. Wu (Ed.), *Biomedical engineering and cognitive neuroscience for healthcare: Interdisciplinary applications* (pp. 337–344). Hershey, PA: Medical Information Science Reference. doi:10.4018/978-1-4666-2113-8.ch035

Tashiro, M., Okamura, N., Watanuki, S., Furumoto, S., Furukawa, K., Funaki, Y., … Yanai, K. (2011). Quantitative analysis of amyloid ß deposition in patients with Alzheimer's disease using positron emission tomography. In J. Wu (Ed.), Early detection and rehabilitation technologies for dementia: Neuroscience and biomedical applications (pp. 220-230). Hershey, PA: Medical Information Science Reference. doi:10.4018/978-1-60960-559-9.ch029

Taylor, B. W. (2014). Decision-making and decision support in acute care. In C. El Morr (Ed.), *Research perspectives on the role of informatics in health policy and management* (pp. 1–18). Hershey, PA: Medical Information Science Reference. doi:10.4018/978-1-4666-4321-5.ch001

Thatcher, B. (2012). Intercultural rhetorical dimensions of health literacy and medicine. In *Intercultural rhetoric and professional communication: Technological advances and organizational behavior* (pp. 247–282). Hershey, PA: Information Science Reference. doi:10.4018/978-1-61350-450-5.ch009

Tiwari, S., & Srivastava, R. (2014). Research and developments in medical image reconstruction methods and its applications. In R. Srivastava, S. Singh, & K. Shukla (Eds.), *Research developments in computer vision and image processing: Methodologies and applications* (pp. 274–312). Hershey, PA: Information Science Reference. doi:10.4018/978-1-4666-4558-5.ch014

Toro-Troconis, M., & Partridge, M. R. (2010). Designing game-based learning activities in virtual worlds: Experiences from undergraduate medicine. In Y. Baek (Ed.), *Gaming for classroom-based learning: Digital role playing as a motivator of study* (pp. 270–280). Hershey, PA: Information Science Reference. doi:10.4018/978-1-61520-713-8.ch016

Trojer, T., Katt, B., Breu, R., Schabetsberger, T., & Mair, R. (2012). Managing privacy and effectiveness of patient-administered authorization policies. *International Journal of Computational Models and Algorithms in Medicine, 3*(2), 43–62. doi:10.4018/jcmam.2012040103

Übeyli, E. D. (2010). Medical informatics: Preventive medicine applications via telemedicine. In M. Cruz-Cunha, A. Tavares, & R. Simoes (Eds.), *Handbook of research on developments in e-health and telemedicine: Technological and social perspectives* (pp. 475–489). Hershey, PA: Medical Information Science Reference. doi:10.4018/978-1-61520-670-4.ch022

Übeyli, E. D. (2011). Telemedicine and biotelemetry for e-health systems. In *Clinical technologies: Concepts, methodologies, tools and applications* (pp. 676–692). Hershey, PA: Medical Information Science Reference. doi:10.4018/978-1-60960-561-2.ch304

Vahe, M., Zain-Ul-Abdin, K., & Türel, Y. K. (2012). Social media as a learning tool in medical education: A situation analysis. In V. Dennen & J. Myers (Eds.), *Virtual professional development and informal learning via social networks* (pp. 168–183). Hershey, PA: Information Science Reference. doi:10.4018/978-1-4666-1815-2.ch010

Vivekananda-Schmidt, P. (2013). Ethics in the design of serious games for healthcare and medicine. In S. Arnab, I. Dunwell, & K. Debattista (Eds.), *Serious games for healthcare: Applications and implications* (pp. 91–106). Hershey, PA: Medical Information Science Reference. doi:10.4018/978-1-4666-1903-6.ch005

von Lubitz, D. (2010). Healthcare among the people: Teams of leaders concept (ToL) and the world of technology-oriented global healthcare. In S. Kabene (Ed.), *Healthcare and the effect of technology: Developments, challenges and advancements* (pp. 145–177). Hershey, PA: Medical Information Science Reference. doi:10.4018/978-1-61520-733-6.ch010

von Lubitz, D. (2011). The teams of leaders (Tol) concept: The grid, the mesh, and the people in the world of information and knowledge-based global healthcare. In E. Kldiashvili (Ed.), *Grid technologies for e-health: Applications for telemedicine services and delivery* (pp. 65–104). Hershey, PA: Medical Information Science Reference. doi:10.4018/978-1-61692-010-4.ch004

Vouyioukas, D., & Maglogiannis, I. (2010). Communication issues in pervasive healthcare systems and applications. In A. Coronato & G. De Pietro (Eds.), *Pervasive and smart technologies for healthcare: Ubiquitous methodologies and tools* (pp. 197–227). Hershey, PA: Medical Information Science Reference. doi:10.4018/978-1-61520-765-7.ch010

Walczak, S., Brimhall, B. B., & Lefkowitz, J. B. (2010). Nonparametric decision support systems in medical diagnosis: Modeling pulmonary embolism. In M. Hunter (Ed.), *Strategic information systems: Concepts, methodologies, tools, and applications* (pp. 1483–1500). Hershey, PA: Information Science Reference. doi:10.4018/978-1-60566-677-8.ch095

Walczak, S., Brimhall, B. B., & Lefkowitz, J. B. (2011). Diagnostic cost reduction using artificial neural networks. In *Clinical technologies: Concepts, methodologies, tools and applications* (pp. 1812–1830). Hershey, PA: Medical Information Science Reference. doi:10.4018/978-1-60960-561-2.ch614

Wang, G., Cong, A., Gao, H., Zhang, J., Weir, V. J., Xu, X., & Bennett, J. (2012). Medical imaging. In Z. Abu-Faraj (Ed.), *Handbook of research on biomedical engineering education and advanced bioengineering learning: Interdisciplinary concepts* (pp. 634–712). Hershey, PA: Medical Information Science Reference. doi:10.4018/978-1-4666-0122-2.ch015

Watanabe, Y., Tanaka, H., & Hirata, K. (2013). Evaluation of cognitive function in migraine patients: A study using event-related potentials. In J. Wu (Ed.), *Biomedical engineering and cognitive neuroscience for healthcare: Interdisciplinary applications* (pp. 303–310). Hershey, PA: Medical Information Science Reference. doi:10.4018/978-1-4666-2113-8.ch031

Watfa, M. K., Majeed, H., & Salahuddin, T. (2012). Healthcare applications for clinicians. In M. Watfa (Ed.), *E-healthcare systems and wireless communications: Current and future challenges* (pp. 49–69). Hershey, PA: Medical Information Science Reference. doi:10.4018/978-1-61350-123-8.ch003

Weigel, F. K., Rainer, R. K., Hazen, B. T., Cegielski, C. G., & Ford, F. N. (2012). Use of diffusion of innovations theory in medical informatics research. *International Journal of Healthcare Information Systems and Informatics*, 7(3), 44–56. doi:10.4018/jhisi.2012070104

Whitaker, R. (2013). Securing health-effective medicine in practice: A critical perspective on user-driven healthcare. In R. Biswas (Ed.), *Clinical solutions and medical progress through user-driven healthcare* (pp. 35–50). Hershey, PA: Medical Information Science Reference. doi:10.4018/978-1-4666-1876-3.ch005

Wilkowska, W., & Ziefle, M. (2011). User diversity as a challenge for the integration of medical technology into future smart home environments. In M. Ziefle & C. Röcker (Eds.), *Human-centered design of e-health technologies: Concepts, methods and applications* (pp. 95–126). Hershey, PA: Medical Information Science Reference. doi:10.4018/978-1-60960-177-5.ch005

Xuan, X., & Xiaowei, Z. (2012). The dilemma and resolution: The patentability of traditional Chinese medicine. *International Journal of Asian Business and Information Management*, 3(3), 1–8. doi:10.4018/jabim.2012070101

Yamamoto, S. (2010). IT applications for medical services in Japan. In W. Pease, M. Cooper, & R. Gururajan (Eds.), *Biomedical knowledge management: Infrastructures and processes for e-health systems* (pp. 327–336). Hershey, PA: Medical Information Science Reference. doi:10.4018/978-1-60566-266-4.ch024

Yan, B., Lei, Y., Tong, L., & Chen, K. (2013). Functional neuroimaging of acupuncture: A systematic review. In J. Wu (Ed.), *Biomedical engineering and cognitive neuroscience for healthcare: Interdisciplinary applications* (pp. 142–155). Hershey, PA: Medical Information Science Reference. doi:10.4018/978-1-4666-2113-8.ch015

Yang, J. (2014). Towards healthy public policy: GIS and food systems analysis. In C. El Morr (Ed.), *Research perspectives on the role of informatics in health policy and management* (pp. 135–152). Hershey, PA: Medical Information Science Reference. doi:10.4018/978-1-4666-4321-5.ch009

Yang, W., Gao, Y., & Wu, J. (2013). Effects of selective and divided attention on audiovisual interaction. In J. Wu (Ed.), *Biomedical engineering and cognitive neuroscience for healthcare: Interdisciplinary applications* (pp. 311–319). Hershey, PA: Medical Information Science Reference. doi:10.4018/978-1-4666-2113-8.ch032

Yap, K. Y. (2013). The evolving role of pharmacoinformatics in targeting drug-related problems in clinical oncology practice. In *User-driven healthcare: Concepts, methodologies, tools, and applications* (pp. 1541–1588). Hershey, PA: Medical Information Science Reference. doi:10.4018/978-1-4666-2770-3.ch077

Young, J. W., Thapaliya, P., & Sapkota, S. (2013). Caught in the middle: The divide between conventional and alternative medicine. In R. Biswas (Ed.), *Clinical solutions and medical progress through user-driven healthcare* (pp. 26–34). Hershey, PA: Medical Information Science Reference. doi:10.4018/978-1-4666-1876-3.ch004

Yu, J., Guo, C., & Kim, M. (2010). Developing a user centered model for ubiquitous healthcare system implementation: An empirical study. In J. Rodrigues (Ed.), *Health information systems: Concepts, methodologies, tools, and applications* (pp. 1243–1259). Hershey, PA: Medical Information Science Reference. doi:10.4018/978-1-60566-988-5.ch077

Yu, J., Guo, C., & Kim, M. (2011). Towards a conceptual framework of adopting ubiquitous technology in chronic health care. In J. Tan (Ed.), *Developments in healthcare information systems and technologies: Models and methods* (pp. 214–231). Hershey, PA: Medical Information Science Reference. doi:10.4018/978-1-61692-002-9.ch015

Zaheer, S. (2014). Implementation of evidence-based practice and the PARIHS framework. In C. El Morr (Ed.), *Research perspectives on the role of informatics in health policy and management* (pp. 19–36). Hershey, PA: Medical Information Science Reference. doi:10.4018/978-1-4666-4321-5.ch002

Zhang, H. H., Meyer, R. R., Shi, L., & D'Souza, W. D. (2012). Machine learning applications in radiation therapy. In S. Kulkarni (Ed.), *Machine learning algorithms for problem solving in computational applications: Intelligent techniques* (pp. 59–84). Hershey, PA: Information Science Reference. doi:10.4018/978-1-4666-1833-6.ch005

Zhang, W. (2011). YinYang bipolar quantum bioeconomics for equilibrium-based biosystem simulation and regulation. In *YinYang bipolar relativity: A unifying theory of nature, agents and causality with applications in quantum computing, cognitive informatics and life sciences* (pp. 266–297). Hershey, PA: Information Science Reference. doi:10.4018/978-1-60960-525-4.ch009

Zhang, Z., Gao, B., Liao, G., Mu, L., & Wei, W. (2011). The study of transesophageal oxygen saturation monitoring. In *Clinical technologies: Concepts, methodologies, tools and applications* (pp. 2191–2200). Hershey, PA: Medical Information Science Reference. doi:10.4018/978-1-60960-561-2.ch813

Zhao, B., Zhang, D. S., & Zhao, Y. Z. (2013). Construction competitiveness evaluation system of regional BioPharma industry and case study: Taking Shijiazhuang as an example. In T. Gao (Ed.), *Global applications of pervasive and ubiquitous computing* (pp. 80–88). Hershey, PA: Information Science Reference. doi:10.4018/978-1-4666-2645-4.ch009

Zheng, K., Padman, R., Johnson, M. P., & Hasan, S. (2010). Guideline representation ontologies for evidence-based medicine practice. In K. Khoumbati, Y. Dwivedi, A. Srivastava, & B. Lal (Eds.), *Handbook of research on advances in health informatics and electronic healthcare applications: Global adoption and impact of information communication technologies* (pp. 234–254). Hershey, PA: Medical Information Science Reference. doi:10.4018/978-1-60566-030-1.ch015

Zhou, F., Yan, J., Wang, Y., Li, F., Xia, C., Guo, R., & Yan, H. (2011). Digital auscultation system of traditional Chinese medicine and its signals acquisition: Analysis methods. In L. Liu, D. Wei, & Y. Li (Eds.), *Interdisciplinary research and applications in bioinformatics, computational biology, and environmental sciences* (pp. 183–193). Hershey, PA: Medical Information Science Reference. doi:10.4018/978-1-60960-064-8.ch016

Zijlstra, W., Becker, C., & Pfeiffer, K. (2011). Wearable systems for monitoring mobility related activities: From technology to application for healthcare services. In C. Röcker & M. Ziefle (Eds.), *E-Health, assistive technologies and applications for assisted living: Challenges and solutions* (pp. 244–267). Hershey, PA: Medical Information Science Reference. doi:10.4018/978-1-60960-469-1.ch011

Zimmer, J., Degenkolbe, E., Wildemann, B., & Seemann, P. (2013). BMP signaling in regenerative medicine. In Bioinformatics: Concepts, methodologies, tools, and applications (pp. 1252-1281). Hershey, PA: Medical Information Science Reference. doi:10.4018/978-1-4666-3604-0.ch064

Zouag, N. (2014). Patterns of migration of medical doctors from MENA and ECE to EU economies with descriptive analysis of relatives wages. In A. Driouchi (Ed.), *Labor and health economics in the Mediterranean region: Migration and mobility of medical doctors* (pp. 124–138). Hershey, PA: Medical Information Science Reference. doi:10.4018/978-1-4666-4723-7.ch005

Zouag, N., & Driouchi, A. (2014). Trends and prospects of the moroccan health system: 2010-2030. In A. Driouchi (Ed.), *Labor and health economics in the Mediterranean region: Migration and mobility of medical doctors* (pp. 314–336). Hershey, PA: Medical Information Science Reference. doi:10.4018/978-1-4666-4723-7.ch013

Zybeck, K. L. (2013). A question of degrees: Collecting in support of the allied health professions. In S. Holder (Ed.), *Library collection development for professional programs: Trends and best practices* (pp. 145–163). Hershey, PA: Information Science Reference. doi:10.4018/978-1-4666-1897-8.ch009

Compilation of References

Aaronson, S. (2014a, May 21). *Why I am not an integrated information theorist (or, the unconscious expander)* [Web log post]. Retrieved from Shtetl-Optimized, http://scottaaronson.com/blog

Aaronson, S. (2014b, May 30). *Giulio Tononi and me: a phi-nal exchange* [Web log post]. Retrieved from Shtetl-Optimized, http://scottaaronson.com/blog

Aaronson, S. (2015, November). *The Unconscious Expander*. Paper presented at The Integrated Information Theory of Consciousness: Foundational Issues, Workshop, New York, NY.

Altmann, E. M., & Trafton, J. G. (2007). Timecourse of recovery from task interruption: Data and a model. *Psychonomic Bulletin & Review*, *14*(6), 1079–1084. doi:10.3758/BF03193094 PMID:18229478

Alvermann, D.E., Smith, L.C., & Readence, J.E. (1985). Prior knowledge activation and the comprehension of compatible and incompatible text. *Reading Research Quarterly, 20*(4), 420-436.

Ambrose, S. A., Bridges, M. W., DiPietro, M., Lovett, M. C., & Norman, M. K. (2010). *How Learning Works. Seven Research-Based Principles for Smart Teaching*. John Wiley & Sons.

Ames, C. (1990). Motivation: What teachers need to know. *Teachers College Record*, *91*, 409–472.

Anderson, J. R. (1996). A simple theory of complex cognition. *The American Psychologist*, *51*(4), 355–365. doi:10.1037/0003-066X.51.4.355

Anderson, J. R., Byrne, M. D., Douglass, S., Lebiere, C., & Qin, Y. (2004). An integrated theory of the mind. *Psychological Review*, *111*(4), 1036–1060. doi:10.1037/0033-295X.111.4.1036 PMID:15482072

Anderson, J. R., Corbett, A. T., Koedinger, K. R., & Pelletier, R. (1995). Cognitive tutors: Lessons learned. *Journal of the Learning Sciences*, *4*(2), 167–207. doi:10.1207/s15327809jls0402_2

Anderson, M. L. (2003). Embodied Cognition: A Field Guide. *Artificial Intelligence,* *149*(1), 91–130. doi:10.1016/S0004-3702(03)00054-7

Ansorge, U., Kunde, W., & Kiefer, M. (2014). Unconscious vision and executive control: How unconscious processing and conscious action control interact. *Consciousness and Cognition, 27,* 268–287. doi:10.1016/j.concog.2014.05.009 PMID:24960432

Ari, C., & DAgostino, D. P. (2016). Contingency checking and self-directed behaviors in giant manta rays: Do elasmobranchs have self-awareness? *Journal of Ethology, 34*(2), 1–8. doi:10.1007/s10164-016-0462-z

Aristotle, . (2004). *Rhetoric* (T. W. Rhys, Trans.). Dover Publications.

Armstrong, A. M., & Dienes, Z. (2013). Subliminal understanding of negation: Unconscious control by subliminal processing of word pairs. *Consciousness and Cognition, 22*(3), 1022–1040. doi:10.1016/j.concog.2013.06.010 PMID:23933139

Arnold, M. B. (1970). Perennial Problems in the Field of Emotion. In *Feelings and Emotion* (pp. 169–185). New York: Academic Press.

Arpaly, N., & Schroeder, T. (2014). *In Praise of Desire.* Oxford, UK: Oxford University Press.

Ashby, W. R. (1954). Design for a brain. John Wiley & Sons. doi:10.5962/bhl.title.6969

Ashby, W. R. (1952). *Design for a brain* (1st ed.). New York: John Wiley & Sons.

Audi, R. (1993). *Action, Intention, and Reason.* Ithaca, NY: Cornell University Press.

Avila-Garcìa, O., & Cañamero, L. (2005). Hormonal modulation of perception in motivation-based action selection architectures. In *Proceedings of the symposium Agents that Want and Like: Motivational and Emotional roots of Cognition and Action* (pp. 9–17). University of Hertfordshire.

Baars, B. (1988). *A Cognitive Theory of Consciousness.* Cambridge, UK: Cambridge University Press.

Baars, B. J. (2002, January). The conscious access hypothesis: Origins and recent evidence. *Trends in Cognitive Sciences, 6*(1), 47–52. doi:10.1016/S1364-6613(00)01819-2 PMID:11849615

Baars, B. J. (2005). Global workspace theory of consciousness: Toward a cognitive neuroscience of human experience. *Progress in Brain Research, 150,* 45–53. doi:10.1016/S0079-6123(05)50004-9 PMID:16186014

Baars, B. J., & Franklin, S. (2009). Consciousness is computational: The Lida model of global workspace theory. *International Journal of Machine Consciousness, 1*(1), 23–32. doi:10.1142/S1793843009000050

Baars, B. J., Ramsøy, T. Z., & Laureys, S. (2003, December). Brain, conscious experience and the observing self. *Trends in Neurosciences, 26*(12), 671–675. doi:10.1016/j.tins.2003.09.015 PMID:14624851

Baddeley, B. (2008). Reinforcement learning in continuous time and space: Interference and not ill conditioning is the main problem when using distributed function approximators. *Systems, Man, and Cybernetics, Part B: Cybernetics. IEEE Transactions on, 38*(4), 950–956.

Baranes, A., Oudeyer, P. Y., & Gottlieb, J. (2015). Eye movements reveal epistemic curiosity in human observers. *Vision Research, 117*, 81–90. doi:10.1016/j.visres.2015.10.009 PMID:26518743

Bargh, J. A., & Morsella, E. (2008). The Unconscious Mind. *Perspectives on Psychological Science: A Journal of the Association for Psychological Science, 3*(1), 73–79.

Barrett, A. (2014). An integration of integrated information theory with fundamental physics. *Frontiers in Psychology, 5*(63). PMID:24550877

Barrett, L. F. (2006). Valence is a basic building block of emotional life. *Journal of Research in Personality, 40*(1), 35–55. doi:10.1016/j.jrp.2005.08.006

Barron, A. B., Søvik, E., & Cornish, J. L. (2010). The roles of dopamine and related compounds in reward-seeking behavior across animal phyla. *Frontiers in Behavioral Neuroscience, 4*, 1–9. doi:10.3389/fnbeh.2010.00163 PMID:21048897

Barron, K., & Harackiewicz, J. (2001). Achievement goals and optimal motivation: Testing multiple goal models. *Journal of Personality and Social Psychology, 80*(5), 706–722. doi:10.1037/0022-3514.80.5.706 PMID:11374744

Barsalou, L. W. (2008). Grounded cognition. *Annual Review of Psychology, 59*(1), 617–645. doi:10.1146/annurev.psych.59.103006.093639 PMID:17705682

Bass, L., Clements, P., & Kazman, R. (2012). Software Architecture in Practice (3rd ed.). Addison-Wesley.

Bauer, R., Zubler, F., Pfister, S., Hauri, A., Pfeiffer, M., Muir, D. R., & Douglas, R. J. (2014). Developmental self-construction and self-configuration of functional neocortical neuronal networks. *PLoS Computational Biology, 10*(12), e1003994. doi:10.1371/journal.pcbi.1003994 PMID:25474693

Bayne, Y., Cleeremans, A., & Wilken, P. (2009). *The Oxford Companion to Consciousness.* Oxford, UK: OUP. doi:10.1093/acref/9780198569510.001.0001

Berridge, K. C. (2004). Motivation concepts in behavioral neuroscience. *Physiology & Behavior*, *81*(2), 179–209. doi:10.1016/j.physbeh.2004.02.004 PMID:15159167

Binzegger, T., Douglas, R. J., & Martin, K. A. C. (2007, November). Stereotypical Bouton Clustering of Individual Neurons in Cat Primary Visual Cortex. *The Journal of Neuroscience*, *27*(45), 12242–12254. doi:10.1523/JNEUROSCI.3753-07.2007 PMID:17989290

Bionik, V.-F. (2012). Biomimetics – Conception and strategy – Differences between bio- mimetic and conventional methods/products. *VDI-Handbuch Bionik, 1*, 1-1. Retrieved from https://www.vdi.de/richtlinie/vdi_6220_blatt_1-bionik_konzeption_und_strategie_abgrenzung_zwischen_bionischen_und_konventionellen/

Block, N. (2011). Perceptual consciousness overflows cognitive access. *Trends in Cognitive Sciences*, *15*(12), 567–575. doi:10.1016/j.tics.2011.11.001 PMID:22078929

Bohl, V., & van den Bos, W. (2012). Toward an integrative account of social cognition: Marrying theory of mind and interactionism to study the interplay of Type 1 and Type 2 processes. *Frontiers in Human Neuroscience*, 6. PMID:23087631

Bongard, J., Zykov, V., & Lipson, H. (2006, November). Resilient Machines Through Continuous Self- Modeling. *Science*, *314*(5802), 1118–1121. doi:10.1126/science.1133687 PMID:17110570

Born, J., & Wilhelm, I. (2012, March). System consolidation of memory during sleep. *Psychological Research*, *76*(2), 192–203. doi:10.1007/s00426-011-0335-6 PMID:21541757

Borst, J. P., & Anderson, J. R. (2013). Using model-based functional MRI to locate working memory updates and declarative memory retrievals in the fronto-parietal network. *Proceedings of the National Academy of Sciences of the United States of America*, *110*(5), 1628–1633. doi:10.1073/pnas.1221572110 PMID:23319628

Bösser, T. (1987). Learning in man-computer interaction: A review of the literature. In *Esprit Research Reports* (Vol. 1). Heidelberg, Germany: Springer-Verlag. doi:10.1007/978-3-642-83233-8

Bösser, T. (2013). A discussion of 'The Chunking of Skill and Knowledge' by Paul S. Rosenbloom, John E. Laird & Allen Newell. In B. A. Elsendoorn & H. Bouma (Eds.), *Working Models of Human Perception* (pp. 411–418). San Diego, CA: Academic Press.

Bourke, V. J. (1964). *Will in Western thought*. New York: Sheed and Ward.

Bromberg-Martin, E. S., & Hikosaka, O. (2009). Midbrain dopamine neurons signal preference for advance information about upcoming rewards. *Neuron*, *63*(1), 119–126. doi:10.1016/j.neuron.2009.06.009 PMID:19607797

Burmakin, E., Fingelkurts, A. A., & Fingelkurts, A. A. (2009). Self-organization of dynamic distributed computational systems applying principles of integrative activity of brain neuronal assemblies. *Algorithms*, *2*(1), 247–258. doi:10.3390/a2010247

Cabanac, M. (2010). The Fifth Influence. The Dialectics of Pleasure. iUniverse Books.

Cabanac, M. (1971). Physiological role of pleasure. *Science*, *173*(4002), 1103–1107. doi:10.1126/science.173.4002.1103 PMID:5098954

Cabanac, M. (1992). Pleasure: The common currency. *Journal of Theoretical Biology*, *155*(2), 173–200. doi:10.1016/S0022-5193(05)80594-6 PMID:12240693

Cabanac, M. (2000). Pleasure, the prerational intelligence. In H. Ritter, H. Cruse, & J. Dean (Eds.), *Prerational Intelligence: Adaptive Behavior and Intelligent Systems Without Symbols and Logic* (pp. 201–213). Dordrecht: Kluwer Academis Publishers.

Canabal, D. D., Song, Z., Potian, J. G., Beuve, A., McArdle, J. J., & Routh, V. H. (2007). Glucose, insulin, and leptin signaling pathways modulate nitric oxide synthesis in glucose-inhibited neurons in the ventromedial hypothalamus. *American Journal of Physiology. Regulatory, Integrative and Comparative Physiology*, *292*(4), 1418–1428. doi:10.1152/ajpregu.00216.2006 PMID:17170237

Cannon, W. B. (1929). Organization for physiological homeostasis. *Physiological Reviews*, *9*, 399–31.

Cao, S., Qin, Y., Jin, X., Zhao, L., & Shen, M. (2014). Effect of driving experience on collision avoidance braking: An experimental investigation and computational modelling. *Behaviour & Information Technology*, *33*(9), 929–940. doi:10.1080/0144929X.2014.902100

Cao, S., Qin, Y., Zhao, L., & Shen, M. (2015). Modeling the development of vehicle lateral control skills in a cognitive architecture. *Transportation Research Part F: Traffic Psychology and Behaviour*, *32*, 1–10. doi:10.1016/j.trf.2015.04.010

Carter, R., Aldridge, S., Page, M., Parker, S., Frith, C., & Frith, U. (2010). *Das Gehirn: Anatomie, Sinneswahrnehmung, Gedaechtnis, Bewusstsein, Stoerugen* (K. Hofmann & J. Wissmann, Trans.). Dorling Kindersley.

Chalmers, D. (1995). Facing up to the problem of consciousness. *Journal of Consciousness Studies*, *2*.

Chalmers, D. (1996). *The Conscious Mind*. New York: Oxford University Press.

Chalmers, D. (in press). The combination problem for panpyschism. In L. Jaskolla & G. Bruntup (Eds.), *Panpsychism. Oxford University Press*.

Chalmers, D. J. (1995). Facing up to the problem of consciousness. *Journal of Consciousness Studies*, *2*, 200–219.

Chalmers, D. J. (1995). Facing up to the Problem of Consciousness. *Journal of Consciousness Studies, 2*, 200–219.

Chella, A. (2013). LIDA, Committed to Consciousness. *Journal of Artificial General Intelligence, 4*(2), 28–30.

Chella, A., Frixione, M., & Gaglio, S. (2008, October). A cognitive architecture for robot self-consciousness. *Artificial Intelligence in Medicine, 44*(2), 147–154. doi:10.1016/j.artmed.2008.07.003 PMID:18715770

Chella, A., & Macaluso, I. (2009, January). The perception loop in CiceRobot, a museum guide robot. *Neurocomputing, 72*(4-6), 760–766. doi:10.1016/j.neucom.2008.07.011

Chikhaoui, B., Pigot, H., Beaudoin, M., Pratte, G., Bellefeuille, P., & Laudares, F. (2009). Learning a song: An ACT-R model. *International Journal of Computer, Electrical, Automation, Control and Information Engineering, 3*, 1784–1789.

Clark, A. (1997). *Being there: putting brain, body, and world together again*. London, UK: MIT Press.

Clark, A. (1998). Embodied, situated, and distributed cognition. In W. Bechtel & G. Graham (Eds.), *A companion to cognitive science* (pp. 506–517). Malden, MA: Blackwell.

Clarke, J., Grumberg, O., & Peled, D. A. (1999). Model Checking. MIT Press.

Cleeremans, A. (2008). Consciousness: the radical plasticity thesis. *Prog Brain Res., 168*, 19-33.

Cleeremans, A. (2011). The Radical Plasticity Thesis: How the Brain Learns to be Conscious. *Frontiers in Psychology, 2*, 86.

CMMI Product Team CMMI for Development. (2006). Retrieved November 25, 2015, from http://www.sei.cmu.edu/pub/documents/06.reports/pdf/06tr008.pdf

Cognition and Technology Group at Vanderbilt. (1994). From visual word problems to learning communities: Changing conceptions of cognitive research. In K. McGilly (Ed.), *Classroom lessons: Integrating cognitive theory and classroom practice* (pp. 157–200). Cambridge, MA: MIT Press/Bradford Books.

Cohen, E. B. (1999). Reconceptualizing Information Systems as a Field of the Transdiscipline Informing Science: From Ugly Duckling to Swan. *Journal of Computing and Information Technology, 7*(3), 213–219. Retrieved from http://elicohen.info/uglyduckling.pdf

Cohen, M., & Dennett, D. (2011). Consciousness cannot be separated from function. *Trends in Cognitive Sciences, 15*(8), 358–364. doi:10.1016/j.tics.2011.06.008 PMID:21807333

Cohen, M., & Dennett, D. (2012). Response to Fahrenfort and Lamme: Defining reportability, accessibility and sufficiency in conscious awareness. *Trends in Cognitive Sciences*, *16*(3), 139–140. doi:10.1016/j.tics.2012.01.002

Corns, J. (2014). Unpleasantness, motivational oomph, and painfulness. *Mind and Language, 29*(2), 238-254.

Costa, V. D., Tran, V. L., Turchi, J., & Averbeck, B. B. (2014). Dopamine modulates novelty seeking behavior during decision making. *Behavioral Neuroscience*, *28*(5), 556–566. doi:10.1037/a0037128 PMID:24911320

Courtland, R. (2014). Can the human brain project succeed? *IEEE Spectrum*, *9*(July). Retrieved from http://spectrum.ieee.org/tech-talk/computing/hardware/can-the-human-brain-project-succeed

Cousot, P., & Cousot, R. (1977). Abstract Interpretation: A Unified Lattice Model for Static Analysis of Programs by Construction or Approximation of Fixpoints. *Proceedings of the 4th ACM SIGACT-SIGPLAN Symposium on Principles of Programming Languages*. ACM. doi:10.1145/512950.512973

Cowan, N. (2008). What are the differences between long-term, short-term, and working memory? *Progress in Brain Research*, *169*, 323–338. doi:10.1016/S0079-6123(07)00020-9 PMID:18394484

Craig, A. D. (2013). An interoceptive neuroanatomical perspective on feelings, energy, and effort. *Behavioral and Brain Sciences*, *36*(06), 685–686. doi:10.1017/S0140525X13001489 PMID:24304783

Craig, A. D. (2015). *How do you feel? An interoceptive moment with your neurobiological self*. Princeton University Press. doi:10.1515/9781400852727

Crick, F. (1995). *Astonishing Hypothesis: The Scientific Search for the Soul*. Scribner.

Crick, F., & Koch, C. (2003). A framework for consciousness. *Nature Neuroscience*, *23*(2), 119–126. doi:10.1038/nn0203-119 PMID:12555104

Csikszentmihalyi, M. (1978). Attention and the Holistic Approach to Behavior. In The Stream of consciousness: scientific investigations into the flow of human experience (pp. 335-358). New York: Plenum Press.

Damasio A. R. (1994). *Descartes' Error: Emotion, Reason, and the Human Brain*. Bard, an Avon Book.

Damasio, A. (1994). *Descartes*. New York: Gosset/Putnam Press.

Damasio, A. (1999). *The Feeling of What Happens. Body and Emotion in the Making of Consciousness*. London: Heinemann.

Damasio, A. R. (1994). *Descartes' Error: Emotion, Reason, and the Human Brain.* New York: GP Putnam's Sons.

Damasio, A. R. (2003). *Looking for Spinoza: Joy, Sorrow, and the Feeling Brain.* Harcourt.

Damasio, A. R. (2010). *Self Comes to Mind: Constructing the Conscious Brain.* New York: Pantheon Books.

Day, T. A. (2005). Defining stress as a prelude to mapping its neurocircuitry: No help from allostasis. *Progress in Neuro-Psychopharmacology & Biological Psychiatry, 29*(8), 1195–1200. doi:10.1016/j.pnpbp.2005.08.005 PMID:16213079

de Gardelle, V., & Kouider, S. (2009). Cognitive theories of consciousness. In W. Banks (Ed.), *Elsevier Encyclopedia of Consciousness.* Elsevier. doi:10.1016/B978-012373873-8.00077-3

De Sousa, R. (2011). *Emotional Truth.* New York: Oxford University Press, Inc.

Dehaene, S., Changeux, J. P., Naccache, L., Sackur, J., & Sergent, C. (2006). Conscious, preconscious, and subliminal processing: A testable taxonomy. *Trends in Cognitive Sciences, 10*(5), 204–211. doi:10.1016/j.tics.2006.03.007 PMID:16603406

Dehaene, S., & Naccache, L. (2001, April). Towards a cognitive neuroscience of consciousness: Basic evidence and a workspace framework. *Cognition, 79*(1–2), 1–37. doi:10.1016/S0010-0277(00)00123-2 PMID:11164022

DeLancey, C. (2002). *Passionate Engines: What Emotions Reveal About Mind and Artificial Intelligence.* Oxford, UK: Oxford University Press. doi:10.1093/0195142713.001.0001

Dennett, D. (1990). *Quining Qualia.* In W. Lycan (Ed.), *Mind and Cognition* (pp. 519–548). Oxford, UK: Blackwell.

Dennett, D. (2005). *Sweet dreams: Philosophical obstacles to a science of consciousness.* Cambridge, MA: The MIT Press.

Dennett, D. C. (1990). Cognitive Wheels: The Frame Problem of AI. In M. E. Boden (Ed.), *The philosophy of artificial intelligence* (pp. 147–171). Oxford, UK: Oxford University Press.

Dennett, D. C. (1991). *Consciousness Explained.* Boston: Little, Brown and Company.

Di Paolo, E. A. (2000). Homeostatic adaptation to inversion of the visual field and other sensorimotor disruptions. In J-A. Meyer, A. Berthoz, D. Floreano, H. Roitblat & S W. Wilson (Eds.), *From Animals to Animats,Proc. of the Sixth International Conference on the Simulation of Adaptive Behavior.* MIT Press.

Di Paolo, E. A. (2003). Organismically-inspired robotics: Homeostatic adaptation and natural teleology beyond the closed sensorimotor loop. In K. Murase & T. Asakura (Eds.), *Dynamical Systems Approach to Embodiment and Sociality*. Adelaide, Australia: Advanced Knowledge International.

Distefano, S., Milano, P., & Mazzara, M. (2015). Neuromodulating Cognitive Architecture. *Conference Paper*.

Donchin, E., & Coles, M. G. H. (1998). Context updating and the p300. *Behavioral and Brain Sciences, 21*(1), 152–154. doi:10.1017/S0140525X98230950

Douglas, R. J., & Martin, K. A. (2004). Neuronal Circuits of the Neocortex. *Annual Review of Neuroscience, 27*(1), 419–451. doi:10.1146/annurev.neuro.27.070203.144152 PMID:15217339

Douglas, R. J., & Martin, K. A. C. (1990, September). Control of Neuronal Output by Inhibition at the Axon Initial Segment. *Neural Computation, 2*(3), 283–292. doi:10.1162/neco.1990.2.3.283

Douglas, R. J., & Martin, K. A. C. (2009). Inhibition in cortical circuits. *Current Biology, 19*(10), 398–402. doi:10.1016/j.cub.2009.03.003 PMID:19467204

Douglass, S. A., & Mittal, S. (2013). A framework for modeling and simulation of the artificial. In A. Tolk (Ed.), *Ontology, Epistemology, and Teleology for Modeling and Simulation* (pp. 271–317). Heidelberg, Germany: Springer-Verlag; doi:10.1007/978-3-642-31140-6_15

Douglas, V. I., & Peters, K. G. (1979). Clearer Definition of Attentional Deficit. In G. A. Hale & M. Lewis (Eds.), *Attention and cognitive development*. New York: Plenum Press. doi:10.1007/978-1-4613-2985-5_8

Duch, W., Oentaryo, R. J., & Pasquier, M. (2008). Cognitive architectures: Where do we go from here? In P. Wang, B. Goertzel, & S. Franklin (Ed.), *Proceedings of the First AGI Conference* (pp. 122-136). Memphis, TN: IOS Press.

Edelman, G. (1989). *The remembered present: A biological theory of consciousness*. New York: Basic Books.

Edelman, G. (1989). *The Remembered Present: A Biological Theory of Consciousness*. New York: Basic Books.

Edelman, G., & Tononi, G. (2000). *A universe of consciousness: How matter becomes imagination*. New York: Basic Books.

Edwards, R. B. (1979). *Pleasures and Pains*. Ithaca, London: Cornell University Press.

Eklund, Nichols, & Knutsson. (2016). Cluster failure: Why fmri inferences for spatial extent have inflated false-positive rates. *Proceedings of the National Academy of Sciences*.

Emmeche, C. (2002). The chicken and the Orphean egg: On the function of meaning and the meaning of function. *Sign Systems Studies, 30,* 15–32.

Fahrenfort, J., & Lamme, V. (2012). A true science of consciousness explains phenomenology: Comment of Cohen and Dennett. *Trends in Cognitive Sciences, 16*(3), 138–139. doi:10.1016/j.tics.2012.01.004 PMID:22300549

Fingelkurts, A. A., Fingelkurts, A. A., & Neves, C. F. H. (2012). Machine consciousness and artificial thought: An operational architectonics model guided approach. *Brain Research, 1428,* 80–92. doi:10.1016/j.brainres.2010.11.079 PMID:21130079

Fisher, R. A. (1930). *The genetical theory of natural selection: a complete variorum edition.* Oxford University Press. doi:10.5962/bhl.title.27468

Fowler, M. (2002). *Patterns of Enterprise Application Architecture.* Addison-Wesley.

Franchi, S. (2015). Ashbian Homeostasis as non-Autonomous Adaptation. *SASO 2015 Ninth IEEE International Conference on Self-Adaptive and Self-Organizing Systems.*

Franchi, S. (2013). Homeostats for the 21st Century? Simulating Ashby Simulating the Brain. *Constructivist Foundations, 9*(1), 93–101.

Frankfurt, H. G. (2004). *The reasons of love.* Princeton, N.J.: Princeton University Press.

Franklin, S. & Patterson, F. (2006). The lida architecture: Adding new modes of learning to an intelligent, autonomous, software agent. *pat, 703,* 764–1004.

Franklin, S. (1997). Autonomous Agents as Embodied AI. *Cybernetics and Systems, 28*(6), 499–520. doi:10.1080/0196972971260029

Franklin, S., Ramamurthy, U., D'Mello, S. K., McCauley, L., Negatu, A., Silva, R., & Datla, V. (2007). LIDA: A computational model of global workspace theory and developmental learning. In *AAAI Fall Symposium on AI and Consciousness: Theoretical Foundations and Current Approaches* (pp. 61-66). Arlington, VA: AAAI Press.

Franklin, S., Strain, S., McCall, R., & Baars, B. (2013). Conceptual commitments of the LIDA model of cognition. *Journal of Artificial General Intelligence, 4*(2), 1–22. doi:10.2478/jagi-2013-0002

Freeman, E., Bates, B., Sierra, K., & Robson, E. (2004). *Head First Design Patterns.* O'Reilly.

Frégnac, Y., & Laurent, G. (2014). Where is the brain in the Human Brain Project? *Nature, 513*(7516), 27–29. doi:10.1038/513027a PMID:25186884

Freund. (2014). Numerical simulation of flowing blood cells. *Annual Review of Fluid Mechanics.*

Friston, K. J. (2010). The free-energy principle: A unified brain theory? *Nature Reviews. Neuroscience*, *11*(2), 127–138. doi:10.1038/nrn2787 PMID:20068583

Friston, K., Schwartenbeck, P., FitzGerald, T., Moutoussis, M., Behrens, T., & Dolan, R. J. (2013). The anatomy of choice: Active inference and agency. *Frontiers in Human Neuroscience*, *7*, 1–18. doi:10.3389/fnhum.2013.00598 PMID:24093015

Froese, T., & Stewart, J. (2010). Life after Ashby: Ultrastability and the autopoietic foundations of biological individuality. *Cybernetics & Human Knowing*, *17*(4), 83–106.

Gallagher, S. (2015). The new hybrids: Continuing debates on social perception. *Consciousness and Cognition*, *36*, 452–465. doi:10.1016/j.concog.2015.04.002 PMID:25952957

Gamez, D. (2010). Information integration based predictions about the conscious states of a spiking neural network. *Consciousness and Cognition*, *19*(1), 294–310. doi:10.1016/j.concog.2009.11.001 PMID:20018526

Gamma, E., Helm, R., Johnson, R., & Vlissides, J. (1998). *Design Patterns CD: Elements of Reusable Object-Oriented Software*. Addison-Wesley.

Geist, M., & Pietquin, O. (2013). Algorithmic survey of parametric value function approximation. *Neural Networks and Learning Systems. IEEE Transactions on*, *24*(6), 845–867.

Gentner, D., Loewenstein, J., & Thompson, L. (2003). Learning and transfer: A general role for analogical encoding. *Journal of Educational Psychology*, *95*(2), 393–405. doi:10.1037/0022-0663.95.2.393

Gibson, J. J. (1979). *The Ecological Approach to Visual Perception*. Hillsdale, NJ: Lawrence Erlbaum Associates.

Gick, M. L., & Holyoak, K. J. (1980). Analogical problem solving. *Cognitive Psychology*, *12*(3), 306–355. doi:10.1016/0010-0285(80)90013-4

Gigerenzer, G., Hertwig, R., & Pachur, T. (Eds.). (2011). *Heuristics: The foundations of adaptive behavior*. New York: Oxford University Press. doi:10.1093/acprof:oso/9780199744282.001.0001

Gill, G., & Bhattacherjee, A. (2007). The Informing Sciences at a crossroads: The role of the Client. *Informing Science Journal*, *10*, 17–39.

Goldsmith, T.C. (2014). *The evolution of aging*. Academic Press.

Gossman, J., & Eliasmith, E. (2016, February22). Optimizing Semantic Pointer Representations for Symbol-Like Processing in Spiking Neural Networks. *PLoS ONE*, 1–18.

Gottlieb, J., Oudeyer, P. Y., Lopes, M., & Baranes, A. (2013). Information-seeking, curiosity, and attention: Computational and neural mechanisms. *Trends in Cognitive Sciences*, *17*(11), 585–593. doi:10.1016/j.tics.2013.09.001 PMID:24126129

Gregory, R. L. (1988). Consciousness in science and philosophy: conscience and con-science. In Consciousness in Contemporary Science. Oxford, UK: Oxford Science Publications.

Gu, X., & FitzGerald, T. H. (2014). Interoceptive inference: Homeostasis and decision-making. *Trends in Cognitive Sciences*, *18*(6), 269–270. doi:10.1016/j.tics.2014.02.001 PMID:24582825

Halbrügge, M., Quade, M., & Engelbrecht, K.-P. (2015). A predictive model of human error based on user interface development models and a cognitive architecture. In N. A. Taatgen, M. K. van Vugt, J. P. Borst, & K. Mehlhorn (Ed.), *Proceedings of the 13th International Conference on Cognitive Modeling* (pp. 238-243). Groningen, The Netherlands: University of Groningen.

Hattie, J., & Timperley, H. (2007). The power of feedback. *Review of Educational Research*, *77*(1), 81–112. doi:10.3102/003465430298487

Heidrich-Meisner, V., & Igel, C. (2008). Similarities and differences between policy gradient methods and evolution strategies. *ESANN*, 149–154.

Hills, T. (2006). Animal foraging and the evolution of goal-directed cognition. *Cognitive Science*, *30*(1), 3–41. doi:10.1207/s15516709cog0000_50 PMID:21702807

Hills, T., & Butterfill, S. (2015). From foraging to autonoetic consciousness: The primal self as a consequence of embodied prospective foraging. *Current Zoology*, *61*(2), 368–381. doi:10.1093/czoolo/61.2.368

Hinton, G. E., Dayan, P., Frey, B. J., & Neal, R. M. (1995). The wake- sleep algorithm for unsupervised neural networks. *Science*, *268*(5214), 1158–1161. doi:10.1126/science.7761831 PMID:7761831

Hinton, G. E., Osindero, S., & Teh, Y. (2006). A fast learning algorithm for deep belief nets. *Neural Computation*, *18*(7), 1527–1554. doi:10.1162/neco.2006.18.7.1527 PMID:16764513

Hinton, G. E., & Salakhutdinov, R. R. (2006). Reducing the dimensionality of data with neural networks. *Science*, *313*(5786), 504–507. doi:10.1126/science.1127647 PMID:16873662

Hochreiter, S., & Schmidhuber, S (1997). Long short term memory. *Neural Computation*, *9*(8), 1735–1780.

Hochreiter, S., Bengio, Y., Frasconi, P., & Schmidhuber, J. (2001). Gradient flow in recurrent nets: the difficulty of learning long-term dependencies. *A field guide to dynamical recurrent neural networks.*

Hoel, E., & Marshall, W. (2015, November). *How the macro beats the Micro.* Paper presented at The Integrated Information Theory of Consciousness: Foundational Issues, Workshop, New York, NY.

Hofstadter, D. (2007). *I am a strange loop.* New York: Basic Books.

Hohpe, G., & Woolf, B. (2004). *Enterprise Integration Patterns: Designing, Building, and Deploying Messaging Solutions.* Addison-Wesley.

Hohwy, J. (2014). The neural organ explains the mind. In *Open MIND.* Frankfurt am Main, Germany: MIND Group.

Hollenstein, M., Koenig, T., Kubat, M., Blaser, D., & Perrig, W. J. (2012). Non-conscious word processing in a mirror-masking paradigm causing attentional distraction: An ERP-study. *Consciousness and Cognition, 21*(1), 353–365. doi:10.1016/j.concog.2012.01.005 PMID:22289507

Hornik, K., Stinchcombe, M., & White, H. (1989). Multilayer feedforward networks are universal approximators. *Neural Networks, 2*(5), 359–366. doi:10.1016/0893-6080(89)90020-8

Howison, J., & Herbsleb, J. D. (2015). Scientific software production: incentives and collaboration. *Proceedings of the ACM 2011 conference on Computer supported cooperative work.* doi:10.1016/j.jss.2015.07.027

Howison, J., Deelman, E., McLennan, M. J., da Silva, R. F., & Herbsleb, J. D. (2015). Understanding the scientific software ecosystem and its impact: Current and future measures. *Research Evaluation.*

Innopolis University Presentation. (2014). Retrieved November 25, 2015, from http://innopolis.ru/files/docs/uni/innopolis_university.pdf

Izhikevich & Edelman. (2008). Large-scale model of mammalian thalamocortical systems.*Proceedings of the national academy of sciences.*

Jackendoff, R. (1987). *Consciousness and the computational mind.* Cambridge, MA: MIT Press.

Jaeger, H. (1998). Todays dynamical systems are too simple (Commentary on Tim van Gelders The dynamical hypothesis in cognitive science). *Behavioral and Brain Sciences, 21,* 643–644. doi:10.1017/S0140525X98401730

James, W. (1927). *Psychology.* New York: Henry Holt and Company.

Jirsa, V. K. (2004). Connectivity and dynamics of neural information processing. *Neuroinformatics*, *2*(2), 183–204. doi:10.1385/NI:2:2:183 PMID:15319516

Johnson-Laird, P. N. (1980). Mental models in cognitive science. *Cognitive Science*, *4*(1), 71–115. doi:10.1207/s15516709cog0401_4

Johnston, V. (1999). *Why We Feel. The Science of Human Emotions*. Reading, MA: Perseus Books.

Jordan, J. S. (2003). Emergence of self and other in perception and action. *Consciousness and Cognition*, *12*(4), 633–646. doi:10.1016/S1053-8100(03)00075-8 PMID:14656506

Jordan, J. S. (2008). Toward a theory of embodied communication: Self-sustaining wild systems as embodied meaning. In I. Wachsmuth, M. Lenzen, & G. Knoblich (Eds.), *Embodied Communication in Human and Machines* (pp. 53–75). Oxford, UK: Oxford University Press. doi:10.1093/acprof:oso/9780199231751.003.0003

Jordan, J. S. (2013). The wild ways of conscious will: What we do, how we do it, and why it has meaning. *Frontiers in Psychology*, *4*. doi:10.3389/fpsyg.2013.00574 PMID:24027543

Jordan, J. S., & Ghin, M. (2007). The role of control in a science of consciousness: Causality, regulation, and self-sustainment. *Journal of Consciousness Studies*, *14*(1-2), 177–197.

Jordan, J. S., & Day, B. (2015). Wild systems theory as a 21st century coherence framework for cognitive science. In T. Metzinger & J. M. Windt (Eds.), *Open MIND: 21*. Frankfurt am Main, Germany: MIND Group; doi:10.15502/9783958570191

Jordan, J. S., & Ghin, M. (2006). (Proto-) consciousness as a contextually-emergent property of self-sustaining systems. *Mind & Matter*, *4*, 45–68.

Jordan, J. S., & Vinson, D. (2012). After nature: On bodies, consciousness, and causality. *Journal of Consciousness Studies*, *19*(5-6).

Kahneman, D., Diener, E., & Schwartz, N. (1999). *Well-Being: The Foundations of Hedonic Psychology*. New York: Russel Sage Foundation.

Kaku, M. (2014). *Die Physik des Bewusstseins: Uber die Zukunft des Geistes*. Rowohlt Verlag GmbH.

Kane, Hohman, Cerami, McCormick, Kuhlmman, & Byrd. (2006). Agile methods in biomedical software development: a multi-site experience report. *BMC Bioinformatics, 7*(1).

Kant, I. (1798). Anthropology from a pragmatic point of view (M. J. Gregor, Trans.). The Hague, The Netherlands: Martinus Nijhoff.

Kant, I. (1929). Selections (T. M. Greene, Ed.). New York: Charles Scribner's Sons.

Kant, I. (1983). *Ethical Philosophy the complete texts of GROUNDINGS for the METAPHYSICS of MORALS and METAPHYSICAL PRINCIPLES OF VIRTUE (Part II of the Metaphysics of Morals)* (J. W. Ellington, Trans.). Hackett Publishing Co.(Original work published 1785)

Katz, L. D. (2005). Three Faces of Desire. *Philosophical Reviews, University of Notre Dame*. Retrieved 14 September 2015 from http://ndpr.nd.edu/review.cfm?id=3861

Kauffman, S. (1995). *At Home in the Universe*. New York, NY: Oxford University Press.

Kelly, D. (2015). Scientific Software Development Viewed as Knowledge Acquisition: Towards Understanding the Development of Risk-Averse Scientific Software. *Proceedings of the ACM 2011 conference on Computer supported cooperative work*. ACM.

Kelso, J. A. S. (1995). *Dynamic patterns*. Cambridge, MA: MIT Press.

Kenny, A. (1963). *Action, Emotion, and Will*. London: Routledge and Kegan Paul.

Khazeev, M., Rivera, V., & Mazzara, M. (2016). Usability of AutoProof: a case study of static debugging. *The 5th international Conference in Software Engineering for Defense Applications*.

Kihlstrom, J. F. (1987). The cognitive unconscious. *Science*, *237*(4821), 1445–1452. doi:10.1126/science.3629249 PMID:3629249

Kihlstrom, J. F. (1994). The rediscovery of the unconscious. In H. Morowitz & J. L. Singer (Eds.), *The mind, the brain, and complex adaptive systems* (pp. 123–143). Reading, MA: Addison-Wesley Publishing Co, Inc.

Kihlstrom, J. F., Mulvaney, S., Tobias, B. A., & Tobis, I. P. (2000). The emotional unconscious. In E. Eich, J. F. Kihlstrom, G. H. Bower, J. P. Forgas, & P. M. Niedenthal (Eds.), *Cognition and emotion* (pp. 30–86). New York: Oxford University Press.

Kirkpatrick, S., Gelatt, C. D., & Vecchi, M. P. (1983). Optimization by simulated annealing. *Science*, *220*(4598), 671–680. doi:10.1126/science.220.4598.671 PMID:17813860

Kiryazov, K., Lowe, R., Becker-Asano, C., & Randazzo, M. (2013). The role of arousal in two-resource problem tasks for humanoid service robots. In RO-MAN, 2013 IEEE (pp. 62-69). IEEE. doi:10.1109/ROMAN.2013.6628532

Koch, C. (2009). *A "Complex" Theory of Consciousness*. Retrieved 2015-10-24, from http://www.scientificamerican.com/article/a-theory-of-consciousness/

Koch, C. (2014, June 1). *Giulio Tononi and me: a phi-nal exchange* [Web log post]. Retrieved from Shtetl-Optimized, http://scottaaronson.com/blog

Koch, C. (2015, November). *Some Counterintuitive Predictions Arising from IIT*. Paper presented at The Integrated Information Theory of Consciousness: Foundational Issues, Workshop, New York, NY.

Koch, C. (2013). *Bewusstsein*. Berlin: Springer Berlin Heidelberg. doi:10.1007/978-3-642-34771-9

Koch, C., & Tononi, G. (2013). Can a photodiode be conscious? *The New York Review of Books, 3/7*(13).

Koch, C., & Tsuchiya, N. (2007). Phenomenology without conscious access is a form of consciousness without top-down attention. *Behavioral and Brain Sciences, 30*(5-6), 509–510. doi:10.1017/S0140525X07002907

Koedinger, K. R., Anderson, J. R., Hadley, W. H., & Mark, M. A. (1997). Intelligent tutoring goes to school in the big city. *International Journal of Artificial Intelligence, 8*, 30–43.

Komer, B., & Eliasmith, C. (2016). A unified theoretical approach for biological cognition and learning. *Current Opinion in Behavioral Sciences, 11*, 14–20. doi:10.1016/j.cobeha.2016.03.006

Kondratiev, D., Tormasov, A., Stanko, T., Jones, R., & Taran, G. (2013). Innopolis University – a new IT resource for Russia.*Proceedings of the International Conference on Interactive Collaborative Learning (ICL)*. doi:10.1109/ICL.2013.6644718

Konstan, D. (2006). *The Emotions of the Ancient Greeks: Studies in Aristotle and Classical Literature (Robson Classical Lectures)*. Toronto: University of Toronto Press. doi:10.3138/9781442674370

Kouider, S., & Dehaene, S. (2007). Levels of processing during non-conscious perception: A critical review of visual masking. *Philosophical Transactions of the Royal Society of London. Series B, Biological Sciences, 362*(1481), 857–875. doi:10.1098/rstb.2007.2093 PMID:17403642

Kuchins, A. C., Beavin, A., & Bryndza, A. (2008). *Russia's 2020 Strategic Economic Goals and the Role of International Integration*. Washington, DC: Center for Strategic and International Studies.

Laird, J. E. (2008). Extending the Soar cognitive architecture. In P. Wang, B. Goertzel, & S. Franklin (Ed.), *Proceedings of the First AGI Conference* (pp. 224-235). Memphis, TN: IOS Press.

Laird, J. E. (2012). *The Soar cognitive architecture*. Cambridge, MA: MIT Press.

Laird, J. E., Newell, A., & Rosenbloom, P. S. (1987). Soar: An architecture for general intelligence. *Artificial Intelligence, 33*(1), 1–64. doi:10.1016/0004-3702(87)90050-6

Lane, D. M. (2012). Persistent autonomy artificial intelligence or biomimesis? In Autonomous under-water vehicles (auv), 2012 ieee/oes (pp. 1–8). doi:10.1109/AUV.2012.6380719

Langley, P., Laird, J. E., & Rogers, S. (2009). Cognitive architectures: Research issues and challenges. *Cognitive Systems Research, 10*(2), 141–160. doi:10.1016/j.cogsys.2006.07.004

Lattanze, A. (2008). *Architecting Software Intensive Systems: A Practitioner's Guide*. Auerbach. doi:10.1201/9781420045703

Lau, H. C. (2008). A Higher-Order Bayesian Decision Theory of Perceptual Consciousness. *Progress in Brain Research, 168*, 35–48. doi:10.1016/S0079-6123(07)68004-2 PMID:18166384

Lewis, R. L. (1993). An architecturally-based theory of sentence comprehension. *Proceedings of the Fifteenth Annual Conference of the Cognitive Science Society* (pp. 108-113). Boulder, CO: Lawrence Erlbaum.

Limb, C. J., & Braun, A. R. (2008). Neural Substrates of Spontaneous Musical Performance: An fMRI Study of Jazz Improvisation. *PLoS ONE, 3*(2).

Llinás, R. R. (2001). *I of the Vortex. From neurons to Self*. Cambridge, MA: MIT Press.

Locke, J. (1690/1824). An Essay Concerning Human Understanding. London: Baldwin. doi:10.1093/oseo/instance.00018020

Locke, D. (1982). Beliefs, Desires and Reasons for Actions. *American Philosophical Quarterly, 19*, 241–249.

Loveland, D. W. (1978). *Automated Theorem Proving: A Logical Basis (Fundamental Studies in Computer Science)*. Elsevier North-Holland.

Lövheim, H. (2012). A new three-dimensional model for emotions and monoamine neurotransmitters. *Medical Hypotheses, 78*, 341–348.

Lowe, R., & Kiryazov, K. (2014). Utilizing Emotions in Autonomous Robots: An Enactive Approach. In Emotion Modeling (pp. 76-98). Springer International Publishing.

Lowe, R., Montebelli, A., Ieropoulos, I., Greenman, J., Melhuish, C., & Ziemke, T. (2010). Grounding motivation in energy autonomy: a study of artificial metabolism constrained robot dynamics. In ALIFE (pp. 725–732). Odense: The MIT Press.

Lowe, R. (2013). Designing for Emergent Ultrastable Behaviour in Complex Artificial Systems – The Quest for Minimizing Heteronomous Constraints. *Constructivist Foundations*, *9*(1), 105–107.

Lowe, R. (2016). The Role of Allostasis in Sense-Making: A Better Fit for Interactivity than Cybernetic-Enactivism? *Constructivist Foundations*, *11*(2), 251–254.

Lowe, R., & Ziemke, T. (2011). The feeling of action tendencies: On emotional regulation of goal-directed behaviour. *Frontiers in Psychology*, *346*(2), 1–24. PMID:22207854

Maguire, P., Moser, P., Maguire, R., & Griffith, V. (2014) Is consciousness computable? Quantifying integrated information using algorithmic information.*Proceedings of the 36th Annual Conference of the Cognitive Science Society*. Austin, TX: Cognitive Science Society.

Manicka, S., & Di Paolo, E. A. (2009). Local ultrastability in a real system based on programmable springs. In *Advances in artificial life.Proceedings of the tenth European Conference on Artificial Life (ECAL09)*. Berlin: Springer.

Marcus, G. (2013, June 6). How much consciousness does an iphone have? *The New Yorker*. Retrieved October 28, 2015, from www.newyorker.com/tech/elements/how-much-consciousness-does-an-iphone-have

Marks, J. (Ed.). (1986). The Ways of Desire: New Essays in Philosophical Psychology on the Concept of Wanting. Chicago: Precedent Publishing.

Marr, D. (1982). *Vision: A computational investigation into the human representation and processing of visual information*. San Francisco, CA: W. H. Freeman.

Marsh, K. L., Richardson, M. J., & Schmidt, R. C. (2009). Social connection through joint action and interpersonal coordination. *Topics in Cognitive Science*, *1*(2), 320–339. doi:10.1111/j.1756-8765.2009.01022.x PMID:25164936

Massimini, M. (2005, September). Breakdown of Cortical Effective Connectivity During Sleep. *Science*, *309*(5744), 2228–2232. doi:10.1126/science.1117256 PMID:16195466

McCarthy, J. (1968). Programs with Common Sense Proceedings of the Teddington Conference on the Mechanization of Thought Processes. In M. Minsky (Ed.), *Semantic Information Processing* (pp. 403-418). Cambridge, MA: MIT Press.

McEwen, B. S. (2004). Protective and Damaging Effects of the Mediators of Stress and Adaptation: Allostasis and Allostatic Load. In J. Schulkin (Ed.), *Allostasis, Homeostasis, and the Costs of Adaptation*. Cambridge University Press. doi:10.1017/CBO9781316257081.005

McEwen, B. S., & Wingfield, J. C. (2003). The concept of allostasis in biology and biomedicine. *Hormones and Behavior*, *43*(1), 2–15. doi:10.1016/S0018-506X(02)00024-7 PMID:12614627

McFarland, D. (2008). *Guilty Robots, Happy Dogs*. New York: Oxford University Press.

McFarland, D. (2008). *Guilty Robots, Happy Dogs: The Question of Alien Minds*. Oxford, UK: Oxford University Press.

McFarland, D., & Bösser, T. (1993). *Intelligent Behavior in Animals and Robots*. The MIT Press.

McFarland, D., & Spier, E. (1997). Basic cycles, utility and opportunism in self-sufficient robots. *Robotics and Autonomous Systems*, *20*(2-4), 179–190. doi:10.1016/S0921-8890(96)00069-3

Melhuish, C., Ieropoulos, I., Greenman, J., & Horsfield, I. (2006). Energetically autonomous robots: Food for thought. *Autonomous Robots*, *21*(3), 187–198. doi:10.1007/s10514-006-6574-5

Meyer, B. (2009). *Touch of Class: Learning to Program Well with Objects and Contracts*. Springer Publishing Company, Incorporated. doi:10.1007/978-3-540-92145-5

Miller, C. S., & Laird, J. E. (1996). Accounting for graded performance within a discrete search framework. *Cognitive Science*, *20*(4), 499–537. doi:10.1207/s15516709cog2004_2

Miller, G. A., Galanter, E., & Pribram, K. H. (1960). *Plans and the structure of behavior*. New York: Holt, Rinehart and Winston. Inc. doi:10.1037/10039-000

Mill, J. S. (1957). *Utilitarianism* (O. Priest, Ed.). New York: Macmillan. (Original work published 1861)

Minsky, M. (2007). *The emotion machine: Commonsense thinking, artificial intelligence, and the future of the human mind*. Simon & Schuster.

Montemayor, C., & Haladjian, H. H. (2015). *Consciousness, Attention, and Conscious Attention*. Cambridge, MA: MIT Press. doi:10.7551/mitpress/9780262028974.001.0001

Moon, J., & Anderson, J. R. (2013). Timing in multitasking: Memory contamination and time pressure bias. *Cognitive Psychology*, *67*(1-2), 26–54. doi:10.1016/j.cogpsych.2013.06.001 PMID:23892230

Muntean, I., & Wright, C. D. (2007). Autonomous agency, AI, and allostasis. *Pragmatics & Cognition*, *15*(3), 485–513. doi:10.1075/pc.15.3.07mun

Nanay, B. (2013). *Between Perception and Action*. Oxford, UK: Oxford University Press. doi:10.1093/acprof:oso/9780199695379.001.0001

National Research Council. (2000). *How people learn: Brain, mind, experience, and school*. Washington, DC: National Academy Press.

Nguyen, S. M., & Oudeyer, P.-Y. (2013). Socially guided intrinsic motivation for robot learning of motor skills. *Autonomous Robots*, *36*(3), 273–294. doi:10.1007/s10514-013-9339-y

Novak, J. (1998). *Learning, creating, and using knowledge: Concept maps as facilitative tools in schools and corporations*. Mahwah, NJ: Erlbaum.

O'Reilly, A. G., Roche, B., & Cartwright, A. (2015). Function over Form: A Behavioral Approach to Implicit Attitudes. In Z. Jin (Ed.), *Exploring Implicit Cognition: Learning, Memory, and Social Cognitive Processes*. IGI Global. doi:10.4018/978-1-4666-6599-6.ch008

Oatley, K., & Johnson-Laird, P. N. (1987). Towards a Cognitive Theory of Emotions. *Cognition and Emotion*, *1*(1), 29–50. doi:10.1080/02699938708408362

Oatley, K., & Johnson-Laird, P. N. (1996). The communicative theory of emotions: Empirical tests, mental models, and implications for social interaction. In L. L. Martin & A. Tesser (Eds.), *Striving and feeling: Interactions among goals, affect, and self-regulation*. Hillsdale, NJ: Erlbaum.

Oizumi, M., Albantakis, L., & Tononi, G. (2014). From the phenomenology to the mechanisms of consciousness: Integrated information theory 3.0. *PLoS Computational Biology*, *10*(5), e1003588. doi:10.1371/journal.pcbi.1003588 PMID:24811198

Olsson, J. (2015). *An evaluation of the integrated information theory against some central problems of consciousness, Bachelor Degree Project*. University of Skövde.

ORegan, J. K., & Noë, A. (2001). A sensorimotor account of vision and visual consciousness. *Behavioral and Brain Sciences*, *24*(5), 883–917. doi:10.1017/S0140525X01000115 PMID:12239892

Oudeyer, O. (2013). *Object learning through active exploration*. Hal.Archives-Ouvertes.Fr.

Ovsich, A. J. (1998a). Outlines of the Theory of Choice: Attitude, Desire, Attention, Will. *Intelligent Control (ISIC), 1998. Held jointly with IEEE International Symposium on Computational Intelligence in Robotics and Automation (CIRA), Intelligent Systems and Semiotics (ISAS), Proceedings* (pp. 503-510). doi.org/doi:<ALIGNMENT.qj></ALIGNMENT>10.1109/ISIC.1998.713713

Ovsich, A. J. (1998b). Outlines of the Theory of Choice: Attitude, Desire, Attention, Will. *Proceedings of the 1998 Twentieth World Congress of Philosophy.* Retrieved 14 September 2015 from http://www.bu.edu/wcp/Papers/Acti/ActiOvsi.htm

Ovsich, A. J. (2012). Mathematical Models of Desire, Need and Attention. In *Proceedings of AISB/IACAP World Congress 2012.* Retrieved from http://events.cs.bham.ac.uk/turing12/proceedings/03.pdf

Ovsich, A., & Cabanac, M. (2012). Experimental Support of the Mathematical Model of Desire. *International Journal of Psychological Studies., 4*(1), 66–75. doi:10.5539/ijps.v4n1p66

Pan, W., Schmidt, R., Wickens, J. R., & Hyland, B. I. (2005). Dopamine cells respond to predicted events during classical conditioning: Evidence for eligibility traces in the reward-learning network. *The Journal of Neuroscience, 25*(26), 6235–6242. doi:10.1523/JNEUROSCI.1478-05.2005 PMID:15987953

Pascarella, E., & Terenzini, P. (2005). *How college affects students: A third decade of research.* San Francisco: Jossey-Bass.

Pfutzner, H. (2014). *Bewusstsein und optimierter Wille.* Berlin: Springer Berlin Heidelberg.

Pickering, A. (2010). *The cybernetic brain: Sketches of another future.* Chicago, IL: University of Chicago Press. doi:10.7208/chicago/9780226667928.001.0001

Pitonakova, L. (2013). Ultrastable neuroendocrine robot controller. *Adaptive Behavior, 21*(1), 47–63. doi:10.1177/1059712312462249

Plutchik, R. (1980). *Emotion. A psychoevolutionary Synthesis.* New York: Harper & Row.

Powers, W. T. (1973). Quantitative analysis of purposive systems: Some spadework at the foundation of scientific psychology. *Psychological Review, 85*(5), 417–435. doi:10.1037/0033-295X.85.5.417

Prinz, J. J. (2004). *Gut Reactions: A Perceptual Theory of Emotion.* Oxford University Press.

Prinz, J. J. (2005). A neurofunctional theory of consciousness. In A. Brook & K. Akins (Eds.), *Cognition and the brain: Philosophy and neuroscience movement* (pp. 381–396). Cambridge, UK: Cambridge University Press. doi:10.1017/CBO9780511610608.012

Putnam, H. (1975a) The meaning of 'meaning'. In Mind, language, and reality (pp. 215-71). Cambridge, UK: Cambridge University Press. doi:10.1017/CBO9780511625251.014

Putnam, H. (1960). Minds and machines. *Republished in Putnam, 1975b,* 362–385.

Putnam, H. (1975b). *Mind, Language, and Reality*. Cambridge, UK: Cambridge University Press. doi:10.1017/CBO9780511625251

Putnam, H. (1988). *Representation and Reality*. Cambridge, UK: Cambridge University Press.

Rado, S. (1964). Hedonic Self-Regulation of the Organism. In R. G. Heath (Ed.), *The Role of Pleasure in Behavior* (pp. 257–264). New York: Harper & Row.

Raffone, A., & Pantani, M. (2010, June). A global workspace model for phenomenal and access consciousness. *Consciousness and Cognition, 19*(2), 580–596. doi:10.1016/j.concog.2010.03.013 PMID:20382038

Reggia, J. A. (2013). The rise of machine consciousness: Studying consciousness with computational models. *Neural Networks, 44*, 112–131. doi:10.1016/j.neunet.2013.03.011 PMID:23597599

Resnick, L.B. (1983). Article. *Mathematics and Science Learning, 220*, 477-478.

Reynolds, R. F., & Bronstein, A. M. (2003). The broken escalator phenomenon: Aftereffect of walking onto a moving platform. *Experimental Brain Research, 151*(3), 301–308. doi:10.1007/s00221-003-1444-2 PMID:12802549

Roberts, S., & Pashler, H. (2000). How persuasive is a good fit? A comment on theory testing. *Psychological Review, 107*(2), 358–367. doi:10.1037/0033-295X.107.2.358 PMID:10789200

Robins, A. (1995). Catastrophic forgetting, rehearsal and pseudorehearsal. *Connection Science, 7*(2), 123–146. doi:10.1080/09540099550039318

Robinson & Berridge. (2015). *Wanting vs Needing* (2nd ed.). International Encyclopedia of the Social & Behavioral Sciences. doi:10.1016/B978-0-08-097086-8.26091-1

Rolls, E. T. (2010). *Consciousness, Decision-Making and Neural Computation*. In A. Hussain & J. G. Taylor (Eds.), *Cutsuridis, Vassilis* (pp. 287–333). Perception-Action Cycle, Germany: Springer.

Rosenblatt, F. (1958). The perceptron: A probabilistic model for information storage and organization in the brain. *Psychological Review, 65*(6), 386–408. doi:10.1037/h0042519 PMID:13602029

Rosenthal, D. (2009). *Concepts and definitions of consciousness. In Encyclopedia of Consciousness*. Amsterdam: Elsevier.

Rubinshteòin, S. L. (1957). *Bytie I soznanie; o meste psikhicheskogo vo vseobshcheòi vzaimosvþiÆazi þiÆavleniòi materialñnogo mira*. Moskva: Izd-vo Akademii nauk SSSR.

Russell, B. (1921). *The Analysis of Mind*. London: G. Allen & Unwin, Ltd.

Russell, J. A. (2003). Core affect and the psychological construction of emotion. *Psychological Review*, *110*(1), 145–172. doi:10.1037/0033-295X.110.1.145 PMID:12529060

Sakarya, O., Armstrong, K. A., Adamska, M., Adamski, M., Wang, I., Tidor, B., & Kosik, K. S. et al. (2007). A post-synaptic scaffold at the origin of the animal kingdom. *PLoS ONE*, *2*(6), 506. doi:10.1371/journal.pone.0000506 PMID:17551586

Schach, S. R. (2011). *Object-Oriented and Classical Software Engineering* (8th ed.). New York, NY: McGraw-Hill.

Schroeder, T. (2004). *Three Faces of Desire*. Oxford, UK: Oxford University Press. doi:10.1093/acprof:oso/9780195172379.001.0001

Schueler, G. F. (1995). Desire. Its Role in Practical Reason and the Explanation of Action. Cambridge, MA: MIT Press.

Schulkin, J. (2004). *Allostasis, homeostasis, and the costs of physiological adaptation*. Cambridge University Press. doi:10.1017/CBO9781316257081

Schulkin, J. (2011). *Adaptation and well-being: Social allostasis*. Cambridge University Press. doi:10.1017/CBO9780511973666

Schwartz, D. L., & Bransford, J. D. (1998). A time for telling. *Cognition and Instruction*, *16*(4), 475–522. doi:10.1207/s1532690xci1604_4

Searle, J. (2013, January 10). Review of the book *Consciousness: confessions of a romantic reductionist*, by C. Koch. *New York Review of Books*.

Seth, A. K. (2013). Interoceptive inference, emotion, and the embodied self. *Trends in Cognitive Sciences*, *17*(11), 565–573. doi:10.1016/j.tics.2013.09.007 PMID:24126130

Seth, A. K. (2014). The Cybernetic Bayesian Brain. In *Open MIND*. Frankfurt am Main, Germany: MIND Group.

Shanahan, M. (2006). A cognitive architecture that combines internal simulation with a global workspace. *Consciousness and Cognition*, *15*(2), 433–449. doi:10.1016/j.concog.2005.11.005 PMID:16384715

Shanahan, M., & Baars, B. (2005, December). Applying global workspace theory to the frame problem. *Cognition*, *98*(2), 157–176. doi:10.1016/j.cognition.2004.11.007 PMID:16307957

Shannon, C. E., & Weaver, W. (1949). *The mathematical theory of communication*. Urbana, IL: University of Illinois Press.

Sherrington, C. S. (1908). Reciprocal innervation of antagonistic muscles. thirteenth note.-on the antagonism between reflex inhibition and reflex excitation. *Proceedings of the Royal Society of London. Series B, Containing Papers of a Biological Character, 80*(544), 565–578. doi:10.1098/rspb.1908.0053

Silver, D., Huang, A., Maddison, C. J., Guez, A., Sifre, L., van den Driessche, G., & Hassabis, D. (2016, January). Mastering the game of Go with deep neural networks and tree search. *Nature, 529*(7587), 484–489. doi:10.1038/nature16961 PMID:26819042

Simon, H. A. (1967). Motivational and emotional controls of cognition. *Psychological Review, 74*(1), 29–39. doi:10.1037/h0024127 PMID:5341441

Singh, S. P., Jaakkola, T., & Jordan, M.I. (1994) Learning without state-estimation in partially observable markovian decision processes. *ICML*, 284–292.

Skoggard, I., & Waterson, A. (2015). Introduction: Toward an Anthropology of Affect and Evocative Ethnography. *Anthropology of Consciousness, 26*(2), 109–120. doi:10.1111/anoc.12041

Sloman, A. (2001). Beyond shallow models of emotion. *Cognitive Processing, 2*(1), 177–198.

Snaider, J., McCall, R., & Franklin, S. (2011). The LIDA Framework as a General Tool for AGI. In D. Hutchison et al. (Eds.), *Artificial General Intelligence* (Vol. 6830, pp. 133–142). Berlin: Springer Berlin Heidelberg. doi:10.1007/978-3-642-22887-2_14

Sober, E., & Wilson, D. S. (1999). *Unto others: The evolution and psychology of unselfish behavior*. Harvard University Press.

Spinoza, B. (1955). *On the Improvement of the Understanding. The Ethics. Correspondence*. New York: Dover Publications, Inc.(Original work published 1674)

Sprague, J., & Stuart, D. (2000). *The speaker's handbook*. Fort Worth, TX: Harcourt College Publishers.

Spranger, M., Thiele, C., & Hild, M. (2010). Integrating high-level cognitive systems with sensorimotor control. *Advanced Engineering Informatics, 24*(1), 76–83. doi:10.1016/j.aei.2009.08.008

Staddon, J. (2014). *The new behaviorism*. Psychology Press.

Staude, M. (1986). Wanting, Desiring and Valuing: The Case against Conativism. In J. Marks (Ed.), *The Ways of Desire: New Essays in Philosophical Psychology on the Concept of Wanting* (pp. 175–198). Chicago: Precedent Publishing, Inc.

Sterling, P. (2004). Principles of allostasis: optimal design, predictive regulation, pathophysiology and rational therapeutics. In J. Schulkin (Ed.), *Allostasis, Homeostasis, and the Costs of Adaptation*. Cambridge University Press. doi:10.1017/CBO9781316257081.004

Sterling, P. (2012). Allostasis: A model of predictive regulation. *Physiology & Behavior, 106*(1), 5–15. doi:10.1016/j.physbeh.2011.06.004 PMID:21684297

Strawson, G. (2010). Mental Reality. Cambridge, MA: MIT Press.

Sutter, H. (2005). The free lunch is over: A fundamental turn toward concurrency in software. *Dr. Dobbs Journal, 30*(3), 202-210.

Sutton, R. S. (1988). Learning to predict by the methods of temporal differences. *Machine Learning, 3*(1), 9–44. doi:10.1007/BF00115009

Tagliazucchi, E., Chialvo, D. R., Siniatchkin, M., Brichant, J.-F., Bonhomme, V., ... Laureys, S. (2015, September). *Large-scale signatures of unconsciousness are consistent with a departure from critical dynamics*. arXiv:1509.04304

Tailor, C. C. W. (1986). Emotions and Wants. In J. Marks (Ed.), *The Ways of Desire: New Essays in Philosophical Psychology on the Concept of Wanting* (pp. 217–231). Chicago: Precedent Publishing.

Taketani, M. (1971). On formation of the Newton Mechanics. *Progress of Theoretical Physics, 50*(Supplement), 53–64. doi:10.1143/PTPS.50.53

Talanov, M. (2015). Neuromodulating Cognitive Architecture: Towards Biomimetic Emotional AI. *2015 IEEE 29th International Conference on Advanced Information Networking and Applications*. http://doi.ieeecomputersociety.org/10.1109/AINA.2015.240

Taylor, J. G. (2010). Article. In V. Cutsuridis, A. Hussain, & J. G. Taylor (Eds.), A Review of Models of Consciousness (pp. 335–357). Perception-Action Cycle, Germany: Springer.

Tegmark, M. (in press). Consciousness as a state of matter. *Chaos, Solitons, and Fractals*.

Thagard, P., & Steward, T. C. (2014). Two theories of consciousness: Semantic pointer competition vs. information integration. *Consciousness and Cognition, 30*, 73–90. doi:10.1016/j.concog.2014.07.001 PMID:25160821

Thelen, E., & Smith, L. B. (1994). *A dynamic systems approach to the development of cognition and action*. Cambridge, MA: MIT Press.

Thompson, R. (2010). Das Gehirn: Von der Nervenzelle zur Verhaltenssteuerung (A. Held, Trans.). Spektrum Akademischer Verlag.

Thomson, R., Pyke, A., Trafton, J. G., & Hiatt, L. M. (2015). An account of associative learning in memory recall.*Proceedings of the 37th Annual Conference of the Cognitive Science Society*. Austin, TX: Cognitive Science Society.

Tononi, G. & Koch, C. (2014). *Consciousness: Here, There but Not Everywhere*. Arxiv, 15.

Tononi, G. (2014, May 30). *Why Scott should stare at a blank wall and reconsider (or, the conscious grid)* [Web log post]. Retrieved from Shtetl-Optimized, http://scottaaronson.com/blog

Tononi, G. (2015, November). *Integrated Information Theory: An outline and some ontological considerations*. Paper presented at The Integrated Information Theory of Consciousness: Foundational Issues, Workshop, New York, NY. doi:10.4249/scholarpedia.4164

Tononi, G., & Koch, C. (2015). Consciousness: here, there and everywhere? *Philosophical Transactions of the Royal Society, Philosophical Transactions B*. doi:10.1098/rstb.2014.0167

Tononi, G. (2004). An information integration theory of consciousness. *BMC Neuroscience*, *5*(1), 42. doi:10.1186/1471-2202-5-42 PMID:15522121

Tononi, G. (2008). Consciousness as integrated information: A provisional manifesto. *The Biological Bulletin*, *215*(3), 216–242. doi:10.2307/25470707 PMID:19098144

Tononi, G., & Edelman, G. (1998). Consciousness and complexity. *Science*, *282*(5395), 1846–1851. doi:10.1126/science.282.5395.1846 PMID:9836628

Trafton, J. G., Hiatt, L. M., Harrison, A. M., Tamborello, F., Khemlani, S. S., & Schultz, A. C. (2013). ACT-R/E: An embodied cognitive architecture for human robot interaction. *Journal of Human-Robot Interaction*, *2*(1), 30–55. doi:10.5898/JHRI.2.1.Trafton

Tschacher, W., & Dauwalder, J.-P. (Eds.). (2003). *The dynamical systems approach to cognition: concepts and empirical paradigms based on self-organization, embodiment, and coordination dynamics*. Singapore: World Scientific. doi:10.1142/5395

Tulving, E. (1985). Memory and consciousness. *Canadian Psychology*, *26*(1), 1–12. doi:10.1037/h0080017

Turner, M., & Fauconnier, G. (2002). *The Way We Think. Conceptual Blending and the Mind's Hidden Complexities*. Basic Books.

Valen, L. (1973). A new evolutionary law. *Evolutionary Theory*, *1*, 1–30.

Vallverdú, J. (2012). Subsuming or Embodying Emotions?. In J. Vallverdú (Ed.), *Creating Synthetic Emotions through Technological and Robotic Advancements*. IGI Global Group. doi:10.4018/978-1-4666-1595-3

Vallverdu, J. (2015). *A cognitive architecture for the implementation of emotions in computing systems*. Biologically Inspired Cognitive Architectures. doi:10.1016/j.bica.2015.11.002

Vallverdú, J. (2016). *Bayesians Versus Frequentists. A Philosophical Debate on Statistical Reasoning*. Springer. doi:10.1007/978-3-662-48638-2

Vallverdu, J., Talanov, M., Distefano, S., Mazzara, M., Manca, M., & Tchitchigin, A. (2016). NEUCOGAR: A Neuromodulating Cognitive Architecture for Biomimetic Emotional AI. *International Journal of Artificial Intelligence*, *14*(1), 27–40.

van Gaal, S., de Lange, F. P., & Cohen, M. X. (2012a). The role of consciousness in cognitive control and decision making. *Frontiers in Human Neuroscience*, *6*, 121. doi:10.3389/fnhum.2012.00121 PMID:22586386

van Gaal, S., & Lamme, V. A. (2012). Unconscious high-level information processing: Implication for neurobiological theories of consciousness. *The Neuroscientist*, *18*(3), 287–301. doi:10.1177/1073858411404079 PMID:21628675

van Gelder, T. J. (1998). The dynamical hypothesis in cognitive science. *Behavioral and Brain Sciences*, *21*(05), 1–14. doi:10.1017/S0140525X98001733 PMID:10097022

van Rooij, I., Bongers, R. M., & Haselager, F. G. (2002). A non-representational approach to imagined action. *Cognitive Science*, *26*(3), 345–375. doi:10.1207/s15516709cog2603_7

Varella, F., Thompson, E., & Rosch, E. (1991). *The embodied mind: cognitive science and human experience*. Cambridge, MA: MIT Press.

Vernon, D. (2013). Interpreting Ashby–But which One? *Constructivist Foundations*, *9*(1), 111–113.

Vernon, D., Lowe, R., Thill, S., & Ziemke, T. (2015). Embodied cognition and circular causality: On the role of constitutive autonomy in the reciprocal coupling of perception and action. *Frontiers in Psychology*, *6*. PMID:26579043

Vilunas, V. K. (1976). Psychology of the Emotional Phenomena. Moscow: Moscow University.

Wallin, N. L., & Merker, B. (2001). *The origins of music*. MIT Press.

Wegner, D. (2002). *The Illusion of Conscious Will*. Cambridge, MA: MIT Press.

Weiss, J. (1997). The role of pathogenic beliefs in psychic reality. *Psychoanalytic Psychology*, *14*(3), 427–434. doi:10.1037/h0079734

Whitmore, A., Choi, N., & Arzrumtsyan, A. (2015). Open source software: The role of marketing in the diffusion of innovation. *Information Technology and Control, 38*(2).

Wigfield, A., & Eccles, J. (2000). Expectancy-value theory of achievement motivation. *Contemporary Educational Psychology, 25*(1), 68–81. doi:10.1006/ceps.1999.1015 PMID:10620382

Wilson, A. D., & Golonka, S. (2013). Embodied cognition is not what you think it is. *Frontiers in Psychology, 4.* PMID:23408669

Wiltshire, T. J., Lobato, E. J. C., Jentsch, F. G., & Fiore, S. M. (2013). Will (dis) embodied LIDA agents be socially interactive? *Journal of Artificial General Intelligence, 4*(2), 42–47.

Wiltshire, T. J., Lobato, E. J., McConnell, D. S., & Fiore, S. M. (2014). Prospects for direct social perception: A multi-theoretical integration to further the science of social cognition. *Frontiers in Human Neuroscience, 8.* PMID:25709572

Wingfield, J. C. (2004). Allostatic Load and Life Cycles: Implications for Neuroendocrine Control Mechanisms. In J. Schulkin (Ed.), *Allostasis, Homeostasis, and the Costs of Adaptation.* Cambridge University Press. doi:10.1017/CBO9781316257081.011

Winkielman, P., & Schooler, J. W. (2011). Splitting consciousness: Unconscious, conscious, and metaconscious processes in social cognition. *European Review of Social Psychology, 22*(1), 37–41. doi:10.1080/10463283.2011.576580

Wirzberger, M., & Russwinkel, N. (2015). Modeling interruption and resumption in a smartphone task: An ACT-R approach. *i-com, 14,* 147-154. doi:10.1515/icom-2015-0033

Young, P. T. (1961). *Motivation and Emotion.* New York: John Wiley & Sons, Inc.

Zatorre, R. J., Chen, J. L., & Penhune, V. B. (2007). When the brain plays music: Auditory–motor interactions in music perception and production. *Nature Reviews. Neuroscience, 8*(7), 547–558. doi:10.1038/nrn2152 PMID:17585307

Ziemke, T., & Lowe, R. (2009). On the Role of Emotion in Embodied Cognitive Architectures: From Organisms to Robots. *Cognitive Computation, 1*(1), 104–117. doi:10.1007/s12559-009-9012-0

Zimmer, C. (2010, September 20). Sizing up consciousness by its bits. *The New York Times.* Retrieved October 28, 2015, from www.nytimes.com/2010/09/21/consciousnesss.html

Zimmerman, B. J. (2001). Theories of self-regulated learning and academic achievement: An overview and analysis. In B. J. Zimmerman & D. H. Schunk (Eds.), *Self-regulated learning and academic achievement* (2nd ed.; pp. 1–3). Hillsdale, NJ: Erlbaum.

Zubler, F., & Douglas, R. (2009). A framework for modeling the growth and development of neurons and networks. *Frontiers in Computational Neuroscience, 3*. doi:10.3389/neuro.10.025.2009 PMID:19949465

Zykov, S. (2015). Enterprise Applications as Anthropic-Oriented Systems: Patterns and Instances. In *Proceedings of the 9th KES Conference on Agent and Multi-Agent Systems: Technologies and Applications*, (pp. 275-283). Springer. doi:10.1007/978-3-319-19728-9_23

Zykov, S. (2009). Designing patterns to support heterogeneous enterprise systems lifecycle. In *Proceedings of the 5th Central and Eastern European Software Engineering Conference in Russia (CEE-SECR)*. doi:10.1109/CEE-SECR.2009.5501184

Zykov, S. (2010). Pattern Development Technology for Heterogeneous Enterprise Software Systems. *Journal of Communication and Computer, 7*(4), 56–61.

Zykov, S. (2015). Human-Related Factors in Knowledge Transfer: A Case Study. In *Proceedings of 9th KES Conference on Agent and Multi-Agent Systems: Technologies and Applications (KES-AMSTA-2015)*, (pp. 263-274). Springer. doi:10.1007/978-3-319-19728-9_22

Zykov, S., Shapkin, P., Kazantsev, N., & Roslovtsev, V. (2015). Agile Enterprise Process and Data Engineering via Type-Theory Methods. In *Proceedings of the 5th International Symposium ISKO-Maghreb*.

About the Contributors

Jordi Vallverdú, Ph.D., M.Sci., B.Mus, B.Phil, is Tenure Professor at Universitat Autònoma de Barcelona (Catalonia, Spain), where he teaches Philosophy and History of Science and Computing. His research is dedicated to the epistemological, cognitive and ethical aspects of Philosophy of Computing and Science and AI. He is Editor-in-chief of the International Journal of Synthetic Emotions (IJSE). He has written several books as author or editor: (2009) Handbook of Research on Synthetic Emotions and Sociable Robotics: New Applications in Affective Computing and Artificial Intelligence, (2010) Thinking Machines and the Philosophy of Computer Science: Concepts and Principles, (2012) Creating Synthetic Emotions Through Technological and Robotic Advancements, (2015) Bayesian vs. Frequentist Statistics. In 2011 he won a prestigious Japanese JSPS fellowship to make his research on HRI interfaces at Kyoto University. He was keynote at ECAP09 (TUM, München, Germany), EBICC2012 (UNESP, Brazil) and SLACTIONS 2013 (Portugal).

Manuel Mazzara is a dedicated and flexible individual with commitment to research and passion for teamwork, tutoring and coaching. In 2000 he was a system administrator at CS Labs in Bologna and in 2003 he worked as SW Engineer at MS in Redmond where he developed his technical skills for then building a more theoretical background with his PhD in Bologna. During this period, he also worked as a teacher and consultant (banking and private business). In 2006 he was an assistant professor in Software Engineering at the University of Bolzano (Component-based Development and Software Reliability). In 2007 he worked as a Project Manager at the Technical University of Vienna (Semantic Web and Discovery). From 2008 to 2012 Manuel encountered the most challenging and exciting situations of his life working with Newcastle University on the DEPLOY project. This project involved several partners Europe-wide with 4 of them coming from the most varied industrial scenarios: Bosch, Siemens, SAP and Space Finland. The objective was deploying software engineering techniques into the industrial process to guarantee stronger products reliability. In 2012 Manuel also served as a Computer Scientist at UNU-IIST in Macao while still being with Newcastle as a Visiting Researcher. Manuel worked on the automatization of the immunization process for third world countries and on e-health and sustainability projects related to the UN "Agenda 21". This experience was fundamental to grow form a technical, managerial and human point of view. In 2013/14 he also worked on remote assistance and telemedicine domotics tools with Polytechnic of Milan and as a teaching fellow at the same university before joining Innopolis and ETH. Manuel is a versatile individual who does not spare himself when running the extra mile is needed. His technical and interpersonal skills are demonstrated by the long list of collaborations and by the recommendations of his colleagues, business partners and students.

Max Talanov is the acting head of the Intellectual Robotics department, Republic of Tatarstan, Russian Federation Information Technology and Services. Highly-creative AI researcher/architect/designer/developer and team leader with 16 years of professional experience. Has experience in development of machine understanding applications, automation of code generation, web-based and client-server and web-services based enterprise applications and management of small teams. Specialties: AI, Affective computation, Affective Computing, Machine cognition, Machine reasoning, Natural Language Processing, Semantic technologies, Scala, Java, Python, C++.

Salvatore Distefano is an Associate Professor at University of Messina and a Professor Fellow at Kazan Federal University. He authored and co-authored more than 140 scientific papers in international journals, conferences and books. He took part to national and international projects such as Reservoir, VisionCloud, CloudWave (EU FP7) Beacon (H2020) and SMSCOM (FP7 EU ERC Advanced Grant). He is a member of several international conference committees and editorial boards, among others the IEEE Transactions on Dependable and Secure Computing. Since 2001 he taught more than 30 courses on parallel and distributed systems, dependability and performance evaluation, and software engineering for undergraduate, graduate and PhD students, mentoring more than 50 students. His main research interests include non-Markovian modeling; dependability, performance and reliability evaluation; Quality of Service; Service Level Agreement; Parallel and Distributed Computing, Cloud, Autonomic, Volunteer, Crowd, Anthropic Oriented Computing; Big Data; Software and Service Engineering.

* * *

Roman Bauer is currently an MRC Fellow at Newcastle University (UK), with a research focus on retinal development. He devises and analyses computational and statistical models of how neural tissue evolves during development, in order to better understand the dynamics leading to healthy and pathological states. These models incorporate the bidirectional interaction between genetic rules and physical laws of the extracellular environment. Since these detailed models are often very demanding from a computational point of view, his research also involves modern computing approaches and industrial collaboration (https://biodynamo.web.cern. ch/). Roman studied Computational Science and Engineering (MSc, 2008) at ETH Zurich (ETHZ), Switzerland. He then undertook his doctoral studies at the Institute of Neuroinformatics (University of Zurich and ETHZ) on the topic of neural self-organization. Afterwards, he moved to Newcastle University to continue working on computational modeling of neural development.

Ivo Boblan is the head of the junior research group MTI-engAge and of the Compliant Robotics Lab MTI-FabLab (www.BioRobotikLabor.de) in the Control Systems Group, part of the Department of Electrical Engineering and Computer Science at the Technische Universität Berlin. His research interests in the field of biorobotics focus on the areas of Bionik, passive/active compliant systems, robust control, robotics and human-robot interaction.

Vincent Cialdella is currently pursuing a master's degree in Cognitive and Behavioral Sciences at Illinois State University with a focus on perception and action. Recently, he was awarded an internship opportunity with the Air Force Research Laboratory where he worked with cognitive architectures.

Francis Fallon is an Assistant Professor in the Department of Philosophy at St. John's University in New York City.

Leonard Johard is a researcher with a dedication to strong artificial intelligence, neural computation, robotics, and reinforcement learning. Current projects include the development of new actor-critic learning algorithms for robotics, mathematical dream models and the development of software for large-scale biological simulations.

J. Scott Jordan received his PhD in cognitive psychology and the neurophysiological basis of perception at Northern Illinois University in Dekalb, Illinois in 1991. In 1992 he was awarded an Alexander von Humboldt Post-doctoral Fellowship and spent a year in Prof. Dr. Hans Kornhuber's neurophysiology lab at the University of Ulm in Germany studying the relationship between event-related brain potentials and memory and attention. In 1998-1999 he spent a year at the Max Planck Institute for Psychological Research in Munich, Germany studying the relationship between action planning and spatial perception, and in 2006, spent a semester as a Scholar-in-Residence at the Center for Interdisciplinary Research at the University of Bielefeld in Germany working in a research group entitled, "Embodied Communication in Humans and Machines." His empirical research continues to focus on the relationship between spatial perception and action planning, with an increasing emphasis on social influences. His theoretical work (i.e., Wild Systems Theory) focuses on moving scientific psychology away from the current computational-ecological debate, toward an integrated framework that conceptualizes organisms as embodiments of the phylogenetic, cultural, social, and developmental contexts from they emerged and in which they sustain themselves.

Emilio Lobato is a current Master's student at Illinois State University studying Cognitive and Behavioral Science. He researches social cognition, specifically focusing on scientific literacy and human-robot interaction.

Robert Lowe has had published over 50 peer-reviewed articles and his interests lie in emotion theory and empirical research, computational modeling and cognitive architecture development. He currently works at the University of Gothenburg and University of Skövde in Sweden.

Alexander J. Ovsich has a degree in physics, and works in informatics. His main research interests are choice theory, hedonic philosophy and psychology, and their application to Artificial Intelligence. He has developed mathematical models of attitude, desire, need, attention and will effort, published on those subjects, and presented on them at national and international symposiums including World Congress of Philosophy 1998, IEEE ISIC/CIRA/ISAS Joint Conference 1998, 5th Lanzarote International Scientific Workshop 2008, AISB/IACAP World Congress 2012, 17th International Conference on Cognitive and Neural Systems 2013, CEPE-IACAP Conference 2015. He wrote a Foreword to Prof. Michel Cabanac's book "The Fifth Influence. The Dialectics of Pleasure".

Alexandra Weidemann is a PhD candidate and research assistant in the group "MTI-engAge" at Technical University Berlin.

Sergey V. Zykov is an Associate Professor at the National Research University – Higher School of Economics, Moscow, Russia. He has completed his PhD thesis on ERP software systems implementation methodology in 2000. Sergey is also an Associate Professor at the National Nuclear Research University MEPhI. He has eleven years with ITERA Oil and Gas Group of Companies, including Vice-CIO and Enterprise Portal Manager positions. Sergey is the author of five books on enterprise software development, he has also published over 50 papers in proceedings.

Index

   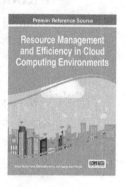

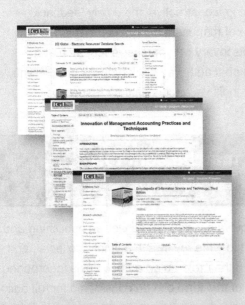